The Politics of Crowds

An Alternative History of Sociology

When sociology emerged as a discipline in the late nineteenth century, the problem of crowds constituted one of its key concerns. It was argued that crowds shook the foundations of society and led individuals into all sorts of irrational behaviour. Yet crowds were not just something to be fought in the street; they also formed a battleground over how sociology should be demarcated from related disciplines, most notably psychology. In *The Politics of Crowds*, Christian Borch traces sociological debates on crowds and masses from the birth of sociology until today, with a particular focus on the developments in France, Germany and the USA. The book is a refreshing alternative history of sociology and modern society, observed through society's other, the crowd. Borch shows that the problem of crowds is not just of historical interest: even today the politics of sociology is intertwined with the politics of crowds.

CHRISTIAN BORCH is Associate Professor at the Department of Management, Politics and Philosophy, Copenhagen Business School, Denmark. His Ph.D. was on the history of modern crime semantics, in which he studied how notions of crime and criminals evolved in the twentieth century and what responses were adopted to deal with crime. In his more recent research Borch has focused on crowds, architecture and urban theory. He has published widely on these issues as well as on key social theorists such as Gabriel Tarde, Niklas Luhmann and Peter Sloterdijk. He is co-founder and editor-in-chief of *Distinktion: Scandinavian Journal of Social Theory*.

The Politics of Crowds

An Alternative History of Sociology

Christian Borch

CAMBRIDGE
UNIVERSITY PRESS

CAMBRIDGE UNIVERSITY PRESS
Cambridge, New York, Melbourne, Madrid, Cape Town,
Singapore, São Paulo, Delhi, Mexico City

Cambridge University Press
The Edinburgh Building, Cambridge CB2 8RU, UK

Published in the United States of America by Cambridge University Press, New York

www.cambridge.org
Information on this title: www.cambridge.org/9781107625464

First published 2012
Reprinted 2012
First paperback edition 2013

A catalogue record for this publication is available from the British Library

Library of Congress Cataloguing in Publication Data
Borch, Christian.
  The politics of crowds: an alternative history of sociology / Christian Borch.
    p.   cm.
  ISBN 978-1-107-00973-8 (Hardback)
  1. Crowds.   2. Crowds–History.   I. Title.
  HM871.B67 2012
  302.33–dc23

                                                        2011043657

ISBN 978-1-107-62546-4 Paperback

Contents

Acknowledgements

Just as the behaviour of crowds cannot be reduced to the act of a single person, so this book would not have come about without the generous help and support of a number of people and institutions. First of all, the research behind the book was made possible by a four-year grant from the Carlsberg Foundation, one of the central bastions when it comes to ensuring basic research in Denmark. I truly appreciate the Foundation's interest in and commitment to the project which allowed me to excavate the more or less forgotten sociological tradition of crowds and masses.

During the process of writing the book I have benefited from discussions with colleagues first at the Department of Sociology, University of Copenhagen, and subsequently at the Department of Management, Politics and Philosophy, Copenhagen Business School, Denmark. Friends and colleagues from these and other departments who have followed and encouraged the research include Henning Bech, Margareta Bertilsson, Ole Hammerslev, Uffe Lind, Frederik Thuesen and Sébastien Tutenges. I am particularly grateful to Bjørn Schiermer Andersen and Marius Gudmand-Høyer for several stimulating reflections on the project. I also owe a special thanks for ongoing discussions on crowds to Urs Stäheli who introduced me to the field of crowds when I was an exchange student at the University of Bielefeld, Germany, quite some years ago. Urs' original work continues to be a rich source of inspiration.

Some of the ideas presented in this book have previously been vented at lectures and seminars at the European University Viadrina Frankfurt (Oder), Goldsmiths, Oxford University, Stockholm University, the Technical University of Darmstadt, University of Basel, University of Copenhagen, University of Hamburg, University of Westminster and Yale University. I am grateful to the various audiences for their valuable comments.

I am highly indebted to Tiina Arppe and Carl-Göran Heidegren who read and commented on select chapters. Their thoughtful suggestions generated significant improvements of the argument. The same applies to two anonymous Cambridge University Press readers who offered constructive criticism and several extremely valuable suggestions. It goes without saying that none of these scholars are to blame for any remaining shortcomings. I would also like to express my gratitude to Martin Barr for careful copy-editing.

Last but certainly not least I owe the greatest thanks possible to my wife Susanne for her persistent encouragement and incredible patience, year after year after year. The book is dedicated to her.

The book draws on some of my previous articles on the history and analytical potentials of crowd theory. These articles include: 'Urban Imitations: Tarde's Sociology Revisited', *Theory, Culture & Society* 22(3) (2005), 81–100; 'The Exclusion of the Crowd: The Destiny of a Sociological Figure of the Irrational', *European Journal of Social Theory* 9(1) (2006), 83–102; 'Crowds and Pathos: Theodor Geiger on Revolutionary Action', *Acta Sociologica* 49(1) (2006), 5–18; 'Crowds and Total Democracy: Hermann Broch's Political Theory', *Distinktion: Scandinavian Journal of Social Theory* 13 (2006), 99–120; 'Crowds and Economic Life: Bringing an Old Figure Back in', *Economy and Society* 36(4) (2007), 549–73; 'Market Crowds between Imitation and Control', *Theory, Culture & Society* 24(7–8) (2007), 164–80 (co-authored with Jakob Arnoldi); 'Modern Mass Aberration: Hermann Broch and the Problem of Irrationality', *History of the Human Sciences* 21(2) (2008), 63–83; 'Body to Body: On the Political Anatomy of Crowds', *Sociological Theory* 27(3) (2009), 271–90; and 'Between Destructiveness and Vitalism: Simmel's Sociology of Crowds', *Conserveries mémorielles* 8 (2010). While none of these articles reappear here in the form of separate book chapters, some of the ideas they present have been incorporated in discussions throughout the book. Since the present book also adds substantial amounts of new material, the whole is much more than the sum of the above-mentioned parts.

Introduction: the crowd problem

The apogee and disappearance of a problem

The famous German sociologist Georg Simmel is often counted as one of the founding fathers of the sociological discipline. He has earned this honour not least as a result of his original conception of society, centred on notions such as sociation and reciprocal effects. But he has also achieved the name of a founding father because he pursued his distinctive sociological programme in stimulating analyses of virtually every social phenomenon one might think of (money, fashion, cities, art, individualism, meals, picture frames, etc.). In the light of the extraordinary variety of topics he analysed, it is interesting to observe that, in his seminal 1917 essay entitled 'Grundfragen der Soziologie' ['Fundamental Problems of Sociology'], Simmel asserted that '[i]t is one of the most revealing, purely sociological phenomena that the individual feels himself carried by the "mood" of the mass, as if by an external force' (1950a: 35, 1999e: 97–8). This observation echoed a widespread belief in the early twentieth century. At that time crowds and masses formed a central concern for a great number of sociologists, and this had been the case since the inception of crowd psychology in the 1890s. Indeed, countless working hours were poured into the attempt to understand the phenomenon of crowds and to arrive at still more refined conceptualizations of these collective eruptions.

The importance attributed to the phenomenon of crowds by Simmel and his contemporary colleagues is striking when compared to the neglect which has surrounded the crowd in sociological thinking since the 1970s. To give a rough idea of the rather marginal role played by the crowd today, one might look to the work of grand sociologists such as Pierre Bourdieu, Jürgen Habermas or Niklas Luhmann, three significant figures in the sociological landscape since the late 1960s. Despite the fact that each of these prominent scholars was born around 1930, and therefore experienced the Second World War and its mass hysterias as adolescents, and even if each of these social scientists has scrutinized modern society in numerous books and articles, none of them places the problem of crowds centrally in their work. Certainly, none of them would subscribe to Simmel's assertion that the crowd experience embodies 'one of the most revealing, purely sociological phenomena'.

I am aware that the epochal rupture I am intimating here is – from crowds constituting a core sociological topic to becoming practically excluded from the span of sociological attention – exaggerated. It is certainly possible today to identify sociologists and social theorists who take crowd behaviour seriously. At the same time, it can hardly be disputed that something radical has happened in terms of the significance attributed to crowds and masses in sociological thinking. From forming a problem or topic that chief general sociologists were occupied with, the crowd has been relegated to a specialized sub-sub-field of analysis. It might be argued that this is a destiny shared by several subject matters that were central to the forming years of sociology, but this does not make the development of the notion of crowds any less baffling. This is why I am interested, in this book, in how this transformation came about. Why is it that crowds and masses constituted a crucial problem for sociologists and social theorists one century ago, but seem to sustain themselves in the margins of contemporary sociological thinking? Why has the crowd problem in effect been marginalized in sociology?

Two immediate answers lend themselves to these questions. To begin with, it might be argued that the contemporary disinterest in crowds – or more precisely, the exclusion of the crowd from the central domains of sociological analysis – is due to the disappearance of crowds and masses as actual or perceived social phenomena. If crowds do not make up a vital part of social life (any longer), then why include them as a key sociological occurrence? Another reason why present-day sociologists do not pay primary attention to crowds might be that the explanatory models associated with classical approaches to crowds are deemed obsolete today. The sophistication of contemporary thinking may simply have moved significantly beyond the theoretical and analytical understandings characteristic to former modes of study, thereby endowing these with a stuffy aura.

Neither of these lines of explanation can be wholly discarded, but at the same time, neither of them is fully satisfactory. For example, even today, the mass media recurrently report on new mass events, explicitly labelled thus, typically in the form of mass protests, mass disasters such as panic at large festivals, pilgrims who are trampled down, traders who are captured by crowd moods, etc. This illustrates that crowded events have *not* disappeared, although, to be sure, their expressions and modes of formation may differ from that of their earlier counterparts.

What the reference to the increasing sophistication of sociological theory concerns, it is true, is that sociologists often stand on the shoulders of previous scholars, something that allows for all sorts of corrections and modifications that might materialize in more refined approaches. But to the dismay of some, it would be premature to believe that the development of sociological theorizing is only driven by a move towards greater explanatory force and conceptual rigour. Such a view would ignore the political struggles that impinge on which directions sociological theory takes and what phenomena and problems it elevates to the level of key concerns.

Instead of understanding the gradual dissolution of crowd theory on the basis of a narrative of either scientific progress or changing social realities, this book proposes a different take: I am interested in understanding the evolution of sociological crowd thinking as a history of internal disciplinary endeavours (the relentless efforts to arrive at more precise and adequate conceptions of crowds and masses, the shifting theoretical and analytical emphases as well as the politico-theoretical struggles to define the proper demarcations of the sociological discipline), but with a view to the broader social and political transformations that are pertinent to the evolution of sociological thinking. As I will flesh out in more detail below, I describe this as *a history of sociological crowd semantics*, which refers to the concepts, explanatory models, political preferences, etc. that are part of the sociological discussions of crowds.

Writing semantic history

Even though the crowding together of people can be identified at all times and in every culture, it was only with the advent of modern society that genuinely theoretical approaches were developed which tried to explicate in systematic form the emergence, constitution and implications of crowds and masses. More specifically, the crowd surfaced as a theoretical concept at the end of the nineteenth century, i.e. more or less at the same time as sociology, the discipline devoted to the study of modern society, gained footing. The intimate connection between crowds and modernity has been accurately described by Jeffrey T. Schnapp and Matthew Tiews in their introduction to a collection of crowd essays. 'In some deep and essential sense', they write, 'crowds *are* modernity. Modern times are crowded times. Modern man is the man of the crowd' (2006: x, italics in original). This is no fortuitous observation. As Schnapp and Tiews go on to argue, '[t]he era of popular sovereignty, industrialization, and urbanization saw the rise of a constellation of new forms of mass assembly and collective social action' (2006: x–xi), which triggered a scholarly interest in the new social and political multitudes. Although the concern with these multitudes rumbled throughout the nineteenth century, it was only at the turn of the century that a distinctive scientific programme was instituted under the heading of crowd psychology. Contrary to previous academic and non-academic engagements with multitudes, crowd psychology was not content with mere descriptions of collective behaviour; it aimed more ambitiously to *explain* these collective spectacles.

In the present book, I take this crowd psychology as my starting point. More specifically, I wish to trace the evolution of sociological crowd semantics from the inception of crowd psychology in the late nineteenth century to the present day. To this end, the book rests on an analytical approach which hybridizes inspirations from Michel Foucault, Niklas Luhmann and Robert K. Merton, and which, methodologically as well as in terms of its contributions, presents a piece of historical sociology of knowledge and science.

Different disciplines offer different notions of semantics. In this book, the notion of semantics is adopted from Luhmann who inherited it from the conceptual historians Otto Brunner, Werner Conze and especially Reinhart Koselleck. In his historical work, developed alongside his more abstract theorizing on the nature of modern society, Luhmann studied the relations between societal structure and specific semantic histories. Luhmann basically asserted that semantics, defined as the concepts or vocabulary with which society describes itself, or more formally as the 'forms of meaning that communication treats as worth preserving' (1995: 282), always develops in close interaction with society's fundamental set up, its societal structure. According to Luhmann, this structural edifice is constituted by society's so-called primary mode of differentiation. In his historical studies, he focused particularly on the semantic effects induced by the transition from a pre-modern, hierarchical mode of differentiation to a modern society, defined by a functional differentiation of operationally autonomous subsystems of politics, economy, religion, science, law, etc. (see also Borch 2011). For example, Luhmann demonstrated, the semantics of individuality underwent a profound transformation in the transition from traditional to modern society. As an effect of this structural change, an individual's individuality was no longer defined by the affiliation to a specific societal strata (social class), but rather conceived as something to be shaped and maintained independently of former class ties (Luhmann 1989). Somewhat similarly, the present book purports, modernity instigated a new way of conceptualizing the relation between the one and the many, which amounts to saying that crowd semantics emerged as a distinctively modern semantics, arguably even as *the* semantics of modernity.

Although there was in principle nothing in Luhmann's conception of semantics and societal structure that prevented him from examining semantic trajectories *within* (and beyond) modern society, his actual studies were preoccupied with understanding the, admittedly important, semantic implications of the transition from pre-modern to modern society. The reason for this self-imposed limitation was that, for Luhmann, the fundamental structure of modern society, its functional differentiation, has not (yet) been replaced by a new primary mode of differentiation. Consequently, no radical semantic changes were likely to have been brought about within modern society. Accepting that view would make the current enterprise of understanding the history of sociological crowd semantics a fairly easy venture: if nothing significant has happened since the coming of modern society and its crowd semantics, then this semantics is likely to have lived a quiet, steady life. Things turn out to be more complex, however, and this is why, for present purposes, Luhmann's analytical approach is relevant merely as a general framework that emphasizes that semantics is not independent and free-floating, but carries some link to broader societal structures.

Given the inability to pursue the objectives of the present book fully on grounds of Luhmann's approach, and in order especially to account in more detail for semantic transformations within modern society, I supplement the Luhmannian framework with insights provided by Robert K. Merton's seminal contributions to the sociology of knowledge and science. Faithful to this sociological tradition Merton was aware that knowledge, not least of a sociological bent, does not evolve autonomously; directly or indirectly, it retains a relation to its social and cultural context. In contrast to what he saw as a tendency in previous studies to give credit only to how science affects society (and not the other way round), Merton approached the science–society intertwinement by stressing 'the *reciprocal* relations between science, as an ongoing intellectual activity, and the environing social and cultural structure' (1970: xi, italics in original).

The present investigation does not pretend to be able to perform a reciprocal analysis where sociological crowd semantics is studied in terms of how social and cultural events impinge on its development *and* vice versa. I follow Merton in the sense that I pay attention to internal as well as external dynamics, i.e. to how sociological crowd semantics has developed as an internal continuous engagement with previous semantics (including a variety of disciplinary and institutional aspects pertaining to this) and to how this semantic development has been related to an external socio-political environment. But more modestly than what Merton called for, my primary interests lie in the internal dimension and in how the semantic developments are (also) responses to and influenced by broader social contexts, whereas there will be no systematic examination of how crowd semantics has fed back onto external social, cultural and political developments. Moreover, I admit, for reasons I shall come back to below, the historical contextualization will figure centrally mainly in the first four chapters, whereas it will play a less prominent role in the remainder of the book.

As is probably clear from this, there are many aspects of Merton's approach to the study of scientific knowledge that find no equivalent in the present investigation. To mention just one in addition to what has already been alluded to, this book is informed by a purely qualitative methodology, whereas Merton argued for the active use of statistical data to test qualitative conclusions. In his retrospective 1970 preface to his seminal 1938 study *Science, Technology and Society in Seventeenth Century England*, Merton stated that:

The quantitative orientation [of Merton's book] is designed, so far as possible, to put interpretative ideas on trial by facing them with suitable compilations of statistical data, rather than relying wholly on selected bits and scraps of evidence that too often catch the scholar's eye simply because they are consistent with his ideas. (1970: xv)

I do not deny the gains of this dual methodological approach, nor do I disagree with the need for coping with the problem Merton identifies in this quote, the resolution to which he found statistical data befitting. However, accumulating quantitative data is not a universal tool that suits any analysis of semantic trajectories. To be sure, one might trace the destiny of the notion of crowds by counting how many articles on the topic are published in leading journals. Yet while quantitative data might shed some light on the ebbs and flows of sociological interests, their nature does not permit a doorway to understanding qualitative semantic changes, which is what I hope to furnish with this book. Needless to say, abandoning a statistical supplement to the qualitative profile of this inquiry does not amount to saying that I believe one to have fallen into the trap of making biased selections that merely confirm my hypotheses (nor does it mean, it must be added, that quantitative data are a bulletproof means of steering clear of this always-present challenge). But rather than using statistical data to handle this potential problem, I have attempted to avoid the trap by compiling a comprehensive archive of sociological and social–theoretical literature on crowds – and not merely some random 'bits and scraps'. I will flesh out in more detail how this archive is constructed in a moment, but first I wish to say a few words on the final key inspiration guiding my approach, namely the work of Michel Foucault.

Just as I included Merton to add specificity to Luhmann's overall framework, so I turn to Foucault to continue further down the funnel of analytical accuracy. Thus, inspired by Foucault, the main semantic lines I aim to explore are those which revolve around a *problematization* of crowds and masses. The notion of problematization was coined by Foucault to describe a particular way of examining the history of thought (see Foucault 1989, 1992, 1997, 2001). He developed the notion in his final years to capture, in retrospect, the analytical intentions behind much of his previous work and to establish the common methodological thread running through his various studies. In Foucault's own words:

What I tried to do from the beginning was to analyze the process of 'problematization' – which means: how and why certain things (behavior, phenomena, processes) became a *problem*. Why, for example, certain forms of behavior were characterized and classified as 'madness' while other similar forms were completely neglected at a given historical moment; the same thing for crime and delinquency, the same question of problematization for sexuality. (2001: 171, italics in original)

Problematizations do not emerge out of the blue, entirely disconnected from their historical configuration. Quite the contrary, Foucault stressed, a problematization should be seen an 'an "answer" to a concrete situation which is real' (2001: 172). That said, one cannot infer from a specific historical situation to a particular problematization (Foucault 2001: 173). There is never just one possible problematization of a given historical context, although the latter may render some problematizations, some answers/responses, more probable than others. Following Luhmann's definition of contingency as that which is 'neither necessary nor impossible' (1989: 45), problematizations can therefore be said to assume a contingent (rather than arbitrary) relation to the historical configuration.

Another aspect of problematization must be highlighted. In an excellent reconstruction of Foucault's notion of problematization, Marius Gudmand-Høyer notes that a problematization analysis should not only attend to how and why certain phenomena become a problem, but also to the 'embedded normativity' of any problematization (2009: 7). In making this point, Gudmand-Høyer refers to Foucault's opening lecture in the 1978 course *Security, Territory, Population*, where Foucault posited that there is hardly 'any theoretical or analytical discourse which is not permeated or underpinned in one way or another by something like an imperative discourse' (2007: 3). Extrapolating this to problematizations, this amounts to saying that there is no problematization which does not in some way or other contain an imperative dimension. The problematization of something (e.g. crowds) typically entails an implicit or explicit articulation of a favoured solution to the observed problem, for example, in the form of suggestions for how to deal with the problem in practice.

Against this background, the history of sociological crowd semantics to be studied in this book might now be rephrased as an investigation of the destiny of the crowd as a sociological problem. That is, I wish to study sociological crowd semantics by exploring how crowds and masses have been problematized within sociology. This generates the following questions to be examined in the book: how did the crowd emerge as a problem for sociological analysis, and under what (social, political, scholarly/disciplinary) conditions? How has the problematization of crowds changed since the late nineteenth century, and in response to which historical contexts? What embedded normativities characterize the problematization of crowds? Which alternative semantics have been introduced in the light of the altering problematizations of crowds? Finally, and relatedly, why did the crowd cease to form a key problem in sociology, and what forms do present-day problematizations of crowds adopt?

I mentioned above that the investigation of these questions is based on a comprehensive archive, the composition of which I will now describe in more detail. To begin with, I should note that, even though I am committed to examining more than just a few 'bits and scraps of evidence', I make no pretensions to having obtained a full coverage of the literature on crowds and masses; nor is the ambition of the investigation to arrive at a complete inclusion, though. A full coverage must be abandoned if only for pragmatic reasons. Due to the central role that the problem of crowds occupied in early sociological thinking, it is virtually impossible to map out every account and discussion of crowds. Of course, a great number of books and articles make explicit reference to crowds and masses (along with all sorts of derived and neighbouring notions) in their titles, rendering them easily traceable, but very often sociological discussions of the crowd topic appear in contexts which provide no surface indication that this or that text actually contributes to the semantics of crowds. To give but one example, Robert Michels' *Political Parties: A Sociological Study of the Oligarchical Tendencies of Modern Democracy* does not immediately stage itself as playing a part in the history of sociological crowd semantics (1959). Yet in this book Michels actually adopted a classical problematization of crowds in order to illuminate a phenomenon not previously examined, namely the tendency of political parties to succumb to elite rule. The existence of vast amounts of similar material, which seems to be at most secondarily concerned with crowds and masses, but which nevertheless contains central contributions to the history of sociological crowd semantics, poses great challenges to the methodological design of the present study. Put very simply, the question is what to include and what not, and how to search for relevant material?

As a first demarcation, the archive focuses on academic texts, i.e. written contributions, since my interest is in the development of scholarly (sociological) crowd semantics.[1] Narrowing the study to scholarly texts obviously only marks a first small step forward when it comes to constructing an archive for the inquiry. More specifically, therefore, I have concentrated on texts that are generally canonized as key contributions to sociological crowd semantics. This applies, for instance, to Gustave Le Bon's *The Crowd*, Robert E. Park's *The Crowd and the Public* and Theodor Geiger's *Die Masse und ihre Aktion*, to mention but a few; but also canonized texts are included whose *sociological* status might be contested, such as Sigmund Freud's *Ego Analysis and Group Psychology* and Elias Canetti's *Crowds and Power*. In addition to such landmark texts the archive comprises a plethora of 'minor' contributions, many of which subscribe to, reflect on, modify or criticize the canonized milestones. Texts belonging to this latter category have typically been identified through library keyword searches or via cross-referencing in other texts. Quantitatively, the 'minor' texts constitute the bulk of the archive, and much has been included here to ensure an extensive picture of the history of sociological crowd semantics. However, and this is critical to set in stone, I am not interested in every enunciation on crowds and masses, but rather in the main lines of problematization that the history of sociological crowd semantics exhibits. So although detours might (and will) appear, it is and remains the grand semantic trajectories – or plateaus, as I shall call them below – that constitute my central concern in this book.

When it comes to grasping the historical contexts of sociological crowd semantics, I rely on secondary sources in the form of books and

---

[1] Obviously, one would have to consult other sources as well if one were to understand the broader social and political role of crowds in modern history. For example, Jeffrey Schnapp has demonstrated the creative ways in which crowds have served as a socio-political imaginary on political posters (2005). Similarly, work by Lesley Brill and Michael Tratner has explored the significant status of crowds in twentieth-century movies (Brill 2006; Tratner 2008). Given the present purposes, I will leave out such material.

articles written by historians. However, at times I also have recourse to literature (typically, novels) when accounting for the interrelatedness between scholarly semantics and its socio-political environment. The reason for this is that academic conceptions and literary representations of crowds display close links historically (see in particular Esteve 2003; Plotz 2000; Schettler 2006). Especially during the nineteenth century, literary representations served as inspiration for subsequent crowd theory. But the influence also ran in the opposite direction, as literary representations did much to popularize the negative, frightening images of irrational crowds that characterized a lot of early crowd semantics. The intimate connection between literature and scholarly crowd semantics is further manifested in the fact that some key crowd scholars had literary backgrounds, including Hermann Broch and most notably Canetti, who was awarded the Nobel Prize in literature in 1981.

Crowds in history

There is a long and weighty tradition of dealing historically with the problem of crowds. In the following I shall discuss some of the most eminent contributions to this rich body of literature, partly in order to position the present investigation vis-à-vis existing studies, and partly to set the basis for explicating the main arguments of the book.

Let me begin by noting one of the crucial analytical implications of my approach. Even if crowd semantics is embedded in specific historical situations, the focus on problematization makes evident that the present book is not about real crowds and their actual behaviour (see also Foucault 1992: 11). The investigation does not intend to map the various forms and expressions that crowded behaviour has assumed in modern society, nor is the objective to explain the dynamics underpinning these modes of actions. This sets the present book radically apart from one of the most renowned lines of inquiry that takes a historical interest in crowds, and which emanates from the work of Georges Lefebvre. In a seminal article from the early 1930s, entitled 'Revolutionary Crowds' (1965), Lefebvre critically interrogated the image of crowds, which had been put forward by nineteenth-century thinkers such as Hippolyte Taine and especially Gustave Le Bon (to be discussed in detail in Chapter 1). Lefebvre's point was that, when confronted with historical evidence, several of Le Bon's and Taine's fundamental ideas could not be sustained. In particular, Lefebvre questioned if the French Revolution, often referred to as the emblematic outburst of crowd action, could be adequately described as the behaviour of hypnotized, hence involuntary, crowds such as Le Bon assumed. Contrary to this image, Lefebvre found it more apposite to account for the revolutionary events on the basis of a notion of voluntary assemblies (see also 1973).

George Rudé, writing some decades later and being deeply indebted to Lefebvre, took over the baton. In influential books such as *The Crowd in the French Revolution* (1959) and *The Crowd in History* (1981), Rudé too disputed the validity of Le Bon's and Taine's claims when tested against actual historical data. Rudé identified particularly two problems in Taine's and Le Bon's accounts. First, he argued, these scholars conceived of crowds as composed largely of criminal, deranged and pathological individuals (Rudé 1959: 219). Yet, Rudé could show, on the basis of careful historical analyses of the composition of the crowd that stormed the Bastille, the occupational status of these rioters and their motives, this was factually incorrect. Second, Taine and Le Bon put too much emphasis on the role of leaders. To be sure, Rudé conceded, when scrutinizing actual crowd events:

Leaders, too, played a part in giving the crowd cohesion and unity and in guiding and directing its energies. Yet they probably never enjoyed the lonely eminence nor played the outstanding role ascribed to them in such events by Taine and Le Bon. (1981: 247)

Lefebvre and Rudé's central contribution was to understand crowds, not as abstractions, but as real historical phenomena triggered by the energies of the actual masses 'from below'. Also belonging to this tradition, E. P. Thompson (1971) argued for taking seriously the *moral* background of actual crowd behaviour. In his seminal work on eighteenth-century food riots, Thompson suggested that these riots were not performed by mad criminals, nor were they mere irrational responses to poverty. Much more, he asserted, the kind of crowd action manifested in these riots was disciplined, deliberate and most importantly, it was legitimate in the sense that 'the men and women in the crowd were informed by the belief that they were defending traditional rights or customs', which added up to a decided 'moral economy of the crowd' (1971: 78, 94). Similarly, Eric Hobsbawm's historical work challenged some of the central ideas put forward by classical crowd theorists. In particular, Hobsbawm demonstrated that the *revolutionary* aspirations usually ascribed to crowds are often exaggerated when confronted with historical evidence. Indeed, he stated, in *Primitive Rebels: Studies in Archaic Forms of Social Movement in the 19th and 20th Centuries*:

Normally it [the urban mob] may be regarded as *reformist*, insofar as it rarely if ever conceived of the construction of a new order of society, as distinct from the correction of abnormalities and injustices in a traditional old order. (1971: 7, italics added)

Not all historical studies of crowds subscribe to the Lefebvre–Rudé–Thompson–Hobsbawm tradition.[2] One example is Mark Harrison's intriguing historical analysis of *Crowds and History: Mass Phenomena in English Towns, 1790–1835* (1988). Among other things, and somewhat parallel to what literary scholars have shown, Harrison establishes an interesting connection between popular conceptions of crowds in the early nineteenth century and subsequent theorizing. Specifically, he contends that 'fear of mass "contagion" of spectators by rioters, expressed in the early nineteenth century, was a precursor of the theories of crowd psychology to be developed at the end of the century by LeBon and others' (1988: 313).[3]

Many other historical investigations of crowds could be listed, including Charles Tilly's seminal work, which will be discussed in Chapter 7. However, the aim of this admittedly all too brief account of some of the existing historical studies of crowds is not to present an extensive review, but rather to give a sense of a line of inquiry that differs from the one I pursue in this book: although I study real semantics, I do not venture into an analysis of actual crowds and their actual behaviour. I readily accept that some, perhaps even a majority, of the theoretical problematizations I examine might not match up to the historical realities they purport to account for, but this is a discrepancy which matters little to the present project. By way of analogy, a history of physics or economics that neglected ideas, which were later contested or proved wrong, would be wholly inadequate. Writing a history of knowledge and science entails

---

[2] Moreover, there have been heated disputes among historians about the extent to which the French Revolution is best understood by means of the Marxian approach that Lefebvre's work inspired. While, for example, Albert Soboul would follow in the footsteps of Lefebvre and study the Revolution on the basis of a Marxist framework that stresses the import of class relations and socio-economic tensions, other historians such as especially Alfred Cobban and François Furet have argued for alternative interpretations, highlighting among other things the need for understanding the Revolution in view of broader, cross-national political and ideological dimensions. I will not elicit this debate in any detail, though, as it concerns the Revolution rather than crowds and their status.

[3] Harrison's book puts forward a critical examination of the work of Rudé, Thompson and Hobsbawm and their attempt to shake the predominantly negative images of crowds as advanced by Le Bon and others. For example, Harrison (1988: 12) observes Rudé replicates one of the biases he attributes to Taine and Le Bon, in that he conflates crowds with rioting mobs. As a result Rudé not only ignores the possibility that crowds could be non-aggressive but also that crowds could be essentially non-political (a parallel critique is voiced by Holton 1978: 225–6). The same objection applies, Harrison argues, to the work of Thompson, who tends to equate crowds with riots, as well as to Hobsbawm who, despite stressing the reformist rather than revolutionary character of the crowd, is almost exclusively concerned with the mob's rioting or rebellious acts, thus in effect confirming the violent image of mass behaviour he disputes (see Hobsbawm 1971: 108–25).

a commitment to take seriously ideas that were considered valid in a certain epoch, even if these ideas might not stand a subsequent reality test.

Not being concerned with actual crowds is one thing. Even more radically, perhaps, the book does not even presume that crowds and masses actually exist as real, tangible phenomena. However, nor does it contend the opposite, namely that there is no such thing as crowds and masses. Therefore I am only partly in agreement with Raymond Williams when he asserts that '[t]here are in fact no masses; there are only ways of seeing people as masses' (1963: 289). I find this negative statement just as presumptuous as its positive counterpart. In fact, although I refrain from considering the ontological status of crowds in the present study, I am convinced that for performative reasons the positive claim has more to offer than the negative one. Thus, when people describe themselves and others in crowd and mass terms, this is likely to have performative effects on their subsequent behaviour. Schnapp and Tiews corroborate this view when arguing that, today, the classical idea of crowds operates as an icon; one which is activated, for instance, when collectivities seek to act in ways they believe reflect 'true' crowd behaviour (Schnapp and Tiews 2006: xi). I will return to this performative aspect in the Epilogue.

Just as I renounce judging the ontological status of crowds, so I follow John S. McClelland's (1989: 8) example and abstain from basing the inquiry on a particular definition of crowds and masses. The argument is that the definitions pertaining to various problematizations change over time, and this is likely to produce very different ideas of what constitutes crowds, masses, mobs, etc. It is my hope that tracing these movements will elucidate the *politics of definition* which relate to the field of crowd semantics, for, indeed, defining specific phenomena in crowd terminology is not innocent. A remark by Mark Harrison may illustrate this point, although the quote refers more to common language than to scholarly semantics:

Those people watching a football match are termed a crowd, but those gathered in the Albert Hall are referred to as an audience. Skinheads are said to roam in gangs, company directors assemble in groups. A large number of pickets behaving in a threatening manner may be termed a mob, but a large number of policemen charging with batons will almost never be so described. (1988: 5)

The politics of definition finds a parallel manifestation on the level of demarcating the proper disciplinary boundaries, something that merits particular attention in the light of the present study. Using late-nineteenth-century crowd *psychology* as the entry into the study of *sociological* crowd semantics thus begs the question of how to establish what counts as sociological. In what sense do psychological deliberations form part of the annals of sociology? No clear answer can be given to this question, since the demarcation of the sociological terrain has been contested throughout history. I therefore also purposely refrain from offering an explicit definition of 'sociology'; instead I operate with a broad conception and address the problem of disciplinary delineation in a historical–explorative manner. In fact, as I shall demonstrate in the book, one of the remarkable aspects of the history of crowd semantics is that it provides a doorway to studying the repeated attempts to mark out the proper and legitimate fields of sociological research. Thus, the crowd has often functioned as a tactical marker: as a subject matter through which to circumscribe and police the boundaries of sociology; for instance, by excluding specific positions because of their purportedly psychological or literary (meaning non-scientific) nature.

Since the topic of crowds has played a part in the struggles over how (or how not) to delineate sociology from adjacent disciplines I will need at times to discuss scholarly crowd semantics which, in the eyes of some sociologists, might not fall within the sociological confines. This applies in particular to the examination of more recent crowd semantics. Thus the gradual disappearance of the crowd from the centre of sociological analysis, which was mentioned at the beginning of this introduction, may bear witness to a diminishing sociological interest in crowds during the final decades of the twentieth century. However, crowd semantics has not disappeared altogether from social theory, if the latter term designates a broader category than sociology and one not so occupied with disciplinary divisions. In fact, crowds and masses may be most heavily debated today by scholars who would not first and foremost be called sociologists, but rather social and political theorists. In order to provide a full account of the history of sociological crowd semantics, an outlook is therefore required on how the notion of crowds has moved (or been shoved) to other fields within the social–theoretical realm.

A number of scholars have been attentive to the politics of definition pertaining to the history of the notion of crowds as well as to how it has been mobilized to detach sociology from other disciplines. I think in particular of the following, on whose broad shoulders I stand: Susanna Barrows' *Distortion of Mirrors: Visions of the Crowd in Late Nineteenth-Century France* (1981); Helmuth Berking's *Masse und Geist: Studien zur Soziologie in der Weimarer Republik* (1984); Daria Frezza's *The Leader and the Crowd: Democracy in American Public Discourse, 1880–1941* (2007); Helmut König's *Zivilisation und Leidenschaften: Die Masse im bürgerlichen Zeitalter* (1992); John S. McClelland's above-mentioned *The Crowd and the Mob: From Plato to Canetti* (1989); Serge Moscovici's *The Age of the Crowd: A Historical Treatise on Mass Psychology* (1985); and Jaap van Ginneken's *Crowds, Psychology, and Politics, 1871–1899* (1992). These books have all added significant layers to the understanding of the history of crowd thinking, and I have benefited a lot from them in my own attempt to trace the evolution of sociological crowd semantics. At the same time, these investigations have narrower horizons than the present book, either because they focus on shorter time-spans or more limited geographical contexts, or because they are less inclusive in terms of the number of theoretical positions they cover.

The argument

I have said a lot so far about what constitutes the objectives of this investigation. In the following I would like to give a brief outline of the general argument I present in the book. The central argument has five dimensions, a couple of which have already been touched upon.

First of all, I posit, *sociological crowd semantics is essentially a problematization of modern society and its social and political set-up.* I have already established an intimate relation between modernity and crowds above, but this link may now be described in more accurate terms. Thus, I assert, sociological crowd semantics displays a recurrent problematization of modernity as a fundamentally unfinished project, to put it in Habermasian parlance. From its very inception, the notion of crowds has referred to the dark side of modern society: to something which is intrinsic to the edifice of this social order, and which is associated with all sorts of negative features – and therefore looked upon with terror. Of course, there are notable exceptions to this image, but it is remarkable how seldom crowds are conceived as a *solution* to the challenges of modern society rather than as the embodiment of its immanent dangers. The negative image of crowds is simply so strong that positive counter-images stand out as exceptional. It is also obvious that the crowd-related problematizations of modern society have changed over time. For example, the semantic shift from co-present crowds to dispersed masses, which became increasingly dominant from the 1930s onwards, reflects an altered conception of society, namely one in which the mass media gain significantly in social and political prominence. The point I am getting at here is that the crowd may be seen as a diagnostic category: it offers a lens or prism on how sociology has observed modern society and its social and political constitution at different times. Consequently, the history of sociological crowd semantics examined in this book amounts, in effect, to an investigation of how sociology has diagnosed modern society. And since the crowd is often observed as the dark side of modern society, the resulting diagnoses tend to be perpendicular to some of the most celebrated narratives of sociological analysis. Most notably, perhaps, a diagnosis of modern society, which revolves around classical conceptions of crowds, takes an almost opposite stand to Max Weber's (2001) famous claim about modern society's increasing rationalization.

Indeed, second, one of the main reasons why the notion of crowds has provoked continuous anxiety is that it is associated with *irrationality, violence* and *de-individualization*. Crowds have typically been depicted as entities that run amok in wild rage and whose members are so carried away by the mood of the multitude, as the opening Simmel quote would have it, that they are beyond the reach of rational arguments. This image was particularly strong at the turn of the nineteenth century, but it retained its hold in much sociological crowd semantics throughout the twentieth century and was easily adopted by the semantic transition from crowds to masses. The negative features ascribed to crowds, particularly irrationality and de-individualization, have produced an image of modern society that differs markedly from the rationalization pattern projected by Weber.[4] But they also contribute a great deal to explaining the destiny of the crowd in sociological thinking. Most importantly, it is due to these purported qualities that the crowd has been conceived as a problem rather than something that merits endorsement. Indeed, in much crowd semantics, the crowd is looked down upon, and it is perceived as a phenomenon to be forestalled so as to avert irrationality and de-individualization from taking firm hold of modern society. But in addition to being discredited according to intellectual (its irrationality) or moral/legal (its violence) yardsticks, the crowd also seems to present a *political* matter of concern. In fact, a central reason why the crowd poses a problem is that it challenges particular political ideas. Most notably, the supposedly de-individualizing nature of crowds questions the ideal of the constituent liberal subject. This concern is expressed most vividly, I claim, in American sociological crowd semantics, which struggles to conceive of collective behaviour in ways that do not compromise the

---

[4] It might be debated whether non-rationality or a-rationality are more apt terms than irrationality to describe crowds. Some scholars explicitly prefer non-rationality or a-rationality over irrationality when accounting for crowds and masses. I adhere to the notion of irrationality because especially early sociological crowd semantics tended to portray the crowd not merely in terms of a momentary absence of rationality, such as non-rationality or a-rationality would suggest, but rather as a decisively hysteric, insane, atavistic entity, which constituted the very antagonism to the civilized, rational order. This alleged irrationality has been contested by several sociologists and historians, as I shall come back to on more occasions, but this does not change its status as one of the paradigmatic images of the crowd.

ideal of the autonomous liberal subject. On this basis, I find it warranted to suggest that the challenge posed to the notion of the liberal subject by the classical image of the crowd is (at least partly) responsible for the crowd topic's gradual expulsion from the central sociological agenda.

Third, a central battlefield for the fight against anti-liberal sentiments has been constituted by the notion of *suggestion*. Early crowd psychology often posited that the irrationality, violence and de-individualization of crowds could be explained as effects of hypnotic suggestion. When people form a crowd, so the argument went, a transformation takes place where they become hypnotized by the leader and readily submit to whatever he or she fancies. This hypnotic suggestion is the reason why the crowd members' rational faculties are momentarily annulled and why they are driven to irrational and violent acts. Similarly, suggestion implies de-individualization, as it transforms the crowd members into mere automatons, devoid of any distinctive individual characteristics. While the notion of suggestion played a key explanatory role in early crowd psychology it was heavily contested by much subsequent sociology and social psychology. The reference to suggestion, with its underlying emphasis on features that countered rather directly the ideal of the constituent subject, was hard to digest for liberal sociologists who launched a vendetta against the suggestion concept, eventually rendering it sociologically inappropriate. Suggestion experienced a similar career within psychology, as psychologists too questioned the notion, so that in the end it was endowed with an air of long-superseded, scarcely scientific views on hypnosis. In the book, I demonstrate how suggestion became a key target in the battle over the conception of crowds and over the demarcation of the sociological discipline.

I should note that my interest in how the history of sociological crowd semantics is intertwined with the destiny of the notion of suggestion is guided by the underlying intuition that the latter's fate was undeserved. To be sure, crowd psychologists often referred to suggestion in a rather vague sense. Even so, it seems to me (as I have just intimated) that the critique that was vented against the notion often tended to be based on political discomfort as much as on academic arguments. Yet I do not find the destiny of suggestion unjust simply because the political agenda seemed to penetrate the academic discussion, and in some instances perhaps be more important than that. More crucial, I believe that the notion of suggestion holds greater sociological potentials than the critics granted it. The scope of the book does not permit me to flesh out these potentials, but I shall offer a few notes on the issue in the Epilogue when discussing how crowd thinking might be given fresh life in contemporary sociology.

Fourth, the exclusion of the crowd from the centre of sociological attention did not happen overnight. It was *a gradual, non-coordinated process*, where, step by step, ever new nails were hammered in the coffin. This means that when I discuss all kinds of minor shifts in the history of sociological crowd semantics, these should always also be assessed in the light of how they added to the general movement towards rendering the sociological problematization of crowds increasingly peripheral.

Fifth, and in continuation of the first four points, the book presents *an alternative history of sociology*, i.e. a history observed not from the winner's point of view, as it were, but from the perspective of the defeated, namely the crowd problem which occupied a central role in early sociological debates but came to be marginalized due not least to the politics surrounding the crowds. Moreover, the book constitutes an alternative history of sociology in the sense that it attends to and reinterprets the work of sociologists who are usually acknowledged for very different contributions to sociological debates, but who also – though less well known – have a share in the history of crowd semantics.

Together these five dimensions form the bricks of the argumentative arch of the book. It is my hope that, even if these dimensions are specific to the present investigation, they may be relevant beyond the realm of crowds. I aspire in other words to capture a history of scholarly semantics whose fundamental features and dynamics might be identified in other semantic trajectories within sociology, or which might serve as a template for understanding intellectual developments in other disciplinary domains.

Let me end this introduction with a brief overview of the structure of the book. The chapters are structured around what I call key *semantic plateaus*. The notion of plateaus serves to indicate that semantic formations or trajectories can assume a more or less coherent (but not necessarily uniform) shape, while overlapping to some extent with others in time, space and content. In other words, although the plateaus have separate characters (i.e. problematize crowds in rather similar ways), the boundaries between them need not always be strictly defined. One consequence of this is that although the first chapters focus on crowd semantics in France, Germany and the USA, respectively, some overlaps occur, meaning for instance that a French theorist such as Georges Sorel is discussed in the chapter on German crowd semantics because his work is closely affiliated with one of the semantic strands I identify in the German plateau.

It is trivial but needs to be said: the genealogy of crowd semantics I present in this book emphasizes some branches and developments at the expense of others. This is reflected in semantic plateaus I examine.

Rather than following a strict chronological outline where, for instance, the destiny of late-nineteenth-century French crowd semantics is traced through a systematic study of semantic developments throughout twentieth-century French sociology, I attend to what I claim are the most central semantic plateaus in the history of sociological crowd semantics. That is, I focus on those semantic developments which, I contend, have made the greatest difference and ignore others which have had lesser bearings on the overall history. One implication of this is a certain temporal asymmetry in the discussion of French, German and American crowd semantics. For example, in the examination of French problematizations of crowds a central fixture is the late-nineteenth-century dispute between Gabriel Tarde and Émile Durkheim, whereas in Germany the most significant contributions to sociological crowd semantics are located some decades later, namely in the Weimar era.

Looking more at the specific chapters, Chapter 1 takes a 'pre-sociological' view in that it maps some of the French discussions that formed the backdrop to the late-nineteenth-century sociological debates on crowds. The chapter pays particular attention to Gustave Le Bon's crowd psychology and the scholarly and historical circumstances surrounding it. I categorize Le Bon as pre-sociological because the crowd debates were only really transplanted onto the sociological domain by his contemporary Gabriel Tarde. Chapter 2 examines Tarde's work on crowds and discusses how crowd semantics was allocated a pivotal role in the Tarde–Durkheim debate on the proper understanding of sociology and its possible demarcation from psychology. A note on chronology is warranted here. Some of Tarde's central writings of crowds pre-dated Le Bon's work in this field. I nevertheless discuss Le Bon before Tarde and do so for two reasons. One is that Le Bon came to embody early crowd psychology. It was not least his account that subsequent debates revolved around, either affirmatively or negatively. The other reason for this slight reversion of chronology relates to what I referred to as the pre-sociological status of his work. While popular in non-academic circles, Le Bon did not enjoy recognition in the formal sociological community. Here Tarde's status was entirely different, at least for some time, meaning that he was in a better situation to endow the crowd semantics that Le Bon popularized with sociological capital.

While the semantic plateaus discussed in Chapters 1 and 2 have their epicentres in turn-of-the-nineteenth-century French developments, Chapter 3 performs a spatiotemporal shift: it studies the German crowd semantics that took off in the 1890s, but culminated in the Weimar years. Specifically, the chapter analyses how different lines of thinking on crowds, one inspired by psychology, another by Marxism, formed the basis for the apex of sociological crowd semantics in the Weimar years, represented by the work of Theodor Geiger. Like Durkheim, Geiger wished to enact a strong differentiation between sociology and psychology, and the notion of crowds came to play a central role in this endeavour. But compared to the French problematizations of crowds, which tended to be associated with a conservative outlook, the Weimar debates assumed a more leftish orientation. The same phenomenon, that of crowds, was in other words approached from different political horizons in the two countries.

Chapter 4 covers more or less the same era, i.e. the time-span from the 1890s to the 1930s, but explores the US American setting. Here, I argue, the problematization of crowds was related to a larger problematization of urbanization that burgeoned in the nineteenth century. This gave rise among other things to strategies that aimed to reform cities and their purported crowd tendencies. While key notions from the European crowd semantics had a leverage on how the American scholars conceived of crowd phenomena, the American debates soon acquired a particular accent that struck more liberal tones. Thus, especially Chicago School sociologists with Robert E. Park in the lead argued for seeing crowds, not as incarnations of irrationality, but as vehicles for the liberation of individuals and for the creation of new modes of sociality. This amounted to a rationalization and normalization of crowd phenomena which planted the seeds for more radical notions of rational crowd behaviour in the 1950s, 1960s and 1970s. The chapter also explores some of the charges that were aired against sociological crowd semantics, and which formed part of the struggles on how to conceive of sociology in a legitimate manner.

In the first four chapters on France, Germany and the USA, I strive to understand the semantic developments on the basis of how the problematization of crowds was embedded in specific social and political contexts. This broader contextualization of crowd sociological semantics has less prominence in the final four chapters. The central reason for this is that, after the 1930s, the main sociological discussions on crowds are no longer easily separated along national–geographic lines. This is due among other things to the practical circumstance that the rise of Hitler made many European scholars emigrate to the USA. This did not completely eradicate national differences, but the main semantic plateaus assumed more cross-national forms. For example, Chapters 5 and 6 discuss the semantic transition from crowd to mass, captured by the diagnosis of the so-called mass society. Here, I claim, the important semantic developments were not so much responses to specific national problematizations, but rather to what was seen as general tendencies that went across singular countries, not least the perceived threat of totalitarianism.

The various theories that make up the semantic plateaus explored in Chapters 5 and 6 share several features. Above all, they are all premised on the idea that traits which were previously ascribed to crowds of co-present people now applied to much larger settings where physical co-presence was neither necessary nor possible. This was the essential shift enacted in the transition from crowd to mass semantics. But the semantic plateaus of the two chapters also championed the common idea that the emergence of mass society contained deep-seated totalitarian impulses. The semantic plateau analysed in Chapter 5 argued that this totalitarian inclination resulted from mass society's suspension of previous class differences. In mass society, it was argued, differences between elites and masses are no longer operative, but there are also no moral or cultural values to guide the behaviour of masses. In this morass of moral decline, cultural dissolution and annulment of class distinctions totalitarian propensities thrive, so the problematization went.

In contrast to the discussions of *crowds* the *mass* society semantics did not seek to delineate a particular sociological field, defined in opposition to for example psychology. On the contrary, the debates on mass society tended to cater to a non-specialization of disciplinary horizons. This is particularly visible in Chapter 6 where I examine a semantic plateau which unravelled the complexities and totalitarian propensities of modern mass society and which did so on the basis of a *mélange* of sociology and psychology/psychoanalysis. The Frankfurt School's work – including its problematization of the purported isolation that burgeons in modern mass society and which renders people susceptible to anti-democratic, totalitarian influence – occupies a central place in this discussion, but some of the critique it was confronted with is also attended to.

The fading relevance of country-specific socio-political contexts does not entail that the context of crowd semantics became altogether obsolete as if the problematization of crowds evolved in a vacuum. It is more correct to say that other contexts took over. In continuation of discussions from Chapters 2, 3 and 4, Chapter 7 examines how broader academic developments within history and sociology impinged on conceptions of crowds and collective behaviour in American sociology from the late 1950s onwards. In spite of the mass society semantics, a range of scholars began to conceive of crowds in their physical composition anew. One prominent example of this was Elias Canetti's work, but in spite of all his originality, Canetti left hardly any imprint on sociological debates. Much more influential were a wave of collective behaviour scholars who challenged previous notions of irrational crowds and suggested a more rational understanding instead. This rationalization of crowd and collective behaviour was aligned with historical work which stressed the purposive nature of crowds. Despite all intentions, the upsurge in sociological work on crowds and collective behaviour did not manage to put crowds (back) on top of the sociological agenda. Quite the contrary, the notions of crowds and collective behaviour slowly faded into the background, ousted not least by a waxing interest in social movement studies. It is this peripheral status that the notion of crowd holds to this day, I claim.

Chapter 7 pays particular attention to developments within American sociology since this is where the 'mainstream' (an unsatisfactory and dubious term, I admit) trajectories of the discipline are defined today. While the chapter basically analyses the dying twitch of sociological crowd semantics, Chapter 8 demonstrates that an alternative (mainly European) plateau can be identified, which, stretching from the late 1970s until today, has tried to unearth mass dynamics under postmodern conditions. This semantic plateau enlivens the semantics of masses, but does so in ways that oppose mainstream conceptions and methodologies in sociology. Moreover, postmodern mass semantics revolves around a political predicament which I analyse on the basis of the notion of post-politics. That is, these postmodern theories suggest that the contemporary masses have entered an era where traditional notions of politics are suspended or bypassed. This does not amount to a dismissal of crowd and mass semantics. Quite the contrary, these theories agree, an adequate understanding of contemporary society and politics must take seriously the state, operations and desires of the masses.

Finally, in the Epilogue I briefly summarize a few of the book's main findings and chart some directions for what a future sociology might look like, which does not necessarily place the notion of crowds centre stage, but which does take it more seriously than is presently the case in most sociological analysis.

1   Setting the stage: crowds and modern French society

In an infamous dictum Alfred North Whitehead noted that Western philosophy is but 'a series of footnotes to Plato' (1978: 39). A similar maxim might be championed with respect to the problematization of crowds. In the *Republic* Plato compared the *plēthos*, the political mass of citizens, to an animal that scorns knowledge and makes itself heard instead through a 'voice of anger and of appetites, that is to say, of all that is not rational' (Foucault 2010: 212; Plato 1994: 214–15 (493a–4a)). This critical appraisal of crowds has been echoed in much subsequent social and political theory. John S. McClelland has even suggested 'that political theorizing was *invented* to show that democracy, the rule of men by themselves, necessarily turns into rule by the mob', leaving the stamp of a 'profoundly anti-democratic bias' on much Western political thought (McClelland 1989: 1, 2, italics in original). Anti-democratic or not, throughout history problematizations of political order have often been framed within a horizon of crowds, masses, mobs and multitudes.[1] And more often than not, these problematizations have conceived of crowds and masses as something to be avoided, directed,

---

[1] A few selected snapshots from pre-twentieth-century political philosophy will suffice. Niccolò Machiavelli's general objective can be said to lie in transforming the mob into a republic people (McClelland 1989: 72–81). Thomas Hobbes' *Leviathan* envisioned 'the Multitude ... united in one Person' (1991: 120), a concurrence forged to grant every individual lasting security and peace. The notion of multitudes received new emphasis in Baruch Spinoza in his ardent defence of democracy (e.g. 2002). Some 150 years later, in an 1836 essay entitled 'Civilization', John Stuart Mill observed a correlation between civilization and masses, which was believed to change the conditions of modern politics since 'power passes more and more from individuals, and small knots of individuals, to masses: ... the importance of the masses becomes constantly greater, that of individuals less' (Mill 1859: 163). As Asa Briggs (1985: 38–9) notes, Mill replicated this diagnosis in *On Liberty*, when asserting that '[a]t present individuals are lost in the crowd ... The only power deserving the name is that of masses, and of governments while they make themselves the organ of the tendencies and instincts of masses' (Mill 1948: 58). Somewhat similarly, in 1846 Søren Kierkegaard employed a crowd vernacular to describe the 'present age' as one containing a 'leveling' power (1978: 84; see also Welge 2006: 350–1).

transformed.[2] This was also the key image propagated by Gustave Le Bon whose work became almost synonymous with the psychology of crowds that burgeoned in the 1890s. In the present chapter, I shall discuss the main tenets of Le Bon's crowd theory, explore its inspirations and examine its biopolitical ambitions, so as to characterize the edifice on which subsequent sociological crowd semantics was built (or tried to tear apart).

Before delving into Le Bon's theorizing on crowds, it might be helpful briefly to sketch the social and intellectual backdrop to his work. It is no coincidence that crowd psychology took off in the 1890s, nor that it was anchored in a largely (but not exclusively) French context. The French Revolution in 1789 instigated an unstable political century where observers began to acknowledge the political role of crowds, so that, gradually, reflections on the French Revolution became intertwined with the problematization of crowds. In order to give a sense of this, I start out with some observations on the historical context in which crowd psychology emerged. Given the focus on Le Bon and the background for his theorizing, this contextualization will have a one-sidedly French twist.

Crowds in an age of revolutions

In France, the storming of the Bastille on 14 July 1789 and the radicalized revolutionary years that followed suit marked the most famous steps in a longer revolutionary march, which included the July Revolution of 1830, the 1848 insurrections and the 1871 upheaval as other landmark events. These events were the signposts in a politically highly unstable century where the political regimes changed constantly: from the First Republic, which counted the Convention (1792–5), the Directory (1795–9) and the Consulate (1799–1804); over the First Empire (1804–14); the First Restoration (of Bourbon monarchy) (1814–15);

---

[2] Some of the largely negative undertones associated with crowds have old etymological roots. For example, Latin has two words for crowds that carry pejorative connotations. *Turba* refers to the disorder and tumult of crowds, while *vulgus* denotes the lower classes with their allegedly inferior intelligence and moral standards (Sofroniew 2006a, 2006b). As a contraction of *mobile vulgus*, the term *mob* has inherited some of the derogatory qualities of *vulgus*. But through its association with *mab*, 'meaning "a woman of loose character" in the sixteenth century' (Wang 2006: 188), *mob* is also a gendered category, a feature that will play some role in the problematizations to be examined in this book. *Multitudo*, a third Latin word for crowds, originally referred to the crowd as an exclusively numerical entity, but eventually came to be endowed with a qualitative meaning, signifying the body politic, as in Hobbes (Schuyler 2006). For more thorough etymological and semantic accounts, see Briggs (1985), Hill (1974) as well as the entries in Schnapp and Tiews (2006).

the Second Restoration (1815–30); the July Monarchy (1830–48); the Second Republic (1848–52); the Second Empire (1852–70); to the Third Republic (1870–1940). Add to this the social instability, caused in part by famine and poverty, which worked as a constant propagator of political turmoil, and which itself was propelled by increasing industrialization and urbanization.

One index of the social and political unrest can be found in the number of strikes that workers organized. In their analysis of strikes in France from 1830–1930, Edward Shorter and Charles Tilly demonstrate the existence of nineteenth-century strike waves peaking in 1833, 1840, 1869–70, 1893 and 1899–1900 (1974). Generally speaking, the number of strikes as well as the number of participants increased greatly throughout the century. As a vestige of the magnitude of the phenomenon, Shorter and Tilly register fifty-five strikes in 1833 and 634 in 1893 (1974: 107–18). Importantly, strikes were not an exclusively Parisian affair. Even if Paris was the centre for much strike activity, the vast majority of the strikes were executed in other parts of France.

Historians have suggested conflicting explanations of the strike activity, from seeing strikes as a reaction to deprivation to interpreting them, as Shorter and Tilly (1974: 343) do, as a means of political action, aimed not so much at the individual employers, but rather at the government. For present purposes, the actual reasons behind the strikes matter little. I am more interested in the fact that, throughout the nineteenth century, strikes were often linked to crowd behaviour. One of the most renowned accounts of how workers on strike formed a crowd took on a literary attire, as it was put forward in *Germinal*, the famous book by the French novelist Émile Zola, who was acclaimed by his contemporaries as 'the epic poet of crowds' (Barrows 1981: 112).[3] *Germinal*, which was published in 1885, described how, at the end of the Second Empire, a community of poor miners was led on a long-term strike by the influence of a newcomer, the book's protagonist, Étienne Lantier. Inflamed by contemporary socialist ideals, Étienne opens the eyes of his fellow miners to the injustices they suffer. Triggered by an ill-concealed cut in wages, he organizes a strike, which at first is characterized by passive resistance, but escalates in violent crowd action and confrontations with soldiers, a point at which Étienne's authority and oratory control over the crowd vanishes. However, neither the passive resistance nor the eruption of violence brings about any immediate improvement for the workers, who eventually return to work.

---

[3] While I shall only discuss *Germinal* here, Naomi Schor (1978) has argued that the crowd theme is at the heart of much of Zola's fictional work.

Germinal's significance lies not least in its naturalistic approach. Zola had studied the historical conditions of miners closely, and had had the chance to visit a mine in 1884. Moreover, the strike described in the book was modelled around an actual mining strike at Anzin, which Zola observed first-hand, and where 12,000 workers went on strike between 19 February and 16 April, 1884. This temporal displacement, the use of an 1884 occurrence as a template for describing events that allegedly took place around one and a half decades earlier, was compensated for by the fact that in 1869 two huge coal strikes broke out, which too could be said to bear some resemblance to the strike portrayed in *Germinal* (Lethbridge 1993: x). In combination, these 1869 and 1884 events weaved a backcloth that ensured that *Germinal*, despite being a work of fiction, would evoke a sense of immediate recollection among its readership. Indeed, Zola believed that his work offered a realistic representation of social conditions and even argued that his writings approximated 'quasi-scientific evidence' (Lethbridge 1993: xii). However, *Germinal*'s main realistic feature may not so much be its account of strikes and mining conditions at the end of the Second Empire; its chief realism may lie instead in how it conveyed a widespread belief that strikes and crowd behaviour were intimately tied and in how it portrayed popular images and fears of revolutionary crowds, whether or not these had any real socio-historical foundation.

The revolutionary references were flagged already in the title of the book. Germinal thus refers to the seventh month (21 March to 19 April) in the new republican/revolutionary calendar that was introduced in 1793, and which set the proclamation of the Republic in 1792 as Year I. More specifically, the name of Germinal alludes to the famous so-called Germinal risings where a crowd of some 10,000 people marched on the Convention, the national assembly of 1792–5, to protest against famine, an event that took place on 1 April 1795, i.e. on 12 Germinal, Year III. These revolutionary undertones of Zola's novel were easily recognized by its French audience. His point of recalling the Germinal risings in a novel whose action was located at the end of the Second Empire was to establish an uninterrupted path of revolutionary aspirations running from the early years of the French Revolution right up to 1885 when *Germinal* was published. In Robert Lethbridge's words, '[r]ather than being circumscribed by its origins in specific events of 1869 and 1884 [the strikes mentioned above], the novel accommodates the conflicts of the century extended, by a process of repetition, from 1789 onwards' (1993: xi). More specifically, as industrialization gained firmer footing in France throughout the nineteenth century, and unionization and socialist as well as anarchist movements grew stronger, the old revolutionary objectives were now appropriated and modified by the workers whose strikes and uproars formed a stepping stone for the climax arrived with the Parisian Commune in 1871. Indeed, for Zola, 'the savagery of 1871 could be interpreted as the culmination of strains and tensions which imperial dictatorship had tried to suppress', and which crowds of workers on strike had reacted against during the Second Empire (Lethbridge 1993: x–xi). In this sense, *Germinal* was not merely about the very epoch in which its action unfolded, but just as much a literary problematization of a century engulfed with revolutionary desires, unleashed, many believed, in the form of crowd behaviour.

The novel's reference to popular images of revolutionary crowds is vivid in the following description of striking miners, an account which adeptly connected the French Revolution, the Second Empire and the 1884 Anzin 'model' strike:

Then the men hove into view, a raging mob 2,000 strong, pit boys, hewers, and wastemen [different groups of mining workers], a compact mass tumbling forwards like a single body, whose discoloured breeches and ragged woollen jerseys merged into a single mud-coloured mass. Only their burning eyes and the dark holes of their gaping mouths could be seen as they sang the 'Marseillaise', and the verses tailed off into a vague bellowing, echoing to the beat of their clogs clattering over the hard ground. Over their heads, among the spikes of the iron bars that stabbed at the air, they passed an axe, keeping it upright; and this single axe, flaunted like the battle standard of the band, took on the sharp profile of a guillotine blade against the light evening sky. (Zola 1993: 348)

Germinal reproduced several other popular images of crowds. For example, the book evoked a sense of contagious dynamics underlying the violent rage ('[t]heir rancour had swollen gradually but poisonously within them, and now it burst like a boil. Year after year of starvation spilled over into a feverish hunger for murder and destruction', 1993: 333–4).*Germinal* also depicted the crowd as being at the mercy of instincts rather than succumbing to rational guidance, something which was emphasized by Zola's tendency to suggest an 'alcoholic thirst of mobs' (Barrows 1981: 101). Moreover, women were presented as particularly susceptible to the crowd's alleged frenzy ('[t]he women screamed in delirium', 1993: 285) and as more violent than their male counterparts once captured by the crowd.[4] Finally, while Zola, due to his socialist sympathies, generally portrayed the crowd of miners on strike as one whose acts were largely explained and justified by the

---

[4] Zola's gendering of the crowd is analysed in Barrows (1981: 102–4, 106) and Schor (1978: 87–103).

exploitation of the workers, he also used *Germinal* to recall the night-marish perspective that the revolutionary crowd constituted to the bourgeois observer, for whom:

The women would scream, and the men would look gaunt as wolves, their fangs drooling and gnashing. Yes, these same rags and the same thunder of clogs, the same terrifying pack of animals with dirty skins and foul breath, would sweep away the old world, as their barbarian hordes overflowed and surged through the land. There would be blazing fires, not a stone of the towns would be left standing, and they [the bourgeoisie] would become savages again, living out in the woods, once the poor had enjoyed their great orgy and garnered their harvest, sucked the women dry and sacked the cellars of the rich. (1993: 349)

This was no distorted fear simply stemming from Zola's pen. Quite the opposite, as will be evident throughout this chapter, the quote appositely epitomized the animalistic and barbarian image of crowds that circulated in late-nineteenth-century bourgeois spheres. One notable propagator of such fearful sentiments towards crowds was the French historian, Hippolyte Taine.

Taine was one of many intellectuals who pondered over the revolutionary course France had taken since 1789. How to characterize and explain this development, it was asked, and how to establish a more stable path? These questions prompted themselves with greater urgency after 1871. In July 1870 France had declared war on Prussia, but a humiliating defeat at Sedan, which included the capture of the emperor, Napoleon III, seriously discredited the regime, and the Parisian people went on the streets to demand a new beginning. Soon a group of deputies of a moderate bent proclaimed the Third Republic, in part to prevent revolutionaries from seizing power (Price 1993: 190). Yet the revolutionary inclinations were far from subdued as would soon be obvious. Although the French were in effect beaten, the war continued, and from 19 September 1870 to 28 January 1871, the Prussian troops kept Paris under siege. The capital was defended by the National Guard, consisting in large part of men from the working classes. Eventually, Paris was lost, as was Alsace-Lorraine, and France accepted peace. Meanwhile, however, insurrections broke out in Paris. For some time tensions had intensified between the National Guard and the national government, reaching a provisional culmination on 18 March when, after two weeks of Parisian resistance to the government's attempt to take over the National Guard's cannon, the people revolted. On 26 March 1871, the Parisians elected the Commune, a self-governing, patriotic if revolutionary body of socialist (though not exclusively so) leaning. The national government, led by Adolphe Thiers, had with-drawn to Versailles but now sent in its troops to recapture Paris and suppress the revolution. This resulted in the so-called 'bloody week' from 21–7 May 1871, which ended with Versailles' victory over the revolting crowds. The triumph came at a high cost, though. In the words of François Furet:

The Communards, retreating from west to east, set fire to the Tuileries, and then burned the Conseil d'État, the Cour des Comptes and finally the old Hôtel de Ville; they shot hostages, including the archbishop, Monseigneur Darboy. The Versailles troops, for their part, gave no quarter: from the 26th, Paris was the theatre of a real manhunt, in which several thousand 'suspects', including women and children, were killed without trial: the grisly tally is not statistically exact, but the figure of 20,000 dead is probable. Furthermore, 40,000 prisoners were dumped in mostly primitive conditions. (1992: 504)

This veritable massacre and destruction that took place in the confrontation between the revolutionary crowds and the government forces had immense repercussions. In particular, bourgeois observers like Taine were in shock (see Van Ginneken 1992: 31). However grave previous insurrections had been throughout the nineteenth century, the 1871 Commune riots went beyond the wildest fears. The Commune made evident that the revolutionary crowds constituted an ever-present threat to society and civilization. As Furet puts it:

the last uprising in the French revolutionary tradition was also the one which created the most fear and shed the most blood, as if it formed the ultimate exorcism of a violence which had been an inseparable part of French public life since the end of the eighteenth century. In this Paris in flames, the French Revolution bade farewell to history. The bourgeoisie, however, took the opposite view: it was proof of the terrifying threat which increasingly hung over their destiny, and over the future of civilization. (1992: 506)

This was the context that lent Zola's *Germinal* its sense of portraying the tensions leading to revolutionary excess, and which urged Taine to dig into France's revolutionary past. Robert K. Merton has suggested that Gustave Le Bon, whose work will be discussed below, was 'often analyzing the behavior of crowds in the Third Republic under the guise of examining the behavior of crowds during the [1789] Revolution' (1960: xxvii). Something similar can be said of Taine. It was the 1871 events that led Taine to embark on his investigation of *Les Origines de la France Contemporaine*, the second part of which was devoted to (and entitled) *The French Revolution* (Taine 2002, originally published between 1878 and 1884).

Taine's contribution consisted in a kind of historical diagnosis of the revolutionary inclinations. The medical reference to diagnosis is deliberate, for Taine's goal was 'therapeutic: to make a diagnosis, write a prescription, find a "social form" that the French people might take on' (Ozouf 2002: xi). More specifically, Taine, a great believer in the positivist sciences that burgeoned at his time, sought to inaugurate a historical approach which was centred on psychological dimensions. He envisioned a kind of psychohistory, a sort of 'pure psychology', as he put it, applied to historical phenomena, including the French Revolution (quoted in van Ginneken 1992: 44).

Taine was far from the first historian to analyse the revolutionary past of France. But, he felt, previous investigations had ignored one important agent, the crowd, and were therefore inadequate both with respect to their descriptive–historical qualities and when it came to suggesting remedying action. Only by taking into account the political psychology of the mob could the revolutionary events be fully understood – and future insurrections prevented. Taine established an intimate link between revolutionary events and crowd behaviour at the very beginning of *The French Revolution*. Thus the first section of the book, significantly named 'Spontaneous Anarchy', opened with a description of how, on the night of 14 July 1789, power had not only:

slipped from the hands of the King ... it lay on the ground, ready to the hands of the unchained populace, the violent and overexcited crowd, the mobs which picked it up like some weapon that had been thrown away in the street. (Taine 2002: 3)

Taine went on to detail how the 1789 events amounted to a brutal 'dictatorship of a mob' (2002: 40). At the base of this view was a problematization of democracy. The good society, Taine posited, is one governed by a minority of nobles whose dignity is naturally given. Replacing such a hierarchical order with the rule of the masses would create an obvious obstacle to 'the safety and prosperity' of society because it would no longer be possible to set a natural example for and educate the multitude (2002: 166). Even worse, he believed to demonstrate, popular government is bound to dissolve into arbitrary and violent destruction.[5] Despite his insistent claims to objectivity,[6] this highly critical attitude towards democracy bears witness to the conservative and aristocratic or elitist tenets of Taine's approach (see e.g. van Ginneken 1992: 48). The conservative elitism of Taine is echoed in the remedies he

---

[5] This was meant as a critique, in essence, of Jean-Jacques Rousseau and the Enlightenment tradition which, in Taine's eyes, had seeded the revolutionary intent. Taine's scene with Rousseau and the Enlightenment is examined at length by McClelland (1989: ch. 5).

[6] In the preface to *The French Revolution*, Taine made the following statement about his investigation: 'This is history, and nothing more, and, if I may fully express myself, I esteem my vocation of historian too highly to make a cloak of it for the concealment of another' (2002: xxxvi). History, yes, but clearly also *politicized* history.

envisioned. France could only enter a stable path, he argued, if power was placed in the hands of a true nobility, conscious of its obligations. Alternatively, institutions such as the church or the family should be allocated a pivotal role (Barrows 1981: 83).

According to Taine, the rule of mobs that could be identified in the French Revolution – and, by extension, in the 1871 Paris Commune – signified an entire '*dissolution*' of society (2002: 3, italics in original). This is but one illustration of Taine's inclination to see crowd behaviour as an evolutionary regression. As van Ginneken (1992: 25–6) notes, Taine was well informed about recent developments in evolutionary theory and followed the attempts – by scholars such as Herbert Spencer – to apply the principles of evolution to the understanding of social phenomena. Taine's observations of how France's revolutionary course had effected a leap down the evolutionary ladder went hand in hand with his conservative predisposition; it showed the Revolution not from the perspective of equality and liberty but rather as a barbarous collapse of society.

This is one of the points where Zola and Taine entered different semantico-political avenues. Zola was in fact very inspired by Taine's historiographic objectives. This was visible to some extent in *Germinal*, where Zola's accounts of striking crowds shared many of the same pejorative features that were aired in Taine's work. Nonetheless, the underlying political agendas differed markedly (see Barrows 1981: 107–8). While Taine insisted on the unambiguously negative effects of revolutionary crowds, Zola was at pains to outline the miserable conditions that contemporary workers were living under. This lent a sense of legitimacy to the behaviour of striking crowds, just as it pointed to the need to actually destabilize those societal structures which, for Zola and like-minded spirits, served to suppress workers and maintain societal inequality. Hence the optimistic tone resonating in the title of *Germinal*, which not merely alluded to the famous 1792 uprisings. It also referred, Zola said, to a 'patch of sunlight ... It represents a revolutionary April, the flight of a decrepit society toward springtime' (quoted in Barrows 1981: 108). Taine's account was not imbued with any such hopes for a germinating future of social equality.

While at odds politically, Taine and Zola sided with one another when it came to how they described crowds. In particular, they subscribed to the same rudimentary psychology of crowds. In addition to being violent, revolutionary and destructive, Taine portrayed crowds and crowd members as 'bewildered sheep' who are 'carried away by their delirium' and instincts; they were said to be spontaneous 'brutes gone mad', led by 'blockheads who have become insane' (2002: 409). Indeed, the crowd purportedly produced a 'paralysis of the brain', a gravity which was emphasized by the allegedly 'contagious' nature of masses (2002: 410, 18). Much of this idiom was reproduced in *Germinal*. But Taine's influence went beyond Zola. Taine thus represented and further propagated a semantic horizon that was widely endorsed in both academic and non-academic circles, and which also formed the backdrop to much of the crowd psychologists' later theorizing. Specifically, van Ginneken (1992: 47–51) has shown, Taine's study of *Les Origines de la France Contemporaine* was extremely influential in the social, political and psychological thinking of his time as well as in the years following his death in 1893. Of greatest interest for present purposes is his salience to crowd psychologists such as Le Bon. Barrows (1981: 85) even suggests that 'Taine stood as the hero and model for crowd psychologists', so ramifying was the approval that his descriptions of barbarous crowds met.

Still, Taine's (as well as Zola's) psychology of crowds remained rudimentary, not least when compared to the work of subsequent scholars. His problematization of crowds was first of all political, dressed in apparently objective historical guise; it was not scientifically explanatory in the sense that he aimed to understand the underlying dynamics of crowds. What Taine failed to incorporate – hence merely making him a precursor of the crowd theoretical tradition I focus on in this book rather than an 'associate' in his own right – is the theoretical reservoir of hypnotism and suggestion, the main ingredients in the breakthrough of crowd psychology as a distinctive scholarly branch. Taine certainly was aware of some of the important developments in the French discussions of hypnotism, but this knowledge was never transformed into more than superficial observations. As Barrows remarks, 'he cared less about analyzing the dynamics of crowd psychology than simply labeling it as pathological. Taine simply stated that passions were contagious, without asking why they were' (1981: 86; see also McClelland 1989: 151–2).

What was it more specifically that Taine did not incorporate in his work? What were the discussions on hypnotism about? In answering these questions it might be helpful to note that ever since Franz Anton Mesmer's 1775 work on magnetism, there had been lively medical debates in France, Germany, England and elsewhere on whether patients could be treated through magnetic sleep and whether all or only particular individuals were susceptible to magnetization (Ellenberger 1970: 57ff.). In the 1880s some of these questions were readdressed in a new dispute, this time revolving around hypnotism, a concept that was invented in 1843 on the basis of elaborations on mesmerism. Briefly put, the matter of this new dispute was whether all persons were susceptible to hypnosis or only certain pathological individuals. The debate found its institutionalized expression in the views of two conflicting schools, the Salpêtrière School versus the Nancy School. The name of the former was derived from the Salpêtrière Hospital in Paris where its leading figure, Jean-Martin Charcot, applied hypnosis to cure patients. According to Charcot, it was only possible to hypnotize hysterics, as the specific organic predisposition that was believed to cause hysteria was also said to be key to the effective use of hypnosis (see van Ginneken 1992: 143–4). The Charcot position on hypnosis and its restricted range of employment dominated the French debates during the 1880s. However, the competing framework put forward by the Nancy School gradually gained momentum and in the early 1890s it had taken the lead position – partly facilitated by the death of Charcot in 1893.

The main figures of the Nancy School were August Ambroise Liébeault and Hippolyte Bernheim. In his local practice in a village close to Nancy Liébeault had proved successful, for many years, in curing patients through hypnosis. Contrary to the claims of Charcot, Liébeault maintained that hypnosis was applicable also to non-hysterics. In addition to this, he argued that hypnotism is based essentially on suggestion (Barrucand 1967: 93). In 1882 the renowned professor Bernheim visited Liébeault to witness his method and was soon convinced about its potentials. Elaborating on Liébeault's work, Bernheim took his colleague's perspective in a more theoretical direction but he, too, argued that hypnosis was an effect of suggestion, defined in Bernheim's voluminous textbook, *Hypnotisme, Suggestion, Psychothérapie*, as the '*act through which an idea is introduced to the brain and accepted by it*' (Bernheim 1891: 24, italics in original). According to this theoretical framework, the application of hypnotic suggestion was not restricted to certain pathological individuals, e.g. hysterics, whose specific predisposition was essential for hypnosis to be successful. By contrast, Bernheim believed, everyone is susceptible to hypnosis and suggestion, although not necessarily to the same degree.

Bernheim's theory had crucial implications. By arguing that hypnotic suggestion was no pathological phenomenon, he extended its explanatory potential to all social spheres. It suddenly became possible to understand developments in the legal field, in politics, economics, etc. as a result of suggestion (Barrows 1981: 123–4). This led to a veritable explosion in the public and scholarly interest in hypnotism in the 1880s and 1890s, in France as well as in other countries (see Ellenberger 1970: 164–5; van Ginneken 1992: 144–5). And this interest also became formative to the crowd psychology that was to develop in the 1890s.

Le Bon's crowd psychology: inspirations and concerns

One of the scholars who employed the perspective of the Nancy School to understand the behaviour of crowds was Gustave Le Bon. He initially received medical training but soon decided not to pursue a practical medical career. Instead he devoted his energy to present and synthesize in a popularly accessible style a broad spectrum of scientific theories of his time. In his brilliant and authoritative biography of Le Bon, Robert A. Nye characterizes him as 'the supreme scientific vulgarizer of his generation' (1975: 3); vulgar at least in the eyes of the established academic world, which did not see his work as quite as scientifically robust as he did himself – a fact that caused much bitterness on the part of Le Bon. Nye also rightly notes that although Le Bon had left the practical medical world behind, his medical background reverberates in many of his writings. This shows in the great influences from Liébeault and Bernheim that can be identified in his crowd theory. But it is visible as well in his deep concern with what he diagnosed as the pathological state of the contemporary civilization, the reason why, similar to Taine, 'a search for the elusive remedy for France's sickness remained a central fixture' in his thought (Nye 1975: 14).

After a series of publications on race, alcoholism, civilization, intelligence and criminals, dating from the early 1860s onwards, Le Bon embarked on the crowd issue.[7] The most paradigmatic outcome of this part of his work was published as the essay that would associate his name ever since with crowd psychology, the 1895 book on the *Psychologie des foules*, in English translation, *The Crowd: A Study of the Popular Mind* (Le Bon 1960). The book stirred much debate, partly because Le Bon was accused of plagiarism, and partly because he was the first who really managed to synthesize the previous discussions of crowds in an accessible yet scientific language that brought the topic (and its purported significance) far beyond the academic world.[8] In fact, Nye suggests, Le Bon's book on crowds might well have 'been one of the best-selling scientific books in history' (1975: 3). Looking less to sales figures than to impact, Gordon Allport has alleged that Le Bon's book is, '[p]erhaps the most influential book ever written in social psychology' (1954: 26).

---

[7] Le Bon's pre-crowd studies are examined in Barrows (1981: 163–8), Llobera (2003: 87–94), Nye (1975) and van Ginneken (1992: 132–8).

[8] Accusations that Le Bon ripped off the insights of other scholars but nevertheless claimed full originality were advanced among others by the Italian criminologist Scipio Sighele, whose work will be briefly touched on below. Le Bon's plagiarism is discussed in Barrows (1981: 181–2), McClelland (1989: 197) and van Ginneken (1985, 1992: 119–26), but is not crucial to the present investigation.

Le Bon did not turn to the crowd topic by accident. A number of specific historical events led him in that direction. As Merton has argued:

the consequential historical events that made Le Bon's observations and ideas immediately and immensely popular were ... the same events that largely led him to those ideas. It is these events, also, that produced the resonance between Le Bon and his public. (1960: xviii–xix)

In very general terms, Le Bon shared Taine's concern with France's revolutionary past – as well as with the more recent manifestations of what appeared to be deep-seated revolutionary proclivities. For example, the Paris Commune had left an enduring imprint on Le Bon. But Le Bon was equally worried about a range of other and more recent developments. Van Ginneken lists three concerns in particular (1992: 149–71).[9]

One was related to the so-called Boulanger affair (for a full account of this affair, see Seager 1969, on which the following is based in part). Boulanger was a charismatic general, who was appointed minister of war after the 1885 elections, and who soon earned widespread popularity, within the army as well as with the general public. When, in 1887, Boulanger was forced to resign for internal cabinet reasons, people took to the streets to demand his reappointment. When he was subsequently exiled to the provinces, more than 20,000 people came to the Gare de Lyon to show their support and block the tracks. This apparent defeat, his expatriation from the centre of French politics, was not the end to Boulanger's political life, though. He would soon return, stronger than ever. Thus, in 1888, a Republican Committee of National Protest was set up to restore his political role and to sponsor his candidacy in by-elections. The Committee ran an efficient propaganda office and a movement of Boulangism swept the country, culminating in January 1889 when he won more than 245,000 votes in one Parisian district. As a further indication of his popularity, around 30,000 devotees allegedly assembled later that night in front of the restaurant where Boulanger was celebrating his victory. One of Boulanger's main achievements was his broad appeal: 'he stood as the hero of royalists, revisionists, the military, and some sectors of the working class, and perhaps most important, as the symbol of the discontent with the Third Republic', a discontent that augmented and intensified those years (Barrows 1981: 14). Not surprisingly, the government saw Boulanger's spectacular success as an express threat, and rumours of a *coup d'état* began to circulate. In order to pacify Boulanger, a campaign was

---

[9] The following also draws on Barrows (1981), Merton (1960) and Nye (1975).

orchestrated against him by his political enemies, and faced with the threat of being arrested, he fled to Belgium.

Although the Boulanger movement did not subvert the state, the entire affair was a clear illustration, for Le Bon, that the masses were readily seized by a charismatic leader – it even seemed as if they were yearning for one – and that this combination of leader and crowd could be extremely hazardous to the political order. What frightened the conservative Le Bon in particular about Boulanger was his ability, through 'plebeian rhetoric' (van Ginneken 1992: 161), to gather followers from many parts of the political spectrum, and not only among the usual revolutionary/socialist suspects. At the same time, Merton observes, Le Bon also took notice of the fickleness of the crowds who, after Boulanger had fled, soon turned their interest from Boulanger to other things, such as the Universal Exposition in 1889 (Merton 1960: xxv). One fad, *in casu* the instantaneous rise of Boulanger, was easily replaced by another.

Less of a fad was the second major concern that added to Le Bon's interest in the crowd topic, namely the ever-firmer footing of socialism in France and internationally. Socialist viewpoints were not new, but around 1890 a new wave of socialist organization attracted attention and fear, depending on political leaning. In 1889, the Second International was formed in Paris, which among other things demanded an eight-hour working day and declared 1 May to be the International Workers' Day. The 1 May demonstrations of 1890 gathered some 100,000 participants in Paris alone, which, however, was only one-third of what London furnished (van Ginneken 1992: 163). The demonstrations turned out rather quiet, arguably because of the heavy pre-emptive measures that had been taken by the government 'to avert what it believed would be a proletarian uprising, a resurgence of the Commune' (Barrows 1981: 25). For present purposes, the fears that the new socialist organization and its 1 May events generated are of greater importance than the actual demonstrations. Thus, for conservative observers such as Le Bon, the fact that the workers had managed to join forces on an international scale and that they were capable of organizing nationwide demonstrations (and increasingly began to propose the general strike as a new weapon) rendered the danger of revolution extremely present; suddenly the socialists seemed endowed with powers far surpassing those they had previously been equipped with. All the faith the workers put in these developments was, in other words, equalled by a bourgeois fear of no lesser magnitude.

According to van Ginneken, the third socio-political impetus behind Le Bon's devotion to crowd psychology was a feeling of anti-parliamentarianism that swept across France between 1892 and 1894 (1992: 167). Much confidence in the political establishment had been lost in some serious examples of corruption. While some discontent had previously been articulated in the Boulanger movement, increasingly it found other means of expression, particularly in anarchist bombings and assassinations. Police headquarters, cafés, restaurants, etc. were targets of such anarchist attacks. 'Strikes and demonstrations reached their apogee in the early nineties', writes Barrows (1981: 40); but 'so did anarchist terrorism', which culminated with the assassination in June 1894 of the President of the Third Republic, Sadi Carnot. In contrast to strikes and demonstrations, much of the anarchist action was conducted by singular individuals rather than in concert, which seemed to rule out the existence of crowd impulses. At the same time, however, there was a clear sense that the anarchist attacks came in waves, suggesting that some collective fever was in fact active.

In addition to these three historical developments, Le Bon's interest in the crowd topic was triggered by a waxing scholarly problematization of crowds. Taine played a central role here and is often referred to in *The Crowd*. But other more recent intellectual currents were of no less import to Le Bon. In the early 1890s, for example, a number of criminologists started to look into the crowd issue. Criminology emerged as a distinctive scientific discipline in the 1880s, baptized through Raffaele Garofalo's 1885 book *Criminology* (1968). In its early form, the discipline bore the stamp of the Italian criminal anthropologist, Cesare Lombroso, and his so-called positivist school, which counted scholars such as Enrico Ferri and Raffaele Garofalo. Lombroso had revolutionized the scholarly debates on crime by arguing that it was possible to single out specific so-called born criminals on the basis of their particular characteristics. Yet by paying close attention to individual criminals, Lombroso had left crimes committed by collectives largely unexplored. This neglect would soon be remedied by the Italian criminologist Scipio Sighele.

A student of Ferri, Sighele subscribed in many respects to the Lombrosian tradition, but he combined it, in his 1891 *La Foule criminelle*, with more collective–psychological notions such as contagion, suggestion and imitation so as to explain the crimes committed by crowds (Sighele 1897, 1901). Contrary to most other crowd psychologists, Sighele preferred the Salpêtrière approach to suggestion, and argued that suggestion cannot impel individuals to commit crimes; it can merely provoke those criminal acts for which the person is predisposed (1897: 175). Sighele used this point to argue for a special combination of crowd psychology and a refined criminological positivism, where the crimes of crowds were explained in part by suggestion, and in part by predispositions.[10]

Sighele reproduced many views on crowds as they had been advanced by e.g. Taine and Zola. He also drew on the French sociologists Alfred Espinas and Gabriel Tarde, the latter of whom had addressed the crowd issue from within a criminological (though anti-Lombrosian) horizon in his *Penal Philosophy* from 1890 (1968). I shall discuss Tarde's contribution to sociological crowd semantics at length in Chapter 2. For now the important point to observe is that Sighele added to a growing scholarly literature on crowds, and that his work itself inspired new contributions such as Henry Fournial's *Essai sur le psychologie des foules* (1892).[11] Crucially, therefore, when Le Bon embarked on the crowd issue, he did so against a backdrop of an existing, if only embryonic, crowd theorizing. Le Bon's central feat was to synthesize the nascent semantics and to rearticulate it in a pointed form.

An era of crowds

For Le Bon and other conservative observers, the experiences with Boulangism, socialism and anarchism conveyed the impression that France was in the middle of a vast historical transformation. A dangerous cocktail had been stirred, which laid bare that revolutionary sentiments, especially in the guise of collective formations, constituted a persistent challenge to the Third Republic and, more generally, to the notion of a civilized society. French society and its political regime seemed anything but stable; they were marred by the continuous threat of collapse and overthrow from within. It was against this backdrop of 'transition and anarchy' that Le Bon formulated his reflections on crowds (1960: 14). Thus, the anarchy had a face, as crowds had gradually materialized as the major source of social power:

While all our ancient beliefs are tottering and disappearing, while the old pillars of society are giving way one by one, the power of the crowd is the only force that nothing menaces, and of which the prestige is continually on the increase. The age we are about to enter will in truth be the ERA OF CROWDS. (1960: 14)

---

[10] Another difference to the conservative French scholars was Sighele's socialist inclinations. For more extensive discussions of Sighele's contribution to crowd theory, see Barrows (1981: 127ff.), McClelland (1989: 162ff.), Poggi (2002: 718–19), Stewart-Steinberg (2003) and van Ginneken (1992: ch. 2).

[11] Fournial's work is examined by Barrows (1981: 131–4) and van Ginneken (1992: 100–29), both of which also discuss Espinas.

Le Bon shared Taine's conviction that crowds signify revolutionary intent. The inherently revolutionary aspiration attributed to crowds was apparent throughout *The Crowd*, which, through repeated references to the French Revolution – as well as to the revolutionary century that followed – posited that, in practice, crowds are synonymous with insurrection. Indeed, Le Bon played on the entire bourgeois register of fear and terror when highlighting how, '[g]iven the growing influence of crowds and the successive capitulations before them of those in authority', the 'history of the Commune of 1871' was bound to be repeated in the near future (1960: 165). A similar emphasis on the opposition between the civilized bourgeois society, on one side, and the unruly crowds, on the other, was apparent in statements such as: 'Civilisations as yet have only been created and directed by a small intellectual aristocracy, never by crowds. Crowds are only powerful for destruction. Their rule is always tantamount to a barbarian phase' (1960: 18).

This fearful attitude towards crowds was interlaced with the alarm that the growth of socialism evoked in Le Bon. He quite simply feared the rule of crowds because he believed it to be closely linked to socialist inclinations and to calls for democracy and egalitarianism. And, Barrows notes, what united a number of his writings was a profound critique of socialism and a 'rejection of equality' (1981: 187). In *The Psychology of Peoples*, published in 1894 (i.e. one year before *The Crowd*), Le Bon left no doubt as to the hazard posed by crowds and socialism in conjunction:

Socialism appears to-day to be the gravest of the dangers that threaten the European peoples. It will doubtless complete a decadence for which many causes are paving the way, and it will perhaps mark the end of Western civilisation. To appreciate its dangers and its strengths, it is not the teachings it spreads abroad that must be considered, but the devotion it inspires. Socialism will soon constitute the new faith of the suffering masses … This great religious entity of to-morrow sees the crowd of its faithful increase every day. (Le Bon 1974: 225, 226)[12]

This quote makes plain that, even though Le Bon proclaimed that he pursued the study of crowds in a 'purely scientific manner' (1960: 3), his investigation was carried out under the influence of a specific political agenda, as in Taine's case. The quote further shows that, by connecting the rise of crowds and socialism, Le Bon in effect established an intimate relation between modern society and the prevalence of crowds. He basically argued that rather than being mutually exclusive, modernity and the rule of crowds constituted one another. That is, modern society

---

[12] The interrelation of crowds, religiosity and socialism was later further examined by Le Bon in his *Psychology of Socialism* (2001, originally published in 1898).

was intimately tied to forces that tried to enact a societal breakdown from within. This was the real calamity. But this is also where the sociological importance of Le Bon's endeavour transpired, for if he were correct, the study of crowds would amount to an investigation of modernity as such.

What were the characteristics of crowds, then? To begin with, said Le Bon, it is important to understand that a crowd is not a mere collection or gathering of individuals, but rather a distinctive psychological entity; a mental unity of people who may or may not be present at the same location but who, however temporarily, are subjected to a collective mind. More specifically, Le Bon posited, the crowd is characterized by three interrelated qualities. First, the crowd exerts an 'invincible power' over the individual crowd member 'which allows him to yield to instincts which, had he been alone, he would perforce have kept under restraint' (1960: 30). The second defining feature of the crowd was contagion. The contagious aspect – which was present in 'every sentiment and act' of the crowd (1960: 30) – contributed to the weakening of the individuality of the crowd members. In the crowd, the person's 'conscious personality vanishes' (1960: 23). Contagion was, finally, an effect of suggestibility. This entailed that, being in the crowd, the individual would cease to be governed by his or her will. By contrast, he or she was 'paralysed' by the 'magnetic influence given out by the crowd' and transformed into a mere 'automaton', driven by suggestions, instincts and impulses rather than reason (1960: 31, 32).

This alleged impulsiveness of crowds, their readiness to succumb to any suggestion, was in Le Bon's eyes the main reason why they readily engaged in 'bloodthirsty' activity (1960: 37). Crowds simply have no (moral or other) barriers that prevent them from regressing into barbarian violence. According to Le Bon, the Boulanger affair was a vivid illustration of this:

It is crowds that have furnished the torrents of blood requisite for the triumph of every belief. It is not necessary to go back to the historic ages to see what crowds are capable of in this latter direction. They are never sparing of their life in an insurrection, and not long since a general, becoming suddenly popular, might easily have found a hundred thousand men ready to sacrifice their lives for his cause had he demanded it. (1960: 37; see also 75–6)

In his discussion of suggestibility Le Bon subscribed to the work of Bernheim rather than Charcot. This lent his investigation politico-analytical powers far surpassing those of Taine. Most importantly, the incorporation of the Nancy position implied that everyone could become part of a crowd. It was not merely criminals, poorly educated individuals or other parts belonging to the 'inferior' classes of society that were susceptible to the hypnotic suggestions of crowds; everybody could be paralyzed by and caught in the crowd. In this sense the crowd was highly democratic: it could include and seduce everyone, independently of social position. McClelland (1989: 11) observes that this Le Bonian notion that every social group could turn into a crowd was very frightening to contemporary readers because it annulled the distinction between 'them' and 'us', between those who represented a bulwark against anarchy and those who promoted it. Even the elite, so beloved by Le Bon, could turn into an irrational hazard to society. Le Bon illustrated this point in analyses of specific groups (criminal juries, electoral crowds, parliamentary assemblies) that were composed of people of relatively high status, but which could nevertheless transform into irrational crowds.

Le Bon's reference to suggestion had another important implication. It zeroed in on the relation in crowds between those who are hypnotized and the one who hypnotizes. It stressed, in other words, the relationship between the leader and the crowd, a distinction which had no similar theoretical status in Taine's work. In a chapter devoted to understanding leaders and their means of persuasion, Le Bon characterized the crowd as 'a servile flock that is incapable of ever doing without a master' (1960: 118), thereby ascribing to the leader a constitutive role as the one who ensures the cohesion of the crowd. Le Bon continued by exploring how leaders can exert a powerful suggestion over crowds through the affirmation, repetition and contagion of ideas and sentiments, and how their authority and status rest on prestige.[13] Not every leader would do, however. Crowds purportedly revolt against weak leaders and only accept and submit to strong and powerful ones: 'The type of hero dear to crowds will always have the semblance of a Cæsar. His insignia attracts them, his authority overawes them, and his sword instils them with fear' (Le Bon 1960: 54–5). Le Bon's exposition on leaders suggested an implicit direction for how to cope with the contemporary crisis of crowd rule: understanding the techniques of how to influence crowds was mandatory if their destructive patterns were to be prevented. The underlying Machiavellian credo was not too optimistic, though: 'A knowledge of the psychology of crowds is to-day the last resource of the statesman who wishes not to govern them – that is

---

[13] While this suggested a very personalized conception of the leader, other discussions in *The Crowd* intimated that the suggestion of crowds may also emanate from non-personal sources such as images (Le Bon 1960: 102–3). I shall briefly discuss this suggestive power of non-humans in the Epilogue.

becoming a very difficult matter – but at any rate not to be too much governed by them' (Le Bon 1960: 19).

The Crowd was not just a sweeping account of society at large being under attack. It contained more specific sociological observations as well, as crowds were believed to cause a loss of both rationality and individuality. Indeed, Le Bon maintained, crowds are inherently irrational. 'In crowds it is stupidity and not mother-wit that is accumulated', implying that 'the crowd is always intellectually inferior to the isolated individual' (1960: 29, 33). Individually, the person may be perfectly rational; collectively, rationality transforms and dissolves into irrationality. The intimate connection between crowds and irrationality entailed that living in an era of crowds amounted to being in the middle of a time in which irrationality reigned. This emphasis on the irrational dimensions taking possession of all aspects of human life – i.e. the gradual predominance of affect and sentiments – was crucial to Le Bon and remained an important fixture throughout his work.[14] The loss of rationality in crowds was explained by their contagious and suggestive nature which also accounted for the parallel loss of individuality. In the crowd, individuality is suspended and everyone submits to the suggestive power of the leader. Le Bon's reference to the crowd member as an 'automaton who has ceased to be guided by his will' is a lucid illustration of the semi-determinism which he believed had replaced individuality and critical, individual judgement in crowds (1960: 32).

According to Le Bon, the double loss of rationality and individuality had severe social implications, for crowds would not be capable of original creations and were therefore not positioned to take society forward. Le Bon strongly believed that social advances were attributable solely to great men, the elite. Regrettably, however, the nobility's good advice was wasted on crowds, immune as they were to reason. As he put it in *The Psychology of Peoples*, '[t]he voice of a Galileo or a Newton will never have the least echo among the masses' (Le Bon 1974: 204). Again, this had political undertones, as it was meant as a critique of socialist and democratic ideals. Le Bon's elitist convictions made all collectivist inclinations look highly suspicious to him (2001: 13–14).

One final aspect of Le Bon's general characterization of crowds should be emphasized. While he repeated over and over again the destructive

---

[14] Le Bon's acknowledgement of the affective sides of life was inspired in part by the work of psychologists such as Théodule Ribot, a friend of Le Bon. Nye (1975: 97ff.) notes that this line of influence subsequently aligned Le Bon with the thought of Henri Bergson (also a friend of Le Bon) and equally with the pragmatism of William James. In a letter to Le Bon, Bergson wrote that, 'William James would have been delighted' by his work (quoted in Nye 1975: 99).

and revolutionary aspirations of crowds, he also argued that in reality crowds are profoundly conservative:

> to believe in the predominance among crowds of revolutionary instincts would be to misconstrue entirely their psychology. It is merely their tendency to violence that deceives us on this point. Their rebellious and destructive outbursts are always very transitory. Crowds are too much governed by unconscious considerations, and too much subject in consequence to secular hereditary influences not to be extremely conservative ... In fact, they possess conservative instincts as indestructible as those of all primitive beings. Their fetish-like respect for all traditions is absolute. (Le Bon 1960: 55, 56)

Moscovici has interpreted this as a sign of optimism on the part of Le Bon. If crowds are actually 'tortured by a desire to return to things as they had been in the distant past' (Moscovici 1985: 113), then the clever leader might use this insight to create order by magnetizing the crowd with sentimentalism, myths of tradition, etc. – a strategy which, Moscovici (1985: 114) argues, fascism would later employ.

The biopolitical agenda

In order to stress the irrationality of crowds Le Bon made use of specific strategic discursive associations, declaring, for instance, that crowds are fundamentally feminine. 'Crowds are everywhere distinguished by feminine characteristics' (1960: 39), he stated; and '[t]he simplicity and exaggeration of the sentiments of crowds have for result that a throng knows neither doubt nor uncertainty. Like women, it goes at once to extremes' (1960: 50).[15] Such observations were hardly controversial, echoing as they did a widely accepted impression that women figured centrally in much crowd behaviour. The most infamous example from the revolutionary past was arguably the so-called October days in 1789 when a procession of some 5–6,000 armed women marched from Paris to Versailles to voice their complaints about lack of food to the king. Events like this also formed the backdrop to Zola's gendering of the crowd.

This semantic correlation of crowds and the feminine has been analysed thoroughly by Barrows (1981) who demonstrates how both women and alcoholics constituted important 'metaphors of fear' in late-nineteenth-century France. The female gendering of the crowd

---

[15] See also Le Bon (1960: 35–6, 46). This supposedly feminine character was underscored by the curious fact that the notion of the crowd is in the feminine in both French and German (*la foule* and *die Masse*, respectively). For analyses of the semantic configuration of crowds and femininity, see particularly Barrows (1981: 43ff.) and Moscovici (1985: 110ff.); see also Blackman and Walkerdine (2001: 32), König (1992: 157–68), Laclau (2005: 34–5) and van Ginneken (1992: 234).

therefore contributed to highlighting the threat that the masses were seen to pose to the social order: that masculinity (and all the associated male attributes of progress, reason, civilization, etc.) would turn into its female counterpart (characterized by atavism, irrationality, sentiment, excitement, hysteria and unappeasable sexuality).[16]

Whereas the attribution to crowds of a feminine side has often been observed, it is rarely noted that late-nineteenth-century crowd semantics also associated crowds with stereotypic male characteristics. Although the crowd was not related to a masculine logic of reason, it was often depicted in other male categories. The violent tendencies and the 'barbarian' brutality that Le Bon (1960: 18) ascribed to crowds are examples of this. To be sure, these did not express the kind of civilized behaviour that Le Bon celebrated, but referred instead to masculine categories of combat, force and destruction – in short, primitive, irrational dynamics which, from a cultural and evolutionary point of view, were prior to urbane and cultivated conduct. Yet there is another old, stereotypical male feature of crowds which was not debunked by Le Bon. Occasionally, Le Bon thus informed the reader, crowds might actually act heroically:

It is crowds rather than isolated individuals that may be induced to run the risk of death to secure the triumph of a creed or an idea ... Such heroism is without doubt somewhat unconscious, but it is of such heroism that history is made. (1960: 34; see also 19, 37, 51, 57–9)

This focus on male and female features might serve as the pretext for looking into the more bodily aspects of crowds. For although Le Bon was primarily interested in explaining the psychological constitution of the crowd – its mental unity – his analyses contained numerous references to bodily and organic dimensions.[17] These bodily organic aspects of his crowd theory have received only little attention from subsequent commentators. In the following I shall address these issues, and will do so with the aim of demonstrating that Le Bon's fear of destructive, revolutionary crowds was embedded in what was, in Foucault's terminology, a biopolitical project.[18]

According to Michel Foucault, biopolitics surfaced in the eighteenth century as a growing concern with the population and its well-being. The technologies of this emerging biopolitics centred upon life; they

---

[16] The semantic correlation of masculinity and reason is examined by Seidler (1989, 1994).

[17] At one point, for example, he describes the crowd as 'a new body possessing properties quite different from those of the bodies that have served to form it' (Le Bon 1960: 27).

[18] The following draws on Borch (2009).

tried to bring 'together the mass effects characteristic of a population'; and therefore attended to the 'general biological processes' (Foucault 2003: 249). In order to understand how Le Bon combined his political programme with such a focus on life – that is, to grasp the biopolitical nature of his work – it is important initially to explicate his reliance on a biological framework. A first index of this is his characterization of crowds as 'microbes' and his reference to contagious processes (Le Bon 1960: 18, 30). Moreover, Le Bon's conception of history was embedded in a theory of evolution. It was the very evolutionary progress of the population which, he believed, was threatened by crowds: in the midst of the civilized world, the crowd's savage impulses were said to signify an 'atavistic residuum' (1960: 51). This evolutionary background of Le Bon's theory was highlighted, second, by the importance he ascribed to race and hereditary factors. According to Le Bon, races are fundamentally different, an assertion he employed to add a racial expression to his fear of egalitarianism. 'It is barely a century and a half ago', he wrote in the Introduction to *The Psychology of Peoples*:

that certain philosophers . . . propounded the idea of the equality of individuals and races. This idea, which would naturally be most attractive to the masses, ended by firmly implanting itself in their mind, and speedily bore fruit . . . And yet science, as it has progressed, has proven the vanity of the theories of equality and shown that the mental gulf created in the past between individuals and races can only be filled up by the slowly accumulating action of heredity. (Le Bon 1974: xiv, xv)[19]

Le Bon continued by outlining a hierarchy of races which, hardly surprisingly, placed the 'Indo-European peoples ... among the superior races' (1974: 27). But hierarchies were identified even within races. Some of the (mainly philosophical) ideas which for Le Bon were peculiar to a specific civilization 'rest confined to the upper grades of the nation', whereas other ideas, 'particularly those relating to religious conceptions and politics, go deep down in some instances among the crowd' (1974: 175). On this view, problems were bound to arise when the ideas which guide a civilized race were not only rapidly transformed but replaced by ideas from an earlier evolutionary state. This was what happened when the ideas that had been established over generations through heredity – and which had helped elevate the race to one that acknowledged the

---

[19] The reference to heredity, and thereby to the biological foundation of race, shows that Merton is wrong when he interprets Le Bon's notion of race as 'an ill-conceived idea corresponding loosely to what has since been described as "national character structure"' (Merton 1960: xxxviii). Race in Le Bon is not merely national character; it is, as McClelland (1989: 204) rightly notes, conceived in both cultural *and* biological terms (see also Barrows 1981: 164–5).

fundamental gulf between different individuals and races – were suddenly toppled by the crowds. In this sense crowds constituted a racial threat, an opinion Le Bon highlighted by making a semantic association of equality, democracy, homogeneity and crowds, on one side, and the hereditarily determined heterogeneity of individuals and of races, on the other. As crowds were barbarous in Le Bon's account, their societal rule amounted to an unforgivable assimilation of conflicting racial characteristics and hence, from the vantage point of the superior race, to evolutionary regression (see Llobera 2003: 91ff.; Nye 1975: 43, 49).

These aspects were all united in Le Bon's biopolitical programme which can be formulated thus: in order to prevent an evolutionary degeneration, which would endanger the entire advanced population, it was crucial to combat the crowd and its contagious effects. It was not least the crowd's tumultuous and revolutionary tendencies which constituted a serious danger to the well-being and civilized character of the population – no matter how conservative the crowd might be. In a discussion of traditions, where he exposed the conservative tenet of his biopolitical objectives, Le Bon argued:

A people is an organism created by the past, and, like every other organism, it can only be modified by slow hereditary accumulations ... The ideal for a people is in consequence to preserve the institutions of the past, merely changing them insensibly and little by little. (1960: 82, 83)

This just reiterated the credo stated above. Anything that generates rapid transformations of the organism of the people poses a threat to the organic stability and hence to the people as such. This was the biological rationale behind the anxiety that the crowd microbes engendered.

In Foucault's account of biopolitics, there is an emphasis on its productive aspects, its ambition to create and foster rather than repress and destroy. How is this compatible with Le Bon's political project? Is not Le Bon's book ultimately a Machiavellian manual that advises the statesman on how to combat the revolutionary crowd? And is not this ambition repressive rather than fostering? In order to see that Le Bon did in fact present a biopolitical programme, although with a special accent, it is crucial to take seriously the racial dimension of his work and to acknowledge the way in which race became associated with power during the nineteenth century. Foucault thus demonstrates how the biopolitical interest in life was linked to a biological hierarchy of races, implying that some races should be annihilated insofar as they posed a threat to the valued species. As Foucault explains:

the reason this mechanism can come into play is that the enemies who have to be done away with are not adversaries in the political sense of the term; they are threats, either external or internal, to the population and for the population. In the biopower system, in other words, killing or the imperative to kill is acceptable only if it results not in a victory over political adversaries, but in the elimination of the biological threat to and the improvement of the species or race. (2003: 256)

This is precisely how Le Bon resonated. His assertion that races are fundamentally different implied that they are as a rule incompatible. 'Cross-breeding may be a source of improvement when it occurs between superior and sufficiently allied races, such as the English and the Germans of America', Le Bon admitted, 'but it always constitutes an element of degeneration when the races, even though superior, are too different' (1974: 53). Needless to say, cross-breeding between a superior, civilized race and inferior, barbarian impulses would constitute a threat to the former and should therefore be avoided. It is this specific combination of biopolitics and racism that was at the heart of Le Bon's political programme: the crowd should be combated because it posed a biological danger to the organism of the superior population. Eliminating the devalued crowd microbes was, for Le Bon, the only way to foster the life of the general population/race.

I have tried in this chapter to convey a sense of the socio-historical as well as intellectual currents that formed the backdrop to the emergence of crowd psychology in France in the 1890s, embodied most notably by Le Bon's study. As I have demonstrated, Le Bon's problematization of crowds was framed as an elitist concern with the socialist–revolutionary crowds he believed were about to put an end to the civilized order and transform it into a general chaos of degeneration, violence and irrationality.

Le Bon's crowd psychology proved immensely influential. Its pointed articulation of widespread concerns made it a central resource in (some) academic circles, as Allport's above-mentioned comment attests to. Yet its main significance lay beyond academics. For example, Joseph W. Bendersky has demonstrated how Le Bon's notion of crowds soon penetrated military thought in the USA (2007). More crucially, the kind of crowd psychology Le Bon personified would later be translated into totalitarian attempts to mobilize crowds for political purposes (Borch-Jacobsen 1988: 270, n. 37; McClelland 1989: 292; Stein 1955).

As will be clear in the following chapters, other scholars added further layers to the semantic scaffold that Le Bon had helped to erect. While these scholars may not have been as influential as Le Bon when measured according to popular or political reception, they often had greater success within *sociological* circles. To show this, the next chapter examines how crowd semantics entered French sociology in the late nineteenth century, where the problematization of crowds assumed a key role in discussions of how to draw the proper demarcations for the sociological discipline.

2 Disciplinary struggles: the crowd in early French sociology

The conservative problematization of crowds might have found a widely read advocate in Le Bon, but his popularizing conjunction of existing academic and non-academic concerns and ideas did not really catch on in sociological circles. In that sense Le Bon was and remained an outsider. In the present chapter I argue that crowd semantics, and the associated vocabulary of suggestion and hypnosis, required another scholar to be placed centrally on the sociological research agenda in France. This scholar was Gabriel Tarde, who, as mentioned in the previous chapter, was one of the academic sources Le Bon drew on. I contend that Tarde played a key role in the history of sociological crowd semantics, and that he did so on three accounts.

First, in contrast to Le Bon, Tarde enjoyed plenty of academic capital (at least in his early career), so when he began to study the crowd in some writings from the early 1890s, the topic was readily bestowed with scholarly legitimacy. Second, Tarde's particular sociological programme ascribed a most central and affirmative role to the notion of suggestion, itself linked to his guiding concept of imitation. The transfer of the notion of suggestion, so closely tied to crowd semantics, into the socio-logical realm lent further salience to the crowd topic, for it meant that one of the latter's alleged chief features was located at the base of the social as such. In other words, if Tarde were correct, it could be argued that the crowd should no longer be viewed as the very negation of an ordered society, such as most conservative minds would have it; rather, crowds and society were subjected to the same underlying dynamics. Third, at least in the French context, the sociological legitimacy of crowd semantics at the time rested in great part on Tarde's authority. So when the status of Tarde's theorizing, in particular his reliance on notions such as imitation and suggestion, was severely contested by Émile Durkheim in the 1890s and early 1900s, this was actually the first nail in the coffin of sociological crowd semantics. The ensuing debate between Durkheim and Tarde revolved around the proper delineation of sociology as a discipline. Consequently, whereas Le Bon was the great popularizer of crowd semantics, Tarde was the first scholar whose work on crowds became the battlefield for how to demarcate the sociological discipline.

In this chapter I demonstrate how Tarde conceived of the crowd. I start out by focusing on some of Tarde's criminological writings on crowds, which, similar to the critical outlook of Taine and Le Bon, associated crowds with destructive behaviour. As mentioned above, however, Tarde's broader sociological work also contained, if only implicitly, a positive notion of crowds. This ambiguity between positive and negative views on crowds lies at the heart of Tarde's contribution to sociological crowd semantics and anticipates similar ambiguities in the work of many subsequent scholars. Having established Tarde's basic notion of crowds, I proceed by discussing his reflections on the distinction between crowds and publics. The importance of this distinction became obvious to Tarde after the Dreyfus affair, which had shown how crowd dynamics could be identified in social situations that were not based on physical proximity. But, I suggest, Tarde's interest in publics may also be a reflection of his wish to render his sociological programme more politically attractive in the Third Republic, something that Durkheim managed with great success. The chapter ends with a discussion of Durkheim's negative appraisal of Tarde and crowd psychology, and how Durkheim's attack was aligned with the ambition of demarcating sociology unmistakably from adjacent disciplines (especially psychology).

Tarde's criminological angle

Throughout the 1880s and well into the 1890s, Tarde was highly esteemed by the academic community, both in France and internationally. He had worked for several years as a legal magistrate in Sarlat, not far from Bordeaux, but managed simultaneously to embark on an academic career.[1] Tarde's first scholarly breakthrough was in the field of criminology, where he received widespread acclaim for launching a devastating critique of Lombroso's positivist approach (see Beirne 1987). Briefly put, Tarde asserted that Lombroso's criminal anthropology greatly underestimated the social aspects of crime. Rather than measuring skulls (Lombroso drew on phrenology), one should take seriously that criminal acts are embedded in imitative dynamics, Tarde argued: 'All the

---

[1] For introductions to Tarde that include biographical information, see Clark (1969), Davis (1909) and Milet (1970). The following biographical sketch builds on these sources.

important acts of social life are carried out under the domination of example. One procreates or does not procreate, because of imitation ... One kills or does not kill, because of imitation' (1968: 322).[2]

Jotting down his reflections on crowds just a few years prior to Le Bon, Tarde's theorization was influenced to a large extent by the same historical conditions that shaped Le Bon's thinking. However, van Ginneken contends, Tarde's life in the provinces placed him at a distance to many of the events that stimulated Le Bon's interest in the crowd issue, such as for instance the abortive revolution of 1871, meaning that Tarde's concerns were expressed in a much less confrontational manner (1992: 190–1). Tarde also approached the crowd issue from a different academic perspective than Le Bon. It was in the form of a criminological problematization that Tarde entered the debates on crowds. For Tarde, the crowd posed a twofold problem. First, he believed, the crimes committed by crowds are driven by forces that differ markedly from those guiding the criminal acts of individuals. In *Penal Philosophy* from 1890, Tarde intimated what is at stake in crowds and how easily they turn into criminal entities:

A *mob* [*foule*] is a strange phenomenon. It is a gathering of heterogeneous elements, unknown to one another; but as soon as a spark of passion, having flashed out from one of these elements, electrifies this confused mass, there takes place a sort of sudden organization, a spontaneous generation. This incoherence becomes cohesion, this noise becomes a voice, and these thousands of men crowded together soon form but a single animal, a wild beast without a name, which marches to its goal with an irresistible finality. The majority of these men had assembled out of pure curiosity, but the fever of some of them soon reached the minds of all, and in all of them there arose a delirium. The very man who had come running to oppose the murder of an innocent person is one of the first to be seized with the homicidal contagion, and moreover, it does not occur to him to be astonished at this. (1968: 323, italics in original)

The quote – which was followed by an affirmative reference to the 'never to be forgotten pages of Taine's dealing with the fourteenth of July' (1968: 323) – suggested that, however temporary it might be, the self-organizing power of the crowd is capable of bringing together several individuals in a common spontaneous suggestion, and of leading them to criminal activity. The quote also gave a sense of Tarde's negative view on crowds, emphasized by the semantic correlation of the mob/ crowd with notions such as 'wild beast', 'fever', 'delirium', 'homicidal contagion', etc.

---

[2] He continued by adding, and this was written seven years prior to Durkheim's famous study of suicide, that '[o]ne kills oneself or does not kill oneself, because of imitation; it is a recognized fact that suicide is an imitative phenomenon to the very highest degree' (Tarde 1968: 322).

The critical attitude towards crowd behaviour was very outspoken in two articles from the early 1890s where Tarde addressed the crowd question from an explicitly criminological angle. The first of these articles, 'Les crimes des foules' (1892), which referred to Taine, Espinas, Fournial and Sighele, was a tour de force of negative images of crowds. The crowd was described as a 'female savage'; as an 'impulsive and maniac fool', as 'despotic' and 'intolerant'; as an entity which, allegedly similar to primitives, women and children, was 'essentially dogmatic and passionate', and whose moral and intellectual level was lower than that of isolated individuals; something that was due to the 'extraordinary suggestible' nature of the crowd and its propensity to be easily carried away by 'mental hallucinations' (Tarde 1892: 358, 359, 367, 373, 374). This all entailed that the crowd signified 'a veritable retrogression on the ladder of social evolution' (1892: 356; see also 357–8). The notion of contagion was used repeatedly in the article and seemed to be employed in order to evoke a medical register of pathological developments rather than to describe in a neutral–analytical way the dynamics of imitation. In sum, the article displayed, as Barrows has rightly observed, 'an agitated, almost desperate perspective on crowds' (1981: 145). Clearly, Le Bon had a rich academically sanctioned reservoir to draw upon here when writing *The Crowd* a couple of years later.

Much of what Tarde wrote in this article, and which Le Bon would later radicalize, recalled views and ideas that had already been outlined in *Penal Philosophy*. Both of Tarde's texts addressed the second problem he associated with crowds. In addition to being readily susceptible to criminal activity, the crowd's contagious and suggestive constitution destabilized traditional understandings of liability.[3] Tarde's theory of liability asserted that, although the vast majority of an individual's actions (criminal activity included) consists in imitation of others' behaviour – and therefore, one might say, is caused by society – this does not exempt the individual from liability. This was not the case for crowd behaviour, however, and this is why the question of liability was particularly tricky when it came to individuals who committed crimes while being under the spell of the crowd's suggestive force. '[I]n an excited crowd', Tarde thus contended, 'imitation is absolutely unconscious and blind and contrary to the habitual character of the person who is subjected to it, it is a phenomenon of momentary insanity which lessens responsibility or eliminates it' (1968: 302, n. 1).

---

[3] The question of the legal responsibility of crowds was a much-debated topic in the 1890s. Next to Tarde, Sighele was a leading voice in this debate.

This idea was now further elaborated in 'Les crimes des foules' in which Tarde distinguished between the leader of a crowd and those who are led. Since the leader is the originator of the hypnotic suggestion that spreads rapidly and contagiously in crowds, Tarde argued, he or she bears the main legal responsibility for whatever criminal acts the hypnotized members commit (1892: 380ff.). This distinction between the hypnotizing leader and the hypnotized followers was perhaps not Tarde's invention, but his reflections nevertheless consolidated the conjunction of theories and notions of hypnotism and suggestion, on one side, and analyses of crowd behaviour, on the other. Further, by emphasizing the constitutive role of the leader in crowd behaviour, Tarde made his own important contribution to advancing an essentially Hobbesian horizon of crowd thinking where crowds were seen as small assemblies held together by the Leviathan (see McClelland 1989).

Tarde rehearsed many of his negative views on crowds in another article, 'Foules et sectes au point de vue criminel', published the following year. Once again, the crowd was seen as feminine, destructive and irrational; as intellectually inferior to isolated individuals; and as characterized by spontaneous generation and contagious forces. While this all seemed to point once more to the antisocial nature of crowds, Tarde's insistence on the constitutive role of the leader now made him acknowledge that the suggestive influence of leaders could either take the crowd in a negative or, more rarely, in a positive direction. '[C]ollectivities are susceptible to two opposite excesses', Tarde (1893: 350) wrote, again anticipating Le Bon, namely to 'extreme crime' and, occasionally, to 'extreme heroism'. Moreover, he asserted, not all collectivities are equally susceptible to extreme behaviour. Elaborating on a distinction he had discussed in 'Les crimes des foules', Tarde argued that crowds and sects contain different potentials for destructive and heroic action.[4] Indeed, he said, sectarian corporations by far 'surpass the crowds in the bad and in the good' (1893: 371), which he thought to demonstrate by pointing to the beneficial activities of the Hanseatic League in the Middle Ages and to the revolutionary inclinations of the anarchic sects of his own time. These examples were also illustrative of another fact, namely that, compared to the 1892 article, the 1893 piece embedded the problematization of crowds more firmly in recent historical events. Tarde thus referred to an 1892 wave of anarchist bombings in

---

[4] Tarde had already distinguished between the notions of crowd and sect in *Penal Philosophy*, although not very strongly, as 'the *sect spirit*' was seen here as 'entirely analogous to the *mob spirit [l'esprit de foule]*' (1968: 324, italics in original). On Tarde's distinction between crowd and sect, see Barrows (1981: 148–9).

Paris as one example of how crowds and sects not merely posed a challenge to abstract legal–criminological discussions of liability. Much more importantly, they constituted a very present danger to society which every observer should take seriously.

Tarde's negative characterization of crowds was followed by a general pessimism regarding the possible solution to this problem of violent, criminal and irrational crowd behaviour in modern society. The reference to sects helped little in this regard but merely displaced the problem ('[s]ects are the yeasts of crowds', Tarde asserted; see 1893: 370). Tarde therefore ended 'Foules et sectes au point de vue criminel' with the accurate statement that his analysis had only explored the psychology of crowds and the comparative psychology of crowds and sects. The article had not prescribed any legal or therapeutic measures to handle the problems posed by these crowds and sects (1893: 387). It might be argued that outlining the psychology of crowds and recognizing the significant role of the leader was all that was needed to suggest remedying action. At least this is what Le Bon would later propose. It seems, however, that Tarde did not believe in the capacity of leaders to work as an antidote. The so-called Panama scandal, which was often referred to in 'Foules et sectes au point de vue criminel', seemed to confirm his pessimistic stance. Throughout the 1880s France had spent enormous amounts of money on building the Panama Canal. The project had faced several problems on the level of construction, but especially its financial state of affairs was incredibly unsound. In 1892 it became publicly known that much of the money that had been poured into the project had actually been used to bribe politicians, journalists, etc. so as to prevent them from revealing how serious the troubles were that the whole project confronted. The chief engineer and his colleagues were sentenced to prison, and a profound distrust in politicians ensued (Barrows 1981: 16–17). Enlightened by the Panama scandal, Tarde did not stipulate any means of political action to handle the crowd problem in 1893. Yet he would arrive at a possible solution to the crowd problem some five to eight years later in his investigations of crowds and publics, as I shall come back to later on.

Using crowd semantics as a template for sociological thinking

The respect Tarde won in the field of criminology eventually made him leave Sarlat to take up a position, in 1894, at the Ministry of Justice as the director of the Bureau of Statistics. At that time Tarde's academic interests had already shifted from criminology towards sociology, a shift that had been effected with such success that Tarde's sociological programme soon took a lead position in the contemporary French sociology – i.e., at a time when Émile Durkheim still was, in the words of Bruno Latour, a 'younger, less successful upstart teaching in the provinces' (2002: 117). The acknowledgement of Tarde's work culminated with his appointment in 1900 to the chair of modern philosophy at the prestigious Collège de France in Paris.

Tarde's sociological theory was based on the idea that society rests on an imitative foundation. It is through the imitation of others' ideas, gestures, behaviour, etc. that society emerges, for this imitation establishes a bond of assimilation. Imitation is, in other words, the basic social fact, the fabric of society. As is obvious from this, Tarde did not look upon imitation with admonition. Imitation was no negative term, for Tarde, but precisely a concept that captured the social bond. This understanding of society as a web of imitations was best expressed in Tarde's sociological masterpiece, *The Laws of Imitation*, the first edition of which came out in 1890. Here he asserted that '[s]ociety may therefore be defined as a group of beings who are apt to imitate one another, or who, without actual imitation, are alike in their possession of common traits which are ancient copies of the same model' (1962: 68). Having established that society is imitation, Tarde went on to examine the nature of imitation. This investigation took him to the heart of the debates on hypnotic suggestion where he subscribed explicitly to the position advanced by Bernheim and the Nancy School. Specifically, Tarde argued in a famous definition, '[s]ociety is imitation and imitation is a kind of somnambulism', or suggestion (1962: 87, italics in original). Against this backdrop, Tarde characterized 'the social man as a veritable somnambulist' (1962: 76). Or as he formulated it in a thought experiment:

Let us take the hypothetical case of a man who has been removed from every extra-social influence, from the direct view of natural objects, and from the instinctive obsessions of his different senses, and who has communication only with those like himself or, more especially, to simplify the question, with one person like himself. Is not such an ideal subject the proper one through which to study by experiment and observation the really essential characteristics of social relations, set free in this way from all complicating influences of a natural or physical order? But are not hypnotism and somnambulism the exact realisation of this hypothesis? (1962: 76–7)

The chapter from *Laws of Imitation* in which Tarde developed his notion of the somnambulistic/suggestive imitative basis of society had been published in a previous version as an independent article in *Revue philosophique* in 1884. When transforming this article into a book chapter in *Laws of Imitation*, Tarde took a retrospective look at the first time he had associated imitation with somnambulism and suggestion. The reception of this vocabulary had changed radically, Tarde observed. Thus, back in 1884, he wrote in *Laws of Imitation*:

hypnotic suggestion was but barely spoken of and the idea of universal social suggestion, an idea which has since been so strongly emphasised by Bernheim and others, was cast up against me as an untenable paradox. Nothing could be commoner than this view at present. (1962: 76, n. 1)[5]

It might be argued that the discussion of a hypothetical relation between two persons, the hypnotizer and the hypnotized, is quite detached from debates on people who assemble in crowds, but this is far from being the case. Thus, I wish to argue, Tarde's general sociology of imitation is modelled, in essence, around the notion of suggestive crowds.[6] As an effect, the negative problematization of crowds, which Tarde's criminological writings embody, is complemented by a more positive understanding when the crowd resurfaces in Tarde's sociological considerations. This more positive view can be identified along several axes.

To begin with, besides containing a series of criminological reflections, *Penal Philosophy* outlined a 'social embryology', according to which there are 'two distinct germs of societies, the family and the crowd [*foule*]' (1968: 325, translation corrected).[7] In other words, Tarde suggested, every society can be traced back to one of these two forms, family or

---

[5] In spite of the increasing familiarity with this vernacular, Tarde apologized for the use of the notion of somnambulism: 'This old-fashioned term shows that at the time of the first publication of this passage the word *hypnotism* had not as yet been altogether substituted for somnambulism' (1962: 76, n. 2, italics in original). It should be noted that Tarde was not the first sociologist to refer to somnambulism. Herbert Spencer discussed it in his 1876 *Principles of Sociology* (2002: 138, 424). Imitation, too, had a reception in social theory prior to Tarde's work. In 1872, the British journalist Walter Bagehot analysed the social and political importance of imitation in his famous *Physics and Politics*. According to Bagehot, imitation is particularly strong in primitive societies and among children or uneducated people: 'not only the tendency, but also the power to imitate, is stronger in savages than civilised men' (1872: 101; see also van Ginneken 1992: 198). While Tarde would agree in attributing to imitation a most crucial role in the life of societies, he would oppose Bagehot's idea that the importance of imitation decreases as civilization advances.

[6] I am not alone in establishing this connection between Tarde's general sociology and his conception of crowds. Recently, William Mazzarella has proposed a similar argument, stating that 'Tarde's entire sociology of imitation is a theory of crowd emergence' (2010: 723).

[7] The American edition of *Penal Philosophy* translates 'foule' as mob rather than crowd. I prefer 'crowd' in this context because 'mob' has more pejorative connotations (of rage and dissolution) and thus, in my view, renders Tarde's thought more negative than seems to be intended here.

crowd. The family and the crowd differ from one another in terms of their socio-geographic setting as well as with respect to the kind of imitation they generate. Thus, Tarde posited, the family produces an imitation of customs, a kind of conservative imitation which prevails in the countryside. The crowd, on the other hand, generates imitation of rapidly changing fashions and this type of imitation is primarily to be found in the metropolis: 'in towns the crowd-society [la société-foule] predominates, from all sides come people detached from their home and confusedly brought together' (1968: 326, translation corrected). This metropolitan crowd-society has a revolutionary flavour in the sense that it pays no respect to inherited customs but simply celebrates the latest fads. It follows from Tarde's division between family and crowd that the increasing urbanization in modern society would augment the relative importance of crowd-society and its fashion-imitation.[8]

Yet crowd and family also share certain features, and in the present context these are more important than their dissimilarities. Crucially, claimed Tarde, '[e]very crowd [foule], like every family, has a head and obeys him scrupulously' (1968: 325, translation corrected). Tarde's formulations espoused clear paternalistic undertones, just as the elevation of the family to a societal germ might be said to bear witness to a rather conservative outlook. But these are not the important points for now. I am more interested in the assertion that crowd and family converge in their suggestive constitution. In the crowd as well as in the family, social order is created through the imitation-suggestion that radiates from the leader and father, respectively. And this imitation-suggestion, which takes two distinct forms in the two germs, is then at the base of all other societal dynamics. Precisely the latter point is crucial. It shows that Tarde extended the range of application of the notion of suggestion from the field of crowds to society as such. Put differently, he transferred the explanatory framework, which in the early 1890s was linked primarily to crowd behaviour, to the broader (not necessarily crowded) domain of the social – and in this sense modelled his conception of society and the social around that of the crowd.

By so doing Tarde implicitly proposed a view on crowds that was much more affirmative than the bulk of his criminological writings

---

[8] Nonetheless, Tarde claimed that custom-imitation remains 'preponderant in social life' (1962: 246; see also 249, 253–4, 342–3), and this is why I talk of the increasing relative rather than absolute importance of fashion-imitation. In the case of the crowd he stated that, although its imitation could emerge independently of the family, its maintenance rested on 'the aid of the family' (1968: 325). This emphasis on the constitutive role of the family and its custom-imitation is one of many indications of Tarde's conservative leaning.

suggested. Rather than being a violent, destructive entity, the germ interpretation posited an image where crowds generate sociality; they, too, establish a social bond of assimilation through imitation. This view was expressed unmistakably in *L'opinion et la foule*, where Tarde distinguished between different types of crowds:

> Crowds on the whole are far from deserving the evil reputation which has been attributed to them. If one balances the daily and universal work of crowds of love, above all holiday crowds, with the intermittent and localized work of crowds of hate, in all fairness one has to recognize that the former have done far more to weave or tighten social bonds than the latter have ripped apart this fabric. (I here follow the translation in Barrows 1981: 183; Tarde 1989: 61)

In other contexts Tarde seemed to ascribe this potential for sociality to all crowds, independently of their specific manifestation. For example, in *Laws of Imitation*, Tarde ruminated on the 'perfect and absolute' form of sociality. 'In its hypothetical form', Tarde conjectured, a perfect and absolute sociality 'would consist of such an intense concentration of urban life that as soon as a good idea arose in one mind it would be instantaneously transmitted to all minds throughout the city' (1962: 70). In other words, perfect and absolute sociality would transpire where imitations spread immediately and without friction. While this may certainly be a hypothetical situation, the crowd aspires to be the closest approximation of this pure sociality (Borch 2005: 90; McClelland 1989: 184). So when interlacing Tarde's writings on crowds and sociality, the impression surfaces that no purer manifestation of sociality may exist in practice than the one which is produced by the extremely intense crowd-society.

As a consequence of the claim that society is founded on suggestion, Tarde in effect argued that the annulment of individuality and rationality that was inherent to crowds could be identified more generally in society at large. That is, his notion of somnambulistic imitation threatened to pull the carpet from under the understanding of a constituent subject (personality/individuality) as well as any belief in a rational societal architecture (see Borch 2007). On the one hand, by putting imitation first in his account of how society is constituted, Tarde dismissed the idea of a fixed individuality, as Ruth Leys has rightly observed:

> By dissolving the boundaries between self and other, the theory of imitation-suggestion embodied a highly plastic notion of the human subject that radically called into question the unity and identity of the self. Put another way, it made the notion of individuality itself problematic. (1993: 281)

On the other hand, Tarde's sociology seemed to carve out a space between pure rationality and pure irrationality, as the reference to suggestion might actually break with this dichotomy. This is at least Rosalind Williams' claim when arguing that suggestion, in the Tardean tradition, refers to a 'semiconscious' state:

[Tarde's] theory of semiconscious imitative social behavior represents a vast improvement over the model of *homo œconomicus*, who is supposed to be at once rationally choosing and indefinitely desiring, and also over Durkheim's very similar model of an indefinitely desiring individual restrained only by something external to himself, which is called society. In contrast to the classical economists, Tarde suggests that people are not split between rational choice and irrational desire, but act according to a semiconscious imitation that mingles the two. Tarde suggests that the line between the individual and society, between internal feelings and external restraints, is not so rigid and arbitrary … He sees the mind of the individual as part of an endless social network which in turn contributes to that network, in a dynamic relation of role-setting and role-following. (1982: 349–50)[9]

To sum up, Tarde's emphasis on imitation-suggestion automatically rendered the crowd phenomenon a, if not *the*, principal sociological topic, for the crowd displayed imitation-suggestion of the utmost intensity, and crystallized the very essence of society at a micro-sociological scale. More prominently than other early crowd theory Tarde's position thereby portrayed the crowd as a paradoxical entity (McClelland 1989: 185; Stäheli 2003): the crowd was believed to demonstrate a high degree of sociality but it was also said to generate horrible crimes and to possess an irrational and feminine nature. Hence, for Tarde, the crowd at once signified the manifestation and destabilization of the social (Borch 2005: 91).

To be sure, the more affirmative take on crowds was less pronounced in Tarde's writings than his negative readings. Still, I maintain, the positive understanding of imitation-suggestion that lay at the heart of his sociological theory entailed an implicit appreciation of the crowd, emblematic as the latter was of suggestion. Tarde was one of the first to articulate this ambivalent or paradoxical stance towards the crowd. And although the majority of subsequent crowd theorizing would pay greater attention to the negative than to the positive aspects of crowds, the oscillation between positive and negative qualities would revisit sociological crowd semantics from then on.

---

[9] To be sure, Tarde did acknowledge that 'imitation may be conscious or unconscious, deliberate or spontaneous, voluntary or involuntary. But I do not attach great importance to this classification' (1962: 192). What really mattered for him was that 'man is wrong in thinking that he imitates because he wishes to. For this very will to imitate has been handed down through imitation. Before imitating the act of another we begin by feeling the need from which this act proceeds, and we feel it precisely as we do only because it has been suggested to us' (1962: 193).

From crowds to publics: the political role of sociology

As mentioned several times, Tarde's political orientation was conservative. Rather than being delighted about the sociality of crowd behaviour, he was deeply concerned with the breakdown of sociality it threatened to produce. The fact that Tarde's early criminological problematization of crowds did not propose any therapeutic measures endowed it with a resigned air, and he therefore more or less left the crowd scene to Le Bon. In the late 1890s, however, Tarde returned to the topic, culminating in 1901 with the book *L'opinion et la foule* (1989), which consisted of two articles from 1898 and 1899, respectively, as well as the 1893 article 'Foules et sectes au point de vue criminel', now entitled 'Les foules et les sectes criminelles'. Despite including this pessimistic 1893 text, *L'opinion et la foule* charted new directions for the discussion of crowds and it even struck a few optimistic notes.

Tarde opened the book by drawing a clear distinction between the crowd and the public, between the mainly threatening entity that had already been scrutinized by numerous scholars and the new phenomenon which Tarde pinned his faith on. He delineated several differences between crowds and publics.[10] First of all, crowd and public were said to differ from one another in their physical anchoring, which put them in different places on the socio-evolutionary ladder:

In the lowest animal societies, associations are above all material aggregates. As one goes up the tree of life, social relations become more spiritual . . . Now, in this respect the crowd has something animal about it, for is it not a collection of psychic connections produced essentially by physical contacts? (1969: 278 1989: 32)

The public, on the other hand, was not based on physical proximity. Its imitation-suggestions could work on great distances, and this 'contagion without contact' signified a much more advanced social and mental evolution than the crowd represented, Tarde asserted (1989: 34). The 'simultaneous conviction or passion', which the members of a public share with one another, was made possible in modern society by the invention of printing and, as a more recent development, by newspapers and other means of 'instantaneous transmission of thought from any distance' (1969: 278, 280; 1989: 32, 37).[11] Contrary to the spontaneous

---

[10] Where possible I quote in the following both from the 1989 edition of *L'opinion et la foule* and from the English translation of extracts from *L'opinion et la foule*, published in Tarde (1969).

[11] The public in Tarde has some affinity with the 'public sphere' that Habermas (1989) would later analyse in *The Structural Transformation of the Public Sphere*. Habermas

anarchy of crowds, publics were seen as civilized entities that, if not rational by themselves, at least had the potential to accommodate rational deliberation. In the same vein, Tarde said, 'publics are less extremist than crowds, less despotic and dogmatic too' (1969: 289; 1989: 52). Finally, whereas the crowd was believed to subsume the entire individual and to promote intolerance – 'one is completely taken over, irresistibly drawn along by a force with no counterbalance' (1969: 281; 1989: 38) – publics were associated with no similar de-individualizing powers. Among other things, this entailed that the predominance of publics over crowds that Tarde observed in modern society 'is always accompanied by progress in tolerance' (1969: 281; 1989: 38–9).

By combining the question of physical proximity with that of social evolution, Tarde reiterated the point made in 'Les crimes des foules' (and by Le Bon) that modern crowds constitute an evolutionary regression. 'The crowd is the social group of the past', he contended, 'after the family it is the oldest of all social groups' (1969: 281; 1989: 37).[12] Since, by contrast, the public is not tied to physical co-presence, it can be 'extended indefinitely, and since its particular life becomes more intense as it extends', Tarde observed, 'one cannot deny that it is the social group of the future' (1969: 281; 1989: 38). Tarde's insistence on the modern predominance of publics led him to correct Le Bon's famous assertion. 'I therefore cannot agree with that vigorous writer, Dr. Le Bon', Tarde wrote, 'that our age is the "era of crowds". It is the era of the public or of publics, and that is a very different thing' (1969: 281; 1989: 38).

There were several reasons why Tarde mobilized an interest in publics. The Dreyfus affair, which reached its apogee in 1898–9, had demonstrated that perhaps the greatest dangers to society were no longer to be found in the rage of crowds. Much more severe threats could result from the intervention of the press and its ability to manipulate public opinion. At the same time, such manipulation could only be successfully

---

actually mentions Tarde once in his famous investigation, referring to *L'opinion et la foule*. According to Habermas, 'Tarde was the first to analyze [public opinion] in depth as "mass opinion" ... It is considered [by Tarde] a product of a communication process among masses that is neither bound by the principle of public discussion nor concerned with political domination' (1989: 240). As Schmitz (1987: 296) remarks, this quote demonstrates that Habermas completely misses the crucial point of Tarde's book, that crowd and public should not be conflated but distinguished from one another. In Schmitz's eyes, Habermas' reading is symptomatic of the lack of seriousness with which Tardes' work was met after the Second World War.

[12] He further maintained that, '[t]he family and the horde [*la horde*] are the two points of departure of [social] evolution' (1969: 286, n. 4; 1989: 49, n. 6), thereby recalling the observation he had made in *Penal Philosophy*.

countered by the press itself, which in the Dreyfus affair was made manifest by Zola's famous accusation in 1898. As van Ginneken notes in his discussion of the affair's implications for Tarde (himself a Dreyfusard), the events suggested that '[t]he battle of crowds had turned into a battle of publics' (1992: 217). Tarde's recognition of the ability of publics to generate imitations far beyond the physical setting of crowds was patent in *L'opinion et la foule* where he wrote with implicit reference to the Dreyfus affair that, 'I know of areas in France where the fact that no one has ever seen a single Jew does not prevent antisemitism from flowering, because people there read antisemitic papers' (1969: 282; 1989: 41).

According to van Ginneken (1992: 218), Tarde's change in focus from crowds to publics also reflected an important transformation of his theoretical position during the 1890s. For example, in 'Les crimes des foules' and *Laws of Imitation* Tarde had stressed the suggestive–somnambulistic nature of imitation, thereby establishing a close affinity to hypnotism as well as to the fundamental primacy of the person or point from which the imitation-suggestion radiates (e.g. the leader in relation to crowds). Gradually, however, Tarde seemed to replace the unilateral conception of imitation with a more reciprocal idea, rendering the prefix 'inter' increasingly dominant in his definition of imitation. The introductory remarks to *Psychologie économique* (1902) testify to this. Here society was no longer described in terms of somnambulism and suggestion; rather, society was conceived of as 'a web of interspiritual actions' (Tarde 1902: 1). This new understanding also penetrated his crowd theory. 'In his last articles on crowds', van Ginneken thus concludes, 'imitation came to mean interaction as a continual and *mutual* process' (1992: 218, italics in original). Emphasizing this mutual definition of imitation implies, van Ginneken's analysis suggests, that publics now became more interesting than crowds, as the latter were believed to be constituted by the leader–follower relationship. Dismantling that distinction, publics seemed to be the phenomenon in which true imitation could be identified.

While van Ginneken certainly has a point in observing a somewhat changed conception of imitation in Tarde's work, I find the theoretical implications less pronounced than he does. Most importantly, *L'opinion et la foule* to a large extent replicated the unilateral understanding of imitation that Tarde had left behind, according to van Ginneken. First, Tarde explicitly maintained that in terms of crowd behaviour, it is the leader who leads the crowd with no reciprocity at play (1969: 282; 1989: 40). Second, in the case of publics, Tarde argued, we are no longer faced with the distinction between leader and follower so pertinent to crowds, yet a similar distinction can be observed, namely between the journalist and the public. Contrary to the structural logic of the crowd, the journalist and the public engage in a reciprocal mode of influence. The public may have a bearing on the journalist, just as the journalist impacts on the public: the public reads what the journalist writes and is as such influenced by him or her; but since the reader can replace one newspaper with another, the journalist 'seeks to please' and retain the reader and is thereby disciplined in terms of style, topics, argumentation, etc. (1969: 283; 1989: 41). Even so, Tarde asserted, the reciprocal dynamics transpire on the basis of a unilateral undercurrent. 'The public, then, *sometimes* reacts on the journalist, but he is *continually* acting on his public' (1969: 283; 1989: 41, italics added). This demonstrates, in my opinion, that, although Tarde did modify his understanding of imitation, this was not his primary reason for discussing publics, as this latter topic was approached through the same explanatory horizon as his previous work.

I will argue that Tarde's interest in publics was enthused by a third and more significant motivation, which is related to the underlying political visions of his sociology. It thus seems to me that Tarde's analysis of crowds and publics should not just be seen in the light of the Dreyfus affair and the increasing importance of the press. Rather, by adding to his examination of crowds the phenomenon of publics Tarde acquired an idea of a sociologically informed political intervention for which he had been looking in vain in his previous crowd studies. Bluntly put, the pessimistic tone of his former examination of the crowd problem was now replaced with an optimistic belief in the civilizing abilities of publics. This suited his conservative mind well, but it also made clear that his sociology could contribute positively to society and its stability. In effect, Tarde's sociological framework no longer served as a mere descriptive–analytical diagnosis of the problems confronting society, now it could even point to remedying political action.

What, more specifically, did this political layer entail? One starting point for discussing this is the following account of the relation between crowd and public. Thus, Tarde argued, it may happen that:

an overexcited public produces fanatical crowds which run around in the streets crying 'long live' or 'death' to anything at all. In this sense the public could be defined as a potential crowd. But this fall from public to crowd, though extremely dangerous, is fairly rare. (1969: 281–2; 1989: 39)

By describing the transition from public to crowd as a 'fall', Tarde referred back to the evolutionary regression that was addressed above. More importantly, the quote pointed to the political task Tarde set for sociology. Thus, Tarde's analysis seemed to suggest, rather than prevent, the formation of crowds, and rather than finding means to control them (such as Le Bon would have it),[13] a new political–interventionist agenda materialized which was concerned with the following questions: what can be done to avoid that publics, this alleged bulwark against chaos, this simultaneous 'extension and antithesis' to crowds (Clark 1969: 52), turn into crowds; and how can crowds be transformed into publics (Borch 2005: 96)? By scrutinizing the complex relations between crowds and publics, sociology could help to identify new techniques to stabilize society and thereby protect civilization from unruly, evolutionary degeneration (see also Tarde 1903: 79).

Stipulating this further, Tarde had been convinced by the Dreyfus affair that publics too could stir upheaval. 'The man of one book is to be feared, it has been said; but what is he beside the man of one newspaper!', Tarde asked; '[t]his man is each one of us at heart, or nearly so, and therein lies the danger of modern times' (1969: 283; 1989: 42). In other words, substituting the public for the crowd was no guarantee in itself of a stable society. Several publics had to be created. This would generate deliberation and discussion and prevent too one-sided views from rousing lynching sentiments. According to this argument, a stable society could be achieved politically by supporting the free press, thereby contributing to the boom in publics.

But why is it that Tarde, as I have claimed, was eager to endow his sociological theorizing with suggestions for practical political intervention? The main reason is, I contend, that Tarde's position in the academic system came under increasing pressure. Contrary to his chief opponent, Émile Durkheim, Tarde's sociological programme did not benefit from political attention. As I will come back to in the next section, Durkheim's ever-more central status in the French academic system was cemented not least because his ideas showed a remarkable correspondence to the political ambitions of the Third Republic. This was not the case with Tarde, although his conservative leaning did of course resonate with some bourgeois ideals. On this basis, I find it warranted to suggest that Tarde's attempts in *L'opinion et la foule* to indicate recommendations for political intervention might have been provoked in part by a wish to counter the strong political and academic influence of Durkheim, i.e. to show that Tarde's sociology was also capable of producing valuable suggestions for political action.

---

[13] As Le Bon put it, '[t]o know the art of impressing the imagination of crowds is to know at the same time the art of governing them' (1960: 71).

Crowd theory and sociology: the Durkheim effect

The above discussion of the ambivalence of Tarde's crowd theory intimated that Tarde represented a more nuanced position than Le Bon's much more univocally negative problematization of crowds. That being the case, one might speculate why, viewed in retrospect, it was Le Bon's *The Crowd* which subsequent political leaders would turn to. How can it be, in other words, that Le Bon's treatise became the more widely read one, as compared to Tarde's more balanced outlook? I think that three explanations stand out. One is stylistic, as Le Bon's account was of a more popularizing fashion than Tarde's writings (themselves rather essayistic, though). A second reason is that Tarde's positive notes on crowds are easily overlooked when compared to his negative descriptions. Indeed, by and large, Tarde and Le Bon shared the same frightened image of crowds. When reading Tarde's discussions of crowds, this negative view dominates; and despite a few explicitly positive passages, one has, admittedly, to do some reconstructive work to arrive at an affirmative position. Finally, the relative neglect of Tarde's ambivalent conception of crowds should be viewed in light of the fact that, as has just been touched upon, his academic capital became ever-more contested throughout the 1890s and early 1900s. Thus, when Tarde published *L'opinion et la foule* in 1901 he had practically been dethroned from his leading position in French sociology. This would seriously affect the reception of his work in subsequent sociology, in France as well as abroad. Tarde's decline within the sociological discipline had as an additional consequence that the general sociological attention to crowd behaviour, fragilely associated with the name of Tarde, was shaken. In a sense, therefore, the destinies of Tarde and of the sociological interest in crowds are entangled.

The demise of Tarde might surprise, insofar as the conservative horizon of his sociological programme, and of crowd theory more generally, was actually consonant with the sociological discourse at the time. As Robert Nisbet (1943, 1952) has demonstrated, late-nineteenth-century French sociology was, by and large, animated by conservative concerns about how to restore social order after a century of recurrent insurrections. While this common conservative ground between crowd theory and the established sociological environment was perhaps a way for the former to be recognized in the emerging sociological discipline, a full inclusion and appreciation met with several obstacles, despite Tarde's early influence. Most importantly, in the eyes of sociologists such as in particular Durkheim, whose ambition it was to turn sociology into a distinctive science, crowd theory was rooted in an unfortunate *mélange* of insights, concepts and modes of explanation, which did not warrant scientific acclamation.

Durkheim's critique took several forms. It was aimed overall at the purported psychologism of Tarde, a kind of critique that the latter's definition of sociology as interpsychology readily (but incorrectly) inspired.[14] In more specific terms, Durkheim disapproved of the notions of imitation and contagion, so dear to both Tarde and crowd theory. The critical remarks were voiced in many contexts, of which I shall mention only the most important. In *The Rules of Sociological Method* (1895), Durkheim delimited the domain of sociology to be the study of 'social facts'. According to his famous definition, '[a] social fact is to be recognized by the power of external coercion which it exercises or is capable of exercising over individuals' (Durkheim 1964: 10). The crucial point here was to argue for the existence of an extra-individual, *sui generis* realm of sociality, which is irreducible to individual acts, but which is nevertheless imprinted upon these and regulates them. In a footnote following the definition of social facts, Durkheim turned this understanding of the social explicitly against Tarde's notion of imitation. 'No doubt, every social fact is imitated', Durkheim said:

it has ... a tendency to become general, but that is because it is social, i.e., obligatory. Its power of expansion is not the cause but the consequence of its sociological character ... Moreover, one may ask whether the word 'imitation' is indeed fitted to designate an effect due to a coercive influence. (1964: 11, n. 3)

In other words, for Durkheim, imitation was only interesting when conceived of as an effect of something else, namely social facts. Other charges against Tarde's sociological programme appeared two years later in Durkheim's study *Suicide*. In a chapter devoted to refuting imitation as a general and independent explanation of suicide, Durkheim once again referred explicitly to Tarde. And this time he even argued with reference to crowd phenomena, specifically, to Tarde's discussion, in *Penal Philosophy*, of the imitation that takes places in crowds (Tarde 1968: 322–3). Durkheim's attack was radical; he entirely dismissed Tarde's idea that crowds are characterized by imitation. His main counter-argument was that since the crowd displays a 'new state', it made no sense to describe it in terms of imitation; rather, it should be seen as a 'creation' (Durkheim 1951: 126).

Interestingly, Durkheim's critique of imitation as a key notion to describe crowd behaviour was not founded on an essentially different

---

[14] As I have demonstrated elsewhere, Tarde did in fact succeed in formulating what he labelled a 'pure sociology' (Borch 2005; Tarde 1962: ix).

conception of what a crowd is; at the surface no marked difference was identifiable between how he and the crowd theorists depicted the crowd.[15] Durkheim simply stressed that the transformation taking place in crowds is incompatible with the idea of imitation: 'We know in fact that the mutual reactions of men in assembly may transform a gathering of peaceful citizens into a fearful monster. What a strange imitation to produce such metamorphoses!' (1951: 126). Durkheim conceded that the creation he associated with the crowd might in itself be an effect of imitation, insofar as the crowd displayed a common imitation of a leader. But, he said, it had never been proved that the leader is actually the cause of the crowd's behaviour. Quite the contrary, there were 'very many cases, where the leader is clearly the product of the crowd rather than its informing cause' (1951: 126). This assertion ran counter to Tarde's emphasis on the leader's constitutive role for the crowd which, from Durkheim's point of view, erroneously reduced collective phenomena to individual performances.[16] In Durkheim's eyes, the Tardean model did precisely that: it reduced social facts to individual psychology, and this, Durkheim believed, could not explain collective states. People might imitate one another on an individual – and therefore largely random – basis, but on a larger social scale this mutual imitation would have to be explained sociologically, i.e. by scrutinizing the obligatory nature of social facts.

In a similar vein, Durkheim critiqued the notion of contagion, another key concept in crowd theory. His argument was analogous to the one he had launched against imitation. The reason why we follow a particular act is not that it appears as a contagious 'example before our eyes', but rather because a social fact exercises its power over us (1951: 128). 'Consequently', he stated, 'all these oft-repeated expressions about imitative propagation and contagious expansion are inapplicable and must be discarded' (1951: 128). Although he did not explicitly target the idea of suggestion, the latter was clearly included in the explanatory horizon he dismissed, as it was intimately linked to Tarde's notion of imitation.

However, there was more at stake for Durkheim than merely wishing to demonstrate what he took to be the 'weakness of the theory that

---

[15] See, for example, the following account which came close to what both Le Bon and Tarde had uttered: 'In the midst of the same social group, all the elements of which undergo the action of a single cause or number of similar causes, a sort of levelling occurs in the consciousness of different individuals which leads everyone to think or feel in unison' (Durkheim 1951: 124).

[16] It is likely that the following comment by Tarde in *L'opinion et la foule* was addressed directly, but implicitly at this part of Durkheim's critique: 'It has been contested, wrongly but not without a deceptive appearance of reason, that every crowd has a leader and that in fact it is often the crowd that leads its chief' (1969: 282; 1989: 40).

imitation is the main source of all collective life' (1951: 141). The theory of imitation had to be rejected in order to save sociology as a science, which is clear from the following passage where Durkheim summarized his attack:

We no longer believe that zoological species are only individual variations hereditarily transmitted; it is equally inadmissible that a social fact is merely a generalized individual fact. But most untenable of all is the idea that this generalization may be due to some blind contagion or other. We should even be amazed at the continuing necessity of discussing an [sic] hypothesis which, aside from the serious objections it suggests, has never even begun to receive experimental proof. For it has never been shown that imitation can account for a definite order of social facts and, even less, that it alone can account for them. The proposition has merely been stated as an aphorism, resting on vaguely metaphysical considerations. But sociology can only claim to be treated as a science when those who pursue it are forbidden to dogmatize in this fashion, so patently eluding the regular requirements of proof. (1951: 142)

In other words, explaining crowd behaviour, or any other social phenomenon, by reference to contagious imitation was not merely flawed, according to Durkheim. More devastating, he felt that such an explanatory framework was not even scientific at all!

This critique was interlaced with Durkheim's attempt to free sociology from its literary inspirations. Although he himself briefly supplemented statistical data with literary examples in his study of *Suicide* (1951: 271), it belonged to one of Durkheim's greatest obsessions to supply sociology with a rigorous method and this, he believed, necessarily made any flirt with literary representation entirely illegitimate.[17] This attack hit Tarde as well as crowd theory more generally. As demonstrated in Chapter 1, there was a fusion of literature and science in much early crowd semantics, most noticeable perhaps in the positive academic reception of Zola's *Germinal* (e.g. Sighele 1897: 145, n. 1). In Tarde's case, the close relations to literature were visible also in another sense. He pursued literary ambitions alongside his sociological work and published several poems as well as a utopian novel, *Underground Man* (1905, originally published in 1896), which described the proliferation of imitative social bonds in the aftermath to a future devastating crisis. It seems plain that the author of such a novel, which mixed literary representation with sociological models, and which in the preface to the English translation received laudatory remarks from H. G. Wells, could hardly qualify for Durkheim's respect.

---

[17] I refer here to a debate in early French sociology which has been thoroughly examined in Wolf Lepenies' seminal study, *Between Literature and Science: The Rise of Sociology* (1988).

The 'totally undisciplined mind' of Tarde (Latour 2002: 118) and the literary–essayistic inclinations of much crowd and imitation theory convinced Durkheim that his abandonment of these theoretical horizons was justified. In some of the disputes with Tarde he thus 'repeated the charge that Tarde's work was unscientific' (Lukes 1985: 310). In one article, for example, he bluntly stated that 'I believe in science and M. Tarde does not' (Durkheim 1895: 523; Lukes 1985: 310). This was of course an absurd accusation. Tarde was as firmly devoted to science as his colleague, just not of the fashion that Durkheim championed.[18]

The debate between Tarde and Durkheim on the nature of sociology lasted until Tarde's death in 1904. The exchange of arguments was one thing. The institutional environment was no less important. In the 1890s Tarde was still the more respected scholar of the two and more strongly institutionally anchored than Durkheim (Mucchielli 2000). Yet Durkheim fought his way and gradually advanced up the ladder. As a part of this, Durkheim's institutional backing increased. This support rested on larger socio-political transformations. The lost Franco-Prussian war and the abortive revolution of the Commune had seriously shaken the young Third Republic, which, moreover, was divided between monarchists and republicans in its formative years. Eventually, the republicans triumphed, and they launched a wide number of reforms so as to create social order, boost individual rights and reinvigorate France. For example, laws restricting the press, strike activity, the organization of public meetings, etc. were alleviated. This happened concurrently with attempts to weaken the influence of religion on private and public life. Most significantly, though, the educational system was singled out as a field in particular need of systematic reform. The purportedly outmoded educational system was believed to have played an important role in France's defeat in the Franco-Prussian war, and therefore a comprehensive reorganization of the entire French system of education was instigated (Clark 1968a: 42–3; Wagner 1990: 73–9). As a part of this process a number of promising young scholars were sent to Germany to study in its universities, many aspects of which were then copied in France. Durkheim was one of these talented persons who received a fellowship to study in Berlin and Leipzig (with Wilhelm Wundt), and who returned with fresh ideas for a new take on the educational system.

---

[18] In fact, Lepenies has argued, 'it was precisely his literary inclinations that preserved Tarde from the illusions of dogmatism into which the sciences were lapsing at the turn of the [nineteenth] century' (1988: 56). This dogmatism was the dogmatism of rationalism which had Durkheim as the leading advocate.

Durkheim's influence in the reformed system of education turned out to be overwhelming. According to the Third Republic's proponents, it was crucial to replace any religious leftovers in the universities with purely scientific approaches and further to replace metaphysical beliefs with moral philosophy (Lepenies 1988: 47). Durkheim's 'belief in national reintegration through (secular) education' fitted well with this project (Lukes 1985: 355). So did his conception of sociology as a secular moral science. It was therefore natural, in the eyes of the republicans, to place Durkheimian sociology centrally in the new university structure. As Lepenies has put it, the republicans realized that 'the republic needed a doctrine. One discipline above all seemed in a position to furnish this doctrine: the sociology of Emile Durkheim' (1988: 53). Tarde's sociology of imitation, which in Durkheim's words was founded on 'aphorisms' and 'metaphysical considerations' (1951: 142), had only little to offer in this political climate.

To be sure, the rise of Durkheim and his ideas did not happen without resistance. For example, the transformation of the Sorbonne – to which Durkheim had transferred from Bordeaux in 1902 – into the New Sorbonne, a change that materialized the new politically induced educational agenda where sociology replaced philosophy as 'the key-science' (Lepenies 1988: 54), elicited strong reactions from other disciplines which now saw themselves subjected to the requirements of Durkheimian methodology.[19] The critique of Durkheim's dominance was in vain. The reform of the French educational system led to the near-complete success of Durkheim's sociology, the major principles of which now became widely diffused in the entire system.[20]

Durkheim's increasing dominance was also bolstered by the influence he exerted through the *Année sociologique*, a journal he founded in 1896 and which became the pivotal point for the kind of sociology he and his followers pursued (Clark 1968b; Lukes 1985: ch. 15). In combination with the *Année sociologique*, the adoption of Durkheim's ideas in the French university and educational system furnished him with a remarkable platform for removing one of the remaining obstacles to his absolute

---

[19] Some of the reactions against this development are examined in Clark (1968a) and Lepenies (1988: ch. 2). The latter interprets the conflict as one between literature and science. 'The sociological worker was to replace the original literary genius: this was the real scandal of the New Sorbonne' (Lepenies 1988: 51).

[20] Clark reports that 'Durkheim's course in pedagogy [at the Sorbonne] was declared mandatory (in 1906) for all aggregation candidates in philosophy, thus assuring his influence on the secondary school teaching of philosophy, and preparing the way for further penetration of the secondary school system that took place after the war' (1968a: 55).

dominance: the theoretical work that emanated from the Collège de France where Tarde had his chair in modern philosophy. In spite of its great (traditional academic) prestige the Collège did not enjoy the same political support and educational influence as did Durkheim at the Sorbonne. This was hardly surprising, for much of the Collège environment (including Tarde and Bergson) emphasized the import of irrationality, hypnotism, spontaneity, etc. and thereby opposed Durkheim's unequivocal devotion to rationalism head-on.

The *Année sociologique* was a convenient forum for Durkheim not only to refuse the anti-rationalist bias of his opponents himself, but also to gather a group of supporters who could help to propagate his 'sociological imperialism', as Lukes (1985: 398) has called it.[21] And the institutionalization of Durkheim's sociology – both in the educational system and through the *Année* – did indeed enable him to build a school devoted to his rationalist methodology. This was yet another difference from Tarde and the crowd theorists who, despite some public, but, in Le Bon's case, also political attention, had no similar success in this respect. The implication was that in France, Tardean sociology more or less passed away when Tarde died, and crowd theory thereby lost one of its most skilled representatives within early French sociology.

Durkheim on crowded effervescence

What did this entail for sociological crowd theory? Did Durkheim's critique of imitation and contagion entirely dismiss the crowd from the sociological arena? There is no doubt that Durkheim's intervention did much to undermine the theoretical legitimacy of crowd theory which from then on was marked as unscientific (a fact that did not disqualify it from still receiving popular attention, as Le Bon's case shows). Although expelled from proper academic discussion, crowd theory nevertheless retained some influence. In fact, and as I shall demonstrate in the following, eventually and quite surprisingly Durkheim opened up new avenues for understanding crowd behaviour. Or to be more precise, without admitting it, he ended up resorting to, confirming and reinterpreting many of the insights of the crowd theories of Le Bon and Tarde. This was most significant in his sociology of religion, *The Elementary Forms of the Religious Life: A Study in Religious Sociology* (Durkheim 1947,

---

[21] According to Clark, 'Durkheim and his colleagues evinced great disdain toward most social scientists not collaborating with the *Année* ... and thereby contributed not a little to crystallizing the French social scientific community into outwardly aggressive and inwardly self-satisfied schools' (1968a: 47).

original published in 1912). In his discussion in this book of the origin of totemism Durkheim arrived at descriptions that one can hardly imagine were written by the same person who had previously flatly rejected ideas of contagious imitation. His reservations against such ideas and their associated theoretical horizon now seemed to have vanished. To be sure, Durkheim did not suggest that the religious practices he analysed could be explained on the basis of psychology. He insisted that he advanced a sociological argument, according to which religious beliefs and rituals were caused by society. Despite this classic Durkheimian perspective his sociology of religion nevertheless incorporated ideas and notions that ran counter to his usual demarcations of what constituted a legitimate sociological approach. Indeed, Robert J. Holton has argued, Durkheim's study of religious life 'provided an important justification for crowd study' (1978: 222).

The discussion of Durkheim's adaptation of crowd theory may begin by highlighting the point of departure he shared with Le Bon and Tarde. 'In the midst of an assembly animated by a common passion', he wrote:

we become susceptible of acts and sentiments of which we are incapable when reduced to our own forces; and when the assembly is dissolved and when, finding ourselves alone again, we fall back on our ordinary level, we are then able to measure the height to which we have been raised above ourselves. (Durkheim 1947: 209–10)

This observation was not merely believed to apply to certain exceptional religious events. According to Durkheim, this description was also valid in many other cases and he mentioned as an example the events that followed in the aftermath of the storming of the Bastille (1947: 210; see also 214; Pickering 1984: 391). Further, although Durkheim was careful not to quote any of the French scholars whose work he had previously dismissed, he nevertheless made several affirmative references to one book that shared a great amount of conceptual inspiration with Le Bon and Tarde. This book was written by the Swiss professor, Otto Stoll, and was significantly entitled *Suggestion and Hypnotismus in der Völkerpsychologie* (1904).[22] The central point to note here is that all of a sudden research subscribing to the suggestion doctrine was no longer abandoned as unscientific.[23]

The empirical core of Durkheim's discussion was constituted by Australian religious ceremonies which, as I have indicated, were believed

---

[22] Stoll's work will be briefly examined in Chapter 3. Suffice it to say at this point that the book was a more than 700-page-long exposé on various forms of suggestive phenomena, including the suggestions of crowds.

[23] I take the notion of a 'suggestion doctrine' from Asch (1952: 387ff.).

to have implications far beyond religious practices. At the centre of this analysis was the so-called corrobbori, a religious ceremony that was commonly celebrated by all the families of a tribe or clan and which was clearly distinguished from other phases of social life where families lived separately. During this corrobbori significant transformations could be registered, both on a collective and on an individual level. Echoing Tarde's account of the crowd in *Penal Philosophy*, Durkheim asserted that:

> When they are once come together, a sort of electricity is formed by their collecting which quickly transports them to an extraordinary degree of exaltation. Every sentiment expressed finds a place without resistance in all the minds, which are very open to outside impressions; each echoes the others, and is re-echoed by the others. The initial impulse thus proceeds, growing as it goes, as an avalanche grows in its advance. And as such active passions so free from all control could not fail to burst out, on every side one sees nothing but violent gestures, cries, veritable howls, and deafening noises of every sort, which aid in intensifying still more the state of mind which they manifest ... these gestures and cries naturally tend to become rhythmic and regular; hence come songs and dances ... This effervescence often reaches such a point that it causes unheard-of actions. The passions released are of such an impetuosity that they can be restrained by nothing. (1947: 215–16)

Besides forming a new collective body, the effervescence also had crucial implications for the individual participants. In the corrobbori, 'a man does not recognize himself any longer' (1947: 218). For Durkheim, this was not simply another example of the de-individualizing tendency of the kind Le Bon and Tarde attributed to crowds. In an interesting analysis, Durkheim argued that the effect of the collective effervescence on the singular individuals is not merely negative; it has positive sides as well. To be more precise, the collective power gives way to a *transformation* of the individual. In the collective entity, the individual 'naturally has the impression of being himself no longer. It seems to him that he has become a new being' (1947: 218). Although this is a temporary feeling that lasts only as long as the collective effervescence is maintained, '[a]ll that he knows is that he is raised above himself and that he sees a different life from the one he ordinarily leads', and this life is 'a superior life' (1947: 220, 221). Employing the distinction between the sacred and the profane, which was fundamental to his conception of religion, Durkheim further argued that the collective effervescence opens up two distinct worlds for the individual. One is the profane world 'where his daily life drags wearily along'; the other is the world created by the effervescent collective, and this is a sacred world replete with 'extraordinary powers that excite him to the point of frenzy' (1947: 218).

In addition to recognizing the overall changes that purportedly take place in collectivities, Durkheim's analysis displayed a number of other remarkable similarities with the crowd theories of Le Bon and Tarde. First, on the level of description Durkheim now accepted the import of spontaneous emergence and contagious transmission of gestures and sentiments. His analysis repeatedly espoused the idea that in the collective, 'the emotions provoked by the one extend contagiously to the other' (1947: 219; see also 220, 222, 237, n. 1). Second, Durkheim put great emphasis on the influence that leaders exert on collectives, and slightly refined his previous claim from *Suicide* that the crowd has priority over the leader. Now he granted the leader 'an abnormal over-supply of force which overflows and tries to burst out from him' and pointed to the allegedly mutually reinforcing ping-pong between the leader and the passionate collectivity (1947: 210).[24] Third, in the vein of Le Bon, Durkheim asserted that collectivities are capable of both 'violent and unrestrained actions, actions of super-human heroism or of bloody barbarism' (1947: 211). A fourth convergence between Durkheim on one side and Tarde/Le Bon on the other regards the relation between religiosity and crowds. In *The Crowd*, Le Bon derived from his general analysis the idea that all crowds are characterized by essentially religious sentiments, visible in their 'blind submission, fierce intolerance, and the need of violent propaganda' (1960: 74). And in his books *The Psychology of Peoples* and *The Psychology of Socialism* he saw in socialism a link between crowds and religiosity (Le Bon 1974, 2001). While Durkheim had a more nuanced understanding of religion, he too combined analyses of religiosity and crowd behaviour, although from a different angle than Le Bon. Thus, Durkheim's main focus was on the religious collectives, the religiosity emerging from the effervescence of the corrobbori and its distinction between the sacred and the profane worlds. But, he added, the excitement and coherence created in religious collectives (and continuously affirmed by the use of rituals) is imitated by many other groups so that they can enjoy the fruits of common sentiments as

---

[24] In this context Durkheim also examined the notion of respect and asserted that respect operates by suspending any 'idea of deliberation or calculation' and by making us feel 'obliged to submit ourselves to rules of conduct and of thought which we have neither made nor desired, and which are sometimes even contrary to our most fundamental inclinations and instincts' (1947: 207). This was parallel to Tarde who, in his analysis of hypnotism and imitation, referred to the import of prestige. 'The magnetiser does not need to lie or terrorise to secure the blind belief and the passive obedience of his magnetised subject. He has prestige – that tells the story' (1962: 78). Le Bon advanced a similar argument in *The Crowd*, arguing among other things that prestige can 'exercise a veritably magnetic fascination' on both crowds and individuals (1960: 132).

well. 'This is why all parties, political, economic or confessional, are careful to have periodical reunions where their members may revivify their common faith by manifesting it in common' (1947: 210).

What had happened to Durkheim? Why this sudden alignment with ideas and notions he had rejected fiercely only a few years earlier? One answer could be that while writing the book on religion, his eyes had been opened to the irrational dimensions of social life. This is no compelling explanation, however, for as one of the respected commentators on Durkheim, W. S. F. Pickering, has observed, Durkheim had actually been on the track of these ideas for quite some time (1984: 382).[25] A similar point has been made by Tiina Arppe (2005), who has demonstrated that Durkheim's earlier study of *Suicide* was fraught with references to flux, currents, passions, etc. that worked as a sort of backdrop to his 'return' to these ideas in his sociology of religion. Be that as it may, Durkheim's stance on crowd theory was hard to digest in the sociological discipline which had by then embodied and institutionalized Durkheim's approach. Indeed, his flirt with crowd theory stirred much debate. Pickering describes how several of Durkheim's contemporaries, as well as later commentators, felt that Durkheim's writings on collective effervescence signified a regrettable return to crowd psychology (1984: 395–6; see also Essertier 1927: 17; Llobera 2003: 101; Lukes 1985: 422). According to Pickering, this was an unjustified accusation. To defend Durkheim against this charge of in effect employing crowd theorizing in his sociology of religion, Pickering argues that 'there is no reference to Le Bon and Tarde' in *The Elementary Forms of the Religious Life* (1984: 403). This is correct and so is his observation that, '[i]t is obvious that Durkheim did not want to be associated with such writers' (1984: 403). But the lack of explicit acknowledgement of their work does not necessarily entail that no inspiration is detectable, an inspiration which Pickering also does not completely deny. Durkheim simply concealed it by referring to Otto Stoll rather than Le Bon and Tarde.[26]

An apparently stronger defence of Durkheim's position vis-à-vis the accusation of crowd-psychological inspiration is launched by Pickering

---

[25] On Durkheim's early interest in religion, see also Lukes (1985: ch. 11).

[26] Lukes had a clearer impression than Pickering of Durkheim's relation to the crowd theorists when he wrote in his authoritative biography on Durkheim that, in his study of religion, 'Durkheim was doubtless affected by the crop of studies in crowd psychology that had appeared at the end of the nineteenth century, by Scipio Sighele, Gustave Le Bon and, indeed, Gabriel Tarde among others, but there is no evidence that he was specifically influenced by any of them' (1985: 462). Later on in the biography, Lukes declares that Durkheim had used 'crowd-psychology as the principal mechanism' to explain how religious beliefs and practices are socially determined (1985: 483).

when asserting that Durkheim maintained a clear distinction between assemblies and crowds and that he was actually only interested in the former category. In the words of Pickering:

Nowhere in *Les Formes élémentaires*, and seldom elsewhere, so far as we have been able to discover, does Durkheim use the word *foule*, meaning a crowd or throng. In speaking about collective effervescence, he always uses the words *rassemblement*, an assembling or gathering, and *assemblée*, gathering. (1984: 397, italics in original)

According to this argument, Durkheim might have adopted parts of the vocabulary of crowd psychology, but applied it to an entirely new field of research. I do not find this argument convincing and will propose the opposite claim that Durkheim used the notions of crowd and assembly almost interchangeably, where both account for what was regularly seen as crowd or throng behaviour. A brief look at the ways he described the crowd (*foule*) in *The Elementary Forms of the Religious Life* supports this claim. At one point, for example, he developed a threefold line of argument that included, first, the immediate aftermath to the July 1789 events; second, 'the particular attitude of a man speaking to a crowd'; and finally then the notion of effervescence (1947: 210; see also Lukes 1985: 422). So contrary to what Pickering holds, Durkheim did actually use the word 'foule' to address the semantic reservoir usually associated with crowds; and he did relate this to effervescence. More-over, later on in *The Elementary Forms of the Religious Life*, Durkheim described how:

The violent passions which may have been released in the heart of a crowd fall away and are extinguished when this is dissolved, and men ask themselves with astonishment how they could ever have been so carried away from their normal character. (1947: 231)

It is very hard, I think, to read this passage without evoking the images of crowds and mobs that had been supplied extensively by the tradition of Taine, Le Bon and Tarde. To further support my claim that Durkheim did not distinguish sharply between crowd and assembly one might refer to his critique of imitation in *Suicide*. Here Durkheim fluctuated effort-lessly between the notions of crowd (*foule*) and assembly, and no distinc-tion whatsoever was drawn between the two (1951: 124–6).

Let me add as a final vestige of Durkheim's new embracing of crowd thinking his book *Moral Education* (1961). This book, which was published posthumously in 1925, consisted of a series of lectures on education that Durkheim had offered at the Sorbonne. The first course was given in 1902–3 (but repeated later on), i.e. around one decade prior to the publication of *The Elementary Forms of the Religious Life*. Although these lectures contained a number of classic Durkheimian propositions, they also exposed a surprising endorsement of crowd theory. At one point, for example, Durkheim actually elevated the crowd to being the fundamental problem or concern for sociology:

> Everyone knows how emotions and passions may break out in a crowd [*foule*] or a meeting [*assemblée*], often altogether different from those that the individuals thus brought together would have expressed had each of them been exposed to the same experiences individually rather than collectively ... Now, what we have said of crowds [*foules*], of ephemeral gatherings [*assemblées*], applies *a fortiori* to societies, which are only permanent and organized crowds [*foules*]. (1961: 62)

If society is nothing but a stabilized and organized crowd, this quote suggested, then its characteristics cannot differ markedly from those of the crowd, hence turning crowd theory into a study of the social micro-cosmos, the germ of society. This idea was akin to Tarde's observation of the fundamental social bond created in crowds.[27] Needless to say, Durkheim made no reference to Tarde in this context and he was careful not to draw the implications suggested here. Indeed, as one of the other lectures evinced, Durkheim had a different agenda. He basically wanted to demonstrate the importance of rational discipline. Repeating the essence of the claim quoted above, Durkheim argued that:

> A mob or a crowd [the French original simply says, 'la foule'] is a society, but one that is inchoate, unstable, without regularly organized discipline. Because it is a society the strong emotional forces generated in the crowd are especially intense. Therefore, they move quickly to excesses. A forceful and complex system of regulation is required to enclose them within normal limits, to prevent them from bursting all bounds. (1961: 150)

So while crowds and societies might show clear resemblances in their basic mode of organization, Durkheim suggested, they differ because the crowds' alleged lack of discipline prevents them from being stable entities. By implication, if one has as the political objective to create an orderly society, i.e. a society devoid of irrational crowd elements, then the means to reach this objective are to be found in various techniques of discipline. Discipline, in the form of rationality and moral rearmament, was consequently Durkheim's solution to the problem of irrational crowd rule.

To sum up, Durkheim acknowledged the irrational dimensions of social life but contrary to especially Le Bon, whose recommendations

---

[27] Sighele reached a similar conclusion in 1898, arguing that '[t]he state is indeed only the primitive and savage crowd transformed by centuries of history and social development' (quoted in Park 1972: 10, n. 10; see Sighele 1975: 41).

for manipulative, remedying action capitalized on the irrationality of crowds, he believed that it was possible to actually rationalize and discipline the irrational. And for Durkheim, the problem of irrationality – his eternal enemy in sociology as well as in social life – extended beyond the crowd in the shape of unruly demonstrations, strikes, etc. It reached into the heart of the educational system, the cornerstone of Durkheim's socio-political endeavours: 'A class without discipline is like a mob [*foule*]' (1961: 151). This statement is perhaps the best illustration that Durkheim had come (or been forced) to take the crowd seriously, for if the educational system was possessed by the irrationality characteristic of crowds, then the social, political and theoretical reinvigoration of France that Durkheim and his likes hoped for could not be achieved. Compared to Tarde's call for publics, Durkheim's vision of discipline dug deeper. For Durkheim, it was not sufficient to mould the technical conditions of public debate (in particular newspapers). His argument for a disciplining intervention in the educational system sought to reconfigure the intellectual conditions for what could later be debated publicly.

Although Durkheim seemed to suddenly incorporate insights from crowd theory, this did not really lead to a sociological acceptance of this framework. Durkheim's reinvigoration of crowd themes came at a time when the exclusion of Tarde and crowd theory from sociology had already been successfully accomplished. This might be illustrated through the reception of his general sociology of religion (and the sacred) in French sociology. Among the French sociologists who received his work on religion chiefly positively was the group of intellectuals that gathered in the so-called Collège de Sociologie, which was founded by Georges Bataille, Roger Caillois and Michel Leiris, and which existed in the short period from 1937–9 (for discussions of the work of the Collège, see Arppe 2009; Moebius 2006).

Although this group of people did not subscribe to Durkheim's methods and overall theoretical objectives, they found inspiration in his work on effervescence and the sacred. One example of this inspiration is visible in Caillois' 1939 lecture on the 'Festival' (1988). This lecture referred explicitly to Durkheim's sociology of religion and used it as a starting point for scrutinizing how the festival constituted a sacred event. While Caillois primarily discussed 'primitive' festivals and their organization, the lecture had more general ambitions, namely to show that contemporary festivals – he mentioned the celebration in France of 14 July as well as the Nuremberg rallies in Nazi Germany – were manifestations of the kind of sacred sociality he depicted. In line with the Durkheimian impetus, Caillois characterized the festival as 'eminently favorable to the birth and contagion of an intense excitement';

as 'an orgy, a nocturnal debauch of sound and movement'; and as 'excesses of collective rapture' (1988: 281, 282, 283). This was not meant negatively. Quite the opposite, he posited, 'the festival must be defined as the *paroxysm* of society, which it simultaneously purifies and renews' (1988: 301, italics in original). It is illustrative of the destiny of French crowd semantics after Durkheim that, even if Caillois associated the festival with several features usually ascribed to crowds, he hardly made any explicit reference to crowds. He did talk of the festival as an 'excited throng [*concours*] of people' and as a 'swarming mass [*masse*] of humanity' (1988: 281, 282), but the lecture made plain that the phenomenon could be accounted for irrespective of crowd vocabulary and, even more pronounced, independently of any crowd-theoretical explanations (be it suggestion or something else). What the Collège de Sociologie case demonstrates is, in other words, that although crowd-related ideas continued to appear in the work of French social theorists, the disciplinary politics of social science – the institutionalization of Durkheimian sociology – was powerful enough to undermine the influence and legitimacy of sociological crowd semantics as an explicit frame of reference, at least in France.

Boldly put, this chapter has demonstrated what might be called the rapid rise and fall of crowds in French sociology. Tarde showed the sociological relevance of the crowd topic, whereas Durkheim, at least in his early work, illustrated its irrelevance. Even if Tarde's death implied that sociological crowd semantics lost one of its chief protagonists, Durkheim's success in French sociology did not entail that the crowd topic disappeared from sociology as such. For, although Tarde might have been overtaken by Durkheim in a French setting, he had many admirers abroad. One consequence of this was that the kind of disciplinary politics that surrounded the crowd in turn-of-the-century French sociology would, as the following chapters will corroborate, extend to other countries. The Tarde–Durkheim debate would actually just start the ball rolling. The debates that ensued in Germany offer a clear example of this.

3   Weimar developments: towards a distinctively sociological theory of crowds

It might be that French crowd theory had lost much of its momentum at the beginning of the twentieth century and from then on, by the standards of the heydays of the 1890s, lived an increasingly marginalized life within the academic sociological community. In Germany, by contrast, the sociological debates on crowds really only took off well into the twentieth century. This is not to say that the crowd topic was altogether new in Germany at that time. For example, the German word for crowd, 'Masse', had been introduced in the 1793 German translation of Edmund Burke's *Reflections on the French Revolution* (Lüdemann 2005: 56); and, as in France, the register of crowds and revolutions triggered conservative fears. This anxiety escalated after the 1848 February revolution in France which stirred insurrections in other European countries, including Germany, in March 1848. Helmut König has described how the German establishment observed the 1848 events with sheer panic (1992: 97ff.). While previous uprisings had been seen as the acts of the lower, suburban classes, the March Revolution appeared to ignore social hierarchies: the emerging politico-historical subject of the revolutionary multitude seemed able to absorb even respected citizens (König 1992: 101–2). As a result conservatives and liberals united in a common anxiety which, according to König, was exaggerated when compared to the actual threats. Exaggerated or not, the terror was significant in two respects. It signified the shock that had been released by the revolutionary events, and it demonstrated what for König is one of the most important aspects of the crowd discourse: although the social reality might not have been adequately described as a rule of crowds, the general perception that passionate crowds did in fact pose a severe threat to society was very real (1992: 108–13).

Even if the unruly crowds were portrayed within a vocabulary of irrationality, passion, spontaneity and other notions later adopted by crowd theory, no comprehensive theoretical register yet existed to explain and account for the behaviour of crowds in a scientific language. One of the first attempts to address the nature of crowds was

F. C. Fresenius' 1866 article precisely entitled, 'Die Natur der Masse' (1866).[1] Fresenius' article did not gather a large reception, though. More influential were the French debates on crowd semantics. Particularly the psychological focus on the suggestion of crowds attracted comprehensive attention among German scholars. However, the French impact on the German discussions remained incomplete in the sense that it was blended with and supplemented by new theoretical conceptions, in particular from the sociological realm, which planted the seeds of the strong differentiation between psychological and sociological perspectives on crowds that was characteristic to German crowd theory in the Weimar years (1919–33). In this time period, the German sociological environment exhibited immense collective efforts to understand the social nature of crowds, which, measured on its intensity, was similar to the French debates in the 1890s, but which aimed at transcending the suggestion doctrine underpinning and largely defining the latter.

In this chapter I attend to what I see as the three central (internally composite) layers of German crowd semantics from the second half of the nineteenth century until around 1933. The first two layers may be categorized as pre-Weimar developments, which in conjunction with the historical context surrounding the Weimar republic (especially the November Revolution in 1918) laid the foundation for the third layer, namely the crowd theories developed in the Weimar years. More specifically, the first layer refers to the adaptation in the German-speaking realm of crowd semantics that relied on the suggestion doctrine. The psychological analyses of hypnotic crowd suggestions spread far beyond France and were particularly strong in Germany. Here they were received by sociologists such as Simmel who, while inspired by the French debates, strived to render the understanding of crowds more sociological and less dependent upon a psychological-looking inventory. I claim that the sociological anchoring of Simmel's crowd investigations constituted an important – but, compared to later inventions, ultimately premature – endeavour in German social theory to distinguish between psychological and sociological perspectives on crowds, an attempt which pre-empted the more elaborated theoretical ventures to accomplish this ambition during the Weimar years.

The second layer to be discussed below came more or less simultaneously with many of Simmel's reflections on crowds, but evolved from within an entirely different and much more politically activist setting.

---

[1] See also Geiger (1931: 120; 1931/32: 90, n. 1) who claims that it was Fresenius who coined the term 'crowd psychology'.

This layer was composed of Marxist approaches which, rather than dismissing the crowd because of its purported destabilizing tendencies, elevated it to being an important agent in political struggles. The leftish leaning of this layer and its aim to conceive of crowds from a broad societal and at the same time highly political point of view also anticipated subsequent Weimar developments. The third layer, then, was the compound of crowd semantics that emerged during the Weimar period. From the early 1920s onwards, the suggestion doctrine was considered increasingly problematic. The attack on the French-inspired suggestion perspective came from different angles. On the psychological side, Sigmund Freud launched a thorough critique of the notion of suggestion which he replaced with his concept of libido. And in the sociological camp, both the suggestion doctrine and Freud's alternative psychological explanation of crowd behaviour were deemed inadequate. Indeed, the sociologists struggled to establish a distinctively sociological theory of crowds so as to free the crowd from its embeddedness in what they considered a psychological straightjacket. Situated vis-à-vis the Tarde–Durkheim debate the Weimar scholars might be said to occupy a mediating position. They tallied with Tarde that the crowd issue was of primary sociological importance, but concurred with Durkheim when it came to assessing the sociological value of the notion of suggestion. Compared to the French forerunners, moreover, the Weimar sociologists who took the crowd topic seriously generally entertained a left-wing rather than a conservative outlook. While they did not necessarily share the Marxist scholars' conviction that crowds should be utilized as radical transformative vehicles, they nevertheless granted crowds a positive social function, namely as a means through which to reconcile societal tensions.

I will explore these three layers in turn and conclude the chapter by discussing the implications of the distinctive sociological approach that transpired during the Weimar years.

Adopting and adapting the suggestion doctrine

The nineteenth-century interest in psychology and how to apply psychological perspectives to collective phenomena was not restricted to France and the discussions emanating from the dispute between Bernheim and Charcot. Important psychological work also appeared in Germany and elsewhere. In fact, in a historical analysis of how the notion of suggestion was applied to the study of crowd behaviour, Diana P. Faber has argued that the theoretical foundation for late-nineteenth-century crowd psychology did not originate in France but rather in the

German *Völkerpsychologie* (Faber 1996: 16).[2] *Völkerpsychologie* had been founded by Moritz Lazarus and Heymann Steinthal in 1860 when launching the journal *Zeitschrift für Völkerpsychologie und Sprachwissenschaft* in which they outlined their study object as the historical–comparative investigation of the *Volksgeist* of different peoples. Lazarus and Steinthal defined this spirit (alternatively, mind or mentality) in the first volume of the journal as 'a similar consciousness of many individuals, plus an awareness of this similarity, arising through seminal descent and spatial proximity' (quoted in Allport 1954: 35). Isolated, this definition could be interpreted along the lines of crowd theory, such as Faber suggests. But seeing a distinct foundation for crowd psychology in this is going too far, I think, as no crowd dynamics were really laid bare by it. And even if some vague relationship might be identified between crowd semantics and early *Völkerpsychologie*, this link is practically undermined when considering the work of Wilhelm Wundt who came to embody and refine the discipline (e.g. 1911).

Wundt established a laboratory for experimental psychological research in Leipzig which became famous far beyond the German borders. One of Wundt's admirers was Durkheim, who visited his laboratory on his trip to Germany in 1885–6 and who found significant inspiration in Wundt's work (see Lukes 1985: 90–1). Wundt maintained a rather critical attitude towards the vocabulary underpinning the contemporary crowd theory. In 1892, for example, he published a book entitled *Hypnotismus und Suggestion* in which he discussed the contemporary French and German psychological interest in hypnotism, suggestion and somnambulism (Wundt 1892). Although he had great respect for Bernheim's work, he generally associated hypnotism with occultism and therefore did not grant it much room in his conception of *Völkerpsychologie*. Moreover, the 1892 book focused on the possible experimental gains of hypnotism and on the psychological explanation of suggestion, whereas the application of hypnotic suggestion to the understanding of crowd phenomena was not central to this book. The field of crowd psychology was discussed instead in Wundt's comprehensive multivolume investigation entitled *Völkerpsychologie. Eine Untersuchung der Entwicklungsgesetze von Sprache, Mythus und Sitte*, which was published between 1900 and 1920. In the seventh volume, dedicated to the study

---

[2] There is disagreement as to how to translate the unique German term *Völkerpsychologie* properly into English. Some early translations proposed 'folk psychology' and 'social psychology', but neither of these conveys the meaning very well, and Wilhelm Wundt, one of the discipline's most prominent scholars, disliked the latter term (Greenwood 2004: 48–9). A more apt translation is 'ethnopsychology' (Mandler 2007: 57, n. 9).

of society, Wundt began by discussing the status of sociology versus that of *Völkerpsychologie* (Wundt 1917). He differentiated between different forms of sociology (philosophical, biological, etc.) and argued that 'sociology as crowd psychology' constituted one of these. Wundt did not have much that was positive to say about Tarde and Le Bon, though, and simply dismissed their contribution to sociology as 'speculative' (1917: 15).

While Wundt showed little respect for the crowd psychologists and did not see much potential in hypnotism and suggestion as important topics for the *Völkerpsychologie*, some colleagues in the German-speaking realm judged differently. One was Otto Stoll, a professor of geography and ethnology in Zurich, who had previously studied at Bernheim's clinic in Nancy. In 1894 he published a book entitled *Suggestion and Hypnotismus in der Völkerpsychologie* (Stoll 1894). This was the book which, as I mentioned in the previous chapter, Durkheim drew on in his turn towards the suggestion doctrine in *The Elementary Forms of the Religious Life* (although Durkheim referred to the second enlarged edition of the book, Stoll 1904). Stoll's ambition with the book was to remedy a problem he observed in the existing *Völkerpsychologie*, namely that it had failed to recognize 'what prominent, even fundamental role suggestion has played, and still plays, not only in individual life but also in the psychology of peoples' (1894: 2–3; see also 489, 513). Stoll was particularly interested in crowd suggestions which, he contended, could be observed 'in an unambiguous manner in all places and at all times in the human history' (1894: 14).

Stoll's book offered an extensive analysis of collective suggestive phenomena among various peoples, ranging in space from China, West India and Mexico to Egypt and in time from ancient Greece to post-1789 Europe. Most importantly for present purposes, Stoll applied the notion of suggestion to account for almost any collective phenomenon. Politics (revolutions, fanaticism), economics (speculation, manias, advertising), religion (mysticism, witch trials) as well as more general and everyday phenomena (panic, ecstasy, etc.) were all subject to hypnotic mass suggestion, he argued. Suggestion, for Stoll, amounted to a 'psychological coercion' which he likened to the effect a moving billiard ball has on another ball's course (1904: 701). This image entailed that suggestion was not seen as a pathological phenomenon. The coercion suggestion exercises on our minds was rather '*an entirely normal quality*' (1894: 491, italics in original). In a sense, therefore, Stoll reached the same conclusion as Tarde did (but without the latter's theory of society): social life is characterized by the kind of hypnotic suggestion that is usually associated with crowd behaviour, although in everyday life the suggestions are less intense than in crowds.

While the debates on hypnotic suggestion and crowds within *Völkerpsy-chologie* were of mainly German origin – although interactions with French scholars did of course take place – there were also German-speaking contributions to crowd theory which showed much greater direct inspiration from France. Thus, the emphasis on suggestion that Stoll advanced joined hands with a more general endorsement of the French suggestion doctrine within German crowd-psychology circles (see also König 1992: 150, n. 19). One example of how suggestion entered German debates came via the Russian psychologist and neurologist Vladimir Bekhterev, who was Ivan 'Pavlov's chief rival in the psychoneurological sciences' (Joravsky 1989: 83). Bekhterev (spelled 'Bechterew' in German) graduated in medicine in Russia but also visited some of the leading specialists in Western Europe, including Charcot in Paris and Wundt in Leipzig. He became deeply interested in the phenomenon of suggestion and in December 1897 he delivered a lecture on this topic at the Military-Medical Academy in St Petersburg. The lecture was subsequently published as a monograph and translated into German as *Suggestion und ihre soziale Bedeutung* (Bechterew 1899). A second significantly elaborated version appeared in German translation a few years later under the title *Die Bedeutung der Suggestion im sozialen Leben* (Bechterew 1905).[3] As the titles of both translations indicated, and as Bekhterev himself stated explicitly in the preface to the second edition, suggestion is not merely to be observed in the narrow cases of one-on-one hypnosis; it comprises a much broader phenomenon, detectable in everyday life. He defined suggestion as 'the direct induction of psychic states from one person to another, induction that occurs without participation of the will (attention) of the perceiving person and often even without clear understanding on his part' (1905: 12; 1998: 13). According to Bekhterev, suggestion constitutes a key feature in social life: 'suggestion is a factor deserving of the most careful exploration for the historian and the sociologist, otherwise a whole line of historical and social phenomena will receive incomplete, insufficient, and often even inadequate interpretation' (1905: 142; 1998: 180).

Even if they were not his exclusive concern, Bekhterev paid great attention to the suggestive epidemics of crowds. He was familiar with previous research by Le Bon, Sighele, Tarde, etc. (e.g. 1899: 79; 1905: 132, 140; 1998: 166, 178); described the suggestion of crowds in Le Bonian terms as having a 'microbe'-like character (1899: 82; 1905: 140; 1998: 178; Le Bon 1960: 18); and shared the assertion that crowds are capable of both heroic deeds and violent outbursts. Similar to the

---

[3] In the following I refer to these German versions and to a recent English translation of the third edition of the book. The third edition contains some additional chapters but the main structure and arguments follow the earlier versions.

work of other crowd scholars, moreover, literary representations of crowd behaviour had a bearing on Bekhterev's work. At one point, for example, he referred to Tolstoy's *War and Peace* to illustrate the influence of suggestion on crowds (1899: 79; 1905: 137; 1998: 174–5).[4]

Bekhterev's work was received positively in Germany and constituted one strand of research that placed a premium upon the explanatory power of the suggestion doctrine. Many other scholars endorsed the suggestion doctrine in analyses of crowd phenomena. Besides Bekhterev, Helmut König (1992: 150, n. 19) mentions Willy Hellpach and his book *Die geistigen Epidemien* (1906) as a representative of the French-inspired psychological approach to crowds in Germany. Further examples include, to mention but a few, the discussions of crowds in Theodor Elsenhans' *Lehrbuch der Psychologie* (1912: 400–4); Ernst Trömner's *Hypnotismus und Suggestion* (1913); and Siegfried Sieber's *Die Massenseele* (1918). While these works modified the psychological approach of the French scholars somewhat, the general message they conveyed was unaltered: crowd behaviour could be analysed psychologically, and if suggestion provided no full *explanation* of crowd dynamics, then at least it offered an apt *description* of what went on in crowds.

It was in the context of this current of approaches subscribing to the suggestion doctrine that Simmel outlined his sociological reflections on crowds and collective behaviour. Simmel never devoted an entire article or book to the study of crowds, yet the crowd topic often crops up in his work since he believed the crowd to constitute a perfect entry into the study of sociality.[5] By and large Simmel shared the idea advanced by

---

[4] In his subsequent work Bekhterev increasingly reformulated his observations on crowds in a theory of reflexology. This theoretical framework – which appeared in German translation as *Die kollektive Reflexologie* (Bechterew 1928, original published in 1921) – departed from a critique of subjectivism in sociology and crowd psychology where notions such as the 'mind of crowds' (Le Bon 1960: 25) were common. Bekhterev considered such categorizations of collective entities according to individual–psychological conceptions flawed and wanted to replace them with his new discipline of reflexology which, he claimed, operated on a 'strictly objective ground' (1928: 6). In spite of this critical starting point he nevertheless analysed collective entities, including crowds, as 'united personalities' [*Sammelpersönlichkeit*] (1928: 50ff.), indicating that the difference from the French crowd scholars was perhaps not that great. The complete edition of Bekhterev's collective reflexology – much extended as compared to the German translation cited above – only recently appeared in English translation, and in this edition he located his approach vis-à-vis the work of Le Bon, Steinthal and Lazarus, Tarde, Wundt and others (2001: 29ff.).

[5] Despite the fact that Simmel took the crowd issue seriously, placing it centrally in his sociology, there is hardly any commentary on this part of his work. One exception is Francisco Budi Hardiman (2001: ch. 1). For a lengthy discussion of Simmel's contribution to sociological crowd semantics, see also Borch (2010), on which the following is based.

Le Bon and Tarde that the crowd exposes a particular social form, often characterized by destructive impulses. In the grand opus, *Soziologie*, the first edition of which was published in 1908, Simmel asserted that in a crowd of physically proximate people:

> innumerable suggestions swing back and forth, resulting in an extraordinary nervous excitation which often overwhelms the individuals, makes every impulse swell like an avalanche, and subjects the mass to whichever among its members happens to be the most passionate ... The fusion of masses under one feeling, in which all specificity and reserve of the personality is suspended, is fundamentally radical and hostile to mediation and consideration. It would lead to nothing but impasses and destructions if it did not usually end before in inner exhaustions and repercussions that are the consequences of the one-sided exaggeration. (1950b: 93–4; 1950d: 227–8; 1992: 70, 206)

The resemblance between this quote and the views expressed by Le Bon and Tarde was not coincidental. Simmel was familiar with the work of this tradition. In 1891 Simmel had reviewed Tarde's *Laws of Imitation*, characterizing it as 'thoughtful', 'stimulating', 'creditable' and 'original', and lauding the 'very interesting manner' in which Tarde had demonstrated 'that imitation [is] a kind of hypnotic suggestion' (1999a: 248, 250).

Simmel also reviewed Le Bon's *The Crowd*. He found the explanatory horizon of the book superficial in many respects and complained that Le Bon did not distinguish clearly between the various forms of crowds he described. In spite of this, Simmel praised the book for being a rare attempt to provide 'a psychology of the human being as a mere social creature' (1999b: 354). In terms of the more specific features of crowds, Simmel accepted the Le Bonian scheme on the intellectual and ethical inferiority of crowds (as compared to individuals), something that Simmel elsewhere described as the 'sociological tragedy as such' (1950c: 32; 1999e: 94). Simmel's explanation of this alleged inferiority differed from that of Le Bon, though. Thus, Simmel asserted in a partly evolutionary argument, the psychological qualities which are common to different persons are always the lower ones which have been transmitted hereditarily (see also 1950c, 1999e: 90–1). By implication, when a large and diverse group of people act in unity, as they do while forming a crowd, it is only the primitive and lowest psychological qualities (e.g. feelings and instincts in contrast to intellect and civility) which are certainly present in every member of the group/crowd. It is therefore only these primitive qualities that can be the foundation of the crowd's action, Simmel resonated (1999b: 356–7). Simmel derived two consequences from this argument. First, educational strategies would only matter little vis-à-vis the intellectual and ethical derangement of crowds.

Even the most skilled group of individuals could be expected to fall back on the lowest common denominator. Second, Simmel sided with Le Bon that the 'crowd regime' should be strongly condemned and that it was warranted to 'speak of the idiotic, blunt, insane [*unzurechnungsfähigen*] crowd without these attributes thereby being valid for any of its members' (1999b: 358).

Much of what Simmel had to say about Le Bon drew on ideas that had been put forward in Simmel's 1890 treatise *Über sociale Differenzierung* (1989). In this book, Simmel presented his evolutionary argument that only the lower qualities are common to everybody and that joint action will always be based on precisely these lower traits. Also, the argument on the inability to change the nature of crowds through education was already developed in *Über sociale Differenzierung*. Since crowds are characterized by lower rather than higher qualities, crowds do not respond to rational arguments; in order to manage crowds, Simmel said, one must appeal 'to their feelings' (1989: 210).

While Simmel seemed to treat the notion of suggestion, which was underpinning the work of Tarde and Le Bon, with deference in the early 1890s, this would change just a few years later. A manifest illustration of this appeared in his 1897 review of the German translation of Sighele's book on criminal crowds. Here Simmel objected that suggestion had turned into a 'magic formula', which signified 'superficialities' and was applied mainly by 'dilettantes' (1999c: 389). What disturbed Simmel in the case of Sighele was that the latter used suggestion as the principal, even universal, explanation of crowd behaviour, and that the Italian subsumed other important concepts, such as for instance imitation, under that of suggestion (1999c: 394). Instead of having recourse to suggestion, sociology demanded a more solid foundation, Simmel argued. This is why he proposed the notion of interactions or reciprocal effects (*Wechselwirkungen*) as a more apt concept than imitation and suggestion, arguing that rather than seeing the crowd as the apex of suggestion, it refers to the social event in which 'the purest reciprocal effects take place' (1989: 211).[6] Importantly, this statement evinced, dismissing the concept of suggestion did not entail a devaluation of the crowd topic. Quite the contrary, far from being a marginal social

---

[6] Simmel did not write off hypnotic suggestion entirely. His point was merely that reciprocal effects was a broader, more inclusive and at the same time strictly sociological notion that captured the dynamics of hypnotic suggestion: 'in every hypnosis the hypnotized has an effect upon the hypnotist', hence hypnotic suggestion too 'conceals an interaction [*Wechselwirkung*], an exchange of influences, which transforms the pure one-sidedness of superordination and subordination into a *sociological* form' (1950d: 186, italics in original; 1992: 165).

incident, crowd behaviour was conceived by Simmel to be 'one of the most revealing, purely sociological phenomena' (1950a: 35; 1999e: 97–8). It was in crowds that the most intense reciprocal impulses could be identified, Simmel in effect suggested, thereby elevating the crowd to being the social entity par excellence.

The point of emphasizing reciprocal effects rather than hypnotic suggestion was that the former seemed to carry far less psychological baggage and that it struck more distinctively sociological tones. This did not change much in terms of how crowds were portrayed, though. Simmel still adopted a frightened attitude and described the crowd as a state of exception that 'arouses the darkest and most primitive instincts of the individual, which ordinarily are under control' (1950d: 228; 1992: 206). In fact, in the specific analyses of crowds it remains difficult to tell how Simmel's own approach really differs from that of the crowd psychologists. So, despite the more explicitly sociological gloss he added, König is right in stating that Simmel did not 'go significantly beyond crowd psychology' (1992: 150, n. 19). Accordingly, Simmel's contribution to the history of sociological crowd semantics might be described as a kind of transition work, a sort of stepping stone, which was affiliated with the suggestion doctrine, but which attempted, if only prematurely so, to wrest the crowd out of the hands of the psychologists and to propose a more sociological framing of crowd semantics. In the German context, the latter ambition was only really fulfilled years later by the Weimar sociologists, many of whom drew on and further elaborated Simmelian insights.[7]

Simmel's work is illustrative of how the suggestion doctrine, while gaining a foothold in German psychology in the 1890s and early 1900s, was received with reluctance in sociological circles. This reservation was to grow stronger as the years passed. Importantly, moreover, especially

---

[7] Arguably, Simmel's most unique, though implicit, contribution to crowd theory may be derived from his notion of sociability (*Geselligkeit*) as developed in a 1910 article (1971). Although Simmel did not explicitly address the crowd issue in this essay, several of his statements might be applied to crowd behaviour. He thus identified 'an impulse to sociability in man' and argued that associations [*Vergesellschaftungen*], whatever their specific purpose, 'are accompanied by a feeling for, by a satisfaction in, the very fact that one is associated with others and that the solitariness of the individual is resolved into togetherness, a union with others' (1971: 128). It might be argued that, translated into the crowd realm, the crowd's primary function lies in 'the satisfaction of the impulse to sociability' (1971: 130). On this view, Simmel's analysis suggests that the crowd in its pure sociable form creates 'an ideal sociological world', where 'the pleasure of the individual is always contingent upon the joy of others' (1971: 132). So rather than constituting a threatening alternative to a rational, civilized social order as Le Bon would have it, the crowd seems to give vent to an affective cohesion of rare purity. I have developed this idea further in Borch (2010).

Simmel's attempt to transform observations furnished by work drawing on the suggestion doctrine into a sociological vernacular took place as an almost entirely academic endeavour. That is, Simmel approached the crowd topic not as an ultimately political problem, but rather as a purely intellectual challenge of how to conceive of this particular social occurrence. It might concluded from this that, contrary to the conservative French scholars, Simmel was not personally intimidated by crowds, which is likely to be the reason why he never devoted an entire article or book to the topic. This somewhat distanced view was countered quite manifestly in the second wave of pre-Weimar German crowd semantics represented by the Marxists' approaches to crowds. Similar to Simmel, several Marxist scholars would grant the crowd a central sociological status, but they would add to this overtly activist and political motivations.

Mobilizing mass action

It does not make sense to speak of a unified body of Marxist crowd semantics. Instead a stream of partly overlapping, partly distinctive problematizations of crowds can be identified which share a basic Marxist outlook. What the Marxist approaches have in common is above all that they testify to the 'tactical polyvalence of discourses' that Foucault has called attention to, i.e. 'the shifts and reutilizations of identical formulas for contrary objectives' (1990: 100). Such tactical polyvalence was already visible in nascent form in the difference between Taine and Zola. However, the subsequent layer of Marxist crowd semantics illustrates more clearly that the notion of crowds, which in the 1890s was utilized mainly by conservative scholars to diagnose an alleged threat to bourgeois society, was reinterpreted and revalorized in a new political vocabulary, which eventually turned the crowd into a category that should be endorsed precisely because it could be activated in the overthrow of the bourgeois order.

Arriving at that position would take some time, though. When the notion of masses entered left-wing debates in the mid-nineteenth century, it did so against a background of comprehensive industrialization, urbanization and deprivation. In this context, pauperism became a new object of knowledge and intervention in the fight against immense poverty (Procacci 1991). And in the discussions of pauperism, the notion of 'Masse' was increasingly used to describe the rapidly extending impoverishment which was now conceived of as mass impoverishment. The term 'Masse' was also employed to signify the 'quantitative leap from mob [Pöbel] to proletariat' (König 1992: 126). The notion of the proletariat is closely tied to the work of Karl Marx and Friedrich Engels who, however, can hardly be categorized as crowd/mass scholars. To be sure, Marx and Engels did refer to these notions in their work. For example, they referred extensively to the term 'Masse' in their 1845 critique of Bruno Bauer (Marx and Engels 1974: 82ff.; see also 9, 11), but the notion was applied here in a rather unspecific manner, signifying both an opposition to spirit ('*Geist*'; they followed Bauer on this point) and the totality of actual subjects (Berking 1984: 85; König 1992: 129–30; see also Reiwald 1946: 308–9). Despite such references Marx and Engels' preoccupation lay elsewhere, above all with the concept of classes, and this concept differed markedly from that of crowds/masses, the latter of which were merely to be characterized as 'pre-class' (Günzel 2004: 121; for an extensive discussion of Marx's view on masses and classes, see Rammstedt 1986).

Later Marxist theorists paid greater attention to crowd and mass semantics. One example is Rosa Luxemburg who, besides publishing widely on socialism, revolution, etc., played an active role in the Social Democratic Party of Germany and later co-founded the German Communist Party. In the present context I shall merely attend to Luxemburg's emphasis on the role of mass action. For while Marx and Engels zeroed in on the conditions and struggles of the proletarian class, Luxemburg suggested that spontaneous mass action constituted a central element in the establishment of proletarian class consciousness: the irrational energies of mass action were believed by Luxemburg to form the backdrop to the institution of a proletarian class (Kitschelt and Wiesenthal 1979: 183).

Luxemburg was particularly interested in mass action in the form of a mass strike. In a manuscript entitled 'Massenstreik, Partei und Gewerkschaften' from 1906, she asserted that it was a key task for the Social Democrats in Germany to provide a political leadership which, instead of waiting for 'the spontaneous mass movement [*Volksbewegung*] to fall from the sky', tried 'to *accelerate*' the revolutionary mass strike (1972: 146, italics in original). Luxemburg was ambiguous when it came to outlining precisely how this mobilization of the mass strike should take place. Yet there was no doubt for her that the Social Democratic Party assumed a central role in this, as the party constituted 'the most enlightened, the most class-conscious vanguard of the proletariat' (Luxemburg 1972: 146). Interestingly, this assertion was semantically aligned with the idea that the mass is unconscious and irrational and that the 'blindness of the mass' should be cured through enlightenment strategies (Luxemburg, quoted in Berking 1984: 87).

In some of her later work Luxemburg gave less weight to political leadership and more to the learning processes arising *through the spontaneous act itself* (see Koselleck 1992: 417). In her address at the foundation of the Communist Party on 31 December 1918 she thus stated that:

The mass must learn to exercise power while exercising power. There is no other way to teach it. We are luckily beyond the era where the proletariat should be educated in socialism ... To educate the proletarian masses in socialism means giving lectures and disseminating pamphlets and brochures. No, the socialist proletarian school does not need this. It learns while it acts. (1969: 198)

This praise of the act itself added a further layer to the discussion of enlightenment, for according to the pure activist position, enlightenment would crystallize through the act. This idea was not univocally endorsed in left-wing circles. Co-founder of the Communist Party, Karl Liebknecht thus maintained a notion of the enlightening Party, arguing that the Party should bring about a 'revolutionary enlightenment', which would amount to instigating a 'revolutionary enthusiasm in the masses of workers and soldiers' (1969: 59).

Luxemburg's early reflections on the mass strike resonated with simultaneous calls made by Georges Sorel in France. Sorel was part of an intellectual milieu that stressed the import of affect and non-rationality in human behaviour and which counted people such as Bergson, Le Bon and Ribot (Nicolas and Charvillat 2001; Nye 1973: 427–8). Some of these inspirations were visible in his *Reflections on Violence*, in which he elaborated his idea of the revolutionary myth, the general strike (Sorel 1999; the majority of the essays constituting the book were first published in 1905–6). Sorel, who had previously reviewed Le Bon's *The Crowd* (1895), generally approved of Le Bon, but also emphasized the need for going beyond his ideas.[8] As he put it in *Reflections on Violence*:

Le Bon says that it is a mistake to believe in the revolutionary instincts of the crowd, that their tendencies are conservative, that the whole power of socialism lies in the rather muddled state of mind of the bourgeoisie; he is convinced that the masses will always go to a Caesar. There is a good deal of truth in these judgements, which are founded on a very wide knowledge of history, but the theories of G. Le Bon must be corrected in one respect; they are only valid for societies that lack the conception of class struggle. (Sorel 1999: 124)

Since a recognition of class struggles was not compatible with Le Bon's own political horizon (at least not in any Marxist sense), Sorel had to

---

[8] Nye reports that Sorel's appreciation of Le Bon was testified to in several letters to the latter. This admiration was not quite returned, for 'LeBon did not want to run the risk of alienating the bourgeois politicians whom he hoped would lead France from the brink by any ill-considered praise of a man who lauded violence' (Nye 1973: 436, n. 96).

adapt crowd psychology to socialism himself. The result was a transformation of the psychology of crowds into a syndicalist struggle for a
new morality; a political vision in which, some commentators have
argued, 'Sorel saw the psychological crowd as the intrinsic unit of the
social cataclysm' (Nye 1973: 431). Indeed, 'far from discouraging the
masses', i.e. far from paralyzing them into a conservative, inactive slum-
ber, the primary means of syndicalism, the general strike, was believed
by Sorel to contain so much vitality that it could 'only excite them still
more to rebellion' (1999: 125). While this blend of crowd psychology
and socialist thought was Sorel's invention, it relied heavily on the image
that Le Bon had already propagated (Horowitz 1961: 38).

It might puzzle that, although Sorel shared with Le Bon a strong belief in
the importance of taking seriously the irrational dimensions of social life,
he did not hesitate to elaborate on the unmistakably anti-socialist crowd
psychology of his colleague. However, their opposite political programmes
converged in a critique of recent social–political developments in France.
Most importantly, they shared an utterly critical stance on the French
Revolution as well as a 'hatred for parliamentary socialism' (Nye 1973:
434). Le Bon's critique of the Revolution and socialism grew, as mentioned
in Chapter 1, out of his conservative critique of egalitarianism. But Sorel,
too, despised the French Revolution and the terrors that followed, and
argued along with Alexis de Tocqueville that, contrary to what was commonly assumed, the Revolution did not bring much new but was in fact
fundamentally conservative (1999: 80–1; see also 91–2). This, he asserted,
also applied to the parliamentary socialists of his time. They, too, 'preserve
the old cult of the State; they are therefore prepared to commit all the
misdeeds of the *ancient régime* and of the Revolution' (1999: 103). So
whereas Le Bon's contempt of parliamentary socialism was based on the
fear that it endangered naturally given inequalities, Sorel criticized parliamentary socialists for retaining inequalities and thus for betraying the true
socialism. Syndicalism, and its crowd act of the general strike, was therefore a reaction against both the bourgeoisie and the indolent socialists.

Returning to the German scene, the calls for a mass or general strike
were not received positively in all socialist circles. Most notably, within
the Social Democratic Party, August Bebel and Karl Kautsky
grew increasingly sceptical towards Luxemburg's wish to promote the
revolutionary mass strike, and Kautsky thought it necessary to critically
examine the spontaneous action of unorganized crowds. In 1911, he
published a long essay on this issue, entitled 'Die Aktion der Masse',
later incorporated as a chapter in his book, *Der politische Massenstreik*
(Kautsky 1911, 1914). Contrary to Luxemburg, who did not engage
explicitly with crowd psychology, Kautsky discussed Sighele and

especially Le Bon, whose work he criticized. Among other things, he contested the explanatory value of the notion of suggestion. Instead he argued that spontaneous crowd action arises as a reaction to specific historical conditions, say, famine or losing a war (1911: 80). Importantly, he added, each crowd member must already be excited prior to the crowd action. 'The being-together in the crowd enhances the excitement, but it is not its cause' (1911: 48). The central message conveyed here was that 'spontaneous' crowd action is not all that spontaneous. Kautsky therefore put greater faith in solving fundamental societal tensions through hard party-political work, rather than in believing in the redemptive power of spontaneous mass action.

Adding a further layer to his scepticism, Kautsky discussed two recent developments which, he believed, significantly altered the conditions of spontaneous crowd action. The first was the changes in the capacity and possibilities of the modern army. New weapons as well as novel urban planning (such as the Hausmannization of Paris) made it easier to fight unruly crowds. Second, the introduction of universal suffrage furnished people with a new channel to voice their protest – and in fact supplied the proletariat with a new means of mass (voting) action which was not restricted to specific physical locations (Kautsky 1911: 111–12). According to Kautsky, these developments did not altogether eliminate spontaneous crowd action, but they were likely to have some leverage on its frequency and effectiveness. Kautsky concluded his essay by discussing the practical tactical implications of his analysis. Since, he argued (in implicit opposition to Luxemburg), the spontaneous crowd is fundamentally unpredictable, it would make little sense for the Social Democratic Party to try to organize spontaneous crowd action. The Party should rather seek to strengthen its organizational powers and work for an 'enlightenment of the masses' (1911: 117).

Interestingly, this faith in the power of organization was being contested the very same year (1911) by Robert Michels in his *Political Parties: A Sociological Study of the Oligarchical Tendencies of Modern Democracy* (1959). Michels was active in the German Social Democratic Party from 1903–7 but flirted with Sorelian syndicalism as well (see Beetham 1977a). *Political Parties*, which was based in part on his observations of the German Social Democratic Party, revolved around a problematization of political organization. Michels opened the book by stressing the need for organizing political interests, framing this with special but not exclusive attention to the proletarian masses. As an individual person the worker has no chance of promoting his or her concerns, Michels conceded; assembling in a collective entity is the only realistic way to advance political opinion. Therefore, '[t]he principle of organization is an absolutely essential condition for the political struggle of the masses' (Michels 1959: 22). However, and this was the chief point of Michels' subsequent analysis, this organization itself contains a number of serious drawbacks, the most important being that '[o]rganization implies the tendency to oligarchy ... As a result of organization, every party or professional union becomes divided into a minority of directors and a majority of directed' (1959: 32).

This observation was inspired by the work of the Italian elite theorists Vilfredo Pareto and Gaetano Mosca. Michels had met the latter at the University of Turin when he moved from Germany to Italy in 1907, and Mosca's work prepared the way for his interest in Pareto. Yet whereas Mosca and Pareto had established *that* elites materialize in any society, Michels sought an explanation as to *why* this was so (Milles 1987: 13). To this end he employed crowd psychology (Beetham 1977a: 14; 1977b: 173ff.).[9] Moscovici even reports that in a letter to Le Bon from 23 November 1911, Michels asserted that, in *Political Parties*, 'I have simply applied to political parties and their administrative and political structure the theories that you have so luminously established concerning the collective life of crowds' (quoted in Moscovici 1985: 386, n. 1). Michels repeated this statement in the preface to the second edition of *Political Parties*, published in 1925, categorizing the investigation as 'crowd psychology applied to history' (1970: xxvi).

The inspiration from Le Bon is easy to detect. For example, Michels noted that the crowd 'is always subject to suggestion, being readily influenced by the eloquence of great popular orators', just as he spoke of 'the pathology of the crowd', and observed that the 'individual disappears in the multitude, and therewith disappears also personality and sense of responsibility' (1959: 24, 25; cf. 1926: 332–4). The main innovation added by Michels was his adoption of the crowd-psychological language, typically utilized to account for the temporary crowds of the street, to the phenomenon of *organized crowds* (political parties, unions, etc.).[10]

---

[9] Crowd semantics played a marginal role in Pareto (e.g. 1984: 59, 70). Although he did refer to Taine and Le Bon in his study *The Rise and Fall of Elites* (1991), there was no theoretical discussion of the notion of crowds in this book, nor was the elite theory developed in it based on reflections on elite versus crowd/mass (see Pareto 1991: 87–8, 112–14, n. 29, 114, n. 34). The same is true of Pareto's huge two-volume study *Les systèmes socialistes*, first published in 1902 and 1903 (1965). Things were not altogether different with Mosca. His *The Ruling Class*, originally published in 1895, made occasional reference to Taine's account of the French Revolution and to Tarde's early work on crowds, but the book contained no systematic treatment of crowds or masses (Mosca 1939).

[10] Emphasizing this organized character of crowds anticipated a central point later advanced by McDougall and Freud (see below).

By having recourse to crowd psychology Michels believed himself able to explain why the oligarchic tendency of organizations is bound to materialize. Thus, he argued, the crowd is possessed by a desire and need for leadership. 'In the mass, and even in the organized mass of the labour parties, there is an immense need for direction and guidance. This need is accompanied by a genuine cult for the leaders, who are regarded as heroes' (Michels 1959: 53). On its own, the proletarian mass is not capable of action, he claimed; its unity and ability to act (say, go on strike) is dependent upon the control exercised by a leader. When describing the leader, Michels once again drew on the semantic reservoir of Le Bon. Most importantly, he said, the leader must possess great oratorical qualities, which will ensure that 'the masses, intoxicated by the speaker's powers, are hypnotized to such a degree that for long periods to come they see in him a magnified image of their own ego' (1959: 71).

Michels' reflections on organized crowds also contained implications for discussions of modern democracy. Whereas Le Bon had feared democracy, because he believed it to instigate the rule of crowds, Michels' analysis demonstrated that crowds will never rule. Due to the dynamics of political organization, they are destined to being ruled. Or as he put it, '[w]ith the advance of organization, democracy tends to decline' (1959: 33). As such, Michels' investigation brought to the fore a basic paradox. The workers need to organize in order to make their voice heard, but this organization installs new power structures which limit their political weight.

This cynical lack of belief in democracy that Michels displayed acquired an additional twist in some of his subsequent thought. Thus, Michels gradually sympathized with Italian nationalism and joined Mussolini's party in 1922. These sympathies fed into his scholarly work, where he began to examine the emergence of fascism in Italy – see his 1924 article 'Der Aufstieg des Faschismus in Italien' (Michels 1987a) – as well as the purported 'criteria for the establishment and development of political parties', as the title of a 1927 article put it (Michels 1987b). In the latter article Michels combined his own crowd-theoretical adaptation of elite theory with his friend and colleague Max Weber's work on charismatic leaders (see also Beetham 1977b: 175–7). The resulting analysis was a celebration and explanation of Mussolini's rise to power, but it can also be interpreted in light of its political recommendations. Michels applauded Mussolini for having a charisma that made the Italian masses see him as identical to and constitutive of Italy as such. Moreover, Mussolini had understood that passions are key to political life. 'Passion is a crowd-psychological stimulant. The possession of passion is what constitutes the political advantage of charismatic parties over programme-based parties or parties based on class interests',

Michels wrote (1987b: 300). Investigating fascism also led Michels to revise some of his earlier ideas. Most importantly, Michels adjusted his notion from *Political Parties* that the crowd needs a leader to emerge and maintain itself. The relation between crowd and elite was more reciprocal, he now asserted. Specifically, he argued, the elite depend on the crowd in order to appear legitimate. The elite cannot maintain its power 'without the explicit or at least tacit consent of the crowds' (Michels 1987b: 302). According to Michels, this squared nicely with the 'fascist theory of consent', which abandoned public elections and replaced them with an assessment of the sheer number of party members and of the loudness of 'the direct and spontaneous applause of the people' (1987b: 303). The political implications were clear. In order to appear legitimate, one can dismiss formal elections and simply orchestrate huge mass events where the crowd celebrates the leader. In the words of Joachim Milles, Michels thus 'reinterpreted the rationally given mandate of the voter into an irrational act of acclamation' (1987: 16).

There is obviously a wide stretch from the political agenda underpinning Luxemburg's adaptation of crowd theory to Michels' fascist turn. Disregarding the latter and looking merely at the seemingly heterogeneous corpus of Marxist contributions to crowd semantics, this is not only united by counter-bourgeois objectives. More specifically, this semantic layer is characterized by a much more activist agenda than what was represented by, for example, Simmel or scholars subscribing to the suggestion doctrine. To be sure, Le Bon's grand ambition with *The Crowd* was to endow the statesman with guidelines for how to manage the crowds. Yet the Marxist approaches were more radical than this, as they sought ultimately to attend to crowd semantics so as to transform politics as such. In line with this, the Marxist adaptations cared less about portraying the crowd's proper qualities, just as they paid no attention to how sociology might be demarcated from adjacent disciplines. Indeed, the more practical–activist objectives behind much of the Marxist layer of crowd semantics entailed a genuine disinterest in disciplinary (meaning less overtly political) struggles. While the policing of disciplinary boundaries was no major concern of the Marxist intellectuals examined above, subsequent Weimar scholars would forge a *mélange* of Marxist resources and a profound concern with strict disciplinary separations.

First World War: evoking large-scale sentiments

I have illustrated so far how crowd semantics that drew on the suggestion doctrine was supplemented by Marxist conceptions. These two semantic strands embodied the main approaches to debates on crowds in German thinking from the late eighteenth century until the early 1920s, when things began to change and a new layer of crowd semantics materialized that challenged the suggestion doctrine, in particular. These changes, which took place during the Weimar years, surfaced to some extent as reactions to the aftermath of the First World War.

The significance of the outbreak of the First World War in 1914 is hard to overestimate, both in terms of the immediate reactions it provoked and with respect to its implications for subsequent thinking. With regard to the immediate responses, the war was generally greeted favourably in Germany since there was a widespread conviction that it could foster a new sense of unity.[11] In her biography on Max Weber, Marianne Weber describes how, in July 1914, Weber and the people around him received the information about the upcoming war with optimistic anticipation:

They did not even totally reject the horror of war, for they felt that the release of tensions, the raging of the elements, the adventures, and the breakdown of the world order might somehow be great and inspiring and would release previously confined energies ... it was an hour of the greatest solemnity – the hour of *depersonalization* [*Entselbstung*], of integration into the community. An ardent love of community spread among people, and they felt powerfully united with one another. Having formed a brotherhood they were ready to destroy their individual identities by serving. (1975: 518–19, italics in original; see also Jensen 1998: 147)

Due to this excitement Max Weber immediately reported for service, which is significant given the fact that Weber was no 'rabid national chauvinist', to use Jensen's terms (1998: 147). Interestingly, moreover, as should be clear from the quote, the liberating potentials ascribed to the war and its depersonalized community came very close to customary accounts of how crowds operated. It seemed, in other words, as if minor local crowd sentiments, which were previously feared and abhorred, had suddenly taken hold of broad masses of people, even intellectuals, and were celebrated precisely for their depersonalizing effects.

One of Weber's colleagues who was indeed seized by the mass excitement was Simmel. In a lecture from November 1914, delivered in Strasbourg to where he had just moved to take a position as professor, Simmel expressed how the outbreak of the war filled him with hope (see also Liebersohn 1988: 156–8). The title of the talk, 'Deutschlands innere Wandlung' (Simmel 2003), clearly articulated the expectations he had for the war. While recognizing the obviously terrible and destructive (outer) sides of the war, Simmel was primarily occupied with the

---

[11] I draw in the following on Jensen's (1998: 144ff.) illuminating analysis.

idea that, in terms of its inner edifice, 'Germany is once again full of a great opportunity', namely the possibility of creating 'a new human being [*Menschen*]', a new attitude (2003: 283). In particular, Simmel argued, this new German attitude would grow out of the new 'point of unity and unconditional solidarity' that he believed the war would evoke (2003: 275). As in the case of Weber, Simmel's reflections could be seen as locating, on a general societal or national level, the kind of transition towards depersonalized unity and solidarity, which was usually believed to be typical of the crowd. In brief, the reactions of Weber and Simmel suggest that the First World War helped to prepare the way for a semantic transformation that would be more fully developed by later scholars, namely the transformation from crowd to mass: the features typically associated with crowds of co-present individuals suddenly appeared to seize the entire nation which therefore emerged as a mass.

To be sure, praising war and its alleged crowd/mass effects pre-dates the First World War. This association had been established most notably by the futuristic movement which had been inflamed by Filippo T. Marinetti's famous manifesto that was published in 1909 in *Le Figaro*, and which soon received a positive reception in Germany (Gay 1968: 6). As Christine Poggi has convincingly shown, both crowds and war played important roles for the futurists, although Marinetti and his co-futurists' position was characterized by ambivalence towards both categories (2002). The futurists subscribed to many of the negative accounts of crowds advanced by Le Bon, Sighele and Tarde, and also associated the crowd with feminine attributes. At the same time, however, the political salience of crowds was emphasized; by animating them culturally, 'the futurists sought to incite their audiences to rise up in revolt against the [Italian] government's apparent pacifism and neutrality' (Poggi 2002: 740). The combined celebration of war and crowds was expressed unmistakably in two of the eleven points in Marinetti's manifesto:

9. We will glorify war – the world's only hygiene – militarism, patriotism, the destructive gesture of freedom-bringers, beautiful ideas worth dying for, and scorn for woman . . .

11. We will sing of great crowds excited by work, by pleasure, and by riot; we will sing of the multicolored, polyphonic tides of revolution in the modern capitals . . . and the sleek flight of planes whose propellers chatter in the wind like banners and seem to cheer like an enthusiastic crowd. (1971: 42)

This excitement about crowds meant that Marinetti and the futurists did not share Le Bon's fear that society would be undermined by the rule of crowds. Quite the opposite (and not dissimilar to Marxist images of mass action), if properly moulded, the crowd could act as a liberating force which, by its destructive militaristic behaviour, would produce freedom and help to invigorate society. That said, the underlying biopolitical approach, which suggested that life and crowd behaviour were positively correlated, was curiously aligned with Le Bon's work. But the notion that war, crowds, patriotism, freedom and a new and energetic conception of 'man' were intimately related to one another also resembled the feeling that Weber and Simmel would later be seized by, namely that the First World War was prone to prepare the way for a new society inhabited by a new people living in a crowd-like state of internal unity and harmony.

Obviously, there were several significant differences between Marinetti and the futurists, on the one hand, and Simmel and Weber, on the other. The former believed in war as such (in fact, they aestheticized it in ways the Italian fascists would later exploit), just as they celebrated anything related to machines, speed, etc. Simmel and Weber, by contrast, expressed concerns about the ever-more dominant 'objective culture' (Simmel) and technical rationality (Weber), and they did not endorse war as such, but were merely captured by the sentiments that followed in the immediate aftermath of the declaration of the First World War. Soon all parties grew disillusioned, however (see also Liebersohn 1988: 74–6). The futurists who had welcomed the war eventually saw it as an anticlimax; 'the triumphant fusion of flesh and metal, man and machine' that they had hoped for turned out to produce mass death and disappointing defeats (Poggi 2009: 234).[12] Similarly, Simmel's war enthusiasm did not last. This became manifest in 1917 when he published a book entitled *Der Krieg und die geistigen Entscheidungen*, which contained the 1914 essay 'Deutschlands innere Wandlung', but which also included later and much more pessimistic analyses (Simmel 1999d).

The disillusion was not reserved for the Germans and futurists. The experiences with the First World War signified, as several historians have argued, a mental watershed in all the countries that took part in the war. This was also the case in the UK, although the starting point was very different there than in Germany. Rather than welcoming the war as a revitalizing and unifying event, many British intellectuals conceived it as a genuine catastrophe. This has been thoroughly analysed by Samuel Hynes in *A War Imagined: The First World War and English Culture* (1990;

---

[12] This disappointment did not prevent Marinetti from developing new suggestions for the improvement of the Italian people. Forgacs and Gundle report that in 1930, 'Marinetti launched a campaign against pasta, asserting that it was an unsuitable food for an alert and warrior people' (2007: 242).

see also Jensen 1998: ch. 4). Illustratively, Hynes opens his investigation with the then British foreign minister Sir Edward Grey's famous response to the outbreak of the war: 'The lamps are going out all over Europe. We shall not see them lit again in our time' (1990: 3). The approaching darkness of the war was to some extent counterweighted by the noble and dignified beliefs in honour, glory and patriotism that characterized the British soldiers upon entering the battles. Ultimately, however, the mass slaughter would profoundly question the noble stance and replace it with a feeling of widespread despair and chaos, both at the front and at home.

The war inspired several British scholars to relate crowd semantics and warfare. One example was Sir Martin Conway's *The Crowd in Peace and War* (1915), which, however, in its form and content was somewhat apart from previous academic discussions. More strongly embedded in the existing sociological literature was Wilfred Trotter's *Instincts of the Herd in Peace and War*, first published in 1916 (1975). Drawing on Le Bon, Boris Sidis and others, Trotter zeroed in on the notion of gregariousness, which, he argued, referred to a fundamental biological and sociological instinct that describes the inclination of persons to respond to impulses from the herd. According to Trotter, the war had stimulated an atmosphere where this gregariousness materialized on a grand scale, and where the herd to which the individual attached him- or herself changed from the social class or group to the nation.

Returning to the German situation, the war defeats led to an increasing internal pressure on Wilhelm II, who eventually abdicated in 1918. On 9 November 1918, the Weimar Republic was proclaimed, and a new government took power, led by the Social Democrat, Friedrich Ebert. On the one hand, this prepared the way for a stabilization of the external relations, as marked by the armistice in November 1918 and followed by the Treaty of Versailles which was signed in June 1919. On the other hand, the internal political order was severely shaken. The proclamation of the Weimar Republic was in effect a revolution, hence named the November Revolution, although a rather quiet one at that. A series of insurrections continued the following months, especially from January to April 1919, thereby further destabilizing the already wobbly foundation of the young Republic. In fact, the events following in the months after the November Revolution were far more violent than the initial revolutionary occurrences, and strikes, violent uprisings, occupations, etc. were scattered around the country (for a brief account, see Kolb 1994: esp. 121–2).

Interestingly, the November Revolution itself was greeted widely. Just as the First World War had inspired all sorts of hopes for revitalization and unification, so the November events were seen by many as a fresh start after the catastrophic war. But just as the 1914 hopes were greatly disappointed in the course of the war, so the 1919 uprisings eventually 'dissipated the capital of goodwill that had accumulated in the days of collapse and hope' (Gay 1968: 9). These 1919 uprisings reflected a stern internal opposition on the left. During the war, a leftish faction of the Social Democratic Party had argued passionately against the Party's support for the war. In 1917 this debate culminated with the formation of a new party, the so-called Independent Social Democratic Party. While this party was not itself revolutionary, it sided in its criticism of the Social Democrats with a group of revolutionary Spartacists, led by Karl Liebknecht and Rosa Luxemburg. Since December 1914, Liebknecht had been one of the most prominent and persistent voices against the war within the Social Democratic Party, and his frustration with the Party eventually made him leave it to form the Spartacist group with Luxemburg and others in 1915. In the wake of the November Revolution, the Spartacist movement was transformed into the German Communist Party, founded in December 1918. Liebknecht and Luxemburg pursued a distinctively revolutionary agenda. They were far from satisfied with the new Ebert government and called for a continued revolution, with the explicit aim to establish a Soviet (*Räte*) system. This was not merely talk. In January 1919, Liebknecht and Luxemburg initiated a revolutionary attack in Berlin. They were both killed in the uprisings. Similar insurrections mushroomed in other German cities the following months.

The whole political instability was reinforced by the great economic burdens that the Versailles treaty imposed on Germany, and which not only made it hard for the country to recover, but which also produced widespread bitterness. The economic challenges further intensified with the immense inflation in 1923. This despair inspired Hitler's abortive putsch in Munich in November 1923, which sent him to prison. The Weimar Republic only really entered a phase of stability and economic progress in the following years, but this was only on borrowed time since instability would return with the financial crisis in 1929.

One of few positive notes amid this pervasive sense of political and economic crisis that formed the frail backbone of the Weimar Republic appeared in the arts and in intellectual life more generally. Thus, the political unrest in the early Weimar years was mirrored by a frantic cultural–intellectual revitalization. In philosophy, theatre, architecture, photography, literature, painting, music, etc. new ideas abounded (Dadaism, Bauhau, *neue Sachlichket*, etc.; see the seminal analyses by Durst 2004; Gay 1968; Peukert 1991). Peter Gay has argued that much of what transpired culturally in the Weimar era was actually preconfigured by earlier developments from the 1900s and 1910s. For example, Walter Gropius' Bauhaus architecture of the 1920s was a rather direct continuation of work conducted in the 1910s (1968: 5). According to Gay, therefore, 'the Republic created little; it liberated what was already there' (1968: 6). This seems to underestimate the extraordinarily vibrant currents of creativity of the Weimar years, which varied from the previous decades in their much closer alliance with and response to a burgeoning mass culture (Peukert 1991). The 1920s were characterized by a widespread feeling that the cultural edifice of Germany was crumbling, and that a massification was taking hold of German society as a consequence of metropolitan life, the advance of machines, rationalization and a general technicized 'progress' of modernization, which were all believed to shake the cultural fabric and evolve into a veritable 'Massendasein' (Berking 1984: 30; Peukert 1991). Part of this cultural critique and its relation to crowd and mass semantics constitutes a semantic problematization of its own and will be discussed in more detail in Chapter 5.

I have had recourse to the above-mentioned historical events so as to convey a sense of the socio-political background for the comprehensive interest in crowds that emerged in the Weimar era. Two key dimensions stand out. To begin with, the outbreak of the war had evoked a positive mass atmosphere in Germany, however short-lived it turned out to be due to the mass destructions of the war. This mass dimension would later be even more pronounced when totalitarian movements sought to capitalize on the instability that the war and the Weimar Republic induced. This is the reason for seeing the First World War as 'the watershed that separates the nineteenth-century age of the crowd from the twentieth-century age of totalitarianism', as Arnason and Roberts put it (2004: 28). The reactions to totalitarianism will be analysed in Chapters 5 and 6. However, totalitarianism did not yet form a crucial problem among the Weimar scholars, at least not among the sociologists. Rather than being preoccupied with *mass* discussions, they were still mainly concerned with *crowd* issues. So in spite of the mass atmosphere of 1914, the 1818–19 events had proved the need for a continued investigation of revolutionary crowd behaviour (which was only emphasized by the Russian Revolution in 1917). Even if the Weimar scholars followed different routes in order to arrive at a proper understanding of crowds, they shared the impression that a new theoretical apparatus was needed; the Le Bonian framework, including the suggestion doctrine, was deemed inadequate. The vibrant intellectual atmosphere only added to the impetus to embark on new paths.

In spite of these winds of change, the suggestion doctrine did not totally vanish. It retained some popularity as a general framework (e.g. Seeling 1925) and, more specifically, as an approach to crowd behaviour (e.g. Häberlin 1927: 131–6; Satow 1921: esp. 99–107).[13] Nonetheless, the suggestion doctrine came under increasing attack during the Weimar years. In what follows I shall describe the two most important critiques, namely those propounded by Freud, on the one hand, and by a group of sociologists, represented most notably by Theodor Geiger, on the other.[14] Since the critiques came from different disciplinary backgrounds, and since this disciplinary division would be a key point for the sociologists, I will discuss this layer of anti-suggestion crowd semantics in two tempi.

Freud's crowd psychology

Sigmund Freud's most crucial contribution to the scientific crowd debates is unquestionably his 1921 book *Group Psychology and the Analysis of the Ego*.[15] In order to understand the theoretical ambitions of this essay, it makes sense to open the discussion by going back some thirty years prior to its publication. As mentioned in Chapter 1, Bernheim and the Nancy School were essential to the establishment of early French crowd psychology, but the work of Bernheim also had an immediate leverage on German psychology. Freud, who in 1889 had experienced Bernheim's work personally, played an important role here, as he translated the latter's 1886 book *De la suggestion et de ses applications à la*

[13] As Günzel (2005: 117, n. 19) remarks, Le Bon's work on crowds even had an impact on Jakob von Uexküll's biologically informed treatise on state biology which, referring explicitly to the Frenchman, pointed to the crowd as a symptom of a social disease that might lead to a dissolution of the state (1920: 43).

[14] It might be objected that since Freud was living and working in Vienna, he is not strictly speaking part of the Weimar era. I nevertheless find it warranted to include him in the discussion of Weimar developments because his work was widely debated in Germany as well (see e.g. Gay 1968: 34–7).

[15] As has often been noted, 'group psychology' is no fortunate translation since the German title, *Massenpsychologie und Ich-Analyse*, places the book explicitly in the tradition of *crowd* psychology. The argument of the English translator of Freud's essay, James Strachey, for using 'group' rather than 'crowd' is that, in the essay, Freud aimed to develop a vocabulary to understand unorganized crowds as well as organized groups (Freud 1989: 3, n. 1). Strachey's argument is not unreasonable. Still, since Freud's essay was meant as an explicit response to the *crowd*-psychological tradition, I have decided to modify Strachey's translation. This means that in the following discussion, the German term *Masse* is translated as crowd (except when referring to the title of the essay). I should note that, in his brilliant deconstruction of Freud's crowd essay, Mikkel Borch-Jacobsen opts for an alternative translation, namely *mass* psychology (1988). Together with the work of Serge Moscovici (1985), Borch-Jacobsen's book is, in my opinion, the most important contribution to understanding Freud's crowd psychology and, needless to say, far more thorough than the following brief examination.

thérapeutique into German. Interestingly, in his preface to the translation Freud voiced a fundamental critique of Bernheim. While Bernheim subsumed hypnosis under suggestion and claimed that everyone is susceptible to suggestion, he failed, in Freud's eyes, to account for how suggestion comes about. 'Suggestion itself remains entirely unexplained' by Bernheim, Freud objected (1896: iv, here quoted from the second German edition of the book; see also 1989: 27–8). *Group Psychology and the Analysis of the Ego* might be read as an attempt to solve this problem in the field of crowd psychology. Indeed, Freud stated in this work, referring explicitly to especially Le Bon, the explanation of crowd phenomena offered by previous 'authorities on sociology and crowd psychology is always the same, even though it is given various names, and that is – the magic word "suggestion"' (1989: 26–7). Freud's reservations not only concerned the explanatory potentials of the notion of suggestion; they also reflected a specific political positioning. Recalling how he personally witnessed Bernheim's way of practising suggestion on patients, Freud spoke of the 'tyranny of suggestion' and referred to suggestion as 'an act of violence' where the hypnotized person was a victim in the hands of the hypnotist (1989: 28). On the basis of this 'libertarian protest against the hypnotist's power', as Borch-Jacobsen has called it (1988: 156), the aim of Freud's intervention was to develop a, for him, more convincing explanatory apparatus, which had no recourse to magic and which did not place power so centrally in the equation.[16]

The whole essay was built on the assertion that the difference between individual psychology, on the one hand, and social or crowd psychology, on the other, should be downplayed (Freud 1989: 3–5). Upon close inspection, Freud claimed, individual psychology is always also a social psychology since it is concerned with the individual in his or her relation to other persons. Obviously, the tactical reason guiding this proposal was that, by collapsing the difference between the individual and social/crowd domains, the way was prepared for an engagement with collective phenomena on the basis of individual psychology, in the form of (Freudian) psychoanalysis.[17]

---

[16] According to Borch-Jacobsen, the critique of suggestion was fundamental to Freud's entire psychoanalytical project. 'Indeed, was it not by rejecting suggestion that psychoanalysis had constituted itself *as* psychoanalysis? Does not this very rejection embody the Freudian break with the past?', Borch-Jacobsen asks (1988: 147, italics in original).

[17] This move would be central to other psychologists as well. Similar to Freud, Alfred Adler explained crowd and mass states on the basis of individual psychology (1934: 138). He asserted, for instance, that 'the mass psyche of a generation' was related to experiences during the early years of childhood (1934: 141). Carl Gustav Jung argued differently. While maintaining that the 'psychopathology of the masses is rooted in the *psychology of the individual*', he proposed a theory operating with notions of the collective

What was Freud's alternative to the suggestion doctrine, then? Most importantly, in order to redirect crowd psychology he proposed that suggestion be replaced by the notion of *libido*, that is, 'the energy, regarded as a quantitative magnitude (though not at present actually measurable), of those instincts which have to do with all that may be comprised under the word "love"' (1989: 29). According to Freud, the turn to libido was substantiated by two observations:

First, that a crowd is clearly held together by a power of some kind: and to what power could this feat be better ascribed than to Eros, which holds together everything in the world? Secondly, that if an individual gives up his distinctiveness in a crowd and lets its other members influence him by suggestion, it gives one the impression that he does it because he feels the need of being in harmony with them rather than in opposition to them – so that perhaps after all he does it *'ihnen zuliebe'*. (1989: 31, translation modified)

Freud illustrated this libidinal structure through an examination of two specific types of crowds, namely the Church and the army (the connection between crowds and the army had already been established by Trotter to whom Freud referred). In these as well as in other crowds, Freud posited, the crowd members unite in their common attachment to the leader – 'in the Catholic Church Christ, in an army its Commander-in-Chief', both of which are believed by the crowd members to love 'all the individuals in the crowd with an equal love' (1989: 33). This shared libidinal tie to the leader would then form the basis for the crowd members' mutual identification, Freud continued. It follows from this that Freud attributed a constitutive role to the leader. A similar argument had been advanced by Le Bon and Tarde, but Freud added a twist to this by claiming that the leader him or herself is not part of the crowd.[18] In Freud's words, the crowd members are 'under the influence

---

unconscious and archetypes which he employed to account for why, after the First World War, there existed a general and collective German mob mentality (1947: 3, italics in original). In a sense this went far beyond classical crowd semantics and was aligned more with subsequent mass semantics in that Jung's diagnosis referred to an allegedly nationwide phenomenon. For other discussions on masses and crowds, see also Jung (1935/36: 666–7; 1958: 15).

[18] Borch-Jacobsen has a different interpretation. For him, the only thing really separating Freud's and Le Bon's accounts of the leader is the underlying explanatory apparatus. Le Bon subscribed to the suggestion doctrine, Freud did not (Borch-Jacobsen 1988: 138–46; cf. McClelland 1989). It seems fair to say, though, that Freud's analysis did instigate at least one important move as compared to, for example, Le Bon. According to Moscovici, Freud's model thus implied a shift in emphasis from the crowd as such to its leader: 'In the crowd psychology that Freud worked out, the crowd was very soon to disappear from the field of investigation, to be replaced by a leader, who occupied the dominant, central and ultimately exclusive position on the horizon' (1985: 241).

of a common affectionate tie with a person *outside* the crowd', meaning that the internal coherence is based on the attachment to an external subject (1989: 67, italics added).

Characterizing the Church and the army as crowds entailed a different notion of crowds than what the traditional images of unruly collectives in the streets suggested. This was one of Freud's deliberate attempts to go beyond Le Bon whom, he believed, was mainly concerned with crowds 'of a short-lived character', something which purportedly endowed *The Crowd* with a propensity to ignore more stable and institutionalized kinds of crowds (1989: 21). In order to account for organized crowd behaviour, Freud attended to the work of William McDougall, particularly his book *The Group Mind* (1920). McDougall drew on a variety of sources, including Le Bon, Stoll and especially Tarde, and claimed that the 'increased suggestibility' of crowd members constitutes 'one of the most striking facts of collective mental life' (1920: 58). More appealing to Freud than this endorsement of suggestion was McDougall's argument that '[t]he peculiarities of simple crowds tend to appear in all group life', meaning that a tight connection could be established between seemingly unorganized crowds and organized groups (1920: 67). In Freud's reading this entailed that McDougall prepared the way for a broad conception of crowds, which tended to conflate the notions of crowd and group. Put differently, McDougall's analysis pointed to the need for a psychology which could explain both types at once, and this, Freud believed, was furnished by the libidinal framework.

On the surface, Freud's notion of the crowd appears rather positive. The crowd fulfils specific functions for the individuals and is not a phenomenon which threatens society, nor does it arouse general panic. Quite the contrary, Freud asserted, fear and panic only ensue if the crowd disintegrates, for this dissolves the libidinal tie between the individual crowd members and the leader and, by implication, the identification between the individual and his or her fellow crowd members (1989: 36). Although this positive conception ran counter to the predominantly negative images developed by Le Bon and Tarde, it seems that upon closer inspection, Freud's emphasis on the leader entailed a political problematization of crowds which did not differ markedly from that of the French crowd psychologists. This has been demonstrated by John McClelland. While he agrees that Freud's crowd psychology 'lacks the anti-popular thrust of nearly all of his predecessors in the crowd theory tradition', he nevertheless asserts that it presents 'an extremely dark picture of human collective living', which is not too different from what Freud's forerunners in the field held (1989: 262, 263). McClelland identifies two major reasons for this gloomy outlook.

One relates to the anti-Semitic political environment Freud had experienced in Vienna (see also Moscovici 1985: 223–7). In the 1880s, Georg Schönerer, leader of a pan-German, nationalist movement, had planted the seeds of anti-Semitism in Austrian–Hungarian political life. Schönerer's anti-Semitic agenda attracted a considerable following, but his political influence faded after he was sentenced to prison for an attack in 1888 on the editorial office of the *Neues Wiener Tagblatt,* which he accused of disseminating treacherous, Jewish propaganda (see König 1992: 197). This did not mean the end to anti-Semitism in Vienna, though. A new wave of anti-Semitism was carried forward by Karl Lueger, who, more successful than Schönerer, was elected mayor of Vienna in 1897, and later re-elected. When Lueger died in 1910, one of his political opponents, the Social Democrat Friedrich Austerlitz, gave the following characterization of Lueger: he was 'the first bourgeois politician who recognized the importance of the masses in politics' (quoted in Wistrich 1983: 251; see also König 1992: 197–9; Schorske 1981: 136). It was this mushrooming anti-Semitism which nurtured Freud's political pessimism (see also McClelland 1989: 267).

The second reason for Freud's bleak attitude was founded on his analysis of the so-called primal horde. Freud argued that 'the crowd appears to us as a revival of the primal horde', and the leader of the crowd reincarnates the 'primal father' who, by his authority, ties the crowd together (1989: 70; see also 77, n. 9). This horde may exhibit libidinal ties, but they are not based on pure enjoyment. Quite the opposite, Freud stressed:

the primal father had prevented his sons from satisfying their directly sexual impulses; he forced them into abstinence and consequently into the emotional ties with him and with one another which could arise out of those of their impulses that were inhibited in their sexual aim. He forced them, so to speak, into crowd psychology. His sexual jealousy and intolerance became in the last resort the causes of crowd psychology. (1989: 72)

According to Freud, the 'uncanny and coercive' features of the primal horde reappear in the crowd, for '[t]he leader of the crowd is still the dreaded primal father; the crowd still wishes to be governed by unrestrictive force; it has an extreme passion for authority; in Le Bon's phrase, it has a thirst for obedience' (1989: 76). This desire for submission and authority, which Freud associated with the libidinal structure, endowed his analysis of the crowd with a pessimistic outlook: it intimated that in an era of crowds, authoritarian impulses are likely to proliferate. Consequently, Freud's analysis did not suggest that irrationality is any less significant in modern society than what was proposed by the French crowd theorists. To be sure, Freud did not subscribe explicitly to Le Bon's prophecy about the era of crowds. However, in a certain sense his analysis demonstrated that Le Bon's prediction might be truer than the latter expected. For rather than studying the unorganized crowd of the street, Freud was concerned with organized or institutionalized crowds, notably, the Church and the army. And when such institutions display the characteristics of crowds, then it is hard to conceive of societal domains where the passion for authority and obedience does not feature prominently. In the words of McClelland:

> In Freud's view of it, when a crowd in the ordinary sense of the word finds ways of institutionalizing itself into some kind of permanent life, it does not jack itself up the rungs of the ladder of civilization; quite the reverse: it begins to recapitulate the events of the primal horde after the Ur-slaying. (1989: 263)

In sum, therefore, Freud's crowd psychology, which was meant first and foremost as a theoretical intervention that projected a new conceptual and explanatory apparatus, was characterized by ambiguity. It proposed a fresh and original perspective on the crowd's libidinal organization, thereby pointing to the possibility that people unite in crowd behaviour because of the pleasure they derive from it. Yet this idea was dampened by a simultaneous emphasis on the authoritarian desire which was also said to be central to the crowd. Politically, therefore, the substitution of the suggestion doctrine with that of libido did not change much. Freud's position displayed the same ambivalence as Tarde's analysis: isolated, the crowd sociality is to be commended *as sociality*, but at the same time it contains a dark, irrational side. In a sense Freud's conception of the crowd was even darker than that of his French forerunners, for there seemed to be no institutionalized alternative to crowds in modern society; no publics, such as Tarde suggested.

Establishing distinctively sociological alternatives

Freud's psychoanalytical critique of the suggestion doctrine as well as his alternative conception of crowds opened up new venues for the study of collectivities.[19] A number of Weimar sociologists readily followed these

---

[19] Freud was not alone in searching for a psychological approach to crowds which took leave of the suggestion doctrine. Much less influential than Freud, in 1920 Walther Moede put forward his *Experimentelle Massenpsychologie*, which, contrary to the suggestion doctrine, offered a more psycho-physiological approach to the study of collective phenomena (1973). Moede argued that the stimulus that radiates from one person can be transferred automatically to others in a group, be it optically, acoustically or kinetically. See also Moede (1915).

paths. They utilized the space opened by Freud's critique but extended the critical attitude to encompass his work as well. As mentioned above, the new theoretical orientation was not merely a product of theoretical reflection; it was triggered as well by concrete historical experiences, most notably the 1918 November Revolution (Ebine 2004). Indeed, the Weimar social theorists set themselves a double challenge: how to account for the recent revolutionary crowd events, and how to do so without falling back upon old psychological categories. While the former question was not always made explicit (it worked rather as an implicit backcloth), the latter was a manifest concern in most sociological crowd semantics in the Weimar years.

In addition to Freud's intervention and the revolutionary events, the work of the Weimar sociologists was fuelled by new currents in German sociology that were rather critical of the explanatory framework put forward by Le Bon and Tarde. Most notably, Max Weber demarcated his grand sociological theory of social action explicitly from the crowd and imitation theories of the two French scholars. In the famous opening chapter of *Economy and Society* Weber asserted that even if 'the behavior of an individual is influenced by his membership in a "mass"', this may not qualify for social action, as this behaviour need not be meaningfully oriented towards others (1978: 23).[20] For the same reason, 'the subject matter of studies of "crowd psychology," such as those of Le Bon, will be called "action *conditioned* by crowds"', not social action (1978: 23, italics in the German original). Similarly, the:

mere 'imitation' of the action of others, such as that on which Tarde has rightly laid emphasis, will not be considered a case of *specifically* social action if it is purely reactive so that there is no meaningful orientation to the actor imitated. (1978: 23, italics in the German original)

Weber did recognize exceptions to this clear-cut picture. He conceded that a demagogue may influence a crowd in a way in which 'his mass clientele is affected by a meaningful reaction' (1978: 23). Likewise, consciously imitating a fashion in order to achieve a specific social position is social action. Still, both 'the behavior of crowds and imitation ... stand on the indefinite borderline of social action' (1978: 24).[21] In effect,

---

[20] *Economy and Society* was published posthumously, but Weber, who worked on the fundamental terminological apparatus between 1918 and 1920, finished the opening conceptual chapter before he died in 1920 (see Roth 1978: c–cii).

[21] In the same vein, the type of social action in Weber's categorization which might be said to have the closest connection to crowd behaviour, namely that of 'affectual' social action, 'also stands on the borderline of what can be considered "meaningfully" oriented' (1978: 25).

Weber repeated Durkheim's exclusion of crowd and imitation theory from the realm of proper sociology since neither belonged to the field of social action. While Weber upheld a politer and seemingly more open tone than Durkheim, stating that sociology 'is by no means *confined* to the study of social action', he stressed at the same time that the focus on social action is 'that which may be said to be *constitutive* for [sociology's] status as a science' (1978: 24, translation modified, italics in the German original). In other words, Weber ultimately shared Durkheim's critique that crowd and imitation theory could hardly qualify as scientific.

While Weber was rather explicit about the exclusion of the crowd topic from sociology, the Weimar sociologists to be discussed in the following approached the problem of crowds differently. Rather than dismissing it a priori they offered a sustained theorizing of crowd behaviour and argued that this took place in a distinctively sociological manner. This merely redefined the disciplinary struggles, though, for in a sense the attempt to develop a distinctively sociological theory of crowds was a reiteration of the (Durkheimian) wish to separate out sociology as an independent discipline. The crowd topic operated as a key element in this disciplinary endeavour: if the crowd topic could be wrested from the hands of the psychologists, then any social phenomenon could.

In the following I demonstrate how and with what purposes and implications the Weimar scholars struggled to establish a distinctively sociological account of crowds. I will organize the discussion thematically and analyse what I take to be the most important concerns and contributions of this Weimar sociology. I begin by analysing the idea of conceiving crowds as a specific kind of group. Next I introduce the distinction between active and latent crowds. As a third step I examine Theodor Geiger's attempt to combine a group–sociological approach with an understanding of active and latent crowds. Underlying these various attempts to arrive at a distinctively sociological perspective on crowds was, as König (1992: 154) notes, the ambition to understand crowd behaviour on the basis of an *exact* science (e.g. Geiger 1987: 1; Vleugels 1930: xi). This was precisely what previous approaches had failed to offer, in part, it was intimated, because of the psychological underpinnings of former work.

Seeing the crowd as a group

The notion of groups played an important role in much early German sociology (e.g. Simmel), but came to occupy an ever-more central status in sociological debate on crowds in the Weimar period. A similar movement might be detected in the social or crowd-psychological realm (such as the work of McDougall and Freud demonstrates), but for the Weimar sociologists, the main reason for interpreting crowds in group vocabulary was to establish a purely sociological, meaning non-psychological, understanding of crowds.

Some of the sociologists who argued for a group-based approach to crowds included Alfred Vierkandt (1923: 418ff.) and Gerhard Colm. Here I shall only discuss the latter's influential 1924 article entitled 'Die Masse. Ein Beitrag zur Systematik der Gruppen' (Colm 1924; see also 1931). Colm's main objective with the article was conceptual, namely to develop a conceptual framework of '*pure* sociology', on the basis of which the crowd could be studied as one social group among others (1924: 694, italics in original). Although, as previously mentioned, this sociological interest in crowds was triggered by the surrounding Weimar events, the essay was not fraught with references to the socio-political climate. The few scattered references to the historical situation did not diminish the sociological importance of crowds. The purported group character was, in Colm's eyes, the reason why the crowd qualified for careful sociological consideration, for a 'pure sociology' must be concerned with analysing the various group formations that are possible (1924: 681).

In order to emphasize the sociological nature of his approach, Colm drew on Ferdinand Tönnies' notions of community and society and argued that the crowd constituted a particular kind of group that side-stepped Tönnies' distinction. While, for example, organizations are society groups based on common objectives, and families and erotic relations are community groups characterized by common life experiences, crowds are characterized by a 'mental attachment' which endows them with a unique group character (1924: 684). This mental attachment, Colm was careful to underline, should not be seen as an effect of suggestion. Rather, it amounted to a particular 'we experience' which was conditioned on the presence of a clear objective: 'A multitude of people becomes a crowd when, for example, a cue gives aim and direction to the deeply stirred [and therefore already existing] powers' (1924: 685).

One of the consequences of Colm's attempt to understand the crowd as a specific kind of group was that he evaded the image often associated with the suggestion doctrine, namely that of the crowd as an inherently pathological entity. In itself, the crowd (and its members) is neither laudable nor the opposite, Colm contended. Its value can be both positive and negative, depending on its specific 'historical function'

(1924: 692). Relatedly, he stated, crowds only emerge under specific historical circumstances, namely when there are no other group formations available, or when the existing ones are highly unstable. In one of the article's few references to the socio-political setting of the time, Colm argued that, '[p]recisely in the current situation, many community and society attachments have become so loose that the historical conditions of crowd formations are present' (1924: 692–3). Consequently, Colm saw the uprisings of his time as a struggle for power between crowds and other group formations.

While Colm's study of the crowd as a distinctive group embodied one of the major transformations in Weimar crowd theory, the institution of a firm sociological alternative to psychological approaches, it failed to incorporate another key innovation in Weimar crowd semantics: the distinction between latent and active crowds.

Latent and active crowds

The distinction between latent and active crowds was propagated in particular by Wilhelm Vleugels, one of the most active figures in Weimar crowd theory, who, similar to Colm and Vierkandt, drew on Simmel's formal sociology. Vleugels' first analysis of the crowd topic was developed in a dissertation from 1921 entitled *Masse und Führer*. This book was never published, however, but parts of it appeared in his later work, most notably in his book *Die Masse. Ein Beitragt zur Lehre von den sozialen Gebilden* (1930), which was the culmination of almost a decade's work on the crowd topic.

According to Vleugels, a crowd is a social formation [*Gebilde*] 'whose nature is based on a far-reaching community of feeling [*Gefühlsgemeinschaft*]. Groups of people that do not possess such a mental connection are not crowds in a sociological sense' (1930: 1).[22] When examining the nature of crowds in more detail, Vleugels arrived at his major conceptual contribution, namely the distinction between latent and active or effective (*wirksame*) crowds. The latter were defined by Vleugels as 'a transient formation, which emerges out of a bulk of co-present people who have the same focus, and to which each individual only participates with those parts of the personality that are common to,

---

[22] The notion of social formations was derived from the sociological theory of Leopold von Wiese, who wrote a celebratory preface to Vleugels' book. Von Wiese devoted a chapter of his *Allgemeine Soziologie* to crowds. Among other things, this chapter distinguished between concrete or perceivable crowds and abstract or latent ones (von Wiese 1929: 104–5). For a brief analysis of von Wiese's contribution to crowd theory, see Franke (1985: 71–5).

and dominate, all the individuals' (1930: 36). The personality aspect referred to the unity or coherence that the crowd purportedly brings about. While the effective crowd may emerge out of any social formation, some formations, namely the latent crowds, were 'downright predestined to become an effective crowd at any time' (1930: 8).

Whereas the acts of the latent crowd are performed by relatively conscious individuals, Vleugels posited, the behaviour of active crowds occurs 'unconsciously and compulsory', i.e. it is determined entirely by the collective (1930: 9). Relatedly, the two kinds of crowds were said to differ in the extent to which they absorb their members. Vleugels argued that in its latent state, the crowd is merely one of many social formations that the individual is part of. The individual simultaneously belongs to a family, a workplace, etc. While these various social formations can coexist, it belongs to one of the active crowd's chief features that 'no other social experience takes up so much mental energy of the individual for *the entire duration of the existence* of the respective *formation* as does the real crowd experience' (1930: 10, italics in original). In other words, in its active form the crowd absorbs its individuals so intensely that their participation in all other social formations is entirely suspended. When the crowd is active, the individual is no longer part of a series of simultaneous social formations; their differentiation is annulled and the unity of the crowd reigns.

One further difference between latent and active crowds is worth emphasizing. According to Vleugels (1930: 8–9), latent crowds can be described as communities of feeling. They share some idea, purpose or the like, which they are ready to defend against those who do not subscribe to it. The solidarity, which emerges out of the shared idea, endows the latent crowd with an essentially positive and affirmative attitude. Its members have a belief in a new and improved society; they share a vision of how to create and maintain social bonds. Contrary to this, Vleugels asserted, active crowds are not creative; they are as a rule negative and destructive (1930: 12).

The alleged predestination of the latent crowd to transform into an active one does not in itself suggest under what circumstances this is likely to occur. So what triggers this transition? According to Vleugels (1930: 21), it is the role of leader to prompt the effective crowd; the leader throws the first stone, as he put it, and thereby gives the crowd a direction, a goal, and inspires its mental unity. Vleugels even claimed that a crowd cannot act without a leader. Until the leader appears, the crowd can only exist in its latent form (1930: 39). The importance thereby attributed to the leader did not entail that he or she has unrestricted power over the crowd. Rather, Vleugels stated, some 'mental reciprocities [*Wechselwirkungen*]' seem to be operating whereby the leader may give the mental energies of the crowd a certain direction, but where he or she is him or herself subjected to these energies (1930: 45, 49). This conception of the leader's role differed greatly from that of Freud who placed the leader unambiguously outside the crowd. For Vleugels, by contrast, 'the leader takes up a double position: he is not only outside and above the crowd but also inside it' (1930: 45). And since the leader is part of the crowd, he or she is also influenced by it, which makes the power relation much less clear than in Freud's model.

The significance of Vleugels' distinction between latent and active or effective crowds might best be seen through a comparison with the work of Le Bon who operated with no such separation. In Le Bon, the crowd was always conceived as an active entity. Introducing the notion of latent crowds permitted Vleugels to suggest that crowds may lie dormant. A somewhat similar point had been made by Tarde when he distinguished between crowds and sects, understanding the latter as the yeasts of crowds. Yet, Vleugels' conception in effect posited that latent crowds could assume a less institutionalized form than sects. This all but marginalized the crowd as a sociological topic. Indeed, due to its latency the crowd phenomenon – and hence the threat posed by future active crowds – was likely to be much more prominent than previous observations indicated: a whole reservoir of latent crowds might forge an invisible ticking bomb just waiting to explode into frenzied action. It makes sense to interpret this aspect of the latent–active distinction as a commentary on the Weimar situation, where the political instability fostered a widespread latency for violent crowd action.

Compared to his contemporary colleagues, Vleugels occupied an outsider position in the sense that he cared little about enacting a strong separation between psychological and sociological perspectives on crowds (1922/23: 80; see also 1923; 1930). Also, Vleugels did not adhere to the idea of analysing crowds as groups (1922/23: 81; 1926: 187–8; 1927: 170; see also von Wiese 1924: 24; 1929 for a sharp distinction between crowd and group). This is where the work of Theodor Geiger becomes important, for in a sense he combined – and went beyond – the work of Colm and Vleugels. Geiger outlined a theory of crowds, which analysed crowds as groups and operated with a distinction between active and latent crowds. Further, he offered a more passionate attack on psychological approaches to crowds than his colleagues within sociology.

The revolutionary crowd

It seems fair to say that Theodor Geiger's work, in particular his 1926 book *Die Masse und ihre Aktion. Ein Beitrag zur Soziologie der Revolutionen,* was the culmination of German sociological crowd semantics in the Weimar years. On the one hand, he presented a distinctively sociological understanding of crowds, which was meant as a clear alternative to psychological approaches. On the other hand, the entire socio-political situation of the Weimar Republic had a profound bearing on Geiger's thinking. This historical dimension translated much more directly into his work than was the case for Colm and Vleugels, whose more formal and abstract approaches tended to be less sensitive to the actual historical events (see also Meyer 2001: 80). Add to this that Geiger assumed an active political role which would also leave an imprint on his life and career. Geiger was affiliated with the revolutionary socialist circles who attempted to establish a soviet (*Räte*) republic in Munich in 1919 (Baier 1987; Meyer 2001: 80, 272). He had joined the German Social Democratic Party in 1918, but a growing discontent with its policies – in particular with what he saw as the Party's lacking ability to replace old dogmas with a vocabulary in which to understand and fight the Nazi Party (Trappe 1978: 266) – made him leave it in 1932. Geiger was outspoken in his critique of the National Socialists. So with Hitler's rise to power, Geiger's critical position became increasingly precarious and in 1933 he therefore fled the Nazi regime and emigrated to Denmark.

Geiger's *Die Masse und ihre Aktion* was framed by – and conceived as a theoretical response to – the experiences with the November Revolution in 1918 and its aftermaths (Baier 1987). This was stated unmistakably in the introductory remark that '[t]he *experience* of the revolution means the end of science. And we all *have* experienced a revolution' (Geiger 1987: viii, italics in original). Geiger's point was that it would be impossible for anyone of his time to provide an 'absolutely objective' and 'purely scientific' analysis of revolutions; the experiences of November 1918 were simply too devastating to be approached unaffectedly. Yet that did not preclude decent sociological analysis, Geiger argued. Indeed, the aim of the book was to present a sociological study of the revolutionary crowd by searching for 'its causality in social life itself and in the structure of society' (1987: viii).

To do so necessitated a distinct alternative to psychological approaches to the study of crowds, Geiger contended. In particular Le Bon formed the target throughout *Die Masse und ihre Aktion*, whereas Freud was only mentioned twice. In a devastating critique of the notion of suggestion Geiger argued for reversing the claims of the 'French school': suggestion might take place in crowds, but it can explain neither their constitution nor their behaviour; quite the opposite, suggestion is to be seen as an effect since the 'common belonging to a group [i.e. crowd] is the ground for contagion and effective suggestion'

(Geiger 1987: 175). Similar to Freud, therefore, Geiger questioned the explanatory potentials of the suggestion doctrine. But, contrary to Freud, he was not of the opinion that the proper alternative to suggestion should be found in the psychological realm. In fact, he struggled to avoid precisely that the psychological be used to explain the sociological, and for this reason he was at great pains to analyse the crowd as a particular, objective social entity or association. The demarcation between sociology and psychology Geiger enacted is comparable to Durkheim's general ambition, although the means they pursued differed. Moreover, rather than marginalizing the crowd as Durkheim did in his early work, the November Revolution convinced Geiger that sociology must pay utmost attention to crowds. This revolutionary background reverberated in Geiger's conception of crowds, which referred simply to revolutionary crowds: 'So we name "crowd" the social association which is carried by the destructive-revolutionary induced multiplicity, and for which no particular name has hitherto existed' (1987: 37).[23]

Geiger's starting point was that in order to study revolutionary crowds sociologically, one had to follow Colm's proposal and analyse them as groups (1987: 6). But compared to Colm, Geiger foregrounded a more structural framework, combining as he did the group approach with inspiration from the Marxist layer of crowd semantics – especially Kautsky was seen as a valuable source (1987: vii).[24] Thus not only is the crowd a social group, Geiger posited, its existence is contingent on a particular social and historical context. More specifically, Geiger proposed, with the transition from a pre-modern social order to a class-based modernity, the former's value community (*Wertgemeinschaft*) is annulled. There are no longer any values, and hence no We, that integrate and unite the entire society. On the contrary, the differentiation

---

[23] Thomas Meyer has argued that this constitutive tie between revolutions and crowds was loosened in some of Geiger's later work. For example, in his 1939 textbook *Sociologi* (never translated from Danish), Geiger to some extent discussed the notion of crowds independently of the concept of revolutions (see Meyer 2001: 80, n. 180). Meyer is correct. In three chapters of this book, Geiger's examination of the crowd was separated from the discussion of revolutions. Still, he maintained that crowds are inherently revolutionary (see the final chapter of the textbook which was devoted to a discussion of revolution and revolutionary crowds, Geiger 1939: 664ff., esp. 685ff.). For a more elaborate discussion of changes in Geiger's view on crowds, see Borch (2006a).

[24] The Marxism in Geiger is a contested topic in the Geiger reception. In a discussion of Geiger's later stratification analyses, Rainer Geißler stresses Geiger's anti-Marxist stance (1995). Paul Trappe, on the other hand, argues that an in no way orthodox Marxist inspiration is prevalent in Geiger (1978: 259). It seems fair to say that, in his early work, such as *Die Masse und ihre Aktion*, Geiger drew on a basically Marxist model of class tensions, but neither there nor subsequently did he buy into the full Marxist package.

of values in modern society is the breeding ground for ever-new power struggles. Society is divided into two classes, he continued, the bourgeoisie and the proletariat. The bourgeoisie, the conservative class of the few, attempts to remain in power and to promote the values it represents as the values of the entire society. The proletariat, on the other hand, the progressive–revolutionary class of the many, defies this asymmetrical power structure and refuses to be a mere object of the bourgeois class. This is what makes the proletariat the 'human material of the social association of the crowd' (Geiger 1987: 40).

Geiger stressed that the proletariat is not a crowd in itself; it only constitutes the reservoir from which the crowd may be formed. More precisely, the proletariat covers three dimensions or manifestations. First, it constitutes a technical or mechanized multiplicity.[25] It is mechanized in the sense that it is a subordinate stratum, an object of the bourgeoisie's power and defined negatively in opposition to this. The mechanized multiplicity has no We; it does not form a group with objective characteristics, but is rather the germ out of which the revolutionary crowd might emerge (Geiger 1987: 46). Second, the proletariat can be an organized entity. This is the case when the mechanized multiplicity forms labour unions, cultural institutions, student organizations, political parties, etc. in order to give voice to the revolutionary aspirations. Each of these proletarian organizations constitutes a social group, Geiger said. Finally, the proletariat may materialize as a revolutionary crowd (to be discussed below).

This tripartite differentiation enabled Geiger to analyse two separate aspects of revolutions, their destructive and reconstructive sides. Thus, he claimed, the revolutionary crowd's only concern is to tear apart. It is pure negation. The organized proletariat, by contrast, has a positive function; it seeks to rebuild society after the crowd has carried out its demolition.[26]

In his examination of the revolutionary crowd Geiger followed Vleugels' distinction and argued that the revolutionary crowd is divided

---

[25] Here Geiger drew on Paul Tillich who developed the notion of the technical crowd in his *Masse und Geist. Studien zur Philosophie der Masse* (1922). This book was characterized by a mainly cultural–philosophical or historical perspective and by a strong focus on religion. I will not go into detail with Tillich's book, although its philosophical horizon inspired some of the Weimar sociologists (see Ebine 2004: 166–8). For present purposes it suffices to say that his notion of the technical crowd referred to '*the crowd as an object of impression and technique*' (1922: 8, italics in original), and this definition was the one employed by Geiger.

[26] This idea was similar to what Kautsky had observed in his essay 'Die Aktion der Masse' when asserting that the spontaneous crowd itself was bound only for demolition, and that an organized entity was needed if constructive work were to be carried out.

into two parts, a latent and an active one.[27] This idea was already visible in the title of the book, where Geiger suggested that the crowd must be separated from its action, from its concrete outburst. The distinction between the crowd's latent and active dimensions had several important implications for Geiger. One was that, due to its latency, the crowd actually exists prior to the concrete action. This existence accounts for why people run into the streets; it is not their gathering that creates the crowd, Geiger believed (1987: 78, 86). In the same vein, it is not the revolution that generates the crowd, but the crowd that explodes in revolutionary action.

Moreover, the distinction between the crowd's latent and active phases entailed that the proletariat is simultaneously inside and outside society. In its passive form the proletarian crowd is part of society, although it holds a negative position towards the existing order. However:

In the crowd explosion the massified proletariat places itself consciously and *in reality* outside the existing society. We can, in fact, from the perspective of the at any time existing form of society, characterize the phenomenon of the crowd as a spontaneous 'mass withdrawal' from society. All existing permanent relationships disappear for a moment. During the crowd action and the pure, explosive crowd posture, the massified proletarian even detaches him or herself from the relationship to the proletarian organizations. (Geiger 1987: 75, italics in original; see also 94, 169)

A similar two-sidedness was mirrored in the function that the crowd fulfils in Geiger's view. Recalling the distinction between the proletarian organization and the proletarian crowd, Geiger attributed to the latter a merely destructive function. Yet this destructiveness should not be dismissed in moral terms. Geiger stressed that the crowd's action might be assessed positively from a historical–sociological point of view. 'In its action [the crowd] is destructive and has no independent content of meaning. As a social *life-form*, however, it implies the protest against the mechanization, that is, against the enslavement of people through social objectification' (1987: 168, italics in original). Consequently, a revolutionary crowd might in fact reconcile the social tensions and imbalances that triggered it in the first place.

This also followed from Geiger's analysis of what instigates revolutions. In general, he asserted, revolutions transpire as a result of a tension between society's values and its so-called 'social forms'. By social forms he understood the '*totality of the sociable human creations that are*

---

[27] Geiger did not use the term 'latent crowd' in the book, but it captures what he had in mind (as he later recognized, see 1939: 689).

active at a particular moment' (1987: 56, italics in original). These social forms were said to be 'value-conditioned', but since values change more rapidly than social forms, the latter may be emptied of meaning. They may simply lose their correspondence to the values. According to Geiger, it is such imbalances that pave the way for revolutions. '*Revolution is the overthrow of social forms that have been emptied of meaning and the creation of social forms filled with values … By revolution, therefore, we understand the sudden radical change of social forms*' (1987: 58–9, italics in original). Geiger illustrated this with the French Revolution which, he believed, was the outcome of a tension that emerged with the Enlightenment. Here began a 'revaluation of values' that did not find an equivalent reformation of social forms until the Revolution (Geiger 1987: 56).[28] Observed from this perspective, the revolutionary crowd is neither irrational nor a pathological entity, as Le Bon would have it, but rather a carrier of a 'historically necessary' process (Geiger 1987: 163).

Given the strain of values and social forms, what propels the concrete crowd explosion? What makes the crowd leave its passive mode and turn active and revolutionary? Geiger offered two answers to these questions. First, the crowd explosion may be triggered by events that either increase the hatred (for the bourgeoisie) significantly or make the incoherence of values and social forms apparent. Widespread famine, losing a war, etc. are such events (Geiger 1987: 75). Second, it is the role of the leader to prompt the explosion. Contrary to what Freud argued, however, Geiger was careful to stress that the leader is not equipped with the power to take the crowd wherever he or she wants. The leader merely stimulates the mood of the crowd in such a way that it becomes active. This relation between the leader and the crowd was reflected by the following assertion:

The typical leader of a crowd is not a 'demagogue', he does not consciously and coldly lead the crowd in a certain direction, but is rather himself affected the most by the ecstasy of the crowd experience, is himself the most unconscious person. (Geiger 1987: 149)

This corresponded nicely with Vleugel's analysis of the leader. The leader is an 'exponent of the crowd', and if he or she does not get the mood of the crowd right, he or she obviously cannot be an exponent, and hence no leader, of it (1987: 149).[29]

---

[28] In this vein, Geiger argued that the modern age is the 'historical habitat of the revolution' (1987: 64). Since the beginning of modernity, the values have changed extraordinarily rapidly, whereas the social forms have become increasingly petrified. See also Geiger (1931) for a condensed version of his analysis of revolution.

[29] Geiger subsequently elaborated on this theory of the leader and developed a general conception of the leadership of groups in a book entitled *Führen und Folgen* (1928). The

As mentioned above, Geiger's analysis encapsulates the central endeavours that can be identified in sociological crowd semantics in the Weimar years. He formulated a clear sociological alternative to the psychological approaches; and he did so by profiting from notions that had been advanced in the two former layers of German crowd semantics, in particular Marxist ideas, but also, though more indirectly (and mediated through Colms and Vleugels), input from Simmel's formal approach. One of the central contributions of Geiger is his revalorization of the crowd. Rather than being an entity associated first and foremost with terror, Geiger in a sense rehabilitated the crowd, not so as to mobilize it in practical politics (as for instance Luxemburg), but rather in order to see it in its relation to fundamental tensions in society.

The transformation of the crowd in Weimar sociology

This chapter has analysed three layers of German crowd semantics. Since, I have argued, only the third of these layers, the one surfacing in the Weimar years, constitutes a distinctively German current of sociological crowd thinking, the following concluding reflections will focus merely on this one. Before doing so I should stress that I am of course aware that, as is generally the case in this book, the selection of theorists under consideration in this chapter is indeed that – a selection. This is part and parcel of the semantic approach. Let me therefore add that the kind of ideas presented by Colm, Geiger and Vleugels can also be identified in much other work from this period. One example is Gerhard Lehmann's 'Prolegomena zur Massensoziologie', an article that elaborated on the crowd–group distinction, and in which Lehmann described the crowd as the *'originating problem [Ursprungsproblem] of sociology'* (1932: 40–1, italics in original).[30] A further illustration is Georg Stieler's *Person und Masse. Untersuchungen zur Grundlegung einer Massenpsychologie* (1929). Contrary to what the subtitle suggests, this book was intended as much as a contribution to the sociology of crowds as to crowd psychology. And although proceeding from a Husserlian phenomenological perspective, Stieler ended up subscribing to the same basic notion of his fellow Weimar crowd sociologists: he considered the crowd to be one aspect of a general group problematics.

explicit aim of this book was to destabilize the 'popular opposition between "leader and crowd"' (1928: 6). Leadership, Geiger felt, could be analysed much more broadly and was not merely a question of determining the direction of crowds.

30   See also Lehmann's *Das Kollektivbewusstsein*, which voiced a critique of suggestion (1928: 154ff.).

It goes without saying that there were also exceptions to the pattern outlined here. One such was Mathilde Vaerting's *Die Macht der Massen* (1928), which, to the extent that it built on academic crowd discussions, followed Le Bon rather closely and did not subscribe to the conceptual inventions of the Weimar sociologists. Another was Werner Sombart's examination of the relation between crowd psychology and socialistic propaganda in *Der proletarische Sozialismus*, which reproduced Le Bonian rather than Weimar-sociological views (1924).[31] Similarly, Kurt Baschwitz' book *Der Massenwahn. Seine Wirkung und seine Beherrschung* (1923) had hardly any points of connection to the other Weimar debates. The book presented a mainly historical overview of mass aberrations and only made occasional reference to Le Bon, Freud, etc. Yet another example is Friedrich Wieser's *Das Gesetz der Macht* (1926) which, although cited affirmatively by Vleugels (1930: 3), followed an entirely different agenda. Wieser attempted to expand the insights of crowd psychology to a broader field of masses (or peoples), and to establish a connection between this crowd psychology and notions of the purportedly '*leader peoples [Führervölker] of noble blood*' who were believed by Wieser to determine the course of history (1926: 59, italics in original).

A combination of an affirmative reading of classical crowd psychology with the extension of the crowd concept to encompass much larger, permanent associations could also be found in Ferdinand Tönnies' article 'Die große Menge und das Volk' (1926). Tönnies drew mainly on the work of the 'clever' Le Bon (1926: 279), and transformed his insights into the study of the people (*Volk*). Contrary to Wieser, however, the political undertones of Tönnies' article were more democratic and less proto-totalitarian.[32] While these examples all differed from the kind of crowd semantics I have captured as being specific to the Weimar years, they testify to an immense interest in the crowd topic. That is, they bear witness to the widespread consensus of the time, that an understanding of contemporary society would have to revolve around a problematization of crowds.

When assessing the specific Weimar current in sociological crowd semantics as a whole, ignoring any internal differences between Colm,

---

[31] In his later work, Sombart arrived at somewhat more original conclusions. In *Vom Menschen*, for example, in which he developed a theory of the people, he distinguished between tribe and crowd, both of which were said to be part of any larger peoples (Sombart 1938: 200ff.). In this book Sombart also engaged explicitly with the contributions to crowd semantics in the Weimar years (1938: 442–3, n. 97).

[32] For a comprehensive Tönniesian analysis of crowds, see Günther's *Masse und Charisma* (2005).

Geiger, Vleugels, etc., especially four interrelated politico-scientific dimensions stand out. The first of these concerns the *general political orientation* of the crowd scholars and their view on crowds. In contrast to the largely conservative agenda of classical crowd psychology (Le Bon and Tarde), many Weimar crowd sociologists entertained much more leftish views (see the listing in Käsler 1984: 499–500; see also Berking 1984: 83; König 1992: 150–72). This was no doubt most pronounced in the work of Geiger. Berking rightly notes that especially Geiger's analysis was one great attempt to translate central Marxist class ideas into the vocabulary of crowd theory (Berking 1984: 80). In practice, Geiger tended to equalize class and crowd, in the sense that the revolutionary crowd was believed to serve objective proletarian interests. But no translation is innocent, and nor was Geiger's. What disappeared in the translation were many of the irrational, affective aspects previously attributed to crowd behaviour.

This leads to the second dimension. The functional reading of crowd behaviour – i.e. the assertion that the crowd may reconcile societal tensions – amounted to a *rationalization* of the crowd.[33] The Weimar scholars attributed to the crowd a rational purpose; it was no longer believed to arise as mere irrational and violent emergence, but to prepare the way for social reconstruction.[34] In the same vein, the crowd was no longer seen as the sudden eruption of contagious de-individualizing suggestion; rather, it was observed as an expression of individuals who assemble in *collective rational protest* against social inequalities. This underlying rationalization of the crowd anticipated the development within studies of crowds and collective behaviour in the 1960s (see Chapter 7).

Third, the focus on the socio-structural reasons for crowd action had *implications for critique*. The conservative French crowd psychologists were concerned with the destabilizing aspects of crowds, implying that they were critical of crowds as such. The Weimar sociologists, by contrast, transformed the object of critique from being the crowd in itself to being the social conditions that generate crowd behaviour. That is, the Weimar sociologists turned the sociology of crowds into a social critique, or rather into a critique of the social structures, which are external to, but which purportedly condition, crowd behaviour.

---

[33] This rationalization is rather explicit in Lehmann who ascribed to the crowd a '*rational structure*' in the form of an 'ends–means system' (1932: 56, italics in original).

[34] This functional interpretation leads me to disagree with König when he argues that the Weimar sociologists maintained the pathological image of crowds that Le Bon had propagated (1992: 156). While Colm, Geiger, etc. did not endorse the crowd as an unambiguously positive entity (they were well aware of its destructive tendencies), their entire group-theoretical theorizing effected a *normalization* of the crowd.

This, fourth, reflected a more fundamental difference between the French crowd psychologists and the Weimar sociologists, for the latter's distinctively sociological programme tended to change *the very object of study*. The crowd psychologists analysed the crowd from the point of view of its particular capacities and qualities and observed the kind of sociality which ensues from crowd suggestion. Contrary to this, the Weimar sociologists were so eager to overcome the psychological framework that their substitution of it with a sociological one ended up ignoring the crowd itself. In the sociological accounts the crowd tended to be reduced to something else; it had become an effect of the broader social structures. The causes and dynamics of crowds were not sought in the crowd but in external conditions. Geiger was the most significant representative of this when studying the crowd in the light of 'its causality in social life itself and in the structure of society' (1987: viii). So, contrary to the manifest ambition of the Weimar sociologists, it may be argued that the sociological perspective actually did not take the crowd as seriously as the crowd-psychological programme. This also had implications for the sociological prominence ascribed to the crowd topic. On the one hand, the quantity of the contributions to the sociology of crowds as well as the intensity of the debates suggest that generally speaking the crowd was seen as a key sociological topic in the Weimar years. As mentioned above, there was a general feeling that society could hardly be understood, unless this happened on the basis of some form of crowd thinking. On the other hand, the explanatory horizon, both the group-theoretical angle and the social structure perspective, tended to push the crowd to the background and substitute it with other concepts and concerns.

A further aspect of this 'object of study' discussion regards the attempt to replace the purportedly inadequate suggestion doctrine with sound sociological concepts. For the endeavour to arrive at a more scientific approach seemingly created a greater distance to the empirical phenomenon of crowds. This has been emphasized by König, who calls attention to the fact that the formal sociology of the many Weimar scholars tended to be obsessed with ever-new conceptual distinctions and terminological modifications, whereas they offered only few empirical analyses (1992: 154). To be sure, this non-empirical approach was not very different from the crowd theories of Le Bon, Tarde, Freud, etc. Still, König has a point: the discussions of crowds might never have been as intense as during the Weimar years, but they assumed a rather closed, conceptual character – in spite of the recent revolutionary experiences and in spite of the wish to be able to account for these.

4   Liberal attitudes: crowd semantics in the USA

In his seminal study *The Political Context of Sociology* (1961), Leon Bramson takes as his starting point the observation that although sociologists use the same notions they need not mean the same thing (which should come as no surprise after the preceding chapters). Against this background Bramson shows how the concepts of mass and crowd were endowed with very different political content in early European and US American sociology. Whereas many European scholars had an 'anti-liberal twist' (1961: 16), American sociologists, no less interested in crowds than their European colleagues, tended to approach the crowd topic from a more liberal horizon, stressing the crowd's liberating potentials and its ability to operate as a platform for new institutions.

While Bramson is right that turn-of-the-century American emphases differed from contemporary European concerns, it is difficult to subsume the American alternative under one big, uniform hat of 'liberal' thought. Indeed, not only were different notions of liberalism competing in discussions of crowds. These debates were also interlaced with communitarian problematizations of urbanization, which was seen as the chief seedbed of mass disorder. Much of this converged in the Progressive Era (1890–1920), which signalled new lines for how to deal with urban dangers. Hence, I shall argue, rather than forming a monolith bloc of liberal semantics (as opposed to the 'anti-liberal' European thinking), the problematization of crowds in turn-of-the-century American sociology presented a distinctive *mélange* of concerns with how crowds purportedly: (1) undermined community structures; (2) threatened the ideal of the liberal self-contained individual; but also (3) how crowds might free individuals from narrowing ties and pave the way for new, more progressive social institutions. In the light of the preceding chapters, it is particularly the third point and its interrelations with the others that attract attention.

The present chapter sketches the contours of this specific American adaptation of crowd semantics, with a special emphasis on the period from the 1890s to the 1930s. I begin, however, by outlining the more general nineteenth-century background against which the subsequent sociological theorizing appeared. I argue that particularly the urban problem set the horizon for how American sociologists came to approach the crowd topic. But strong European influences were also manifest, and especially the notion of suggestion generated much debate. The chapter shows how the notion of suggestion was transplanted onto American debates and how it was employed in the problematizing juxtaposition of urbanization and crowds. It is also demonstrated how the First World War instigated a semantic shift, where mass media and propaganda gradually replaced urbanization as the key problem. This echoed a wider transformation that was under way and which will be scrutinized in the following chapters, namely the conceptual transition from crowd to mass society. Indeed, much of what happened in American sociological crowd semantics between 1890 and 1940 is significant not least in view of subsequent developments: some of the chief theoretical inventions of the 1950s and 1960s were predicated, I claim, on ideas that emerged in this earlier phase.

Urban crowds between communitarian anxiety and radical democratic celebration

Nineteenth-century problematizations of crowds had a different socio-historical sense in the USA than in France and Germany. To be sure, the starting point was somewhat similar, given that the USA had its own revolutionary past (1775–83). But unlike the French situation, where the 1789 Revolution instigated a century of recurrent political turmoil, 'Americans regarded their own revolution ... as a success', Dorothy Ross notes (1991: 22). The Civil War (1861–5) and various uprisings throughout the nineteenth century could not demolish the strong belief in the Republic and civic political participation (for those granted political rights). Semantically, there were differences as well. Whereas for French scholars such as Le Bon, crowds, mobs and the people amounted to one and the same thing, namely a highly problematic challenge to an aristocratic order, the American Constitution sanctioned the people as a unanimously positive category. Crowds and mobs, by contrast, typically carried pejorative meanings throughout the nineteenth century, although at times crowds were seen as democratic gatherings as opposed to riotous mobs (Frezza 2007: 12–13).

A related difference is that, in spite of social unrest, labour protest and socialist movements, the question of crowds was not tied exclusively or even primarily to the purported danger of an acute socialist overthrow of American society. Rather the problematization of crowds revolved around what was seen as their breeding ground, namely the explosive urbanization of the American society which took off in the late eighteenth century. In his fascinating study *Urban Masses and Moral Order in America, 1820–1920,* Paul Boyer reports how, for example, Philadelphia grew threefold, New York sixfold in the time-span between 1790 and 1830 (1978: 3–4). The rapid growth of cities continued throughout the nineteenth century, leading to all sorts of concerns with the metropolitan way of life, which, unfamiliar as it was at that point, was looked upon with anxiety. As Boyer explains, the alleged:

strangeness of the city was not simply a matter of size, physical expansion, or even of a shifting demographic profile. The very rhythm and pace of life differed in ways that were as unsettling as they were difficult to define. From the early 1800s on, observers commented on the impersonality and bustle of urban existence, the lack of human warmth, the heedless jostlings of the free-floating human atoms that endlessly surged through the streets. Very early, the realization dawned that the urban order represented a volatile and unpredictable deviation from a familiar norm. (1978: 4–5)

The norm that was put on trial in the cities was that of the quiet communitarian life of the village. Apparently setting aside communitarian values, the cities were conceived of as veritable nests for brutality, crime, poverty, prostitution and other signs of moral disintegration and social disorder – ultimately, even revolutionary anarchy. These negative features were not considered incidental to city life, nor were they conceived of simply as the acts of singular restless individuals. Rather, it was believed that the urban compression of innumerable people was prone to unleash socially destabilizing crowd tendencies. And, in fact, '[t]he period from the 1830s to the 1850s was a time of almost continuous disorder and turbulence among the urban poor', with 'more than 200 major gang wars in New York City alone', and with Baltimore earning the little-flattering nickname 'Mob City' (Boyer 1978: 68).

It was in this context that it was soon argued that the urban wildlife, as it were, should not be allowed to evolve according to its own unregulated and disruptive dynamics. Some form of intervention was deemed necessary, if American society were not to collapse into urban barbarism and anarchy. Most importantly, Boyer demonstrates, comprehensive attempts were carried out to transplant the moral order of the communitarian village to the chaotic cities. These attempts at moral reform took different shapes throughout the nineteenth century. Initially, religious movements were very active, aiming at distributing devotional messages through religious tracts and by founding missions and Sunday schools in the cities. Gradually, the intervention zeroed in on slum areas, the urban poor and their children, with private charity organizations offering assistance to vulnerable families. Eventually, upon entering the Progressive Era at the turn of the nineteenth century, calls were made for governmental rather than private interventions, with a special emphasis on physical environment clearance – all resting on the assumption that moral behaviour would ensue from stimulating physical surroundings (this entire development is mapped by Boyer 1978).

Similar to Zola in France, the American problematization of urban masses was conveyed through and impacted by literary representations. One famous example of this is Edgar Allan Poe's 1840 piece 'The Man of the Crowd'. In this tale, the narrator is gazing through the window of a coffee house, looking at the urban crowd that passes by, when suddenly an old man catches his attention and the narrator, yearning to learn more about the stranger, decides to follow him through the city. Shadowing the old man transforms into a journey that lasts some twenty-four hours and which takes the narrator from beautifully lit public squares to dark quarters of the city characterized by utmost destitution. Yet the journey reveals nothing about the personality and individuality of the old man, whose seemingly aimless wandering about remains a mystery to Poe's narrator. When at the end the narrator decides to stop in front of the old man and look him 'steadfastly in the face', his examining gaze is not returned (Poe 2003: 139). He sees nothing but blankness. So although the old man is, of course, a single individual in the urban crowd, he is portrayed as emblematic of the latter and as representing a link to the city's ever-lurking crimes. Thus, the narrator concludes, the old man 'is the type and the genius of deep crime. He refuses to be alone. *He is the man of the crowd*' (Poe 2003: 140, italics in original). This discursive association of cities, crime and crowds that defy rational explanation here goes nicely hand in hand with the general anxiety of urbanization and its purported disintegration of community ties.

But there seems to be more at stake in Poe's short story. As Mary Esteve has interestingly proposed, the kind of crime that the old man is predisposed for is not simply that of murder or theft. It has a much more political dimension, for the fact that the narrator is unable to discern the rational–individual faculties of the old man entails that:

the narrator effectively banishes him from the political domain, though only to re-install him as an aesthetic agent, a carrier of deeply attractive, mirrorlike blankness. He becomes the embodiment of urban aestheticism, a figure that is permitted to be in but not entirely of liberal democracy. (Esteve 2003: 43)

In other words, Poe's tale suggested that being a man of the crowd essentially meant having only a partial share in the liberal political sphere: urbanization rendered individuals members of a crowd and thereby undermined the individual critical judgement that was required for a person to exercise (still only) his democratic duties.

The underlying fear that urban crowds threatened the Republic's democratic foundation gained support from a series of uprisings in the 1870s, 1880s and 1890s. In combination with continuous urban poverty the rapid industrialization that followed after the Civil War gave way to a series of violent workers' strikes and demonstrations. In 1877, for example, a wave of violent strikes swept the country. With the French Commune of 1871 fresh in mind, these strikes were quickly associated by many observers with the fear of an immediate communist threat to the democratic Republic (see Castronovo 2007: 82–7). A similar vestige of the Commune materialized in May 1886 with the so-called Haymarket riot in Chicago, where a bomb was thrown at the police during a strike rally. The bomb killed one policeman and injured several others. The police responded by shooting four demonstrators and wounding many more (Boyer 1978: 125; see also Ross 1991: 100–1). Events such as these were profoundly disturbing to most observers because the urban problem was now aggravated by the threat of socialism. Indeed, Boyer comments, '[o]n that May evening in Chicago, the triple menace of class warfare, alien radicalism, and urban mass violence came together in one terrifying outburst' (1978: 126). The socialist 'problem' did not diminish in the decade that followed the Haymarket riot. In fact, the tensions between liberals and socialists waxed until the 1896 elections finally settled the conflict to the benefit of the liberals (Ross 1991: 135–6).

As if the lurking socialist powers were not scary enough during the Gilded Age, a new image of the American city emerged in the latter half of the nineteenth century which associated urban life with sexuality and, even more provocatively, loudly endorsed this very feature of the city. The spokesperson for this view was the poet Walt Whitman, whose lifelong project, *Leaves of Grass* (first edition 1855), contained an exposition of urban crowds and democracy that differed markedly from that of most contemporary observers in Europe and the USA.[1] While others feared the masses, Whitman expressed his fascination with the urban crowd. Whereas others saw destructive potentials in crowds, Whitman felt refreshed by the common experience that crowds gave rise to. His portrayal simply embodied the idea that crowds may not be

---

[1] Whitman continuously revised his *Leaves of Grass* and several different editions were published. All quotations in this book are from the so-called 'death-bed' edition (Whitman 2004), originally published in 1891–2. The *Leaves* are divided into a number of poem clusters. The discussion of Whitman draws on Borch (2009).

wild creatures but entities in and through which true sociality and democracy can be created and experienced.[2]

Significantly, Whitman opened *Leaves of Grass* by paying tribute, in 'One's-Self I Sing', to 'the word Democratic, the word En-Masse' (2004: 37). This vision of a democratic order that, akin to the crowd, stressed egalitarianism was present throughout the book. An indication of this appears in 'For You O Democracy' where he explicitly dedicated the poems to the democratic institution: 'For you these from me, O Democracy, to serve you ma femme!/ For you, for you I am trilling these songs' (Whitman 2004: 150). Betsy Erkkila has rightly observed that *Leaves of Grass* 'represents Whitman's ambition to write the Bible of Democracy' (1989: 158). The bible he tried to write and the religion he attempted to found were of a very special kind, however, and one that would appear obscene when compared to most existing religions. For what characterize and unite crowds and democracy, according to Whitman, are their associations with sexuality, bodies and affect.

One of the persistent moral concerns with urbanization in the nineteenth century revolved around the apparently untamed sexuality in cities, which was anchored institutionally in organized prostitution (Boyer 1978). Whitman did not share this concern. He argued that rather than putting sexuality aside in public space, it was crucial to acknowledge and pay tribute to the social import of sexuality and affection. This was stated programmatically in a letter to Ralph Waldo Emerson which was published as the preface to the 1856 edition of *Leaves of Grass*. In this letter, which is likely to have been distressing to Emerson ('human sexuality made Emerson uncomfortable', writes Murphy 2004: xxix), Whitman contended that America needed new 'architects', including poets, to fully work out its existing foundation. To complete the architecture of the country, he said, a transformation of language was required which would take leave of the situation of his time where 'sex, womanhood, maternity, desires, lusty animations, organs, acts, are unmentionable and to be ashamed of' (Whitman 2004: 770). This repression of sexuality 'stands in the way of great reforms', he continued; and he concluded by stating that 'I say that

---

[2] To be sure, if only few, there were forerunners to Whitman when it came to praising metropolitan crowds. The great British poet William Wordsworth, famous for his celebration of nature (mountains, lakes, etc.), had offered a positive account of the crowded city of London in his *The Prelude*, written between 1799 and 1805 (1994: 829). See Esteve (2003: 25) and especially Brand (1991). Moreover, the kind of democracy-via-co-corporeality he lauded might be identified in nascent form in Herman Melville's *Moby-Dick* (2001, originally published in 1851). As Sharon Cameron has demonstrated, Melville's book espoused a bodily notion of relational identity, and, ultimately, democracy (1981).

the body of a man or woman, the main matter, is so far unexpressed in poems; but that the body is to be expressed, and sex is' (2004: 771).

This celebration of sexuality provoked charges of indecency and obscenity, just as one of Whitman's publishers threatened prosecution (Murphy 2004: xxxviii). At the same time, it was precisely this call for highlighting sexuality and bodies that explained Whitman's positive image of urban crowds. The sexual desires that caused much anxiety among his contemporaries were simply one of the main reasons why Whitman lauded the urban masses. For him, the bodily compression of crowds, their dense body-to-body composition, did not evoke displeasure, nor was it seen as a threat to the individual and his or her boundaries. Quite the contrary, in a famous celebration of bodies in 'I Sing the Body Electric', Whitman asserted that, '[t]here is something in staying close to men and women and looking on them, and in the contact and odor of them, that pleases the soul well,/All things please the soul, but these please the soul well' (2004: 130). This pleasure acquired an even more sexual tone in 'Crossing Brooklyn Ferry': 'What is more subtle than this which ties me to the woman or man that looks in my face?/ Which fuses me into you now, and pours my meaning into you?' (2004: 194). According to Whitman, therefore, urban crowds were socially important entities *because* they gave vent to bodily impulses and sexual desires; because they initiated affective, physical contact in public space. This was the reason why crowds may improve the future architecture of society.

Whitman's endorsement of sexuality was not limited to one kind of sexual relations. As James E. Miller has argued, Whitman's 'imagination and vision were omnisexual ... The sexual imaginary of *Leaves of Grass* does not, to the dismay of its psychoanalytic readers, fall into any single category. It is auto-erotic, hetero-erotic, homo-erotic' (1973: 241). The reference to the omnisexual character of Whitman's poetry permits a better understanding of his political programme of democracy. The ambition was not merely to advance auto-, hetero- or homosexual relations, but rather to highlight sexuality as such, in whatever form it may take. Only by placing the body, affect and sexuality at the centre of attention, he believed, was it possible to realize a true democratic society; that is, a society based on 'bonds of comradeship and love' (Erkkila 1989: 181). And since the urban crowd was the public site par excellence, not only for violence and destruction, but also for bodily affect and sexual desire, it became, in Whitman's imaginary, a crucial and positive 'democratic icon' (Esteve 2003: 25).

Contrary to Poe's liberal notion of democracy, which rested in the end on the ability of rational individuals to engage in an exchange of arguments, Whitman's vision was that of a radical democracy, 'a project which works to make agreement synonymous with physiological rapport'

(Esteve 2003: 29). By the same token, rather than following the under-lying tenet of much nineteenth-century French crowd theorizing, that the problematic watershed of modern society was the French Revolution's admittance of the masses into the field of institutionalized politics, Whit-man essentially conceived of politics as a 'non-political, noninstitutional theory of mass democracy [that affirms] the anarchist's faith that formal government can be replaced by the spontaneous action of the people', as George Frederickson has put it (quoted in Esteve 2003: 29). So although Whitman's poems were affirmative, their emphasis on egalitarian bonds of comradeship was easily interpreted as aligned with socialist hopes for a new social order that seriously questioned the existing Republic.

I have spent some time on Whitman to show that a more affirmative, if marginalized, interpretation existed alongside the negative problematiza-tions of urbanization and its purported mass disorder and moral as well as democratic breakdown. As Dana Brand has put it, Whitman 'sought to provide an alternative to the reactionary and fastidious disgust that so many of his contemporaries felt in the metropolis' (1991: 185). To be sure, the position Whitman represented was but a small fish in the big sea of nineteenth-century critical American problematization of urbaniza-tion, crowds and democracy. But, as I shall demonstrate below, the positive image of crowds Whitman expounded had a significant bearing on how crowds were conceived by Robert E. Park, who would play a most central role in early-twentieth-century American sociology. Before getting to Park's theoretical programme, however, I wish to explore how the general problematization of urban crowds became interlaced with specific American adaptations of the European emphasis on crowd suggestion.

Crowds, suggestion and progressive reform: liberal and communitarian concerns

As in Europe, American sociology and psychology witnessed intense discussions of imitation and suggestion at the turn of the nineteenth and beginning of the twentieth centuries.[3] Not all of these debates

---

[3] Rather surprisingly, the impact of the French discussions on imitation-suggestion and crowds go largely unnoticed in the huge volume *Sociology in America* (Calhoun 2007a). Tarde is not mentioned in this book, nor are the debates on imitation-suggestion. Only Le Bon receives a single reference in a discussion on Robert E. Park and collective behaviour. It is falsely stated there, though, that Le Bon 'owed a heavy intellectual debt to Durkheim' and that the field of crowds and collective behaviour has 'Durkheimian roots' (McAdam 2007: 420). As demonstrated in Chapter 2, Durkheim struggled to undermine the theoretical horizon advanced by Le Bon and Tarde, and his late studies on collective effervescence hardly qualify as 'roots' in a field which was already well established.

revolved explicitly around crowds; and not all of the reception of the European ideas was positive. One of the prominent scholars who engaged in an early American discussion of the European experiences with hypnotism and suggestion was William James. In his *Principles of Psychology*, published in 1890 (i.e. the same year as the first edition of Tarde's *Laws of Imitation* came out), he devoted a chapter to hypnotism and theories of suggestion (James 1981: 1194–1214). Though respectful of these ideas, James felt that the notion of suggestion tended to be applied to too many phenomena (1981: 1201, n. 4). More positive tones were struck in the introduction James wrote to the Russian immigrant, Boris Sidis' *The Psychology of Suggestion* (1898). 'There is probably no more practically important topic to the student of public affairs' than that of crowd psychology, James asserted (1898: vii).[4] Although he was 'not convinced of all of Dr. Sidis' positions', he believed the book was crucial, because in it, 'the very important matter of "crowd psychology" is discussed, almost for the first time in English' (James 1898: vii). Not surprisingly, Sidis agreed that his investigation of suggestion was of immense importance:

The study of the subconscious is especially of great value to sociology, because nowhere else does the subconscious work on such a grand, stupendous scale as it does in the popular mind; and the sociologist who ignores the subconscious lacks a deep insight into the nature of social forces. (1898: 3)

Sidis' book was greatly inspired by the French debates on suggestion. Indeed, he said, '[t]he French psychologists seem to be on the track of a rich gold vein' (1898: 1). Despite the fact that there was not a single reference to Tarde in the book, Sidis' theoretical programme was quite similar to that of the Frenchman – although an explicit influence from James was also detectable (the James inspiration is discussed by Frezza 2007: 108–9).

In the first two parts of the book, Sidis excavated the deeper nature of suggestibility and examined the self in the light of the suggestion doctrine. More important for present purposes is the third and final part of *The Psychology of Suggestion*, where Sidis zeroed in on society and social

---

[4] James had expressed an almost identical praise of the study of crowds in an 1897 review of the English translation of Le Bon's *The Crowd*. Although James found that Le Bon's book suffered from various shortcomings, being for example too 'misanthropic and pessimistic', he argued that it was concerned with 'a subject of supreme importance, and ought to be read by everyone who is interested in the problems which popular government presents' (1897: 314, 313). A similar point was made the same year by Arthur F. Bentley in his review of *The Crowd* in the *American Journal of Sociology*. According to Bentley, Le Bon's discussion of heterogeneous crowds such as the jury, the parliamentary crowd, etc. 'will excite the greatest practical interest' (1897: 614).

suggestion. Much of this discussion reiterated ideas already articulated by French scholars. For example, Sidis described how suggestion 'spreads like wildfire', and how it exhibits 'a frenzy of excitement', even a 'furious demoniac frenzy' (1898: 303). He also believed that 'the mob has a self of its own' which 'attracts fresh individuals, breaks down their personal life, and quickly assimilates them' (1898: 304). Finally, Sidis subscribed to the gendering often proposed in crowd semantics; he thus claimed that women are particularly suggestible and therefore also more likely than men to be subsumed by crowds and mobs (1898: 362). Sidis was not alone in this view. As Carroll Smith-Rosenberg has shown, the high suggestibility ascribed to women by European scholars was widely accepted in the USA in the nineteenth century (1972).

Sidis portrayed both crowds and mobs in negative terms, but he also distinguished between the two. The crowd, he said, is characterized by suggestions that have a more ephemeral nature than that of mobs, whose suggestibility is permanent, rendering the mob more dangerous than the crowd (1898: 297). The most significant novelty of Sidis' theorizing lay not in conceptual differentiation, though, but rather in his claim that a specific spatial and physiological dimension is underpinning the correct understanding of the suggestibility of crowds and mobs and their alleged erosion of individuality. 'If anything gives us a strong sense of our individuality', he contended, 'it is surely our voluntary movements' (1898: 299; see also 47, 59). This implied that individuality was seen to a large extent as a practical question of whether a person could move freely or not, an ability that was greatly limited in crowds where many people gather in little space:

Now nowhere else, expect perhaps in solitary confinement, are the voluntary movements of men so limited as they are in the crowd; and the larger the crowd is the greater is this limitation, the lower sinks the individual self. *Intensity of personality is in inverse proportion to the number of aggregated men.* (1898: 299, italics in original)

Sidis' comparison of confinement and crowds drew partly on his own biography. Daria Frezza thus notes that 'before coming to America he had been held in prison for rebelling against both his family's Jewish culture and against the Romanov dynasty' (2007: 109).

In spite of this spatial framing, Sidis did not conceive of suggestion as a specifically urban phenomenon. Many of the examples of suggestion he analysed were gathered from the fields of financial speculation and religious manias. That said, the reference to the pressure on voluntary movement also fed into the problematization of cities. The urban banding of people made free individual space an increasing luxury in the large metropolises, meaning that the very spatial setting of large massified cities buttressed the negative effects crowds were believed to have on individuality. But Sidis' central concern actually had much more gloomy undertones, pointing far beyond urbanization. He believed that, as an unfortunate by-product of increasing modernization and its growing specialization, ever more rules, laws, norms, expectations, regulations, etc. had emerged that each individual had to conform to. This produced a conduct of conduct (Foucault) which likened suggestion:

Man's relations in life are determined and fixed for him; he is told how he must put on his tie, and the way he must wear his coat ... Personality is suppressed by the rigidity of social organization; the cultivated, civilized individual is an automaton, a mere puppet. (1898: 312)

On this view, there is no qualitative difference between the individual who is part of the crowd and the person who lives a normal, civilized life; both are automatons, for both are under the sway of suggestion. The underlying criticism Sidis voiced therefore went much farther than that of the conservative crowd scholars. Rather than fearing that the mob might undermine individuality and civilized society, Sidis warned that civilization itself contains devastating effects on the individual's free life. Today, he said, 'individuality is more and more crushed out', and 'there is no possibility for [the modern individual] to move, live, and think freely' (1898: 311, 312). The political message was clear: the negative crowd effects, aggravated by urbanization, were real and should be taken most seriously, but the increasing regulation of society should be handled with no less caution, as it was prone to lead to the same consequences that were rightly feared in crowds. In other words, Sidis translated the fear of crowds into a liberal critique of the purportedly de-individualizing effects of crowds and social institutions. Hence, he could ask rhetorically, '[l]aws and mobs, society and epidemics – are they not antagonistic? In point of fact they are intimately, vitally interrelated, they are two sides of the same shield' (1898: 312). Or as he put it at the end of the book: '*Society by its very nature tends to run riot in mobs and epidemics. For the gregarious, the subpersonal, uncritical social self, the mob self, and the suggestible subconscious self are identical*' (1898: 364, italics in original).

One way of avoiding abnormal mob suggestion was, so his argument implied, to limit the ways in which individuals are regulated by social institutions. The fewer social institutions (laws, norms, etc.) there are, the freer the individual becomes. The ensuing political programme of Sidis was somewhat cut short or one-sided. His strong belief in the liberal subject – and the critique of social regulation following from this – prevented him from considering the liberating potential of crowds/mobs that Whitman had praised. Crowds and mobs were depicted as de-individualizing and destructive by Sidis, and he ignored the possibility that the target of their destruction could be the very same institutions that he found narrowing. He neglected, in other words, that crowd or mob behaviour might have emancipating capabilities. This liberating dimension was absent in Sidis, but as I shall demonstrate later on, it came to play an important role in the sociological work of Robert E. Park.

The American reception of the notions of imitation and suggestion went far beyond the work of James and Sidis. Much of this discussion revolved around Tarde's work. In his introduction to the English translation in 1903 of *The Laws of Imitation*, Franklin H. Giddings described Tarde as 'a gifted and widely influential author', whose work contained many examples of 'his originality and many-sided knowledge' (1962: vii, vi). Likewise, Giddings' *Principles of Sociology*, first edition published in 1896, drew much on Tarde as well as on Le Bon's description of crowds and crowd suggestion (1909: 14–15, 136–7, 150–1).[5] Similarly, Albion Small reviewed Tarde's *Les lois sociales* (1898; see also Tosti 1900). Small, who was the formative power behind the Department of Sociology at the University of Chicago and who founded the *American Journal of Sociology*, described Tarde as 'a very prominent, perhaps the most prominent, figure just at present among the founders' of sociology (1898: 395). Like the book itself, the review did not pay much attention to crowd behaviour, but discussed instead Tarde's key theoretical notions. In spite of his great respect for Tarde, Small was not entirely convinced by Tarde's theoretical programme; still, he found that imitation-suggestion 'is but one among the unnumbered' ideas 'which is marking out promising lines of social research' (1898: 400).

The notion of suggestion was also discussed at length in Charles Horton Cooley's *Human Nature and the Social Order*, which depicted crowd behaviour along the lines set out by Le Bon and Tarde (1907: 40–1).[6] Similarly, James Mark Baldwin presented an early discussion of imitation, which addressed the work of Sighele and Tarde, among many others (1894; 1897; 1968, first edition published in 1894). Baldwin was

---

[5] In Le Bonian style, Giddings compared the purported intolerance of the crowd to that of 'the savage and the child' (1909: 136). See also Giddings' (1896) collective review of Le Bon, Tarde and others.

[6] See also the sequel to this book, a volume entitled *Social Organization*, where Cooley analysed the relation between 'democracy and crowd excitement' (Cooley 1909: 149ff.). According to Cooley, the crowd excesses that the French crowd theorists had identified in the French political order did not necessarily apply to the American political situation, characterized as the latter was, for Cooley, by the workings of public opinion.

not entirely in agreement with Sighele and Tarde, but drew on their work in order to develop his own understanding of imitation. The differences between Baldwin and Tarde were later examined by Charles A. Ellwood in 'The Theory of Imitation in Social Psychology' (1901; see also French 1904; Tosti 1897). One of these differences concerned their objects of study. Whereas, as Ellwood stated, Baldwin developed his theory 'from the side of individual psychology, through the study of the mental development of the child', 'M. Tarde reached his theories from the sociological side, through the study of the phenomena of crowds, crazes, fads, fashions, and crime' (1901: 722). Irrespective of such differences, Ellwood found both Tarde's and Baldwin's variants of imitation theory lacking in one important respect: they failed to offer any guidance to 'the practical worker, the legislator, the social reformer, and the philanthropist' (1901: 740).

This critique may be said to ignore the practical political implications of Tarde's *L'opinion et la foule* (see Chapter 2). More importantly, though, Ellwood's comment signalled that the USA had entered the Progressive Era where social reforms were a key political but also scientific concern (see e.g. Calhoun 2007b: 10ff.; and in particular Ross 1991). This era, largely covering the period from around 1890 to 1920, was one in which '[f]aith was placed in public discourse on the social progress promised by technical and scientific rationality to restore the smooth and rational functioning of the social machine' (Frezza 2007: 38–9). The emphasis on scientific rationality as a way to counter social irrationality placed a premium on the work of social scientists. Their observations could furnish society with a rational, democratic order, not threatened by large inequalities and their possible irrational consequences (violent outbursts, etc.). In this vein, John Dewey made an emphatic call for seeing education as a constituent part of a democratic order in his *Democracy and Education* from 1916 (1966). Other progressives were more concerned with where to anchor the intervention spatially, and here a widespread consensus ensued that one of the areas most in need of reform was the cities with all their poverty and associated problems (Frezza 2000). This need had been felt with great urgency since the late 1880s where journalists such as Jacob A. Riis had documented how the urban poor, the 'other half', lived in extraordinary density in New York City (see Buk-Swienty 2008). Consequently, it was only a small step for the progressives to interlace the question of democracy and social reforms with that of urban crowds.

One of the central scholars who established precisely this connection was Edward A. Ross who, according to Eugene E. Leach, was 'probably the most widely read social scientist of his day' (1986: 102). Ross' scientific work was profoundly influenced by Tarde. In fact, it seems fair to say that Ross largely translated Tarde's thought into English, and in the preface to his *Social Psychology*, Ross mentioned only one source of inspiration: 'the genius of Gabriel Tarde' (1908: viii). The interest in Tarde and suggestion was also visible in Ross' earlier book, *Social Control* (1901), which translated Tarde's ideas into a distinctively liberal position resonant with the Progressive Era and into an abandonment of socialism (see the seminal analysis by Dorothy Ross 1991: 229–40).

In the present context, the most significant part of Ross' work is his reflections on what he called the 'mob mind'. In an early article on this topic, Ross established a clear connection between the mob mind, urbanization and a jeopardized democracy. 'A mob', his definition read, '*is a crowd of people showing an unanimity due to mental contagion*', the latter being an effect of the mob's suggestibility (Ross 1897: 391, italics in original). While Ross preferred to speak of mobs rather than crowds, the main image he presented was traced almost directly from the crowd writings of Le Bon and Tarde. For example, he attributed to the mob a range of qualities such as criminality, ferocity, intolerance and irrationality, which had all been underscored by the Frenchmen. But while Le Bon and Tarde tended to associate crowds with physical co-presence (despite emphasizing the crowd's psychological nature), Ross went further in making plain that such co-present manifestation was no indispensable feature of mobs. This was visible in the cities. 'It has long been recognized that the behavior of city populations under excitement shows the familiar characteristics of the mob quite apart from any thronging', a phenomenon which was 'due in part to the nervous strains of great cities' (Ross 1897: 393). As if this were not bad enough, giving rise to all sorts of fickleness, impulsiveness, fads and crazes, Ross contended that the urban stimulation of the mob mind shook the very foundation of democracy. 'In a good democracy blind imitation can never take the place of individual effort to weigh and judge', but blind imitation was precisely what transpired with the mob and its unanimity (Ross 1897: 398). Ross was not entirely clear about what to do with this problem, but the best solution he could offer was a call for 'a sage Emersonian individualism, that ... shall embrace men to stand against the rush of the mass' (1897: 398).

While Ross was not particularly specific in terms of how to restore this individualism in practice, he would return to the practical dimension in some of his later work. Most significantly, he devoted a chapter of his *Social Psychology* to 'Prophylactics against Mob Mind'. As indicated by the title, the aim of this discussion was proactive in that it attempted, much more directly than was common among the European crowd scholars, to distil political recommendations from the study of crowd dynamics. Thus, in his search for 'the various conditions that favor the growth of strong, robust individualities proof against mental contagion', Ross (1908: 83) presented an original combination of crowd semantics and the interventionist discourse characteristic of the Progressive Era. Among other things, Ross put great faith in physical conditions, hygiene, sport and exercise: 'Physical health in itself makes for intellectual self-possession. Frequently sickness heightens suggestibility' (1908: 86). Similar to Dewey, he also stressed the need for education and classic *Bildung* as other means to prevent irrational crowd eruption (1908: 84, 85). But Ross also repeated his observation of the tight link between the mob and its urban setting. As in the 1897 article, and similar to Simmel's 1903 account of the metropolis (1950e), Ross stated that '[t]he city overwhelms the mind with a myriad of impressions which fray the nerves and weaken the power of concentration … City-bred populations are liable to be hysterical, and to be hysterical is to be suggestible' (1908: 87). In a word, the very spatial setting was likely to induce mob behaviour, a fact that could be deployed for prophylactic purposes:

In the city some ways of living foster suggestibility, while others check it. It is bad for people to be crowded into barrack-like tenement-houses, for such massing inspires the cheese-mite consciousness, makes the self count for nothing. The best correctives for urban propinquity are broad streets, numerous parks, and the individual domicile with a little space about it; for these preserve the selfhood of the family group and of the individual. (1908: 88)

This call for urban planning as a tool for crowd control went hand in hand with reformist ideals about the improvement of the conditions of the poor, in that it focused precisely on those parts of the city that the poor inhabited. As mentioned earlier in this chapter, the progressive concern with cities was predated by a more general problematization of urbanization throughout the nineteenth century. What was new in the Progressive Era was above all the suggested means of intervention. Rather than focusing on religious measures (Sunday schools and the like), the progressives envisioned a kind of 'positive environmentalism', as Paul Boyer has labelled it (1978: 220). The aim of this strategy was to create 'a population of cultivated, moral, and socially responsible city dwellers' through a series of positive improvements of the physical environment (1978: 190). This was exactly what Ross had in mind when proposing parks, broad streets, etc. Through such measures Ross might be said to at once extend and accommodate Sidis' idea of free movement to the urban realm and to the domain of living conditions. Since the urban poor lived in extreme density in the metropolitan slums, they were particularly susceptible to crowd suggestion. In order, therefore, to prevent crowd and mob behaviour it was crucial to provide the poor with bigger and better living spaces. Restraining the mob mind in this fashion was, as Ross' early article made clear, a way of bolstering democracy.

Ross' sanctioning of Emersonian individualism bears some resemblance to Sidis' clear-cut liberal programme, which centred on protecting the singular autonomous individual. But Ross combined his liberal tenets with an endorsement of more communitarian convictions, a blend that was typical of many progressives. As mentioned previously, throughout the nineteenth century the problematization of urbanization had often assumed a communitarian attire. The urban problem consisted, it was believed, in how the communitarian fabric characteristic of the village dissolved in the modern city. Without his or her community, the individual would disintegrate into a lost, alienated person with no solid foundation. Eventually, therefore, the breakdown of communitarian ties in the metropolis was prone to unleash the whole register of unrestricted violence, moral disintegration, loss of meaning, etc. that communitarian bonds protected against.

The notion of the community gained renewed significance among the progressive social scientists, who introduced it as 'a new basic element in the individual/mass antithesis' (Frezza 2007: 117). That is, the progressives inserted the community as the central fixture that would protect the individual from the city's de-individualizing crowd and mass tendencies. Without a sense of community the individual would be subsumed under the crowd, and this would have devastating effects on liberal democracy, as the individual would make the crowd's rather than his or her own voice heard. Consequently, scholars such as Dewey began searching for 'the Great Community' (1954: ch. 5). In a discussion of 'the question of practical re-formation of social conditions', Dewey argued that '[d]emocracy must begin at home, and its home is the neighborly community' (1954: 211, 213). In Ross' case, the argument was that a strong sense of community strengthens the individual and thereby fences him or her off from crowd and mob behaviour. In Ross' words, '[c]lose relations to a few people – as in the well-knit family – joined to a vivid sense of obligation to the community, seem to be more favorable to stable character than the loose touch-and-go associations of general intercourse' (1908: 88). Even if the metropolis generally induced loose associations between people, urban planning could perform little miracles, Ross believed: more parks and more spacious homes would secure the conditions of establishing and maintaining stable family and community ties.

While much of Ross' thinking on urban crowds was aligned with positive environmentalism, i.e. with an underlying notion of productive power, a power that fosters rather than represses, his problematization of crowds also contained more negative-suppressing elements. Thus, notes Frezza, Ross believed that in order to improve 'the living standards of the masses within American democracy, it was necessary socially, politically and economically to limit immigration as well as to adopt a proeugenics policy' (2007: 129). Throughout the nineteenth century the growth of cities had been propelled by continuous waves of immigration. Boyer reports, for instance, that by 1900, more than 80 per cent of the populace of cities such as Chicago and New York were immigrants or children of immigrants (1978: 123–4). Ross considered this immigration problematic, because it entailed an unfortunate racial *mélange* of moral (American) citizens and immoral (Mediterranean) immigrants (Ross 1991: 233–4). But his underlying eugenic programme reached further, in that it was an integral part of his analysis of the present urban masses. The city not only contained numerous deprived individuals that progressive reforms should liberate from their poor conditions; many of these poor people were characterized by Ross (and many others at the time, see Buk-Swienty 2008) as *degenerates*: 'in the sheltered life of the city live many degenerates that would be unsparingly eliminated by the sterner conditions of existence in the country' (Ross 1908: 58).[7] This conception of inferior people added an extra dimension to Ross' more general prophylactic fight against crowds and mobs. In fact, what materialized here was a semantic correlation of racial inferiority and crowds/mobs: Le Bonian biopolitics adapted to the American context.

Robert E. Park and the Chicago School

While Ross continued in the footsteps of the long tradition that had problematized urbanization and modern mass phenomena, other sociologists advocated a different and more positive take on the city. The most prominent exponent of this position is Robert E. Park, a key representative of the Chicago School who would soon become one of the leading voices in American sociology. Having completed his BA under John Dewey in 1887, Park worked for twelve years as a journalist in cities such as Chicago, Detroit and New York. He then returned to university and studied under Josiah Royce and William James, before

---

[7] This was an almost word-for-word repetition of a statement from 'The Mob Mind', the only difference being that in the former version, Ross spoke of 'mental degenerates' rather than just 'degenerates' (Ross 1897: 393).

moving to Berlin, Strasbourg and Heidelberg to study under scholars such as Simmel and Wilhelm Windelband. In the present context I shall deal primarily with Park's main contribution to sociological crowd semantics, namely his doctoral dissertation which was written in German and completed in 1904, some ten years before Park joined the Department of Sociology at the University of Chicago. The book was entitled *Masse und Publikum. Eine methodologische und soziologische Untersuchung* (Park 1904) and was not translated into English until 1972, as *The Crowd and the Public* (Park 1972). That did not prevent its ideas from being disseminated into American academia, though, and I shall give some indications of how this happened.

Let me begin by noting that in spite of Park's interest in the modern city *The Crowd and the Public* was surprisingly silent on urban matters. The book pursued a conceptual strategy, foregrounding abstract theoretical reflections on crowds and publics, and the sparse empirical contextualizations that appeared (brief references to crusades, the French Revolution, the Dreyfus affair, etc.) did not evoke any urban problematization. Even so, I claim, the city is present as an undercurrent in Park's discussions of crowds and, indeed, his interest in the crowd issue was stimulated by an early fascination with the city. This went back to his pre-academic career as a journalist where he had learned to see the city as an exemplary site for studying modern life. Park's approach to the city was indebted to Whitman's salutary descriptions of urban crowds. In a 1930 lecture entitled 'Walt Whitman', he paid the following tribute to the poet who had had such a tremendous bearing on him when he worked as a young journalist:

A newspaperman, more than most people, I suspect, knows, and feels, and is thrilled by the vast, anonymous and impersonal life of the city ... I began to read with a certain amount of enthusiasm Whitman's musings on the city's surging life ... I felt, as he did, that there was something inspiring, majestic – in the spectacle of the manifold and multitudinous life of the city ... something at once moving and mystical. (quoted in Cappetti 1993: 25)

The link to Whitman and urban crowds was further reinforced when Park was an MA student at Harvard. This was mediated through one of his teachers, William James, who exerted a lasting influence on Park's thinking, especially because of the essay 'On a Certain Blindness in Human Beings' that James read to his students in 1898–9 (James 1970; Lindner 1996: 172ff.; Matthews 1977: 32). In this essay James wrestled with the problem that observers are often incapable of really understanding the meaning inherent in the object they study, an inability which was likely to be echoed in the observations. It was this blindness that he wanted to overcome by suggesting instead a more emphatic and attentive approach. This alternative:

absolutely forbids us to be forward in pronouncing on the meaninglessness of forms of existence other than our own; and it commands us to tolerate, respect, and indulge those whom we see harmlessly interested and happy in their own ways, however unintelligible these may be to us. (James 1970: 268–9)

This request by James later reverberated in Park's positive account of crowd behaviour. In fact, James' essay is likely to have stimulated Park's subsequent decision to focus his doctoral dissertation on the crowd. Thus one of the examples James used to illustrate the meaning of attentive observations of social life was an extract of Whitman's celebration of the urban crowd in *Leaves of Grass*. According to James, Whitman 'felt the human crowd as rapturously as Wordsworth felt the mountains, felt it as an overpoweringly significant presence, simply to absorb one's mind in which should be business sufficient and worthy to fill the days of a serious man' (1970: 261). Park was the prototype of such a serious man, whose mind became absorbed with the crowd. Even if the crowd examined by Park was not flagged as explicitly urban in *The Crowd and the Public*, he certainly approached it in a fashion that emphasized its meaningfulness.

The book's title testified to a strong Tardean inspiration, as it was an almost direct copy of the title of one of Tarde's late essays, namely his 1898 paper 'Le public et la foule', included in *L'opinion et la foule* (1989). *The Crowd and the Public* drew explicitly on Tarde's work – also his *L'opinion et la foule* – and combined it not least with Simmelian insights. As an indication of this double legacy Park wished to embed the discussion of crowds in a theory of 'social groups' and to study 'two basic forms of social units: the crowd and the public' (1972: 5, 6).

The Crowd and the Public opened with a discussion of some of the main positions of contemporary European crowd semantics. This included a brief overview of the work of Le Bon, Rossi, Sighele and Tarde, but it also contained references to theorists such as Sidis and Stoll. Park's outline was loyal to the suggestion doctrine endorsed by these scholars. 'It must be concluded', he conceded, 'that the suggestive influence exerted by people on each other constitutes the deciding characteristic of the crowd; and the social epidemic becomes the typical social phenomenon for collective psychology' (1972: 19). That said, Park preferred a Simmelian notion of reciprocity over that of suggestion. Although he applied the two concepts almost interchangeably – for example, he referred to 'suggestive reciprocity' (1972: 22) – this gave Park's analysis a less psychological flavour than some of the European

contributions. Furthermore, the mere existence of suggestion or reciprocity was not sufficient for crowds to emerge, Park argued. Since all
individuals are subject to suggestion/reciprocity in their daily life (an
argument similar to that of Tarde and Sidis), 'a certain degree of intensity' is required before crowds transpire (1972: 22). This intensity is
what induces 'certain individuals [to] cut themselves loose from society
and join together around a new nucleus of feelings and ideas', around a
new common 'goal' (1972: 22). Crucially, for Park, these feelings and
ideas were not seen as antagonistic to society but rather as new social
bonds. It was in this potentially positive function ascribed to crowds that
Park's theory demonstrated a Whitmanesque legacy.

As the title of the book suggests, Park was particularly interested in the
reciprocity ties of crowds and publics. 'The unity of the crowd', he
asserted, 'is based on the fact that all members of the group are controlled by one common drive evoked by the reciprocal interaction of
these members. This reciprocity works as an inhibiting process suppress-
ing all purely individual impulses' (1972: 50). In the public, by contrast,
'individual impulses and interests *arise out of* the undefined basis of the
common consciousness and develop further in a peculiar reciprocal
interaction' (1972: 50, italics added). So instead of inhibiting individual
impulses such as crowds do, the public creates a common platform upon
which these impulses and interests can emerge. Park observed other
significant differences between crowds and publics. One concerned their
critical capacities. Echoing Tarde, Park thus claimed that the crowd
succumbs uncritically to its collective drive, whereas the public 'is
guided by prudence and rational reflection' (1972: 80). Furthermore,
since the public displays an encounter of individual interests, its
members have to adhere to argumentative logics; the crowd, for its part,
is a podium for 'anarchy in its purest form' (1972: 81).[8]

However, Park also established a number of crucial similarities
between crowds and publics, similarities that were believed to unite
them vis-à-vis other groups. For example, in contrast to other social
groups, crowds and publics have an ahistorical character with no

---

[8] Park maintained that this distinction between the anarchic crowd and the rational public
referred 'only to the form of the collective consciousness, and not to its content', and
therefore, he continued, it did not amount to a value judgement where the public was
preferred over the crowd (1972: 81). This suggested some ambiguity on Park's side.
While there is no doubt that Park generally had a rather positive impression of crowds,
his semantic association of crowds with anarchy and the emphasis on their alleged
opposition to rationality indicate that his refusal to make any value judgement between
crowd and public should be seen merely 'as a formal disclaimer', as Henry Elsner, Jr has
put it (1972: xv).

tradition to lean on. Or to be more precise, 'conceptually, crowd and public precede the other groups; actually, they occur later – they are frequently the form that the other groups take to transform themselves into a new, undefined whole' (1972: 79). The latter point is crucial because it hints at the social function Park attributed to crowds and publics: 'they serve to bring individuals out of old ties and into new ones' (1972: 78). Put differently, '[w]herever a new interest asserts itself amid those already existing, a crowd or a public simultaneously develops; and through this union of groups, or certain individuals from among them, a new social form for the new interests is created' (1972: 80). So, for Park, crowds and publics presuppose the existence of other groups, but they also represent a means to transcend these groups and to develop new social forms, which is likely to happen as a result of conflicting interests.

This functional interpretation is one of Park's main contributions to sociological crowd semantics. Rather than seeing the crowd as an irrational threat to society, he conceived of it as an entity in social evolution through which individuals may generate new social relations. Hence, in Park's account, the crowd did not evoke an image of societal destruction and disorganization, but rather of social creation and reorganization. On this affirmative view, society and democracy were believed to profit from the new social forms generated by crowds. This simultaneously meant that, contrary to Ross' progressive reformist programme, according to which the poor should be freed from their susceptibility to crowd suggestion, Park actually observed the *crowd as a reformative entity* itself. People could emancipate themselves from repressive forms through crowd action.

Although Park's dissertation did not appear in English translation until 1972, his characteristic view on crowds was soon integrated in other immediately influential writings. Most notably, it laid the foundation of some of the crucial distinctions in his and Ernest W. Burgess' *Introduction to the Science of Sociology* (1921), the cornerstone textbook for numerous American sociologists. Park and Burgess did three important things in this book. First, they juxtaposed work conducted by American sociologists with views expressed by European scholars. This applied to the entire book and not only to the sections on crowds. Several of the European inspirations were taken from fields closely related to the crowd discussions. For example, the book contained a long chapter on social interaction with special sections devoted to imitation and suggestion, respectively, comprising extracts from the work of Bekhterev (who, together with Le Bon and Tarde, was one of the figures with most entries in the book's index of names).

Second, the book redefined the study of crowds so that it now counted as a subcategory of the broader, and normatively–politically less discomforting, category 'collective behaviour'. The notion of collective behaviour, which was introduced for the first time in the *Introduction to the Science of Sociology*, was defined as 'the behavior of individuals under the influence of an impulse that is common and collective, an impulse, in other words, that is the result of social interaction' (1921: 865). From now on collective behaviour referred to a distinct research field in American sociology, with subfields such as social unrest, the crowd and the public, crowds and sects, sects and institutions, psychic epidemics, mass movements, etc. (1921: 865ff.).[9] One might suspect that this attempt to subsume the study of the crowd under the larger investigation of collective behaviour amounted to a marginalization of the crowd, but this was not the case. Quite the contrary, for Park and Burgess opened their book by stating that '[s]ociology . . . may be described as the science of collective behavior' (1921: 42). This implied that far from being a marginal sociological topic, the crowd, constituting a paradigmatic example of collective behaviour, belonged at the very heart of the sociological discipline.

Third, the conception of collective behaviour was deeply informed by Park's positive rendering of the crowd (see also Bramson 1961: 60–3). For example, Park and Burgess suggested that 'social unrest', the germ of crowd behaviour, may pave the way for 'a new social order' (1921: 867). This new social order was one which 'released [individuals] from old associations', and in which 'new and strange political and religious movements' could arise (1921: 867). The liberating potentials attributed to crowds were, in other words, intact.[10]

---

[9] Crowd-related issues were also examined under other headings in the book. For example, in a discussion of social control, Park and Burgess argued that milling – the process where 'cattle becomes restless and begin slowly moving about in circles' – could be seen as 'a sort of collective gesture', i.e. as a crude, animalistic example of more developed forms of human crowd behaviour (Park and Burgess 1921: 788). Milling, which had also been briefly mentioned in Park's dissertation (1972: 135), would become a customary reference point in many subsequent discussions of crowd behaviour in American sociology. The same applied to the phenomenon of lynching (see also Park and Burgess 1921: 655). Frezza reports that the lynching of African-Americans, immigrants, union leaders, etc. by 'crowds of white men and women . . . reached its peak between 1884 and 1902', but continued to exist until the 1940s (2007: 75).

[10] Park's interest in the crowd topic continued beyond the publication of the *Introduction to the Science of Sociology*. As an illustration of his close attentiveness to the crowd discussions, one can refer to his double book review of Friedrich Wieser's *Das Gesetz der Macht* and Theodor Geiger's *Die Masse und ihre Aktion* (which, surprisingly, did not refer to Park's *Masse und Publikum*). In spite of Geiger's explicit attempt to free himself from any kind of psychology, Park praised his book for being 'the most important and

One the most significant followers of Park's crowd thinking was his colleague at the University of Chicago, Herbert Blumer, who largely subscribed to Park's image of the crowd but also modified it in certain ways. Blumer shared with Park the predominantly conceptual approach with few explicit empirical references. But more clearly than Park (and Burgess), he represented a move away from studying the crowd to investigating the mass, just as he stressed the joys associated with collective behavior.[11] This was all nicely captured in an article entitled 'Moulding of Mass Behavior through the Motion Picture' (Blumer 1935). Here Blumer defined the mass 'as a homogeneous aggregate of individuals who in their extra-mass activities are highly heterogeneous. In the mass they are essentially alike, are individually indistinguishable, and can be treated as similar units' (1935: 118). This definition evoked the homogenizing and de-individualizing capacities traditionally ascribed to crowds, but Blumer made no reference to suggestion and suggestibility. Still, Blumer attributed to the mass a number of qualities that fall within the semantic register usually associated with crowds. For instance, the mass was said to have 'no culture' and 'no traditions', just as it was characterized, he argued, by the 'absence of effective means of communication' (1935: 118, 119).

This might suggest a rather negative conception and, in fact, Blumer stated, the mass has a negative, even destructive side to it; yet it also contains a positive–constructive dimension. These two poles were united in the masses' role as a transitional agent between community and society forms of life. While Blumer did not relate mass behaviour explicitly to urbanization, his analysis can hardly be understood independently of the problematization of how cities dissolved local community ties. Thus, the central difference guiding Blumer's investigation was that between local culture and folk communities, on the one side, and mass behaviour, on the other. Whereas the well-functioning folk community generates no mass behaviour, masses emerge 'in complex, heterogeneous societies, or in folk societies in a state of disruption' (1935: 116). More specifically, if people's needs cannot be satisfied by the local community, they may find satisfaction through mass action, and this may pave the way for a new social order:

Mass behavior can be thought of as efforts at searching or grouping which arise out of this area of unsatisfied disposition. Mass behavior seems to represent

valuable theoretical treatise that so far has been written in the field of collective psychology' (1928: 645).

[11] The mass was not a clearly defined or distinguished category in Park and Burgess who used the term interchangeably with that of the crowd.

preparatory attempts, however crude they may be, at the formation of a new order of living. It can be thought of as constituting the earliest portion of the cycle of activity involved in the transition from settled folk life to a new social order. (1935: 117)

This was the societal function of the mass. It may be destructive in that it represented a destabilization of folk culture, but it also played a constructive role by creating a new social order in which individuals' needs and desires could be satisfied. The emphasis on the individuals and their desires was specific to Blumer's account, as compared to Park's. Whereas in the latter's emancipating interpretation the crowd may liberate individuals or (more often) groups of individuals, Blumer's focus was strictly on the singular individual: 'The form of mass behavior, paradoxically, is laid down by individual lines of activity and not by concerted action' (1935: 119).[12] So for Blumer, the mass was essentially a rational arbitrator of individual preferences.

Blumer elaborated on his theory in subsequent writings. In a volume entitled *An Outline of the Principles of Sociology*, edited by Park, Blumer contributed a chapter entitled 'Collective Behavior' (Blumer 1939; later republished in a slightly revised version, see 1951). Here he began by clarifying the confusion which Park and Burgess' notion of collective behavior had left by simultaneously referring to sociology as such and to a sociological subfield. According to Blumer, sociology is indeed concerned with collective behaviour, but in the specific sense of investigating 'the social order and its constituents (customs, rules, institutions, etc.) *as they are*'; the subfield of collective behaviour, for its part, focuses on 'the ways by which the social order *comes into existence*, in the sense of the emergence and solidification of new forms of collective behavior' (1939: 223, italics added). Once again, therefore, it was the capacity to create new social forms that Blumer's (Park-inspired) interest in collective behaviour centred on. As Blumer put it, 'in studying collective behavior we [are] concerned with the process of *building up* a social order' (1939: 279, italics added).

Compared to Blumer's previous work, the discussion in 'Collective Behavior' stands out because of its explicit reflections on the concept of the crowd. The text presented a distinction between two types of crowds. The first of these was the so-called 'acting crowd', which was similar to the 'psychological crowd' of earlier crowd semantics (1939: 235). The

---

[12] In a later article, which I shall discuss below, Blumer claimed that this strong individual dimension is one of the points that separate the mass from the crowd. Contrary to the crowd member, the individual in the mass is 'apt to be rather acutely self-conscious' (Blumer 1939: 243).

acting crowd was said to focus its attention on some common objective, say, a specific idea that it aimed to realize. This separated it from the other key crowd category Blumer examined, namely the so-called expressive crowd. This latter type was depicted as introverted; rather than seeking to realize some external goal, it would unleash its energy through expressive, physical movements, such as dancing, where this 'expression of excited feeling becomes an end in itself' (1939: 239).

What I find particularly interesting about this expressive crowd is Blumer's discussion of the individual's experience of being part of it. For once again Blumer did not suggest a negative analysis of de-individualizing tendencies. Quite the opposite, he associated the expressive crowd with 'joy', 'pleasure and exhilaration' (1939: 239). Obviously, Blumer was not the first to ascribe such positive terms to crowds; especially Whitman pre-dated him on this point. Still, Blumer was one of the first within the *sociological* landscape who stressed this positive dimension. Also, there is one important difference between Whitman and Blumer, which relates to the kind of new social order the two types of crowd were believed to make possible. Blumer thus argued that the acting crowd might give rise to a new political order, whereas the expressive crowd was likely to produce a new religious order. According to this scheme, joy, pleasure and ecstasy were reserved for the religious realm, whereas in Whitman's case these categories were also central to political crowds.

One of the crucial implications of Blumer's work was its implicit *normalization* of mass behaviour. Blumer steered clear of a pathological register, in part because he established a research agenda on collective behaviour which did not revolve around hypnosis or suggestion. Furthermore, he presented this mass behaviour as a common experience rather than as an exceptional one. Blumer's work initiated a number of subsequent analyses (e.g. Shibutani 1970), some of which will be examined in Chapter 7.

Propaganda and public opinion: nascent problematizations of mass society

The parts of Blumer's work examined above were published in the 1930s. In the following I would like to wind back time a bit. For while Blumer continued along the paths set out by Park, the progressive ideals that inspired the time of the latter's key crowd writings had faded by 1930. In fact, the entire climate for discussing crowds had already changed in the USA around the outbreak of the First World War. The war's effects on crowd theorizing will be discussed shortly, but let me begin by remarking that more or less at the same time as the war raged in Europe, new winds were blowing that challenged the previous American problematization of crowds and urbanization. This did not transpire over night, but was the result of a gradual reinterpretation of cities which led to an entirely new valorization of their social and political status. This new perspective was epitomized by Robert E. Park's pioneering essay 'The City' (1915), which laid the foundation for a generation of more affirmative urban studies.

Park's text offered a sweeping view of the city, extending from the role of schools and churches to the similarities between urban crowd behaviour and financial speculation on stock exchanges. Most importantly for present purposes, Park acknowledged that local ties were being weakened in cities, with negative effects on crime rates. But this was only one aspect of urbanization, and one which should not be exaggerated. Thus, rather than seeing the city as the breeding ground for moral decline and social disorder, Park was loyal to his Whitmanesque legacy and described how the city paved the way for new forms of excitement, solidarity and moral structures, just as he emphasized how novel liberating opportunities mushroomed in cities. Indeed, he argued, the city furnishes the individual with a particular 'moral climate in which his peculiar nature obtains the stimulations that bring his innate qualities to full and free expression' (Park 1915: 608). Park's view on the city as a socio-spatial configuration that permitted individuals to evade narrowing ties found widespread acclamation, and it did so, Boyer contends, on a background of several interlaced reasons. Among other things, cities were increasingly being portrayed positively in the popular culture of the time, just as urban crime rates were actually falling, meaning that crime statistics supported the more positive images of metropolitan life (Boyer 1978: 285, 286).

These developments questioned progressive ideals of urban re-moralization through positive environmentalism. Indeed, as noted above, the whole progressive movement grew fainter in the 1920s (although stimulus to social reform would gain renewed significance the following decade with the New Deal). In its place, a new basic problematization of cities came to light. Thus, it was argued, the problem of cities was not social disintegration, but rather that people might become too integrated so that conformity would reign and individual traits become blurred as a result. While this might not be a problem of cities as such, it was pertinent to the modern city, as the latter purportedly generated 'its own powerful social-control instrumentalities: the pervasive influence of radio, the movies, and mass-circulation periodicals; the potency of advertising and the emerging field of public relations; the commercialization of mass spectator sports; the standardization of consumption' (Boyer 1978: 289; see also the discussion of the social control performed through advertising in Park 1915: 604–7). Accordingly, the transformation from slum city to technological city effected a transition in semantic problematization from urban proto-revolutionary crowd to urban homogenized, mediatized mass. As Boyer puts it:

> The American city, viewed by generations of moralists as a seething human mass that might explode at any moment, came to be perceived by many in the 1920s as the dwelling place of millions of docile conformists daily subjected to a barrage of influences that shaped their behavior and values in ways they themselves hardly realized. (1978: 291)

So even if the city was discussed in much more affirmative categories than used to be the case in the nineteenth century, it was feared that the liberating potentials attributed to the city were beset by the homogenizing tendencies fostered by modern technology, especially the mass media. Although these discussions originated in problematizations of the modern technological city, they soon transformed into a problematization of mass society more generally, i.e. a society where people might well be crowded together in cities, but where the more important fact about their lives was that their conception of the world was filtered through and distorted by the mass media. Lurking behind this problematization was, as in the nineteenth century, a fundamental concern with the liberal subject whose independence was jeopardized by this development. But in contrast to the preceding century, this concern with the subject no longer revolved around the purported lack of community, but around the apparent excess of mass-mediated social-control technologies.

Blumer was one of the scholars who took seriously the new media landscape. While newspapers had been the primary mass medium for Tarde and Park, Blumer, who was born in 1900, represented a new generation that was acquainted not only with the printed press but also with first-generation electronic mass media in the form of broadcasting and movies (Blumer contributed significantly to the sociological study of movies: see Blumer 1933; Blumer and Hauser 1933). Blumer did not paint a univocally negative picture of the new media that tended to be popular in the cities. He posited, for instance, that the new mass media operated as a functional equivalent to the crowd, but as a positive one: one that gathered people around sentiments, but in a way compatible with – and not as a threat against – a free society (e.g. 1935: 127). At the same time, however, the mass media were not just innocent mediators of entertainment, fashions, lifestyles, attitudes, etc. They could also be used for dangerous political and social-control purposes. Contrary to Tarde, therefore, Blumer did not see the media as a public, i.e. as a balancing means, capable of holding crowd impulses in check; rather, the new media public itself could very well work as a manipulating instrument. Accordingly, the Tardean distinction between the irrational crowd and the rational public could no longer be taken for granted (for Blumer's analysis of the public and propaganda, see 1939: 245–52).

This view resonated with a more general problematization of mass media, propaganda and public opinion. Whereas the notion of public opinion had previously referred to an American equivalent to Tarde's concept of publics (e.g. Ross 1908: 64–5), which qua its rational–deliberative constitution was endorsed by the progressives (Ross 1991: 144), a new and much more sceptical framing evolved in the 1920s. In this reconfiguration, public opinion was no longer lauded as a rational alternative to the irrational crowd. Rather, it was argued, public opinion was embedded in a larger machinery which was anything but emblematic of rationality; in fact, public opinion was seen as an additional cogwheel in the repression of rationality. This new critical stance was a response to the experience with the First World War, which 'turned American attention away from domestic reform and sealed the fate of progressivism' (Ross 1991: 320). More generally, writes Dorothy Ross, 'the awful violence of the war, its glaring denial of modern progress, exposed the inadequacy of social science' (1991: 321). This semantic change and the growing dissatisfaction with progressive ideals were epitomized in the work of Walter Lippmann, another of James' students from Harvard.

In 1914 Lippmann had published *Drift and Mastery*, a book which by and large sympathized with the ideas of the Progressive Era (1961). Yet in particular the Wilson administration's use of propaganda during the First World War had changed his view on modern democracy and progressive reforms (McClay 1993: xxiii–xxiv). A far more critical attitude was therefore outlined in *Public Opinion* from 1922, in which Lippmann studied how public opinion was governed through propaganda and how stereotypes, prejudices, etc. dominated public opinion (1991). Lippmann's critical interrogation of the new media reality zeroed in on a basic socio-epistemological challenge, namely that in modern life people do not have direct access to the world. What they know is mediated by the mass media and public opinion (1991: 26–8). As Lippmann put it at one point:

the mass is constantly exposed to suggestion. It reads not the news, but the news with an aura of suggestion about it, indicating the line of action to be taken. It hears reports, not objective as the facts are, but already stereotyped to a certain pattern of behavior. (1991: 243)

As the quote intimates, Lippmann drew on crowd-theoretical resources (such as Le Bon) to account for how propaganda purportedly worked as a filter separating the reality from people's conception of it ('the pictures in our head').[13] Almost echoing Sidis' critique of civilization, Lippmann basically asserted that the media endow people with a warped picture of the world, a kind of mass hypnosis, as it were. This filtering operation of public opinion, newspapers and the media practically eliminated the individual's free judgement and enhanced the irrationality of modern society, rather than forming a bulwark against it such as Tarde believed. Given that this was the central problem, public opinion and the stereotypes it produced should be restrained. One way of achieving this was, according to Lippmann, to insert an elite, or more precisely 'some form of expertness between the private citizen and the vast environment in which he is entangled' (1991: 378). This, Lippmann believed, would prepare the way for more rationality in politics and hence for a democracy worthy of its name, namely one that was not distorted by the prejudices produced by the press of his time, but which permitted individuals to make up their own mind on a more independent basis. A similar conclusion was reached by scholars such as Harry Elmer Barnes. In a lengthy discussion of Le Bon's contribution to social psychology, Barnes concluded that '[w]ar can be eliminated only when society is brought under the control of that leadership of the real intellectual aristocracy which is needed to guide the crowd mind in times of peace' (1920: 369; see also Ross 1908: 349; Shepard 1909).

It did not take long, however, before Lippmann questioned this call for experts. In *The Phantom Public* from 1925, Lippmann had already lost his faith in expertness, and still did not see any prospects in education and reform either. Likewise, any belief in public opinion was dismissed as naïve, '[f]or when public opinion attempts to govern directly it is either a failure or a tyranny', which suggested that public opinion was but a phantom (1993: 60–1). The conclusion was distressing: 'I set no great store on what can be done by public opinion and the action of masses' (1993: 189).

---

[13] Lippmann's analysis was also indebted to the British political theorist Graham Wallas and referred explicitly to the latter's work (e.g. Lippmann 1991: 24, n. 1). Wallas, who was appointed the first professor of political science at the London School of Economics, counts as one of the founding fathers of modern political psychology (for a brief introduction to Wallas, see Bryder 1989). In the preface to the first (1908) edition of his *Human Nature in Politics*, a book that demonstrated the irrational dimension of politics, Wallas referred to Tarde's *L'opinion et la foule* and *Laws of Imitations* as well as Trotter's work on herd instincts as important inspirations (1929: vi). Similarly, in his subsequent *The Great Society* (1914), in the preface to which he dedicated the book to Lippmann, Wallas devoted an entire chapter to 'the psychology of the crowd'. Here Wallas was very critical of Tarde's notion of imitation and he also found the concept of suggestion of little use and argued instead for a theory of stimulations (1914: ch. 8).

Lippmann's central problematization of public opinion and the mass media painted the contours of the negative effects of a mass-mediated society. The net result of such a society was not too different from the negative effects typically attributed to crowd behaviour. This problematization of mass society would grow stronger in the years to come, as the following chapters will demonstrate. But the parts of it that touched upon the propaganda issue were already being heavily debated in the 1920s. However, not all subscribed to the view that propaganda was 'extraneous to the framework of a democratic society', to use Frezza's formulation (2007: 126). Some had much more faith in the positive implications of propaganda. One such person was Edward L. Bernays, who happened to be Freud's nephew and who brought together Lippmann's interest in public opinion and crowd-theoretical insights.[14] In 1923 he published a book entitled *Crystallizing Public Opinion* which revealed important inspirations from Lippmann's *Public Opinion*.[15] Yet the overall aim of Bernays' work differed markedly from that of Lippmann. Whereas the latter presented an analysis of the conditions of modern democracy, Bernays' contribution was 'primarily a sales pitch, not an exercise in social theory', as Mark Crispin Miller has put it (2005: 17). That is, Bernays demonstrated how crowd semantics might be transplanted to non-political domains, and he did so by utilizing the juxtaposition of crowd and propaganda theory in economic life and, more specifically, in the field of advertising, which grew in importance along with a waxing consumerism. In making this point, *Crystallizing Public Opinion* centred on what Bernays called the 'public relations counsel', i.e. 'a man who somehow or other produces that vaguely defined evil, "propaganda," which spreads an impression that colors the mind of the public concerning actresses, governments, railroads', and many other issues (1923: 11–12). Bernays' investigation mapped

---

[14] Another important scholar who drew on Lippmann was John Dewey who expressed his indebtedness to the former in his *The Public and Its Problems* from 1927 (1954: 116–17, n. 1). In contrast to Lippmann, however, the notion of public opinion did not figure centrally in Dewey's book. More interesting than the link to Lippmann, perhaps, Dewey made an important affirmative reference to Whitman. In his search for a Great Community, which would at the same time bring about a democratic public, Dewey wrote that 'democracy is a name for a life of free and enriching communion. It had its seer in Walt Whitman. It will have its consummation when free social inquiry is indissolubly wedded to the art of full and moving communication' (1954: 184). Dewey did not engage in explicit discussions of crowd theory in *The Public and Its Problems*. Yet he was familiar with discussions in crowd theory and with the work of Le Bon and Tarde; see Dewey (1917; 1922: 60–1).

[15] In the foreword to the book, Bernays listed Lippmann as one of his major sources of inspiration. This list also included scholars such as William MacDougall, Everett Dean Martin and William Trotter (Bernays 1923: v).

the workings of this profession, and such an outline had to take seriously ideas from crowd theory, for only thus, he believed, could one obtain a clear idea of how to manage public relations (see also 1935).[16] Accordingly, Bernays devoted seven chapters of the book to a discussion of 'the group and the herd'.

Bernays' discussion of the public relations counsel pointed to a significant trait of much of the propaganda debate, namely that it contained a much greater focus on leaders than other parts of the American crowd semantics did. Compared to European scholars (from Le Bon to Freud), the interest in the leader's constitutive impact on the crowd was surprisingly absent in the work of Blumer, Park, Ross, Sidis, etc. Not even the fact that some of these scholars endorsed the notion of suggestion made them argue that the suggestion of crowds radiated from some central leader. Arguably, the absence of the leader was due in part to the more liberal orientations which granted the singular individual, crowd member or not, much greater autonomy.

On Bernays' view, the work of the leader/public relations counsel was predicated on the 'fundamentals of public motivation', as he called it (1923: 98ff.). In excavating these fundamentals, Bernays found inspiration in particular in the work of Everett Dean Martin, a social philosopher and Director of the People's Institute in New York. Martin published several contributions to the social psychology of crowds and he combined an inspiration from Le Bon with a liberal approach that did not elevate suggestion and suggestibility to being key explanatory concepts. In his *The Behavior of Crowds: A Psychological Study*, for instance, he stated that 'Le Bon is correct in maintaining that the crowd is not a mere aggregation of people. *It is a state of mind*'; yet the 'controlling ideas of the crowd are the result neither of reflection nor of "suggestion," but are akin to what . . . the psychoanalysts term "complexes"' (Martin 1920: 19–20, italics in original). Drawing extensively on Martin's *Behavior of Crowds*, Bernays conceded that the crowd mind is not only:

to be found . . . when there is a physical agglomeration of people. This fact is important to an understanding of the problems of the public relations counsel, because he must bear in mind always that the readers of advertisements, the recipients of letters, the solitary listener at a radio speech, the reader of the morning newspapers are mysteriously part of the crowd-mind. (1923: 103–4)

---

[16] Bernays was not the first to propose this connection to public relations and advertisement. Leach mentions Walter Dill Scott and Dale Carnagey (later Carnegie) as early forerunners who applied crowd psychology in advertisement theories (1986: 103). Another figure in this field was the congregational minister, Gerald Stanley Lee (1900; 1901; 1913; Lee's work is analysed by Bush 1991).

Contrary to what this might suggest, Bernays did not argue that crowd psychology should simply be instrumentalized for the purposes of ruling people more efficiently, namely through the use of propaganda techniques and public relations. To be sure, 'the public relations counsel ... must constantly call upon his knowledge of individual and group psychology' (1923: 121). But this did not mean that public opinion could be entirely manufactured, such as Lippmann claimed. Rather, the public relations counsel needed some basis, 'some group reaction and tradition in common with the public' he or she would try to affect (1923: 118). For this reason Bernays did not believe in radical transformations of public opinion, but rather in the possibility of realizing or directing existing potentials. Or to be more precise: for Bernays, the role of the public relations counsel was to identify the currents of public opinion and to lead these with the help of communicative means and by '[t]he appeal to the instincts and the universal desires' (1923: 173). 'It is his capacity for crystallizing the obscure tendencies of the public mind before they have reached definite expression, which makes [the public relations counsel] so valuable', Bernays concluded (1923: 173).

Interestingly, Bernays' rejection of general manipulative options made him attribute an almost liberating function to the public relations counsel, again in opposition to Lippmann, whom he otherwise admired: 'Mr. Lippmann says propaganda is dependent upon censorship. From my point of view the precise reverse is more nearly true. Propaganda is a purposeful, directed effort to overcome censorship – the censorship of the group mind and the herd reaction' (1923: 122). According to Bernays, therefore, propaganda could be used to actually affect the crowd mind and to liberate the singular individual from his or her reliance on crowd thinking. Bernays elaborated on this argument in a 1929 debate with Everett Dean Martin, a discussion which was provoked in part by the publication in 1928 of Bernays' sequel to *Crystallizing Public Opinion*, a book straightforwardly called *Propaganda* (2005). Under the heading 'Are We Victims of Propaganda?', Martin and Bernays took very different stances on the relation between propaganda, on the one hand, and freedom, responsibility and individuality, on the other (Martin and Bernays 1929).

Martin presented an utterly negative image of propaganda, observing it as a kind of manipulation which posed a threat to democracy and rationality. 'The propagandist', he said, 'proceeds by utilizing, for ulterior ends, the prejudices and passions and fixed ideas of the mob' (Martin and Bernays 1929: 143). As a result, he argued, propaganda gives rise to intolerance and 'organized crowd insanity' (1929: 144). More importantly, propaganda was opposed to education and responsibility (one of

Martin's preferred topics, see Martin 1920: 281): 'The educator strives to develop individual responsibility; the propagandist, mass effects' (1929: 145). Bernays could not accept this account. He stressed that propaganda serves important social functions. For example, he praised propaganda for enabling 'minorities to break up dominant groups. It is the advance agent of new ideas and new products' (1929: 148). Without propaganda, minority groups 'could never bring their views before the public' (1929: 148). By implication, all groups in society, powerful or not, were equal in the sense that they relied on propaganda in order for them to make their views and interests heard. According to Bernays, however, propaganda was not just important as a liberating-emancipating tool. It also worked, he claimed (again, in clear opposition to Martin), as 'the most effective weapon against intolerance' (1929: 148). So in addition to being a means to manipulate the irrational masses, propaganda actually forged a bulwark against the eruption of irrationality on a large scale (see also Bernays 1938).

Bernays' insistence that propaganda might have a liberating function placed him in the tradition of Park's liberal analysis of crowds. Bernays' particular contribution to this line of reasoning was the argument that in order for groups or crowds to create new social forms they are dependent on mastering the techniques of propaganda. This idea, strangely, associated Bernays with progressive ideals. As he put it in *Propaganda*:

The social settlement, the organized campaigns against tuberculosis and cancer, the various research activities aiming directly at the elimination of social diseases and maladjustments ... have need of knowledge of the public mind and mass psychology if they are to achieve their aims. (2005: 148)

In other words, in order to actualize the ideals of a rational social, political or economic order, one had to pay close attention to theories engaged with the dynamics of irrational crowds. Although this echoed progressive ambitions, it added a significant twist to former principles. Thus, Bernays acknowledged that irrationality was a condition of reform, an unavoidable trait of human life which could not be eliminated (the wet dream of the progressives), but which could be worked with and upon. So when Ross (1991: 322) observes that '[o]ne reflection of the shock of wartime violence and the doubts it threw upon historical progress was the increasing currency of irrationalist psychologies', one may therefore include Bernays in this movement. But there were many others (see e.g. Doob 1935; Doob and Robinson 1935; Lasswell 1927: 225ff.; 1933). In Chapter 6, I shall dig further into the upsurge of psychological approaches. Let me end this discussion, however, by noting that with his optimistic attitude, Bernays in effect enacted a reversal of the critiques of mass society. The modern metropolis with its plethora of mass media did not simply undermine democracy and perform an erosion of individuality. Quite the contrary, the mass media should be seen as more neutral transmitters and moulders which could also serve the interests of the masses and democracy. As the following chapters will show, this optimistic view of mass society would soon be challenged by a series of much more critical studies.

Alternatives to suggestion

As demonstrated above, the notion of suggestion was received rather positively in American sociology in the late nineteenth and early twenti- eth centuries, with Sidis and Park as central advocates in the crowd theory domain. Since early European crowd theory was so tightly linked to the suggestion doctrine, the forthcoming reception of it on US grounds was a significant back-up for the adoption of European perspec- tives on crowds. Yet the theoretical underpinnings of crowd theory were increasingly being contested. Indeed, I will argue, new theoretical cur- rents appeared in the first decades of the twentieth century which dealt the early European as well as American semantics of crowds significant blows. These currents only grew stronger in the course of time, paving the way for ever-more diluted and normalized conceptions of crowd behaviour in American sociology. So while the First World War stimu- lated an interest in irrationality and as such seemed to place crowd theory centrally (as, indeed, it did in the work of Bernays), a series of other developments pulled in the opposite direction. In the following I shall discuss three such developments which, however disparate they might be, all boiled down to an attack on the suggestion framework underlying a great part of the early crowd semantics.

One critical stance against the suggestion doctrine emanated from social psychology, with George Herbert Mead as a key representative. Like his colleagues at the University of Chicago, where he was one of Blumer's teachers, Mead was well acquainted with crowd theory in the Le Bon and Tarde tradition. In 1899, for example, he reviewed the English translation of Le Bon's *Psychology of Socialism* (Mead 1899).[17] Mead was very critical. The psychological programme Le Bon presented in the book was, in its ambition to change the course of society (protect- ing it from the dangers of socialism), deemed just as 'inadequate' as his 'social theory' (1899: 409). The crowd issue also cropped up in the posthumously published *Mind, Self, and Society*, where Mead associated

---

[17] See also the brief references to Le Bon's *The Crowd* in the unpublished review of John Dewey's *Human Nature and Conduct* (Mead 1987).

the mob with violent behaviour and established an opposition between mob and society, stating that 'you could not make up human society out of a herd. To suggest this would be to leave out of account the fundamental organization of human society about a self or selves' (1934: 240; see also Leys 1993: 298–300).

Precisely the notion of the self occupied a central place in Mead's critical encounter with the suggestion doctrine *and consequently* with crowd theory. Mead denied that suggestion was at the base of social behaviour such as Sidis and Tarde professed. This view might only be stated implicitly in Mead's scattered remarks on mobs, but it took an explicit form in his general theory of the social personality, which held that the self is constituted in its relation to other selves. And this theory was developed as a clear alternative to Tardean imitation theory, as Ruth Leys has demonstrated (1993). Leys shows how, on the one hand, Mead presented his theory of the social self as somehow congenial to that of Tarde. At one point, for example, Mead discussed sympathy and argued that '[s]ympathy comes, in the human form, in the arousing in one's self of the attitude of the individual whom one is assisting, the taking the attitude of the other when one is assisting the other' (1934: 299). The concept of sympathy had a clear Tardean flavour (see Tarde 1962: 79), so when Mead explained his theory of the social self in terms of sympathy, he aligned himself with a Tardean tradition – as Mead was well aware of (1934: 299).

On the other hand, however, Mead was careful to stress that the social self was not to be understood in terms of a more or less hypnotic process in which the self unconsciously imitates the other. In *Mind, Self, and Society*, for example, Mead stated that '[i]mitation as a general instinct is now discredited in human psychology' (1934: 52). He discussed the work of Tarde explicitly and dismissed it as operating 'without adequate analysis', and he even characterized the idea of imitation as 'an impossible assumption' (1934: 53). Similarly, in an examination of 'Cooley's Contribution to American Social Thought', Mead touched upon Tarde and asserted that '[a]s a mechanism, imitation proves hopelessly inadequate' (1930: 699). Leys draws two conclusions from this. One is that:

we cannot understand Mead's thought unless we grasp that what is mobilizing and impelling it from beginning to end is the resolve to defeat Tarde's theory of imitation-suggestion as that theory had been represented and also deflected in the work of Baldwin, Royce, Cooley, and others ... Mead's whole project would be undermined if imitation-suggestion proved to be internal to the production of the subject rather than an auxiliary process. (1993: 287)

The other conclusion is that in his attempt to dismiss imitation-suggestion, Mead actually ended up undermining his own ambition of explaining the self via the social. Thus, he argued, the self is not an effect of imitation-suggestion; rather, imitation itself requires that the self be conscious of other selves. In order to imitate, in order to put oneself in another's place, Leys' deconstructive reading of Mead therefore demonstrates, 'the self-identical ego or *subject* is silently presupposed. Which is to say that Mead's attempt to derive the subject from the social will be compromised from the outset' (1993: 292, italics in original).

The crucial point for now is not that Mead may have undermined his own project by assuming the existence of a pre-social subject. More importantly, Mead's rejection of imitation-suggestion was yet another indication of the liberal concern with the singular individual. In Mead's case, too, the suggestion doctrine was considered problematic because of its de-individualizing implications. Crucially, furthermore, it was from within the perspective of social psychology – where the suggestion doctrine had had its most prominent career – that Mead voiced his theoretical attack and reorientation. Mead challenged the doctrine on its own ground, so to speak, and in this way he contributed to a growing American destabilization of the suggestion doctrine.

This, I claim, also had implications for crowd semantics: being a prominent social psychologist Mead's attempt to provide an analysis of the social self independently of any reference to imitation-suggestion suggested that a whole new way of conceiving the relation between self and society was not only possible but necessary – including conceptions of the relation between self and crowd. The fact that Mead's attempt has been deemed unsuccessful by Leys changes little about this. Mead's theorizing on this issue also put the relation between crowds/mobs, the subject and democracy in a new light. Thus, a liberal democratic society was only thinkable for Mead if its alleged basic molecule, the individual self, were preserved:

for Mead the 'higher' or conscious identifications with others that distinguish the intelligent – by which he means the *democratic* – social order from the mob and its 'lower' unconscious identifications occur not mimetically on the basis of a hypnotic 'subjection' but antimimetically on the basis of individual differences – on the basis of the subject. (Leys 1993: 300, italics in original)

This was Le Bon turned upside-down. Whereas the Frenchman feared the hypnotic suggestions of crowds because they signalled the transformation of the aristocratic order into a democratic, egalitarian society, Mead operated with the opposite fear that this democracy was undermined precisely by the imitation-suggestions (i.e. very similar to Edward Ross' argument).

I have focused on Mead as a central figure who challenged the suggestion doctrine within American social psychology. However, he was not alone in this move away from the key explanatory framework of classical European crowd semantics. Floyd H. Allport formulated a different, but equally influential, social–psychological critique of the European crowd semantics. Allport's main critique aimed at the purported 'group fallacy' which assumed the existence of collective minds. According to Allport, '[t]here is no psychology of groups [including crowds] which is not essentially and entirely a psychology of individuals' (1924: 4). Allport thus developed a social–psychological approach to crowds which, similar to Mead, prioritized the individual level.[18] John D. Greenwood has argued that what ensued here was a 'moral individualism', i.e. the belief that it was crucial, on both moral and political grounds, to protect the notion and conception of the individual from supra-individual phenomena (2000: 449ff.; see also 2004: 168ff.).

As indicated previously, this moral individualism also surfaced in Edward Ross' work. This is rather surprising, given the fact that Ross' theorizing was almost directly traced from Tarde. But only 'almost', for even if Ross subscribed to the suggestion doctrine, his adaptation of it introduced an important correction to Tarde's model. Rather than operating, as the latter did, with a plastic notion of the subject, Ross effected a transformation where 'the normative psychological subject was increasingly seen to be coherent, bounded and autonomous, able to withstand social influence', as Lisa Blackman has put it in her illuminating analysis of the Anglo-American reception of suggestion (2007: 585). Indeed, Ross stated in his *Social Psychology*, 'social psychology spurs us to push on and build up a genuine individuality, to become a voice and not an echo, a person and not a parrot' (1908: 4; see Blackman 2007: 586; 2008). The central point is that even if Ross had much greater sympathy with the suggestion doctrine than Mead and Allport, he actually also challenged some of its key implications and modified it so as to make it compatible with a positive valorization of the liberal subject.

The critique voiced by social psychologists such as Mead and Allport constituted one significant blow to the theoretical underpinnings of early sociological crowd semantics. Another important setback came from a growing reorientation in the social sciences towards positivist–objectivist ideals. In her seminal study *The Origins of American Social Science*, Dorothy Ross demonstrates that a 'scientistic movement gained power in the 1920s', which became increasingly visible in Park's work as well as, and particularly, in 'the methodological objectivism' successfully propagated by Giddings (1991: 366, 369, 428–48). While different

---

[18] On Allport's dismissal of the idea of suggestibility, see Leach (1986: 106–7).

sociologists had different emphases, the shift that transpired in American sociology in the 1920s was one that granted positivism a more central role in sociological work, and which relied to a still greater extent on statistics to redeem the nomothetic ambitions. The crucial point for now is that crowd semantics which rested on the notion of suggestion came out as rather inadequate in this development. Not dissimilar to Durkheim's critique of the non-scientific nature of Tarde's work, the growing belief in positivism easily dismissed references to suggestion as speculative and, hence, scientifically illegitimate.

The scientism did provoke reactions and calls for more theory (Bannister 2003: 346). And although such theorizing did re-emerge, this did not lead to a wholehearted rehabilitation of earlier crowd semantics. In fact, from the late 1930s onwards, a third blow was dealt to the theoretical underpinnings of early-twentieth-century American crowd semantics. Once again, a broad theoretical reorientation took place of the American sociological landscape, this time induced by Talcott Parsons' sociological programme. After several years with the Chicago sociologists in a leading position, Parsons' landmark book *The Structure of Social Action* (1937) inaugurated a whole new tradition of American sociological thinking. According to Morris Janowitz, this volume not only symbolized the 'intellectual crisis' of the Chicago School; the book announced that 'a new intellectual format imposed itself on American sociology' (1970: x).[19] Although not explicitly conceived as such, *The Structure of Social Action* in effect undermined the key propositions of the classical European crowd semantics. This was reflected in the concrete analyses as well as in the selection of European writers that Parsons based his work upon (the book was subtitled *A Study in Social Theory with Special Reference to a Group of Recent European Writers*). Let me give just three indications of this. First, Parsons worked out his theory of social action not by looking to scholars such as Le Bon or Tarde, but rather by interpreting the work of Émile Durkheim, Alfred Marshall, Vilfredo Pareto and Max Weber.[20] As mentioned in Chapter 3, Pareto's work was only indirectly linked to crowd theory (mainly via Michels); and even if Durkheim may be said to formulate a 'rudimentary crowd psychology' in his sociology of religion (Lukes 1985: 163, n. 22), there is no doubt that this selection of European scholars represented a clear alternative to Le Bon, Tarde, etc.

---

[19] See also Abbott (1999: 9) and his discussion of the destiny of Chicago sociology.
[20] In *The Structure of Social Action* there was no mention at all of Le Bon (or of Park or Blumer, for that matter), and Tarde was, as Leys notes, only cited once, in a discussion of Durkheim (1993: 281; Parsons 1937: 385, n. 1).

Second, the whole idea of Parsons' book was to formulate a voluntaristic theory of action in which 'the means–end schema' – together with its 'subjective reference' to an ego or self – was considered 'the central framework for the causal explanation of action' (Parsons 1937: 750, 47). This was manifestly different from the semantics of crowds where social action was explained in terms of hypnotic suggestion, thereby undermining the whole idea of a conscious, distinctive self. Finally, and hardly surprisingly, therefore, with one exception there were no discussions of crowds in *The Structure of Social Action*. The lone exception appeared in Parsons' discussion of Durkheim's sociology of religion. Although this part of Durkheim's work contained a positive account of collective effervescence, Parsons was at great pains to defend Durkheim against accusations of being aligned in any fashion with crowd semantics. Thus, Parsons stressed, 'Durkheim's theory of ritual is not anti-intellectual crowd psychology – in fact it is not psychology in any sense' (1937: 437). The categorization of crowd psychology as 'anti-intellectual' speaks for itself.

To sum up, Parsons defined a new theoretical agenda in American sociology, which would assume a key role in the 1960s. Similar to Park, he constructed his programme on recent European sociology, but the inspiration he searched for was no less than perpendicular to the (Tardean) tradition of suggestion which was a defining feature of the classical European crowd semantics. Parsons was not at all interested in crowds, and his theory of social action was, in its voluntaristic focus, an obvious alternative to theories that placed imitation-suggestion at the centre of attention.

I do not want to suggest that the notion of crowds was immediately dispelled from sociology due to the three impediments described above. It is more correct to say that the theoretical climate for discussing crowds was ambiguous. While the suggestion doctrine was being contested and scientism was on the march, both of which developments were questioning early sociological crowd semantics, the First World War and the new mass media pulled in a different direction, as they induced theoretical concerns with collective irrationality. This was further buttressed with Hitler's ascent to power, which led to a veritable boom in crowd-theoretical resources (see the next two chapters).

I have argued in this chapter that American discussions of crowds emerged on the backcloth of a more general problematization of urbanization and how the metropolises purportedly shattered stable, meaningful community structures. As the discussion of propaganda showed, this urban contextualization was gradually reconfigured so that the spatial framing of the urban crowd was superseded by a concern with modern mass phenomena, which although initially located in the cities became less and less spatially bound. Independent of its spatial contextualization, I have argued that, whereas some of the liberal takes on crowds produced a fear of crowds no less heartfelt than that of the alleged 'anti-liberal' Europeans, one of the early American sociologists' chief contributions to crowd semantics lay in the claim that crowds might serve liberating functions. To be sure, Weimar sociologists such as Geiger also argued for such a functional understanding of crowds. Yet in the American context the notion of the crowd's liberating potentials tended to revolve around the individual rather than the group (or class). That is, rather than effecting a *societal* transformation for the better, the crowd could liberate specific *individuals* or pave the way for the realization of specific individual interests.

When scrutinizing the American sociological crowd semantics in the time-span from around 1890 to the 1930s, another contrast to the Weimar debates stands out. Whereas the Weimar scholars were at pains to enforce strict disciplinary boundaries between sociology and psychology, and granted the crowd an exemplary role in that endeavour, the American sociologists generally took a much looser stance on the question of disciplinary separation. In the USA, psychology, social psychology and sociology were deeply entangled; and sociologists did not have strong reservations about (social) psychological perspectives.[21] As James Good has argued, '[i]t was not just that within sociology that social psychological work appeared, but rather that American sociology, certainly during the first three decades of the twentieth century, embodied what has been called a "psychic" approach' (2000: 390). It might be argued that the crowd operated as a 'boundary object' (alongside topics like the self, groups, etc.) that permitted, or even called for, a close interaction between psychological and sociological viewpoints (Good 2000: 391). That said, the close relations between psychology and sociology in early American social theory should not gloss over the struggles that took place. As this chapter has shown, the notion of suggestion was gradually subjected to ever-heavier critique, both within sociology and social psychology. This critique also functioned as a means of disciplinary positioning so that, for example, Parsons could launch an entirely new sociological programme that distanced itself from the theories more positive to the suggestion doctrine.

---

[21] This may explain why Robert Park did not hesitate to characterize Theodor Geiger's explicitly non-psychological *Die Masse und ihre Aktion* as a contribution to 'the field of collective psychology' (1928: 645).

In spite of the obvious particularities of crowd semantics in early American sociology, a more diachronic view that takes into account the semantic trajectories of the 1950s and 1960s reveals that much of what happened in the early phase were actually germs of the subsequent developments. So without anticipating the chapters to come, I find it important to note that the 1890–1920 period should be seen in part as a very important forerunner era: the sociological crowd semantics of the 1950s and 1960s simply cannot be understood independently of the theoretical inventions of this earlier epoch. This is particularly apparent with respect to the individualistic view of the crowd (the problematization of crowds as revolving around the liberal subject) which eventually led to a complete reconceptualization of crowds as entities composed of rational, purposive individuals – implying that, paradoxically, the social was increasingly excluded from social psychology and sociology, a point I shall return to in Chapter 7 (see also Greenwood 2004). To be sure, the rationalistic interpretation of crowds only really gained footing from the 1950s onwards. One might conjecture that this distillation of a pure rational approach was long in coming because of the intermezzos with totalitarianism and the Second World War. Hitler's mobilization of the masses did not exactly invite the notion of an epitomized rationality.

5 From crowd to mass: problematizing classless society

The preceding chapters have analysed the developments in sociological crowd semantics in France, Germany and the USA. The reason for focusing on separate national theoretical contexts was that, despite many overlaps and interconnections, each of these countries produced rather distinct conceptions of and approaches to crowds. The present and the following chapters are not organized strictly around such geographic parameters, the reason being that from the 1930s onwards, crowd semantics is no longer easily delineated according to national background. This is due among others things to the fact that the National Socialist regime forced many German scholars to flee to other countries, especially the USA, thereby blurring what was, say, particular German or American plateaus of crowd semantics in the post-Hitler era (see e.g. Hughes 1975). This is not to suggest that, from the 1930s onwards, the differences in crowd conceptions entirely vanished, creating one uniform body of crowd theorizing. Of course, national differences can be detected. However, in the present chapter I attend less to national particularities in semantic trajectories and more to some of the main cross-national batches of crowd or mass semantics that evolved from the 1930s onwards. Specifically, I will argue that a semantic plateau can be distilled, consisting of three central tropes or problematizations, each of which in its own fashion responded to and sought to capture what was depicted as a transformation of contemporary society into a mass society. Key to the problematization of this societal change was the assertion that modern society should be credited with a number of achievements such as especially technical progress, but that such accomplishments must be seen in the light of their negative side effects, including the erosion of the distinction between elite and non-elite, the related emergence of a new subject, the mass individual, and the proliferation of proto-totalitarian or at least non-democratic impulses.

To be sure, scholars such as Blumer also operated with the notion of mass society, made possible in part by the new mass media landscape. But the problematizations to be analysed in the present chapter sought

to direct attention to more fundamental developments not easily captured with Blumer's analytical lens. Specifically, the first problematization of mass society to be scrutinized below revolved around an
essentially moral concern, personified by José Ortega y Gasset. The next
zeroed in on the question of culture. In spite of the above-mentioned
cross-national tendencies, the cultural problematization of mass society
remained a largely German affair, which in the present chapter will be
studied through the work of Karl Mannheim, a central sociological voice
in the Weimar era. While Ortega and Mannheim conceived of mass
society as a moral or cultural decline, respectively, and argued that mass
society stimulated totalitarian, non-democratic impulses, other scholars
arrived at a similar conclusion, but on the basis of a somewhat different
analytical set-up. Centring especially on the notion of classes in mass
society, Hannah Arendt, William Kornhauser and Emil Lederer asserted
that modern mass society was characterized by dissolving former class
divisions. Rather than signifying a unanimous step forward, they argued,
this classless nature of mass society in fact propelled totalitarian
developments.

The chapter focuses on the time-span from the 1930s to 1960 (with a
couple of detours to the 1920s), since in these decades the mass society
semantics occupied a prominent place in social theory. But the mass
semantics also provoked critical responses. For example, in some of his
post-Second World War work, Theodor Geiger formulated a critique,
which was aimed not least against the positions advanced by scholars
such as Ortega and Mannheim. This critique will be examined at the end
of the chapter.

The emergence of 'mass-man'

One of the most poignant attacks on early-twentieth-century societal
transformations was put forward by the Spanish philosopher José Ortega
y Gasset in *The Revolt of the Masses* which came out in Spanish in 1929
(1960).[1] In this book Ortega developed a conservative–aristocratic
critique of the society of his time and linked it explicitly to the
problematization of masses. Ortega focused on the European context
after the First World War and argued that since the war, Europe had
witnessed 'the accession of the masses to complete social power',

---

[1] The book was based on work Ortega had published during the 1920s. In the present
context, I shall limit myself to *The Revolt of the Masses* since this is the most significant
contribution on Ortega's part to crowd/mass semantics. For an analysis which situates
this book in Ortega's larger œuvre, see Graham (2001: ch. 6).

a development which entailed that 'actually Europe is suffering from the greatest crisis that can afflict peoples, nations, and civilisation' (1960: 11).

Ortega's profoundly pessimistic diagnosis was rooted in the observation that the presence of crowds had altered the larger mental and moral fabric of society. The negative and irrational mentality typically attributed to crowds had simply permeated the entire social body. More specifically, the pervasive physical co-presence of crowds had paved the way for a new type of social being, the mass individual. Ortega's description of this transformation took as its starting point an observation which in particular Sidis had emphasized, namely that the problem of crowds was related to the inability to move freely. In Ortega's vocabulary this was defined as a problem of 'agglomeration, of "plenitude." Towns are full of people, houses full of tenants, hotels full of guests ... What previously was, in general, no problem, now begins to be an everyday one, namely, *to find room*' (1960: 11–12, italics added).

Ortega based his observations of the quantitative increase in masses on demographic data (1960: 50), but also on what he considered a *visual* fact: wherever one looked, one saw people and more people. To be sure, great numbers of people had existed before, but only within the past fifteen years, i.e. from around 1915–30, had they made themselves felt (seen) '*qua* multitude' (1960: 13, italics in original). All of a sudden, Ortega asserted, one could observe the masses in 'the best places' of society: 'The multitude has suddenly become visible, installing itself in the preferential positions in society' (1960: 13).

It was precisely the occupation of the preferential positions by the mass that concerned Ortega, because this new situation signified the erosion of what he saw as the guiding difference of every society, namely that between masses and minorities – which, it might be added, replaced the crowd–psychological distinction between crowd and individual. The distinction between masses and minorities did not refer to 'a division into social classes', but rather to a division 'into classes of men' or characters, specifically, the 'mass-man' and the 'select man' (1960: 15). According to Ortega, a person is mass if he or she 'sets no value' on him or herself and is 'happy to feel as one with everybody else' (1960: 14–15). The select man, on the contrary, 'is not the petulant person who thinks himself superior to the rest, but the man who demands more of himself than the rest' (1960: 15). What had happened over the past fifteen years, Ortega regretted, was that the mass-man had ousted the select man. Indeed, as the title of his book suggested, mass-man had revolted against the idea that he or she should succumb to anyone but him or herself.

When exploring the background for this development Ortega pointed to both ideal and material features. In the realm of ideas, he blamed the invention of human rights in the eighteenth century for having disseminated the notion that 'every human being, by the mere fact of birth, and without requiring any special qualification whatsoever, possessed certain fundamental political rights' (1960: 22). This idea had transformed the entire political climate so that the masses would no longer obey select minorities but now believed in their own (to Ortega's mind, ignorant) aspirations. Compared to Lippmann's wish in *Public Opinion* to insert an elite that should help bring the masses forward, Ortega's diagnosis suggested that the times had long gone when the masses would follow ideas other than their own. On the more material level, he pointed to the economic and technological revolutions which had significantly improved the living conditions for all groups of society. Yet, Ortega complained, the comfortable life had also removed any individual incentive to demand more of oneself; the preservation of well-being had become the only, but severely tranquillizing, objective. In combination, these ideal and material developments had produced a greater percentage of mass-men than ever before and thereby radically altered the constitution of the predominant mental character in society. Nobility with its emphasis on obligations and its striving for personal excellence had been replaced by the mass-man's assurance of his rights and self-sufficiency (1960: 63; cf. Schmitt 2007: 92–5).

Ortega's diagnosis of the implications of this mental transformation was gloomy. The fundamental problem was a moral one. The celebration of rights and the rejection of obligations reflected, in Ortega's eyes, the denial to submit to any higher standards, and this amounted to a grand negation of morality as such. 'If you are unwilling to submit to any norm, you have, *nolens volens*, to submit to the norm of denying all morality, and this is not amoral, but immoral' (1960: 189, italics in original). This negative morality, the disappearance of any moral guidelines, had consequences for the assessment of the mass-man as well as for politics.

With respect to the mass-man, Ortega drew on a vocabulary of barbarism and intellectual inferiority which resembled the semantics advocated by Le Bon and the other classical crowd psychologists. However, in Ortega's case, the barbarism was above all a moral problem. 'It is not a problem of the mass-man being a fool', said Ortega, implicitly dismissing the idea that crowd suggestion and its alleged suspension of rational thought constituted the main concern; '[o]n the contrary, to-day he is more clever, has more capacity of understanding than his fellow of any previous period. But that capacity is of no use to him' (1960: 70).

Having no external yardstick (moral, truth, etc.) in effect rendered the mass-man an intellectual barbarian (1960: 70, n. 1). According to Ortega, this intellectual barbarism of the mass-man was one of many signs of his or her atavism. Civilization had progressed significantly, but the mass-man could not keep pace with that development. 'The actual mass-man is, in fact, a primitive who has slipped through the wings on to an age-old stage of civilisation' (1960: 82). At the same time, paradoxically, it was civilization itself that had 'automatically produced the mass-man' (1960: 107). Civilization had created its own subversive monster: an individual who threatened to undermine the very same social order that had fostered it.

This observation of the paradoxical relation between mass and civilization was parallel to Le Bon's analysis. Akin to Le Bon, moreover, Ortega asserted that the mass was inherently destructive. 'The mass crushes beneath it everything that is different, everything that is excellent, individual, qualified and select. Anybody who is not like everybody, who does not think like everybody, runs the risk of being eliminated' (1960: 18; see also 116). In spite of such similarities, Ortega's analysis differed markedly from that of Le Bon. For example, Le Bon had argued that at times the crowd is capable of moral deeds. In Ortega's opinion, this was an impossibility, and in fact this constituted his main critique of the mass-man. Further, the entire explanatory framework differed. Although Ortega attributed to the mass many of the features that the Le Bonian tradition had emphasized (violence, barbarianism, etc.), he offered no *psychological* explanation of the transformation he diagnosed. Ortega confined himself to a broader, perception-based and philosophical framework that stressed the relations between society and moral character. In contrast to Le Bon, finally, there was no Machiavellian programme underpinning Ortega's analysis. Indeed, the whole point was that the 'intellectual hermetism' of mass-man, his or her objection to any guidance other than their own, had radically eliminated the possibility of ruling the masses from the outside (1960: 73). The mass would only submit to its own impulses, and if it were to have a leader, then this leader would have to mirror the mass in every respect.

This latter point brings me to the second major implication of mass-man's societal predominance, namely the consequences for the political realm. According to Ortega, the emergence of mass-man put liberal democracy under pressure and paved the way for both syndicalist movements and fascist regimes. He described the difference between liberal democracy and these alternatives as one between indirect and direct action. Liberal democracy, he said, was 'the prototype of "indirect action"' (1960: 76), meaning that it was based on the rule of law and, hence, on self-limiting measures. This entailed a respect for minorities.[2] In contrast to liberal principles of discussion and self-limiting measures such as the rule of law, Ortega posited, the mass only knew direct action. He traced this direct action back to 'groups of French syndicalists and realists of about 1900', alluding among others to Sorel (1960: 74; on Sorel, see 184). The direct action advocated by these movements had now become the main approach to political life, Ortega cautioned, with all sorts of violent and destabilizing implications: '"direct action" consists in inverting the order and proclaiming violence as *prima ratio*, or strictly as *unica ratio*' (1960: 75, italics in original).

In addition to this syndicalist threat, Ortega emphasized a point that received widespread resonance in the 1920s and 1930s, namely that the transition into a mass society prepared the way for totalitarian regimes. Mass society entailed, so the underlying claim went, a structural propensity to fascism and other anti-liberal movements. Indeed, Ortega observed, fascism transpired as a 'palpable manifestation of the new mentality of the masses' (1960: 73; Lepenies 1977). Fascism grew out of mass society because it epitomized a political order in which the mass-man did not have to accept anything exceptional. This was visible on the level of the leader, as '[t]ypical movements of mass-men' are 'directed, as all such are, by men who are mediocrities' (1960: 92). Hence, there was no talk in Ortega about a constitutive leader to whom the mass *looked up*. Rather, the mass wanted to see its own mediocrity mirrored in the leader, and fascism readily satisfied that desire.

Ortega did not fool himself into believing that the development he diagnosed could be reversed by advocating traditional moral standards. The only solution he envisioned to the identified problems consisted in sparking fresh life into the European mass mind through a transnational unification of Europe. Only such 'building-up of Europe into a great national State' would make Europe 'start to believe in herself again, and automatically to make demands on, to discipline herself' (1960: 186, 183). Political reform in other words had to drive morality forward. Ortega admitted that creating such a European project was no easy task, which the years following the publication of his book demonstrated all too forcefully.[3]

---

[2] Ortega particularly emphasized this achievement. Liberal democracy 'announces the determination to share existence with the enemy; more than that, with an enemy which is weak. It was incredible that the human species should have arrived at so noble an attitude, so paradoxical, so refined, so acrobatic, so anti-natural' (1960: 76).

[3] The Second World War did not really change Ortega's vision, though. He never tired of promoting the idea of a strongly integrated Europe (see Graham 2001: 316ff.).

Ortega's claim that progress in civilization and technical–material capacity forged a new mass subjectivity was echoed by scholars pursuing rather different theoretico-political agendas. One was Ernst Jünger who oscillated, as Peter Sloterdijk has put it, 'between fascism and stoic humanism' (1983: 818). In his 1932 book *Der Arbeiter*, Jünger argued that a new gestalt had emerged in the twentieth century, the 'absolute work character [*totaler Arbeitscharakter*]' (Jünger 1964: 110). According to Jünger, the work character had permeated the entire social body. It was everywhere to be found, not only in factories, as one would expect, but also in the home, in intellectual activity, etc. A crucial implication of the omnipresence of the work character was that it rendered all previous class distinctions obsolete. This seemed to resemble Ortega's observation of the mass-man expelling the select man and, indeed, Jünger's diagnosis suggested that the transformative role of the crowd had now been replaced by that of the new all-pervasive work character (see also Durst 2004: 147ff.; Günzel 2004: 129–31; Heidegren 1997: 140ff.). However, in Jünger's case the focus was not on whether the individual demanded more or less of him or herself. Also, Jünger's diagnosis was not one of decline. Quite the opposite, in what at times resembled Marinetti's futuristic programme, Jünger saw the technical mobilization of the work character as a means to revitalize Germany in that the work character could bridge technical and spiritual progress. Only thus would the blows administered to Germany during and after the First World War – and which Jünger knew from first-hand experience at the frontline – be remedied and the nation re-emerge as a strong collective entity (see also Durst 2004: 150).

Interesting in this context is the photographic essay, *Die veränderte Welt: Eine Bilderfibel unserer Zeit*, which Jünger published together with Edmund Schultz in 1933. Through a series of photographs, followed by brief texts, the book tried to convey a sense of the transformation modern society had undergone since the First World War. One of the sections of the book was devoted to the changed physiognomy of the crowd, another to the new physiognomy of the individual. While the photographs of the crowds did not suggest a uniform problematization of modern masses, the mass issue was addressed in the section on the individual's new expression. It was stated, for instance, that 'the decay of the individual physiognomy produces a strange world of marionettes' (Schultz and Jünger 1933: 54). The associated pictures alluded to masses (lines of women under cosmetic treatment, lines of mannequin legs, etc.). Yet the overall message was not one of deterioration. Thus, the final sections of the book celebrated, in text and images, mobilization and imperialism as paths to embark on (see also Heidegren 1997).

While Jünger pinned his faith on the mobilization of the work character as a means to install collective strength, Karl Jaspers formulated a critical diagnosis of society that culminated in a call for a specific kind of individual mobilization. In his 1931 book *Die geistige Situation der Zeit*, Jaspers recognized that, since especially the nineteenth century, rationalization, mechanization and technicization had improved living conditions, but they had also produced a veritable 'mass rule' (1999: 34). Although Jaspers characterized Le Bon's analysis of the crowd's impulsivity, suggestibility, intolerance, etc. as 'excellent' (1999: 35), his own focus was more general in character but still related to the de-individualization that Le Bon had analysed. Thus, in Jaspers' account, it made sense to speak of a mass 'when the individual only plays a role as countable', i.e. when the individual is merely conceived of as a number and no attention is paid to his or her personal qualities (1999: 35). Now, the real problem was, as Jaspers saw it, anticipating many Frankfurt School analyses (see Chapter 6), that '[t]he mass order produces a universal Dasein-*apparatus* which destroys the true human Dasein-*world*' (1999: 38, italics in original). In brief, the mass order and its technical '*Sachlichkeit*' (1999: 43, italics in original) was believed to threaten the real core of individual existence since, devastatingly, 'the masses isolate the individual as an atom who *has lost all desire for Dasein*' (I here follow the translation in Durst 2004: 144; Jaspers 1999: 36, italics added). Renouncing existence in this way was obviously too high a price to pay for the technical–material improvements.

Yet because of the undeniable achievements evoked by the age of mechanization Jaspers did not believe it was practically possible to reverse that process. The solution to the problems he observed should rather be found on a more individual level. What was needed, he argued, was a new appraisal and endorsement of being-oneself (*Selbstsein*) rather than betraying oneself by being mass – which was yet another call for resisting the de-individualizing tendencies of the mass. Jaspers trusted that a new solidarity would emerge among people if they were true to themselves and their Dasein (Jaspers 1999: 177–9). *Die geistige Situation der Zeit* was not very detailed about how to achieve this end, though (see also Durst 2004: 146). Jaspers was a bit more specific in his 1949 study *The Origin and Goal of History* where he acknowledged an explicit indebtedness to Ortega (1953: 281, n. 8). In this book Jaspers laid out a diagnostic characterization of his time in which the masses were described as 'a decisive factor' in modern life (1953: 127). Compared to the analysis in *Die geistige Situation der Zeit*, the 1949 book was even gloomier, marked as it was by the experiences of the Second World War. Jaspers clearly feared a return to the totalitarian mass events and now pinned his faith on popular education as a means to avoid mass rule. Popular education was a way of endowing people with skills previously reserved for the aristocracy, he believed, and thereby a way of counteracting mass tendencies. If society failed to make use of such measures, it 'may open the door to inconceivable horrors of abysmal mass existence' (1953: 130).

Mass versus elite: the problem of culture

It was briefly mentioned in Chapter 3 that simultaneous with the cultural revitalization that transpired during the Weimar era a much more dismal notion of cultural decline was being propagated by German social theorists. This pessimism had a long prehistory, and had been nourished in the late nineteenth century by Friedrich Nietzsche, who complained that the modern era of masses amounted to a veritable cultural disaster (for a discussion of Nietzsche's critique of mass culture, see Reschke 1992). This critique reverberated with increasing force after the First World War where a general atmosphere of despair reigned. Many scholars contributed with each brushstroke to the painting of a society in decay. Exponents of this pessimistic outlook included Alfred Weber and Georg Simmel, to mention but a couple. I discussed Simmel's praise of the announcement of the First World War in Chapter 3. It might be argued that the great prospects he attributed to the coming war should be understood against the backdrop of his lamentation of 'the tragedy of culture', which one of his investigations of contemporary culture proclaimed (see Frisby and Featherstone 1997: Part II). While the war was initially welcomed as a motor for cultural revitalization, all such hopes soon evaporated. Signs of this were visible in cultural–critical texts published after the war's devastating effects had crystallized (see also Peukert 1991).

One notable example of this was Oswald Spengler's *The Decline of the West* (first volume published in 1918, second volume in 1922), which alone by its title conveyed a sense of resignation. The book presented a grand philosophy, or rather morphology, of history which claimed that the West had culminated *culturally* and had now frozen as *civilization* which, for Spengler, was nothing but the 'fulfilment and finale of a culture' (1980a: 31). On Spengler's view, the central problem was that the creativity and vitality of the West had come to a halt; the West had reached the end phase of its cultural life cycle.[4] It is important to note that in the German context, the notion of culture had a different and deeper meaning than 'civilization'. While civilization was a sign of (technical) progress, in Germany it was 'regarded as useful, but superficial. Genuine values coincided with *Kultur*, not *Zivilisation*' (Turner 1992: xiv, italics in original). Significantly, moreover, while Spengler saw civilization as a frozen temporal successor to culture, the two terms were generally conceived of as (spatially) coexisting but mutually exclusive phenomena, with Germany representing culture, and France civilization (see e.g. Mann 1956).

The problem of culture was also central to Karl Mannheim who, like Ortega, observed an intimate connection between modern progress and totalitarianism. Born in Hungary and educated in Germany, Mannheim became an important scholar in the Weimar years. Similar to his contemporaries, revolution and growing national-socialist support impacted his personal and academic life. Mannheim experienced the revolution and inception of a *Räterepublik* in Hungary in 1919. When it soon collapsed, he was exiled in Germany, where, however, Nazi regulations eventually led to the suspension of Mannheim from the university, after which he emigrated to London. I mention this because at least the revolutionary experience could well have stirred an interest in crowds, such as it did for sociologists such as Geiger. Yet Mannheim's emphasis was closer to Ortega's diagnosis than to Geiger's programme. Similar to Ortega he believed that society was undergoing a severe transformation which was related to its mass character. And akin to his Spanish colleague, Mannheim analysed this in terms of an opposition between the mass and a select minority. However, whereas Ortega's investigation revolved around a moral problematization, Mannheim conceived of the tension between mass and elite as an essentially cultural problem. Moreover, Mannheim's approach was embedded much more strongly in ongoing sociological debates and drew explicitly on the existing semantics of crowds and masses.

Mannheim's problematization of mass society was put forward, for example, in a 1933 paper entitled 'The Democratization of Culture' (1992). The essay opened by stating that '[a] democratizing trend is

---

[4] Interestingly, the crowd topic played some role in Spengler's cultural–morphological outline. In a discussion of so-called microcosmic entities which, in Spengler's system, were attributed a force of tension that could move history, crowds were seen as '*inspired mass-units*' [*beseelte Masseneinheiten*] (1980b: 18, italics in original). Spengler, whose general intellectual influence came from Goethe and Nietzsche (Farrenkopf 2001: ch. 4; Spengler 1980a: 49, n. 1), described these crowds in a way that resembled classical crowd-psychological ideas.

our predestined fate, not only in politics, but also in intellectual and cultural life as a whole' (1992: 171). Mannheim admitted that this observation might have come as a surprise. After all it was written at a time when major European democracies were under pressure. But, Mannheim argued, this strain was to a large extent preconfigured by democracy itself. It was democracy itself which initiated the waxing totalitarian movements:

> Dictatorships can arise only in democracies; they are made possible by the greater fluidity introduced into political life by democracy. Dictatorship is not the antithesis of democracy; it represents one of the possible ways in which a democratic society may try to solve its problems. (1992: 171–2)

Mannheim's analysis centred on understanding the purported 'fluidity' of democracy and singled out two main features. The first was described in a manner which closely resembled Ortega's examination. Thus, with the advent of universal suffrage – i.e. the effective introduction of *mass democracy* – a new political body had been created which, for Mannheim, in an unfortunate way mixed adept elites and incompetent masses. 'At the early stages of democratization', he recalled, 'the political decision process was controlled by more or less homogeneous economic and intellectual élites' (1992: 172). That was the time of indirect action, as Ortega would put it, where democracy worked well (see also Mannheim 1992: 179). Yet the turn to universal suffrage had produced a wholly new situation, in which elite 'strata and groups whose political thinking is reality-oriented have to cooperate with, or contend with, people experiencing their first contact with politics – people whose thinking is still at a utopian stage ... This must lead to disturbances' (1992: 172). The basic problem was one of learning and of contemporaneousness; the masses had not yet developed a factual conception of politics, and their intervention in politics therefore constituted an obstacle to the implementation of the elite's rational decisions.[5]

This touched upon the second element of the democratic fluidity. Referring to Max Scheler, Mannheim complained that the 'democracy of Reason', which the elite-driven model of indirect democracy stood for, had now been turned into a 'democracy of Impulse', i.e. 'an organ of

---

[5] In Mannheim's own words, '[t]he experiments in adult education throw some light on the senseless way in which people behave in politics. Instead of finding a facile explanation in Le Bon's popular psychology of crowd behaviour, it is wiser to suggest that people who have had no chance of political responsibility are bound to behave foolishly until they have gradually obtained some experience of politics and have learnt to act like responsible adults' (1940: 261–2). While Mannheim thus agreed with Le Bon that the popular masses were foolish, he trusted they could improve through education and experience.

the uninhibited expression of momentary emotional impulses' (1992: 173). This alleged infection of democracy by irrational feelings corresponded to a massification of traits usually ascribed to crowds.

The discussion of rationality (reason) and irrationality (impulses) was further developed in Mannheim's *Mensch und Gesellschaft im Zeitalter des Umbaus* (1935), a book that was considerably expanded in the subsequent English version, *Man and Society in an Age of Reconstruction* (1940), to which I refer in the following. In this book Mannheim made several important points. First, he agreed with Le Bon that in crowds, people are subjected to 'suggestions and contagions' (1940: 61).[6] However, the irrationality attributed to crowds of co-present individuals – an irrationality which resulted from the suggestions – need not necessarily encompass all members of society. One had, in other words, to distinguish between the crowd and the mass. Only the former was inherently irrational, Mannheim believed, although, as the abovementioned problematization of the democracy of impulse made clear, the irrationality could in fact be diffused from crowd to mass. Second, and somewhat surprisingly in the light of the problematization of impulse, Mannheim asserted that irrationality need not be harmful per se. Irrationality and ecstasy were important for the 'pure élan' and 'joy of living' in society and should therefore be counted among the 'most valuable' social phenomena (1940: 62). While irrationality as such was not a problem, Mannheim strongly warned against one particular diffusion of irrationality, namely the dissemination of irrationality into the sphere of politics, a sphere which he thought should be reserved for rationality. Yet precisely this diffusion of irrationality into the political realm had occurred with the advent of modern mass democracy where the rational elites were supplanted by the irrational masses.

Mannheim added further dimensions to the analysis of elites and intellectuals in his other work (e.g. 1991: 136–46), and linked this explicitly to the problem of mass society in articles such as 'The Crisis of Culture in the Era of Mass-Democracies and Autarchies' (1934).[7] In this article, which contrary to the 1933 paper contained explicit references to Le Bon and Sighele and to the Weimar crowd debates (1934: 125, n. 1), Mannheim highlighted several problems relating to elites in mass society. For example, he posited that the exclusiveness of elites had been undermined. The elites no longer constituted

---

[6] According to the German version of the book, these suggestions and contagions were 'empirically provable' (1935: 39).

[7] This paper was later included as a chapter in *Mensch und Gesellschaft im Zeitalter des Umbaus* (1935).

the centre from which new formative ideas emerged and radiated. They merely offered impulses that were seen by the masses as being on a par with other impulses. As Mannheim put it, '[t]he new impulses are snapped up by the indiscriminate masses just *as* impulses, that is, in their still immature form, and then flicker away like all other stimuli that flit about in the crowd' (1934: 111, italics in original). Mannheim considered this erosion of the elites' role to be a major problem. His conception of society was so indebted to an idea of intellectual leadership that he believed the destruction of elite exclusiveness would entail a demand for authoritarian leadership. Accordingly, the suspension of the exclusiveness of elites was said to generate widespread uncertainty:

This general uncertainty, which surrounds all æsthetic, moral, and political judgments, itself provokes the reaction of dictatorial solutions. The majority of individuals cannot bear this large variety of possible viewpoints and opinions, and they therefore long for some form of resolute leadership. (1934: 111)

In a word, Mannheim suggested that the suspension of traditional elite leadership would disintegrate society and produce, as a psychological reaction, a demand for strong, perhaps even totalitarian, leadership.

It was stated above that Mannheim formulated his concerns as a cultural problematization. As the titles of his essays suggest, it was not merely the political realm that was affected and exposed to grave transformations with the advent of masses and democratization. So was, on a deeper level, culture as such. Investigating the 'fundamental, structural differences between aristocratic and democratic cultures' was, therefore, the key sociological task Mannheim set himself (1992: 175). To this end, he examined the cultural differences between two characters, that of the aristocratic individual and that of the democratic individual. According to Mannheim, the former's cultural ideal was one of humanism, non-specialization, 'ecstasy' and 'self-distantiation' (1992: 231, 232), comparable to Ortega's reference to the select individual's submission to standards beyond him or herself. With the advent of the modern, fully democratized society, a new character type had emerged. This democratic individual's cultural ideals were 'work-oriented', emphasized specialization and put no value on self-distantiation (1992: 235).

Interestingly, Mannheim was not entirely sceptical about the emergence of the new society and its character type (see also 1934: 125; 1939: 359). Even if the democratic individual did not yet value the ecstasy that the elite (and Mannheim) endorsed, some 'potentialities inherent in the democratic approach' could actually be identified that would 'appear to be eventually conducive to a new type of "ecstasy" and of true "civilization"' (1992: 240). In analysing these potentialities Mannheim arrived at a much more positive account of mass democracy than many of his other investigations suggested. Most significantly, he argued that 'democratization involves not only a danger, but also, and more importantly, *a supreme opportunity*', not least with respect to the relations between individuals (1992: 242, italics added). This rested on the potential of democratization to undermine previous social distances. All vertical distances between people, i.e. distances in rank, status, etc., formed obstacles to a 'purely "existential" relationship' (1992: 243). Undermining such distances would pave the way for pure social relationships where people could '"love" or "hate" the other as a person, irrespective of any social mask he may wear' (1992: 242). Crucially, however, in order to realize this (quasi-Whitmanesque) potential – this ecstasy, as it were – it was mandatory that vertical (aristocratic) distances not simply be substituted by alternative, horizontal ones:

> The true potentialities inherent in democratization are not yet realized when we put *horizontal* social relationships in the places of *vertical* ones in expressing our person-to-person attitudes and feelings. The real opportunity that democratization gives us consists in being able to transcend *all* social categories and experience love as a purely personal and existential matter. (1992: 243–4, italics in original)

Mannheim was not particularly specific on how to realize this positive potential, which after all assumed a rather exceptional status in his analyses of democracy. He had more to offer in terms of how to deal with the negative problems posed by mass democracy. Like Jaspers and Ortega, Mannheim was well aware that a solution to the problems of democratic culture could not consist in reverting to its aristocratic precursor. In that sense the developments were irreversible; there was no turning back from universal suffrage, for instance. Instead Mannheim suggested a threefold strategy consisting of communitarian revitalization, enlightenment/education and planning, which in conjunction should endow the democratic culture with the virtues of aristocratic culture. What the first part of this strategy concerned, 'numerous small communities' had to be created:

> In this way, the large numbers of people who participate in the political life of fully developed democracy would become rounded individuals, as were the responsible élite members at the stage of incomplete democracy. If these communities of autonomous individuals could achieve a balance among themselves, self-neutralization [of individual autonomy] would gradually recede and disappear. We may look towards the emergence of such a higher type of *fully democratized but no longer massified society* as an ideal. (1992: 196–7, italics added)

This was essentially a socio-spatial strategy which, not too different from Ross' progressive ideals, aimed to shield people from the dangers of massification lurking in the metropolises. If only the cities be broken up in smaller parts, i.e. if only the urban atmosphere be replaced with an (ultimately pre-modern) community order, then its mass effects would no longer dominate. In addition to this strategy, which prescribed a segmentation of the population (compare Foucault 1977: 198), Mannheim recommended enlightenment practices. 'Educating the mass in reality-oriented ways of thinking' was seen as key to teaching the democratic individual about the existence of competing opinions; and such mass awareness of 'the coexistence of rival schools of thought in itself tends to slough off whatever is extreme, one-sided and irrational in each of them' (1992: 199). In an essay entitled 'Mass Education and Group Analysis' (1939), Mannheim elaborated on how to achieve this enlightenment through education, arguing that 'all the competent agencies in our democratic societies, such as churches, schools and social services, must examine our moral standards more scientifically' (1939: 337).[8] Crowd psychology was allocated an important role in this scientific foundation: 'No educational system is able to maintain emotional stability and mental integrity unless it can hold in check the social influences which disorganize community life, and unless it knows something of the psychological and social explanations of crowd behaviour' (1939: 332). A part of the educational strategy also aimed at increasing articulation. Thus, Mannheim asserted, crowd theory had demonstrated that 'the same crowd of people will react differently according as it is organized and articulated in organic groups or appears simply as an inarticulate mass' (1934: 125). The former kind of organized entity was what society should aim to create, Mannheim argued (basically revisiting the Weimar sociologists' semantics of crowds and groups), since the 'weaknesses and shortcomings with which the masses are popularly credited' were 'attributable only to the inarticulate masses' (1934: 125; 1939: 362–3; 1997: 93).

---

[8] Specifically, Mannheim suggested so-called 'group analysis' as a new educational approach to be diffused among these agencies. This was conceived of as a supplement to traditional psychoanalytical treatment. Rather than being concerned with the isolated individual, it focused on the group and group interaction in order to provide a 'more conscious use of social stimulation for improving the individual' (1939: 358). According to Mannheim, the fundamental idea of this kind of group analysis was well known: 'I am sure everyone of us has, at some time or other, had similar experiences of collective release either through attending well directed meetings on sexual reform or other methods of public enlightenment' (1939: 358). I will return to the issue of sexual reform in the discussion of Wilhelm Reich in Chapter 6.

As mentioned above, the final dimension of Mannheim's attempt to solve the problems of mass democracy consisted in an emphatic call for a more deep-seated general (rational) planning of society.[9] Mannheim strongly believed in the possibility of using 'Planning as the Rational Mastery of the Irrational', as the title of a subsection in *Man and Society in an Age of Reconstruction* had it (1940: 265). One of the crucial goals of such a planning strategy was to transform unorganized (irrational) crowd behaviour into organized (rational) group behaviour (1940: 288–9). This could be achieved, he posited, through various means of social control, bureaucracy and parliamentary reform. It would go too far to discuss these suggestions here. The crucial point for now is that Mannheim was firmly convinced that the problems attributed to mass society as well as 'the uncontrolled eruption of crowd behavior', which he characterized as 'the great danger in society', could and should ultimately be handled by rational means. The underlying notion was that, while he at times acknowledged the crowd's positive (vital) and even transformative potentialities (1940: 289), crowd and mass remained problematic phenomena in Mannheim's view; and they did so because they signalled a threat to culture.

The politics of mass society

I have focused on Ortega and Mannheim above, but as already intimated, many other scholars problematized mass society. One example, from the domain of cultural critique, is Arnold Gehlen whose *Man in the Age of Technology*, originally published in 1949 under a different title and then republished in revised form in 1957, presented a critical account of the individual in the modern industrial society (1980).[10] In this book Gehlen referred affirmatively to Ortega's diagnosis of *The Revolt of the Masses*, and accepted, for example, the basic distinction between mass and elite. Gehlen's conservative philosophical anthropology conceived of this opposition in a slightly different way, though. Drawing on Max Scheler's notion of '"pleonexia", signifying simultaneously greed, arrogance, and ambition for power', Gehlen argued that the mass could be characterized by this pleonexia, which was purportedly 'a most

---

[9] Mannheim approached this issue with ever greater emphasis in the course of time, as is visible from the development from the publication of *Mensch und Gesellschaft im Zeitalter des Umbaus* in 1935 to *Man and Society in an Age of Reconstruction* in 1940. During these five years the discussion of planning in the book(s) expanded significantly.

[10] Other contributions along this line included, as Lepenies (1977) notes, Günther Anders' *Die Antiquiertheit des Menschen* (1956, 1987) and Hans Freyer's *Theorie des gegenwärtigen Zeitalters* (1955).

useful term for the social-psychological characterization of our age' (1980: 109). 'Conversely whoever exhibits self-discipline, self-control, whoever possesses detachment and a view of how to transcend himself, belongs to the elite' (1980: 109; the reference to self-discipline and self-control evoked a broader agenda of asceticism, which cannot be touched upon in the present context; see instead Heidegren 2002: 138–9). The societal problem was, Gehlen asserted, that it was hardly possible any more to count on elites; they were hardly any 'defense against the relapse into barbarism' (1980: 158; see also Heidegren 2002; Lepenies 1977).

Compared to Ortega and Mannheim, whose contributions to crowd and mass semantics were written at a time when the totalitarian developments in Europe were unfolding or just about to escalate, Gehlen had a greater temporal distance to the events. This also applied to scholars such as Hannah Arendt who, however, did not subscribe to Ortega and Mannheim's analytical horizon. Like Mannheim, Arendt had fled the Nazi regime. In 1941, she ended up in New York and became part of an exiled academic environment which, due to personal experiences, was passionately interested in understanding the dynamics of crowds, masses and totalitarianism. Arendt's key contribution to this discussion was presented in her voluminous study *The Origins of Totalitarianism* (1951). The book was divided into three parts, devoted to anti-Semitism, imperialism and totalitarianism, respectively.

Similar to Ortega and Mannheim, Arendt described the totalitarian society as one in which previous class structures had vanished. In her account this was a matter of a collapse of a class structure where one's birth determined one's social position as well as political interests. Akin to especially Ortega, Arendt characterized this collapse as a recent phenomenon that had followed in the wake of the First World War (1951: 321). 'In this atmosphere of the breakdown of class society the psychology of the European mass man developed', Arendt wrote, mentioning Le Bon as one of the scholars who had predicted the new era (1951: 309, 310, n. 15a). According to Arendt, one of the most important features of the mass individual was his or her purported loneliness, which was a corollary of the collapse of the class structure:

the masses grew out of the fragments of a highly atomized society whose competitive structure and concomitant loneliness of the individual had been held in check only through membership in a class. The chief characteristic of the mass man is not brutality and backwardness, but his isolation and lack of normal social relationships. (1951: 310)

This loneliness was so crucial to the functioning of totalitarianism, Arendt argued, that where atomization had not yet materialized as a natural outcome of the classless society, as in Germany before Hitler's ascent to power, it had to be fabricated politically (she referred to Stalin and his 'preparation' of Russia for totalitarian rule as a case in point; see 1951: 313–16). Arendt also stressed another precondition for totalitarianism, namely number. Only in countries with 'enough human material' and where 'great masses are superfluous or can be spared without disastrous results of depopulation is totalitarian rule … at all possible' (1951: 304, 305). While this seemed to exclude a number of smaller countries from the danger of totalitarianism, the recent significant population increases that Ortega had noted in his demographic observations, and which also Arendt pointed to, suggested that an 'excess' of human material, as it were, was now widely available.

Arendt's problematization of totalitarianism mainly revolved around Hitler's and to a lesser extent Stalin's regimes. Several other scholars excavated the roots of totalitarianism. Two such scholars were William Kornhauser and Emil Lederer. Each in his fashion, Kornhauser and Lederer stood on the shoulders of Arendt, Mannheim and Ortega, although their main concern was neither with the moral state of mass society nor with its cultural fabric. However, they shared with this trio an interest in political matters, particularly with respect to the consequences of the 'state of the masses', as Lederer put it.

Similar to the case of Mannheim, Arendt and many other European scholars, the rise of the Nazi regime forced Lederer to flee from Germany in 1933. He emigrated to the USA where he played an important role in establishing the European research community at the New School for Social Research in New York.[11] Lederer's key contribution to the development of crowd semantics, his book *State of the Masses: The Threat of the Classless Society*, was completed shortly before he died in 1939 and published in 1940 (1967). In the introduction to the book Lederer presented modern dictatorship as his major research problem. The book's central objective was to explain the rise of modern dictatorship as the result of a mass-related suspension of democracy, but the book also addressed how democratic societies might avoid the trap of dictatorship, i.e. totalitarianism. The fundamental problem Lederer diagnosed was structurally similar to what Ortega and Mannheim problematized. They were concerned with the annulment of the distinction between elite and mass;

---

[11] For a discussion of Lederer's life and work, see Krohn (1995).

Lederer, on his side, argued for the societal need for stratification, although not conceived in terms of elite and mass, but rather as a differentiation into social classes or social groups. According to Lederer, a democratic society is per definition a stratified society, namely one whose dynamics are based on the ability of opposite groups to fight for their interests. This constituted the problem which modern dictatorship posed to society: it had eliminated any opposition and generalized in a homogenizing manner the emotions of the mass.

This had two dimensions. First, Lederer argued along with classical crowd semantics that crowds and masses are uniform entities, i.e. entities in which 'social stratification is effaced or at least blurred' (1967: 31). It is worth noting here that Lederer did not distinguish between crowd and mass, but treated the two synonymously. For example, he stated that, 'I understand by a mass or a crowd a great number of people who are inwardly united so that they feel and may possibly act as a unity' (1967: 30). Moreover, he accepted Le Bon's description of the crowd as a destructive, irrational and non-reflective entity. In previous times, Lederer added, such crowds had appeared in history as temporary occurrences in, for example, revolutions. But, and this was the second dimension, under the modern dictatorship the masses were no longer ephemeral incidents; they had become institutionalized, 'and as institutionalized masses they sweep the dictator into power and keep him in power' (1967: 18).[12] This was precisely the state of the masses, which the title of the book referred to: the masses had been elevated and institutionalized in the totalitarian organization of the dictatorial state, and this had eliminated an overt – and essentially democratic – struggle between classes. In Lederer's own words:

The totalitarian state is the state of the masses ... It is bound to change everything. It has built up a spirit in accordance with the mass-movement: it destroys any potential source of political opposition, and it establishes a center of power which is above and beyond any attack. (1967: 45–6)

This state of the masses amounted to a political institutionalization of the crowd's irrationality. Lederer did not believe that irrationality could be entirely excluded from the political realm. He agreed with Graham

---

[12] According to Lederer, the crowds were mobilized in modern society through the press and mass media propaganda. This allowed for the constitution of what Lederer called 'abstract masses', i.e. crowds that are not physically co-present but who owe their (abstract) unity to some mediator, such as in particular the radio (1967: 43–4). Lederer paid close attention to propaganda, which he described as 'the main means by which crowds are kept together and made to last over a longer period' (1967: 235).

Wallas' observation that irrationality was an integral part of the political (Lederer 1967: 29, n. 1). Still, irrationality could be curbed, but this required the kind of stratification which was undermined by totalitarianism. In the words of Lederer, 'as long as the community is stratified, emotions will be restricted and balanced by arguments, without regard to the political system under which the community lives' (1967: 29). This was essentially a call for plurality; democracy was only possible, in Lederer's eyes, if stratification could be maintained and several groups could make their voice heard.[13] Only thus could democracies avoid sliding into dictatorship.

The pluralism which was implicit in Lederer's position would later form a more explicit concern for William Kornhauser in his investigation *The Politics of Mass Society* (1960). Kornhauser argued that 'insofar as a society is a *mass society*, it will be vulnerable to political movements destructive of liberal democratic institutions; while insofar as a society is *pluralist*, these institutions will be strong' (1960: 7, italics in original). What constituted a mass society in Kornhauser's eyes? In order to arrive at a definition he engaged in a discussion of existing theories on mass society and delineated two major positions, namely a so-called aristocratic and a democratic one. The former, represented by scholars such as Le Bon, Lippmann, Mannheim and Ortega, conceived of mass society as a society in which previous elite dominance had disappeared, hence preparing the way for the rule by unqualified individuals. The democratic viewpoint was no less critical than the aristocratic one, but merely articulated its critique from a different angle. Thus, stated Kornhauser, the democratic concern was not with the former non-elites' ascent to power, but rather with how the 'non-elites may be shielded from the domination by elites' (1960: 30). More specifically, the democratic critique observed an increasing atomization in modern society which was believed to make individuals more susceptible to (totalitarian) elite rule. Kornhauser associated the democratic position with the work of Arendt and Lederer, but the theories to be discussed in Chapter 6 are also variants of the democratic critique of mass society.

Although, for Kornhauser, both positions contained valuable insights, neither the aristocratic nor the democratic viewpoints were fully adequate. The problem with the aristocratic position was, on Kornhauser's view, that it did not take into account the dynamics of the non-

---

[13] This is also why Lederer, despite his socialist sympathies, did not believe in a classless society. Such a society would entail the same problems as totalitarian dictatorships: '[t]he idea of a classless or of an unstratified society is empty. It lacks the tension which is life' (1967: 142).

elites, i.e. the masses. In particular, it could not explain why some parts of the mass might be more prone than others to engage in mass action. Precisely this could be explained by the democratic position with its reference to how atomization may render the masses more liable to be mobilized by the elites. Yet, complained Kornhauser, the democratic position tended to ignore the need for accessible elites, i.e. it disregarded that some elite was necessary in order to mobilize the mass, and this elite would often arise from the mass itself. On the basis of his critical discussion of aristocratic and democratic theories of mass society, Kornhauser arrived at his own position which combined elements from both perspectives. According to Kornhauser's definition, then, '[m]ass society *is a social system in which elites are readily accessible to influence by non-elites and non-elites are readily available for mobilization by elites*' (1960: 39, italics in original).

The emphasis on the accessibility of elites and the availability of non-elites enabled Kornhauser to move closer towards his hypothesis that mass society and pluralist society were radically different. By distinguishing between low–high accessibility of elites and low–high availability of non-elites, he presented a typology of four different ideal types of society (Kornhauser 1960: 40–3). First, in 'communal society' there is a low accessibility of elites (elites are selected according to traditions) as well as a low availability of non-elites (people are bound by kinship). Second, 'pluralist society' is characterized by a high accessibility of elites since many diverse groups may make their voice heard. Yet there is low availability of non-elites because people are divided in autonomous groups and therefore not susceptible to totalitarian rule. In 'mass society', by contrast, there is, as the above-cited definition implied, both a high accessibility of elites and a high availability of non-elites, 'in that there is a paucity of independent groups between the state and the family to protect either elites or non-elites from manipulation and mobilization by the other' (1960: 41). Finally, in 'totalitarian society' the accessibility of elites is low (ensured by a monopoly of power), whereas the availability of non-elites is high – 'people lack all those independent social formations that could serve as a basis of resistance to the elite' (1960: 41).

Importantly, this fourfold separation suggested that mass society should not be equated with totalitarian society. The two were seen as distinct even if mass society might have a propensity to move in a totalitarian direction. This propensity was due to the psychological constitution of mass individuals, argued Kornhauser. Thus, the atomization attributed to mass society was believed to lead to alienation and anxiety which, in turn, produced a high mass suggestibility:

For the individual who lacks a firm conception of himself and confidence in himself does not possess the basis for strong control over himself, and therefore is highly *suggestible* to appeals emanating from remote places. Members of elites as well as non-elites may become self-alienated and suggestible, with the consequence that they are readily attracted to mass movements. (1960: 108, italics in original)

Precisely this process might end in totalitarian aspirations, Kornhauser cautioned, namely if the mass individual submits completely to the group and to the elite that rules it. 'That is to say that whereas the mass man is not totalitarian, he readily may become so' (1960: 112).

A great part of Kornhauser's book was devoted to studying the composition and extension of mass movements in contemporary society. For this purpose he drew on statistical observations from a number of countries. On the basis of this information, he argued that especially people from the lower social strata were likely to be attracted by mass movements. More specifically, he contended, the majority of those who are part of mass movements 'will be found in those sections of society that have the fewest ties to the social order', i.e. among those individuals 'who have the fewest opportunities to participate in the formal and informal life of the community' (1960: 212).[14] This was yet another indicator of the central importance Kornhauser ascribed to alienation in mass society. He defined social alienation as 'the distance between the individual and his society' (1960: 237), and the stronger the social ties were, the smaller this distance (and hence the alienation) would be. This observation pointed to some of the political implications of Kornhauser's analysis: in order to safeguard society against anti-democratic mass politics, measures were needed that would strengthen social ties.[15] This is where pluralism became important, because 'a system of social checks and balances among a plurality of diverse groups operates to protect elites as well as non-elites' (1960: 78). That is, only by securing the subsistence of a great number of groups to mediate between individual and family, on the one hand, and state and society, on the other, was democracy viable. Similar to Lederer, in other words, Kornhauser argued that democracy is constituted on a pluralist foundation. But in contrast to Lederer,

---

[14] For example, unskilled workers were said to be more prone to be part of mass movements than skilled workers; so were unemployed as compared to employed people.
[15] The anti-democratic element was emphasized by Kornhauser in a passage that is worth quoting at length: 'Mass politics occurs when large numbers of people engage in political activity outside of the procedures and rules instituted by a society to govern political action. Mass politics in democratic society therefore is anti-democratic, since it contravenes the constitutional order. The extreme case of mass politics is the totalitarian movement, notably communism and fascism. Less extreme examples of mass politics are McCarthyism and Poujadism' (1960: 227).

Kornhauser did not merely argue for the need for stratification. Rather he made an emphatic call for pluralism and saw a prosperous group life as a way of fighting social alienation and thereby mass movements.

Kornhauser's study is important for several reasons. One is the just-mentioned argument that pluralism may be seen as a means to combat mass tendencies. Another relates to the underlying analyses of social structures and personality profiles that guided his investigation. While Mannheim and Ortega had a keen focus on the characterological shape of 'mass man', they did not develop broader analyses of the dynamics of various societal strata. Lederer did discuss the emergence of new middle classes and their importance for the rise of fascism in Germany (see 1967: 51), but Kornhauser was much more systematic, and also more inclusive in terms of the dimensions he considered. In order to determine the social and psychological background of mass society, he drew heavily on the work of Theodor Adorno, Erich Fromm but also on David Riesman, all of whom will be discussed in Chapter 6. Interestingly, moreover, in a certain sense Kornhauser continued in the footsteps of the Park tradition.[16] He thus asserted that contemporary society was not merely one of social alienation but also one of 'enhanced opportunities for the creation of new forms of association' (1960: 237). In other words, despite all shortcomings, modern society should not be diagnosed in entirely gloomy terms; it also contained emancipatory possibilities, including 'a variety of contacts and experiences that broaden social horizons and the range of social participation' (1960: 237–8). This was an important corrective to the negative image of modern mass society as outlined by especially Ortega, and to a lesser extent Mannheim.

Criticizing mass semantics

Although the mass society semantics was very prominent in the time-span between 1930 and 1960, it was not unanimously accepted. One critique of the notion of mass society was articulated by Theodor Geiger who, in the aftermath of the Second World War, revised his position from *Die Masse und ihre Aktion* (I shall discuss other critical positions in the next chapter). In this early book he had contributed to crowd semantics by arguing that the revolutionary crowd might reconcile social

---

[16] In spite of this inspiration Park was only mentioned once in Kornhauser's book, and only with a brief reference to some of his work on urbanization (1960: 143, n. 15). Blumer played a greater role and his work on collective behaviour was cited positively on more occasions.

tensions and therefore should not be dismissed morally. In his post-war work, especially in the article 'Die Legende von der Massengesellschaft' (1950/51) and in the book *Die Gesellschaft zwischen Pathos and Nüchternheit* (1960), Geiger became increasingly critical of crowd and not least mass semantics. Specifically, he refuted the cultural–critical perspective of Mannheim, Ortega, Spengler and others, which stated that contemporary society was in decay and that civilization was being replaced by an anonymous, passive and atomized mass society. On Geiger's view, this was no satisfactory diagnosis of modern society, partly because it exaggerated the mass character, and partly because it ignored tendencies working in opposite directions (Geiger pointed to increasing intimacy in the private sphere as one trend that opposed the purported massification of public life; see 1950/51: 309–10). More importantly, Geiger not only rejected the contemporary diagnosis offered by mass society theory, he also called into question the epochal rupture it assumed. In particular, he declined what he considered the underlying claim of the cultural-critical proponents of the theory of mass society, namely that mass society was characterized by undermining previous community (*Gemeinschaft*) structures. In Geiger's eyes, this transformative thesis rested on a hopelessly romantic account of the value and predominance of communities (1950/51: 305; 1960: 9). No less romantic was the associated call for revitalizing the community which, he believed, was implicitly or explicitly celebrated as the main remedy of the identified calamities. It might be argued that this communitarian trait was not as dominant in the case of Ortega as in that of Mannheim who had in fact proposed a community strategy as a partial solution to the perils of mass society. However, for present purposes it matters little that Geiger might have painted with a broad brush here since I am merely interested in his problematization, whether or not it was entirely fair.

Geiger countered the cultural critics by arguing that in modern society, the problem is not too little community. Rather there may in fact be too much of it, and he therefore made 'a plea for the *emancipation of the individual from the community*, i.e. for his or her liberation from certain forms of emotional collectivism' (1960: 87–8, italics in original). Geiger delineated two types of collective feelings, corresponding to what he termed primary and secondary groups. In primary groups, where people are intimately associated, collective feelings take the form of sympathy. In a modern social order characterized by functional differentiation and distant social relations (secondary groups), by contrast, sympathy cannot be a dominant force. Here common feelings are expressed by or mediated through the pathos of a common object. What associates people in secondary groups is, in other words, not inter-human sympathy but rather a shared, impersonal passion for the same idea, value, etc. (1960: 96–8).

Geiger offered an in-depth analysis of two such feelings, nationalism and class consciousness, but he also furnished a more principal account of what he considered the main perils posed by communal feelings in modern society. First, he said, all communal pathos is rooted in a particular conception of values. For example, in the case of nationalism, the nation in question is ascribed a higher value than other nations. Second, every value community is fundamentally antagonistically organized, for there is no value, Geiger believed, that is not defined in opposition to other values (1960: 137). Amalgamating on the basis of class consciousness only makes sense when assuming the existence of classes that are opposed to one another.

Geiger's critical position towards collective feelings of pathos followed from these two points. He argued that no value community, no *Gemeinschaft* of pathos, were possible which was not essentially hostile to values that differed from its own. This inherent aggressiveness, this '[v]alue pathos, intensified in separated fronts, becomes a dreadful explosive, a power that destroys society' (1960: 138). Indeed, Geiger warned, '[v]alue community means running around in a black or brown shirt, with a red tie or in uniform' (1960: 142). Against this background, Geiger refused the idea that modern (mass) society must revive communal bonds. This was not only a romantic and sentimental demand, he contended, but a highly dangerous one. On Geiger's analysis, therefore, the solutions proposed by Mannheim, Ortega, etc. would not contribute to minimizing totalitarian tendencies. Quite the opposite, the promotion of communitarian ideals and forms of organization would only enhance the totalitarian impulses they were invented to hold in check.

The emphatic critique of promoting any community of pathos provides an interesting elaboration of Geiger's early theory of revolutionary crowds. While the two analyses took the same point of departure – in the modern, functionally differentiated society there is no longer any value community that unites the entire society – they reached rather different conclusions. *Die Masse und ihre Aktion* was a 'cold' sociological analysis of the social conditions of the emergence and organization of revolutionary crowds. *Die Gesellschaft zwischen Pathos and Nüchternheit*, by contrast, had a clear post-Hitler tone to it and was obsessed by arguing against any tendency towards repeating this dreadful part of history. This difference was expressed most markedly in the evaluation of communal bonds. Thus in the former study Geiger was well aware that the We of the crowd was antagonistically defined and that it operated destructively.

Still he demonstrated – and this was a significant contribution compared to most existing theories on the subject – the revolutionary crowd might be 'historically necessary' (1987: 163). In the latter book, by contrast, Geiger completely denied attributing to the communal pathos (the We of the crowds) any positive social or historical function. As a result he effectively revised his own previous suggestion that the crowd might have a creative value because of its ability to strengthen the community ties in modern society.

Another elaboration regarded the practical solutions for how to deal with and avoid destructive collective tendencies in society. The structural framework of the early crowd book did not suggest how the formation of crowds could be prevented. Since the very organization of modern society was, allegedly, the reason why crowds came into existence, this hardly left any options for practical intervention other than – revolution. Contrary to this, the 1960 book suggested a concrete solution, namely the 'intellectualization of the people' (1960: 149). This proposal would leave the social structure intact and aim, so to speak, to upgrade the conceptual life of individuals so as to make it fit to the modern conditions. However, this Geigerean appeal to rationalism was only scantly developed, and I shall therefore pay no further attention to it.

At first sight, it might appear that the mass society semantics painted a more optimistic picture of modern society than what Le Bon's prophecy of the era of violent, semi-revolutionary crowds entailed. After all, Mannheim, Ortega, etc. were not primarily concerned with screaming crowds running amok in the streets. On closer inspection, however, the notion of mass society was far gloomier than the image conveyed by Le Bon. While Le Bon's theorization by and large evoked the notion of the crowd of the street (although also juries and parliaments were conceived of in crowd terms), the semantics of mass society suggested that modern society did not merely give way to a series of more or less coincidental eruptions of crowd violence. Rather, the utterly discomforting fact of modern society was that its alleged progress and technical advancement effected a deep transformation of the modern subject, of class structures and of the socio-cultural edifice that was seen as a formative basis for both individuals and society. Everything separating up from down and good from bad was eroding. This blurring of differences forged a new subject, the mass individual, it was contended. And this individual was born with a disposition to totalitarianism. In fact, whereas one could strive to resist the seductive–hypnotic force of the crowd, the mass society did not permit any outside. Everybody was captured by the development.

To be sure, the semantic branches studied in this chapter had different accents, and they only constitute a fraction of the sociological work that problematized mass society. As the next chapter will show, a series of alternative positions can be identified which, too, centred on the connection between mass society and totalitarianism. While indeed certain overlaps can be detected between the semantic plateaus examined in the present and the next chapter, some key differences are also visible. Most importantly, I claim, the theories discussed above pivoted around the collapse of class differences, whether conceived as elite/mass or as social stratification more broadly. Also, they tended to respond to developments of the early twentieth century, although it was modern society as such that formed the target of much of the work. Chapter 6, on the other hand, is characterized by a somewhat different temporal horizon, as the emphasis here is mainly on Hitlerism and how the totalitarian dynamics underpinning his rise to power might creep into other societies. Moreover, the theories to be examined in the next chapter tended to employ psychoanalytical inventory in their explanatory apparatuses.

6 Reactions to totalitarianism: new fusions of sociological and psychological thinking

The investigations of totalitarianism that were outlined in the previous chapter were based on the diagnosis of a transformation of society into a mass society, with alleged consequences for morality, culture, etc. The explanatory scheme of this problematization revolved around the (corroding) distinction between elites and non-elites, although the two sides of the distinction were labelled differently by different scholars. Even if this mass society was believed to display, on a grand societal scale, key features traditionally associated with co-present crowds, a profound explanatory transition had taken place where neither the suggestion doctrine nor subsequent Freudian alternatives figured centrally in this semantics of mass society. This distance to psychological understandings was not univocal, however. As the present chapter demonstrates, a plethora of analyses mushroomed from the 1930s onwards that tried to grasp mass society and its inherent totalitarian traits on the basis of a synthesis of sociological and psychoanalytical approaches. Similar to Chapter 5, I locate the most important examples of this semantic plateau in German and US American theories, but once again, national borders play a rather indeterminate (or at least, indeterminable) role since many of the German scholars emigrated to the USA to flee National Socialism.

The chapter opens with a discussion of Wilhelm Reich's work. Reich presented one of the most comprehensive attempts to combine sociological and psychoanalytical insights into an explanatory framework that tried to account for the rise of fascism; more decisively, Reich attempted to explain why people *desired* totalitarianism. While Reich's work was firmly (but controversially) planted in Marxism and psychoanalysis, Hermann Broch espoused a much more autonomous, or idiosyncratic, theoretical horizon, which was undoubtedly related to existing traditions, but also differed profoundly from these. I have included Broch's theory of mass aberration in this chapter for two reasons. First of all, it remains one of the most comprehensive contributions to the history of crowd semantics. Second, and more importantly, it contained a much more practical political superstructure than most other work in this field.

Broch was not content with understanding the social and psychological reasons for totalitarianism; he was equally absorbed in reflections on what political and legal structures might prevent new totalitarian mass delusions in the future.

For reasons I shall only briefly speculate about, Broch's work hardly left any traces in sociological crowd or mass semantics. A much more influential, and also collective, effort was that of the Frankfurt School whose work will constitute the bulk of this chapter. Specifically, I shall attend to the analyses of mass society put forward by Erich Fromm, Siegfried Kracauer, Theodor W. Adorno and Max Horkheimer. Although their approaches to the question of mass society and totalitarianism had different accents, they united in a general critique of mass society and mass culture as restraining freedom and autonomy and leading to proto-totalitarian, anti-democratic attitudes.

The Frankfurt School left a lasting imprint on European and American sociology. But the particular ties between social and psychoanalytical theory, which the School established in the 1930s and 1940s, were not endorsed in all sociological sectors. Looking merely to the American context of the School's work, it might in fact surprise that the Frankfurt scholars succeeded in bringing psychoanalytical impulses into conceptions of mass society. After all, the fact that the suggestion doctrine came under fire in the USA through the work of especially Allport, Mead and Parsons, and that a move towards positivist ideals contributed to pulling the carpet from under psychologically inspired crowd semantics in its more traditional variants, did not seem to invite a veritable upsurge of psychoanalytical inspiration. Yet no single theoretical or epistemological perspective could claim supremacy in the 1930s. The positivism that would become hegemonic after the Second World War, and which would eventually challenge Parsons' status as well, was still being countered by alternative outlooks (Steinmetz 2007: 337–8). And Freud's work was actually positively received in some sociological circles. Illustratively, in 1939 the *American Journal of Sociology* devoted a special issue to the relation between sociology and psychoanalysis (see also Steinmetz 2007: 338). Here Burgess examined 'The Influence of Sigmund Freud upon Sociology in the United States' and concluded that one of the fields where 'the combined use of psychoanalytical and sociological concepts and methods' was 'particularly promising' was crowd and collective behaviour (1939: 373, 374).

I emphasize this because it suggests, as was also indicated in Chapter 4, that the work of the Frankfurt School associates was developed at a time when a certain openness was detectable in the USA with respect to fusing sociology with psychological/psychoanalytical inspirations. However, while the Frankfurt School was strong enough to build and nourish its own approach (all internal differences disregarded), it was not representative of the general sociological landscape from the 1930s onwards. There are several indicators of this, and I shall discuss just two in this chapter. One is the critique that was voiced by American sociologists against the Frankfurt scholars' dismissal of mass society and mass culture. Another is the work of David Riesman, whose analysis of the so-called 'lonely crowd' presented conclusions about contemporary society that showed important resemblances to what the Frankfurt associates observed, but whose analytical approach was based on a particular characterological rather than a Freudian framework. Indeed, and very importantly, Riesman's work was a prime example of a new methodological approach that was becoming increasingly dominant in American sociology and which gave primacy to comprehensive empirical work. As I shall claim in the discussion of Riesman, this marked an opposition to the more theoretical (some would say speculative) approaches to crowd and mass semantics that characterized earlier both Freudian and non-Freudian positions.

The mass psychology of fascism

In 1933, Hitler's seizure of power meant the end to the Weimar Republic. That same year Wilhelm Reich published the first edition of his *Mass Psychology of Fascism* (1975).[1] As was the case for many other scholars at the time, Reich's book was a response to contemporary political events, in particular of course the waxing fascism. Reich fled the Nazi regime in 1934, moved to Norway and then in 1939 to the USA.

The central aim of the book was to understand the socio-cultural conditions that made fascism possible and, on this basis, to provide the means for overcoming and preventing fascist regimes and mentalities. A crucial starting point for Reich's analysis was his dissatisfaction with existing social-theory frameworks – what he referred to as 'social economy' frameworks and which encompassed classical Marxist perspectives, but also other positions that made use of economically oriented explanations. With Reich's own example, a social-economy approach was valuable when it came to explaining that workers go on strike as a reaction to exploitation. But this kind of sociology could not

---

[1] I am quoting the third, revised and enlarged edition from 1942 on which the English translation is based. However, my emphasis will be on ideas already expressed in the 1933 volume. According to Reich, the content of the first edition was still valid – perhaps even more so – in 1942 (1975: 22).

explain why some workers do *not* strike even if they are exploited (Reich 1975: 53). More generally speaking:

social economy can give a complete explanation of a social fact that serves a rational end, i.e., when it satisfies an immediate need and reflects and magnifies the economic situation. The social economic explanation does not hold up, on the other hand, when a man's thought and action *are inconsistent with* the economic situation, are *irrational*, in other words. (1975: 53–4, italics in original)

According to Reich a mass-psychological approach was needed in order to account for these irrational actions. More specifically, some form of fusion of Marxist and Freudian inventory was called for: Marxism alone could not explain the irrational psychological dynamics that induce behaviour, and Freud's programme tended to neglect the larger social structures that interrelated with the libidinal economy.[2] Yet by bringing the two together, new analytical avenues were opened, Reich reasoned. In the preface to the third edition of *The Mass Psychology of Fascism*, he acknowledged his theoretical indebtedness explicitly by describing Freud's psychoanalysis as the mother and Marx's sociology as the father of his new theoretical offspring. But, as he noted, '*a child is more than the sum total of his parents. He is a new, independent living creature; he is the seed of the future*' (1975: 26, italics in original). This new creature was named 'sex-economic sociology'.[3]

The basic idea of this sex-economic sociology was that the socio-economic structure of modern society promoted a specific sexual structure that made the masses particularly susceptible to aggressive, conservative, reactionary impulses. It was this theoretical conception which, on Reich's view, rendered the sex-economic sociology highly

---

[2] By attempting to bridge psychology and sociology, Reich obviously countered Geiger's aim to enact a strict demarcation between the two disciplines. Other combinations of psychology and Marx-inspired thinking included the work of the Russian psychologist Serge Chakotin who, in 1939, published *The Rape of the Masses: The Psychology of Totalitarian Political Propaganda*, which came out in English in a revised edition later that year (1971). Chakotin's psychological approach was not of a Freudian bent, but drew instead on Pavlov's notion of conditioned reflexes.

[3] Reich developed the theoretical combination of Freud and Marxism in more detail elsewhere, for example, in *Dialektischer Materialismus und Psychoanalyse*, first published in 1929. In the preface to the 1934 reprint, Reich could not hide his disappointment that neither of the parents to his theoretical child would accept it. Both Freud and the Communist Party claimed that Marxism and psychoanalysis were incompatible (Reich 1934: 3–4), and in 1933–4 Reich was expelled from both the Communist Party and the International Psychoanalytical Association (Sharaf 1983: 172, 186). Eventually, Reich grew increasingly critical of Freud whom, he believed, betrayed his own original emphasis on the constitutive role of sexuality (Reich 1971: 108–9; see also Deleuze and Guattari 1983: 291–2, n., 331–2).

valuable for a mass-psychological analysis of fascism. In the words of Deleuze and Guattari, Reich's original point was that 'the masses were not deceived, they desired fascism, and that is what has to be explained' (1983: 257).[4] To account for this, Reich made a twofold observation. First, the libido constitutes the fundamental sexual energy and 'the prime motor of psychic life' (1975: 60); second, the enactment of the child's libidinal energy is suppressed by society and repressed by the individual. This societal suppression was believed to work first and foremost through the authoritarian family whose 'moral inhibition of the child's natural sexuality ... makes the child afraid, shy, fearful of authority, obedient, "good", and "docile" in the authoritarian sense of the words' (1975: 64).[5]

On this basis, the political implications of Reich's Freudian thesis begin to crystallize. The suppression of sexuality in the family was believed to have a significant bearing on the individual's psychological constitution and, therefore, on his or her political attitudes. Specifically, the inhibition of sexual energies purportedly produced an unconscious 'conservatism, fear of freedom, in a word, reactionary thinking' in the individual, which 'strengthens political reaction and makes the individual in the masses passive and nonpolitical' (1975: 65). But this was only one part of the story, Reich asserted. In addition to generating an unconscious and *passive* political attitude, the suppression of sexuality also 'creates a secondary force in man's structure – an artificial interest, which *actively* supports the authoritarian order' (1975: 65–6, italics added). Thus, the inhibition of sexuality allegedly urged the individual to seek 'various kinds of substitute gratifications' (1975: 66). According to Reich, the promotion of militarism, well known from the Italian black shirts and the German brown shirts, was guided by this rationale:

From the point of view of mass psychology, the effect of militarism is based essentially on a libidinous mechanism. The sexual effect of a uniform, the erotically provocative effect of rhythmically executed goose-stepping, the exhibitionistic nature of militaristic procedures, have been more practically comprehended by a salesgirl or an average secretary than by our most erudite politicians. On the other hand it is political reaction that consciously exploits

---

[4] Or as Reich formulated it in a subsequent book entitled *The Function of the Orgasm*, '[w]hat is new in Fascism is that *the masses of people themselves assented to their own subjugation and actively brought it about*' (1971: 209, italics in original).

[5] Hence Reich's characterization of the family as the 'authoritarian state in miniature' (1975: 64). Although the family might be the 'most important source for the reproduction of the authoritarian social system' (1975: 65), other societal institutions such as religion were said to work in functionally equivalent ways.

these sexual interests. It not only designs flashy uniforms for the men, it puts the recruiting into the hands of attractive women. (1975: 66)[6]

The quote is telling of Reich's analysis of fascism. In contrast to the 'erudite' politicians (who were nevertheless seen as hopelessly naïve), fascism had understood and capitalized on the alleged fact that the masses could be mobilized for reactionary purposes by offering them a substitute satisfaction of their repressed sexual desires. Against this background, the practical political ambitions of Reich's work ensued:

> Thus, the practical problem of mass psychology is to actuate the passive majority of the population, which always helps political reaction to achieve victory, and to eliminate those inhibitions that run counter to the development of the will to freedom born of the socio-economic situation. Freed of its bonds and directed into the channels of the freedom movement's rational goals, the psychic energy of the average mass of people excited over a football game or laughing over a cheap musical would no longer be capable of being fettered. (1975: 67)

It is interesting to note how much this objective mirrored the programme developed by crowd theorists such as Le Bon and Tarde. Similar to the Frenchmen, Reich subscribed to the idea that the irrational energies of crowds/masses posed a serious threat to the proper order of society. Whereas their analyses were embedded in an aristocratic–conservative–rationalist political programme, Reich put forward an intellectually aristocratic and rationalist perspective where the masses should be emancipated from their false and irrational appreciation of cheap cultural entertainment. That is also the limit to the similarities, for Reich's wish to release sexual energies from inhibiting social institutions was likely to provoke concern among the conservative scholars.

Reich's practical ambitions begged the question of the leader's role. Yet rather than explaining mass aberration through reference to the purported (say, demagogic) qualities of the fascist leader, Reich focused on the more fundamental problem of what structural features could explain that masses would readily turn their devotion to a leader. In addressing that query Reich argued that the social position of the lower middle class in the capitalistic system produced a particular family structure which generated a psychic structure that made it highly susceptible to fascist ideology:

---

[6] The reference to women's attraction to uniforms shows that, while Reich did not reproduce the gendered perspective of Le Bon or Tarde, he replaced the Le Bonian stereotypes with new ones.

Within the [lower middle-class] family the father holds the same position that his boss holds towards him in the production process. And he reproduces his subservient attitude towards authority in his children, particularly in his sons. Lower middle-class man's passive and servile attitude towards the führer-figure issues from these conditions. (1975: 87)

There were two main implications of this. The first was that the lower middle-class individual was said to develop an identification with the leader. 'The more helpless the "mass-individual" has become, owing to his upbringing, the more pronounced is his identification with the führer' (1975: 97). Just as important, second, the more people would adopt the lower middle-class way of life and its sexual inhibitions, the more they would identify with the leader. Taking the full consequences of this idea, Reich charged the contemporary German Social Democrats and labour unions with their attempt to transform industrial workers into lower middle-class workers. Such a change would have significant effects on the general societal sex economy, as 'the average industrial worker differs from the average lower middle-class worker by his open and untrammelled attitude towards sexuality, no matter how muddled and conservative he might be otherwise' (1975: 99). This open sexual attitude rendered the industrial worker anti-reactionary, meaning that the social democratic attempts to elevate the industrial workers to lower middle class in fact undermined potential anti-fascist and anti-reactionary resources in society.

What cure against fascism did Reich prescribe, more specifically? According to his diagnosis of the transformation of industrial workers into lower middle-class workers, one might suspect that Reich would plead for reviving classical industrial-worker life forms. However, he seemed to believe this transition to be irreversible; once the workers had adopted a lower middle-class way of life, they could not be convinced about the virtues of industrial-worker life. Consistent with his overall theoretical framework, Reich therefore proposed an alternative strategy, which he derived partly from the sex-economic sociology, and partly from his practical work as a sex-political reformer. It is important for understanding the context of Reich's sexual reformist work to note that it formed part of a larger sex-political and psychoanalytical movement that flourished in Germany in the Weimar years (Rackelmann 1994). Reich was a leading figure in this movement, which also counted figures such as Erich Fromm. In 1931, Reich played a central role in establishing, within the Communist Party in Germany, the organization Sexpol (Reichsverband für proletarische Sexualpolitik, or the German Association for a Proletarian Sexual Policy). The aim of this organization was to enlighten the proletarian classes about sexual questions. Reportedly, Sexpol became incredibly popular and obtained some 40,000 members (Boadella 1985: 82–3; Sharaf 1983: 163).[7]

It was this practical reformist work that Reich wanted to transplant into an anti-fascist political programme, the aim of which was, in line with the sex-economic sociology, to transform sexuality from being a private issue into becoming a public social matter.[8] Specifically, Reich's reformist programme, his sex politics, proposed a biopolitical transformation: a comprehensive approach was needed where society would sustain itself (and protect itself from the deadly powers of fascism) by freeing individuals from their sexual inhibitions. That is, the healthy progress of society depended on emancipating sexuality in the population. On Reich's view, this could only be realized through an extensive enlightenment strategy that would make people – and especially youths – conscious of their 'sexual misery' (1975: 218, italics in original). This consciousness might hinge on a *crowd* incident to be evoked. Thus, Reich wrote:

When I talk to a sexually inhibited woman in my office about her sexual needs, I am confronted with her entire moralistic apparatus. It is difficult for me to get through to her and to convince her of anything. If, however, the same woman is exposed to a *crowd* atmosphere, is present, for instance, at a rally at which sexual needs are discussed clearly and openly in medical and social terms, then she doesn't feel herself to be alone. After all, the others are also listening to 'forbidden things'. Her individual moralistic inhibition is offset by a *collective atmosphere of sexual affirmation*, a new sex-economic morality, which can paralyze (not eliminate!) her sexual negation because she herself has had similar thoughts when she was alone. (1975: 219, italics in original, translation modified)[9]

---

[7] It must be strongly emphasized that the number of members as well as the entire organizational background and existence of Sexpol has been contested. My description is based on what has been handed down through biographies and discussions on Reich. However, contrary to the Reich biographies by Boadella (1985) and Sharaf (1983), Marc Rackelmann (1994) has proposed a historical reconstruction which suggests that Sexpol had fewer than 10,000 members. Rackelmann also posits that Sexpol was founded later than 1931 and only seems to be referred to in Reich's writings in 1934. Prior to that Reich had played an important role in a similar organization named *Einheitsverband für proletarische Sexualreform und Mutterschutz*. For present purposes the debate on the exact history of the organization is not of vital importance. I am interested instead in how Reich transformed his practical reformist work (of which there can be no discussion) into his mass psychology.

[8] See also Reich's discussion of the topic, published under the pseudonym Ernst Parell (1934).

[9] The German original reads '*Massen*atmosphäre' (Reich 1933: 252) which, in the English version, is translated into '*mass* atmosphere'. This is consistent with the translation's general rendering of 'Masse' into 'mass' rather than 'crowd'. Yet, on precisely this occasion, the emphasis on the rally's physical co-presence suggests that Reich applied the term 'Masse' in the *crowd* sense.

Interestingly, here enlightenment was founded on the crowd experience, rather than being undermined by it. More importantly, though, the quote clearly demonstrates what the anti-fascist programme was up against, from Reich's point of view. A *collective* organization was needed in order to fight the moral inhibitions working in each individual. If only such a collective effort could be enacted, the anti-reactionary effects would be significant, for they would be irreversible: 'the objective loosening of the reactionary shackles placed on sexuality cannot under any circumstances be retightened' (1975: 224). As a positive side effect, Reich noted, this enlightenment programme would activate a new sense of responsibility in the citizen: 'The socially irresponsible man is the man absorbed in sexual conflicts' (1975: 235). So, again, if these sexual conflicts – a function of the tension between desires and inhibitions – could be overcome, people would not wind up desiring a fascist, reactionary regime.[10]

Reich's work paved the way for understanding totalitarianism on the basis of simultaneous Marxist and Freudian theorizing. A similar theoretical fusion was advocated by many other scholars. But, as the following sections will show, Reich stands out as the one who underscored Freud's notion of the social role of sexuality most radically.

---

[10] So far I have discussed ideas from *The Mass Psychology of Fascism* that were already developed in the first edition of the book. In the third, expanded edition Reich maintained his 1933 analysis, but added a new answer to the problem of fascism. The new solution was called 'the natural work-democracy'. The work-democracy was seen as '*vitally necessary* work', defined rather broadly as 'every kind of work that is *indispensable* to the maintenance of human life and the social machinery. Hence, that work is vitally necessary the absence of which would be harmful to or would inhibit the living process' (1975: 414, italics in original). According to Reich, work-democracy was in opposition to politics, so rather than seeking to develop new anti-reactionary ideologies and policies, fascism and reactionary thought should be attacked through the 'fulfilment of the biological life functions of love, work and knowledge' (1975: 423). This battle was yet another variation of the clash between rationality and irrationality. Thus, from Reich's perspective, we have 'vitally necessary work as the rational function of life on the one hand and the emotional plague as the irrational function of life on the other hand. It is not difficult to divine that work-democracy views as being part of the emotional plague all politics that is not based upon knowledge, work and love and that, therefore, is irrational' (1975: 405). The work-democracy shared a number of features with the more strictly sex-economic focus, but also contained, as should be clear from the quotes, a stronger life-philosophical emphasis. Furthermore, as Thyssen (1973: 270) has rightly observed, the opposition Reich introduced between work-democracy and politics suggested a new conception of politics on Reich's side. Whereas the 1933 edition of *The Mass Psychology of Fascism* problematized the passive, unpolitical attitude of the masses, the third edition problematized politics as such.

The political psychology of mass aberration

An analysis of fascism somewhat akin to Reich's was put forward by the Austrian mass psychologist, Hermann Broch. But rather than stressing sexual desires as Reich did, Broch's interest zeroed in on how totalitarian regimes might be explained as redemptions of individuals' basic fear of death. Broch was one of the last figures that embodied the close links between literature and science which have been discussed at various points in the preceding chapters. Indeed, Broch stands out because of his truly multifaceted work. In addition to writing famous novels such as the trilogy *The Sleepwalkers* (1996, originally published in 1931–2) and *The Death of Vergil* (1983, first published in 1945), he also produced numerous essays on philosophy, mass psychology and social and political theory. Broch even incorporated his philosophical and social–theoretical ideas into his fictional work. *The Sleepwalkers* trilogy is a prime example of this, as it included Broch's theoretical views on history in ten essays throughout the book.[11] In a similar vein, *The Death of Vergil* opened with a crowd scene that drew on insights from Broch's mass theory (1983: 12ff.).

Broch's first engagement with the crowd issue was the essay entitled 'Die Straße', published in December 1918 as an open letter to Franz Blei in the latter and Albert Paris Gütersloh's journal *Die Rettung* (1981). The essay was formed as a reaction to the events that took place outside the parliament in Vienna in November 1918 when President Karl Seitz proclaimed the Republic of German Austria.[12] The title of the essay, 'Die Straße', referred to the crowd ('Volksmasse', 1981: 30) that Broch had experienced in front of the parliament. Broch reported how he had managed to escape the crowd, despite being, 'as most people are, very easily susceptible to mass psychoses' (1981: 30). That it was indeed an escape was highlighted by the observation that, although Broch was 'absolutely convinced that the crowd is "beautiful"', it nevertheless

---

[11] To be sure, Paul Michael Lützeler observes, it was not uncommon for novelists in the 1920s and 1930s to integrate philosophical ideas in fiction. Yet Broch not merely synthesized fiction and philosophy, he pursued his philosophical analysis parallel to the fictional story, thereby emphasizing both (Lützeler 1990: 164; see also Weigel 1994). See also Harrington (2006: 5) who quotes Broch for characterizing *The Sleepwalkers* as an 'epistemological novel'. One of Broch's colleagues who blended philosophy and literature was Robert Musil, whose masterpiece *The Man without Qualities* contained several crowd-theoretical reflections (e.g. Musil 1997: 681ff., 1097, 1107). In his brilliant discussion of Musil, Stefan Jonsson argues that Musil's observations in the novel on how reason and affect interrelate found their 'most immediate parallel' in Broch's mass psychology (2000: 261).

[12] For a brief account of the events, see Lützeler (1973: 43–4).

shook him with 'disgust' (1981: 30, 31). It did so because, in Broch's eyes, crowds are not proper communities.[13] A true community is one that has a 'common metaphysical feeling of truth' (1981: 31). Yet this was precisely what the crowd failed to possess, as it was characterized, for Broch, by a fundamentally sceptical attitude (1981: 32).

Here, as in Broch's subsequent work, the question of the crowd or mass was embedded in a discussion of politics. In this early essay, Broch's view on politics was just as sceptical as he claimed the crowd to be. He thus ended up criticizing practical politics for relapsing into 'empty mass slogans' and for sliding into 'the cheap ecstasy of the crowd' (1981: 33). Indeed, the essay had a disillusioned tone to it. It offered 'no manifesto, no instructions as how to behave or act, no avowal ... The text's peculiar rhetoric serves to nullify all alternatives simultaneously and to orient the entire development of history toward this superficiality of the political' (Schmidt-Dengler 2003: 58). As will become clear below, the rise of Hitler forced Broch into changing his view on politics. Consequently, in his later mass theory he pinned his faith on a new politics and added an explicitly political superstructure to his mass analysis. This combination of politics and mass psychology served specific democratic functions for Broch:

Up to now, and with a few exceptions, only the totalitarian political systems have made use of mass psychology; it is time, indeed it is high time, that democracy do the same for its own ends: a truly scientific mass psychology is called upon to become one of the most potent and important instruments of democracy. (1947: 358)

As the quote indicates, Broch's post-1918 work on crowds and masses was developed as a response to Europe's totalitarian experiences throughout the 1930s and 1940s. And similar to many other scholars at this time, Broch, too, had very personal reasons for his interest in mass dynamics.[14] His parents were Jewish (Broch himself converted to Catholicism) and his mother was killed in Theresienstadt. Broch was arrested by the Gestapo in 1938 but managed to emigrate first to London and later to the USA (partly due to the intervention of James Joyce). It was in this American exile that Broch began, in 1939, his systematic studies of mass phenomena.[15] The first product was the 1939 'Proposal for the

---

[13] The crowd's purported lack of community was one of the ideas reappearing in *The Death of Vergil* (Broch 1983: 110).
[14] For comprehensive biographical studies of Broch, see Koebner (1965) and especially Lützeler (1985).
[15] Broch's turn to the crowd topic was no sudden occurrence. Besides the reflections on crowds in the early essay 'Die Straße', Broch had had a recurrent interest in the theme

Founding of a Research Institute for Political Psychology and for the Study of Mass Aberration' which he submitted to Albert Einstein at Princeton University and to Alvin Johnson from the New School for Social Research in New York. Although this proposal was never realized, Broch did receive some funding through Hadley Cantril at the Institute for Public Opinion Research, Princeton University, and this allowed him to carry on with his investigations.

For the next decade Broch was occupied with his mass studies. His work within this field was only published posthumously, though, the most complete edition being the voluminous (more than 560 pages long) *Massenwahntheorie* (1979), which consists of a series of texts written between 1939 and 1948.[16] Broch's mass aberration theory was surprisingly silent when it came to quoting or merely referring to other scholars' work.[17] Yet it may be argued that Broch followed a long tradition from Le Bon to the Frankfurt scholars, which saw crowd and mass phenomena as immanent to modern society, and where the problematization of crowds and masses was therefore seen as inseparable from a problematization of modern society more generally.

The fundamental idea underpinning Broch's mass aberration theory was an ego model, according to which the ego is characterized by an 'urge of life' that has as its ultimate goal to surmount death (1979: 46).[18] Broch argued that there are two basic options available to the individual in his or her attempt to ward off (the fear of) death. The first possibility is related to what Broch termed 'irrationality enrichment' (1979: 14).

---

throughout the years in Austria. For example, he used to discuss crowd-theoretical topics with his friend and colleague, Elias Canetti, who had worked on this theme since the mid-1920s. Canetti and Broch became friends in Vienna in 1932 and Canetti praised his colleague's work. See as an example of this Canetti's laudatory speech at Broch's fiftieth birthday in 1936 (Canetti 1981; see also Sloterdijk 2004: 182ff.). Over the years, however, the relationship between the two cooled down (Hanuschek 2005: 202ff.).

[16] Parts of the theory were published in German in 1955, i.e. around four years after Broch's death in 1951.

[17] However, Lützeler (1979: 580) reports that Broch's correspondence shows that he was familiar with Le Bon's *The Crowd* and also with the more recent contributions to crowd/mass theory such as Adler (1934), Cantril (2002), Freud (1989), Jung (1935/36), Lederer (1967), Ortega (1960), Reich (1975), etc. Lützeler also notes that after Broch met with Alexander Mitscherlich in 1950, he considered the latter congenial with respect to crowd theory. Mitscherlich's contribution to the field was a collection of essays (that originally appeared between 1953 and 1970), published under the title *Massenpsychologie ohne Ressentiment* (1972). Among other things Mitscherlich argued for transferring the notion of crowds and masses from the field of political revolutions to the sphere of consumption. He also voiced a critique of planning as a solution to the problems of modern mass society (e.g. 1972: 54, 71–2).

[18] Hannah Arendt has argued that Broch's 'general anxiety about death' was 'characteristic of the war generation' (1970: 126).

This is a process that produces an irrationality supplement so as to satisfy the individual's instinctive urges, but through which these urges are simultaneously transformed into communal ties (Müller-Funk 2003: 96). For example, love, religion or artistic–aesthetic creations may at once fulfil individual urges and generate a sense of community (Broch 1979: 14, 25). While this first option had a basically constructive nature, the second option held much more destructive potentials. This option, named 'rationality impoverishment', signified a process where the individual becomes incapable of rational conduct, instead of which he or she pursues collective instincts (Broch 1979: 14). This, the theory held, would often happen through joint violent action against what were seen (or constructed) as a dangerous enemy. According to Broch, the externalization and personalization of the fear of death, which was at stake here, could generate mass aberration: 'if a large number of individuals is brought to rationality impoverishment for the same reasons, and if they then become reconciled to such a common urge behaviour, then it is justified to speak of mass aberration' (1979: 14). In short, Broch's model suggested that mass aberration and its collective violence was one of the options available for the individual to protect him or her from the panicking fear of death.

Broch's theory added several layers to this basic framework, including a historical model which aimed to explain the socio-historical conditions under which mass aberration is likely to take place.[19] I have discussed this model and other aspects of Broch's mass aberration theory elsewhere (Borch 2006b, 2008). For present purposes I am more interested in the one part of the *Massenwahntheorie* which set it apart from previous studies, namely its political dimension. Other scholars had offered more or less practical ideas on how to intervene politically in order to prevent totalitarian mass phenomena. Ortega called for a unification of Europe. Mannheim put his faith in political planning. Reich argued for sex-political action. Yet it was Broch who presented the most elaborated proposal for how to avoid totalitarian mass aberration.

This political superstructure to Broch's mass theory was developed in the third part of the *Massenwahntheorie*, which seemingly annulled any scepticism about practical politics he had voiced in the early essay 'Die Straße'. The political superstructure had both theoretical and politically

---

[19]   Broch thereby sought to provide a solution to a problem that Adorno *et al.* would later point to in *The Authoritarian Personality*: 'We may be able to say something about the readiness of an individual to break into violence, but we are pretty much in the dark as to the remaining necessary conditions under which an actual outbreak would occur' (1950: 972).

interventionist dimensions, clearly indicated by its title, 'The Fight against Mass Aberration (A Psychology of Politics)' (Broch 1979: 331). The notion of democracy was attributed a central place in this battle. This had not least practical–empirical reasons. Thus, Broch argued, the experiences with Hitler's Germany had shown a totalitarian attack not just on Jews but also on democracy. To avoid a recurrence a new conception of politics and democracy was required, he believed, one that saw democracy as synonymous with the fight against mass aberration and which exhibited a much greater respect for human rights.

In this vein, Broch developed a comprehensive human rights programme, which opposed capital punishment and denied the legitimacy of 'lawless enclaves' (1979: 500). No human must be denied its legal status and hence no extralegal subjects, no illegal combatants, were tolerable in Broch's system.[20] In addition to this, Broch envisioned a Bill of Duties to supplement or even replace the Bill of Rights, where the former defines the 'freedom responsibilities' of each individual (1978a).[21] 'In the protection of people against their fellow beings', he asserted, 'we find the most effective and perhaps even the only guarantee of the preservation of democracy' (1978a: 260). As Joseph Strelka (1988: 81) rightly observes, Broch's call for a supplementary cluster of duties provided a solution to what Ortega observed as the crucial problem in modern society, namely that people celebrate their rights but refuse any obligations (Ortega y Gasset 1960: 188). Broch did not offer a complete analysis of the content of such duties, however, nor of their practical realization. But he did state that the duties would have to impose certain limits on the rights. For example, there should be limits to free speech. The Bill of Duties required that it be illegal to make hateful and contemptuous utterances against other individuals (Broch 1978b: 379).

In spite of such suggestions, Broch's vision of human rights remained a largely utopian one; and the titles of his essays on the subject matter suggest that he shared this opinion: 'Bemerkungen zur Utopie einer "International Bill of Rights and of Responsibilities"' (1978a, written in 1946), 'Trotzdem: Humane Politik. Verwirklichung einer Utopie' (1978b, written in 1950). One is left with the same impression in the final part of *Massenwahntheorie* where Broch pinned his faith on 'decency' as a 'preliminary stage of the future ethical centripetal value'

[20] Or, in the vocabulary that Agamben would later suggest, no *homo sacer* whom everyone is 'permitted to kill without committing homicide' must exist (1998: 104).
[21] This idea reiterated some Kantian tenets in Broch's early political writings, including the essay 'Die Straße'; see Lützeler (1973: 43–51).

(1979: 531, 533). While this was a noble hope, it was not clear how this decency would manifest itself on a large scale.

Interestingly, in spite of constituting one of the most comprehensive examinations of totalitarian mass aberration, Broch's theorizing hardly left any traces in social theory. This is not to suggest a total ignorance of his work. It was positively received both within and (especially) beyond social theory. Lützeler (2003: 3) thus mentions prominent people such as political scientist Anton Pelinka and publicist Harry Pross (1978) as figures who highlighted Broch's significance in the 1970s. Broch also played an important role in Scandinavian discussions at this time. In Norway, Sverre Dahl, the director of Amnesty International, subscribed to Broch's ideas on human rights, and in Denmark intellectuals such as Villy Sørensen (1961) already celebrated Broch in the 1960s and with additional vigour after the Danish translation, in 1970, of parts of his mass theory (Broch 1970).

Still, these examples remain exceptions to the general picture, and within sociology there was hardly any reception of Broch's work. How can it be that such a comprehensive crowd theory was met with this silence? Arguably, the sociological ignorance reflected the old battle between literature and science: Broch, being a famous novelist, could hardly be taken seriously as a scholar. But it might also be that the intimate connection Broch tried to establish between mass theory and practical political politics – or to be more precise, the shift of attention he enacted from the former to the latter – in effect took him beyond the field of social theory. That is, for all of its emphasis on the historico-psychological problematization of the mass issue, the political and legal solutions he suggested in a sense subverted the *theoretical* engagement with crowds and masses and placed the focus instead on *practical* intervention (an observation which fits nicely with the fact that an Amnesty International director picked up on Broch's ideas). It might also be argued that the Marxist framing of many conceptualizations of totalitarianism that were in vogue at this time rendered Broch, who did not propagate a clear Marxist vision, an outsider. The time was much more in favour of approaches such as those advanced by the Frankfurt School.

Frankfurt orientations: totalitarianism as an escape from mass isolation

It has been demonstrated that Ortega and Mannheim attacked mass society from a moral and cultural standpoint and that Reich formulated his critique of a proto-fascist mass society on the basis of a combination of Marxist and Freudian impulses. These strands of research, which differed not least in their political–ideological preferences, were unified in the work conducted by the group of researchers associated with the Institute for Social Research, which was founded in Frankfurt in 1923, who were exiled to New York in 1933 and returned to Frankfurt in the early 1950s. If Reich found himself struggling with having his theoretical infant recognized by its parents, one would suspect the marriage of basically aristocratic cultural critique and Marxist psychoanalysis to face a no less ill-fated future. However, the Frankfurt School sociologists – including among many others Theodor W. Adorno, Walter Benjamin, Erich Fromm, Carl Grünberg, Max Horkheimer, Leo Löwenthal and Herbert Marcuse – easily bridged what might appear to be a deep gulf. In what follows I will examine how this school of research contributed to the study of crowds and masses. This is no easy task, since, in spite of some common concerns and ideas, the scholars affiliated with the Institute did not subscribe to one unified programme. Quite the contrary, it is well known that the Frankfurt researchers pursued different agendas, had many internal disagreements and that their (individual and collective) thinking developed over time. In the following I will gloss over many of these internal discrepancies and developments, as I am interested in the history of crowd semantics rather than in the genealogy of the Frankfurt School, the history of which has already been written by many others (e.g. Bottomore 2002; Dubiel 1985; Jay 1973). More specifically, I shall focus on how crowd and mass semantics informed and was modified in the Frankfurt scholars' reflections on how a totalitarian mass movement such as Hitlerism could come about.[22]

One influential account of fascism was offered by Erich Fromm who was closely associated with the Frankfurt School in the early 1930s, but cut his ties with the School in 1939 (see e.g. Bottomore 2002: 14, n. 6; Jay 1973: 88ff.). Akin to Reich, Fromm combined a Marxist approach with Freudian psychoanalysis, and he too did so in a way not easily reducible to the inspirational sources. Contrary to Reich, Fromm was highly critical of the libido theory that was at the centre of Freud's crowd

---

[22] I shall be rather selective here, as fascism formed a key research topic among the Frankfurt scholars from the 1940s onwards. The systematic efforts of the 1940s were to some extent preconfigured by studies conducted in the 1930s by Erich Fromm, Max Horkheimer, Herbert Marcuse and Frederick Pollock. Helmut Dubiel particularly mentions Marcuse's 1934 essay 'The Struggle Against Liberalism in the Totalitarian View of the State' as a case in point (1985: 20–3; Marcuse 1988b). This essay discussed the problem of fascism, but did so without really addressing the question of crowds and masses – yet it did observe a connection that several other scholars had emphasized as well, namely that liberalism might in fact prepare the way for totalitarianism (see also Kellner 1984: 96ff.).

psychology. Instead his analytical interest zeroed in on modern individual isolation and its consequences. This was also the topic of his 1941 book *Escape from Freedom*, published in his American exile, in which he put forward an examination of the psychology of Nazism (1941).[23] Fromm's basic claim in the book was that modern society, with its roots in the Renaissance and the Reformation, had emancipated the individual. The modern individual had emerged as a free, independent and rational individual. But this achievement had come at a great price, Fromm argued, for it was followed by an experience of agonizing isolation in the subject. Social, economic and political developments added to this isolation and to the individual's feeling of powerlessness and insignificance. For example, capitalism's alleged drive towards monopolistic centralization had put the individual, whether as a blue-collar worker or as a small or medium-sized businessperson, in a situation of alienation vis-à-vis the huge corporations (1941: 123–8). The same applied to the customer who was confronted with modern techniques of advertisement, which 'smother and kill the critical capacities of the customer like an opiate or outright hypnosis' (1941: 128; see also 251). According to Fromm, the feeling of isolation and insignificance also manifested itself at a more general everyday level. It was reproduced wherever the individual moved, and in whatever he or she turned the attention to:

Vastness of cities in which the individual is lost, buildings that are as high as mountains, constant acoustic bombardment by the radio, big headlines changing three times a day and leaving one no choice to decide what is important, shows in which one hundred girls demonstrate their ability with clocklike precision to eliminate the individual and act like a powerful though smooth machine, the beating rhythm of jazz – these and many other details are expressions of a constellation in which the individual is confronted by uncontrollable dimensions in comparison with which he is a small particle. All he can do is to fall in step like a marching soldier or a worker on the endless belt. He can act; but the sense of independence, significance, has gone. (Fromm 1941: 131–2)

This quote is interesting for several reasons. First, it echoed Simmel's analysis of the city's 'rapidly changing and closely compressed contrasting stimulations of the nerves' (1950e: 414) and resonated with the nineteenth-century American fear of cities as well as with Ortega's observations of how the masses occupied urban space. Second, the reference to the 'one hundred girls' and their accurate synchronization

---

[23] The book was published in the UK in 1942 under the title *The Fear of Freedom* (Fromm 2001).

alluded to Siegfried Kracauer's 1927 essay 'The Mass Ornament' (1975), which merits a brief comment.[24]

Kracauer famously opened this essay with a discussion of the so-called Tiller Girls, an American dance troupe which became famous worldwide in the early twentieth century and gave shows also in Berlin. The troupe owed its name to John Tilly who, in the late-nineteenth-century UK, had invented the kind of precision dance, which accounted for the troupe's popularity, and which consisted of a line of female dancers who performed highly disciplined uniform routines. According to Kracauer, '[t]hese products of American "distraction factories" are no longer individual girls, but indissoluble female units whose movements are mathematical demonstrations' (1975: 67). Kracauer saw the mass ornament of the Tiller Girls as a manifestation of a new social and cultural era. Anticipating Fromm, he compared it especially to the economic realm asserting that the Tiller Girls' 'mass ornament is the aesthetic reflex of the rationality aspired to in the prevailing economic system' (1975: 70). For instance, '[t]he hands in the factory correspond to the legs of the *Tiller Girls*' (1975: 70, italics in original). One of the central points in Kracauer's account was the observation of the de-individualization taking place in the mass ornament. 'Only as part of a mass, not as individuals who believe themselves to be formed from within, are human beings components of a pattern' (1975: 68). Put differently, in mass culture the individual was lost and reduced to the mere movements of legs and arms. Related to this, Kracauer's analysis suggested that there was no outside, no external position to this development. The mass ornament described the entire society. Thus, '[t]he regularity of [the Tiller Girls'] patterns is acclaimed by the masses, *who themselves are arranged in row upon ordered row*' (1975: 67, italics added).[25]

Interestingly, moreover, Kracauer's analysis transplanted the sexual and gender categories of classical crowd theory to the field of mass

---

[24] Kracauer was not formally associated with the Frankfurt School but was a close friend of Adorno and Löwenthal. He had a much more troubled relation with Horkheimer (see Jay 1993). For an introduction to Kracauer, which includes a discussion of his relation with the Frankfurt environment, see Koch (1996). It should be noted that, although the essay 'The Mass Ornament' is today the best-known part of Kracauer's work, it did not receive much attention at the time it was published. It really only became a classic after the 1963 publication of a series of essays that were named after this essay (Kracauer 1963; Reeh 2002: 113).

[25] The standardization inherent to the mass ornament was also emphasized by Kracauer in other contexts. One essay from a series of 1929 texts *The Salaried Masses: Duty and Distraction in Weimar Germany* contended that: '[s]alaried employees today live in masses, whose existence – especially in Berlin and the other big cities – increasingly assumes a standard character. Uniform working relations and collective contracts condition their lifestyle' (Kracauer 1998: 68).

society. Although Kracauer asserted that the Tiller Girls constituted 'sexless bodies' and that their ornamental structure 'no longer has erotic meaning but at best points to the place where the erotic resides' (1975: 67, 68), he nevertheless portrayed the mass ornament as inherently feminine and as characterized by underlying sexual currents. For instance, Kracauer focused on the girls' *legs* rather than on the workers' *hands* and depicted the Tiller Girls in their bathing suits as the crystallization of the mass ornament. According to Andreas Huyssen:

Examples such as these show that the inscription of the feminine on the notion of mass culture, which seems to have its primary place in the late nineteenth century, did not relinquish its hold, even among those critics who did much to overcome the nineteenth century mystification of mass culture as woman. (1986: 192)

Contrary to what this might suggest, Kracauer's analysis was not entirely negative or sceptical about the mass ornament. In contrast to the critical opinion of '[c]ertain intellectuals', among whom one could count most of the Frankfurt scholars, not least Horkheimer (Jay 1993: 377), he argued 'that the *aesthetic* pleasure gained from the ornamental mass movements is *legitimate*' (1975: 70, italics in original). Enjoying and affirming the mass ornament was, in other words, not an expression of false consciousness, but rather a purely valid reaction. The reason for this was, according to Kracauer, to be found in its societal potentiality: the mass ornament offered a step on the way towards a rationalization (and demythologization) of society. Specifically, it offered a way of bringing art and aesthetics into the lifeworld, i.e. into close contact with human beings and their concerns, something he believed to be crucial in order to change society for the better (Jay 1993: 379, 380; Kracauer 1975: 76).[26]

---

[26] Kracauer was well aware that the potentials of the mass ornament could be repressed through manipulation. In much of his later work, especially in his writings on films and fascist propaganda, he demonstrated how Hitler had utilized the medium of films to orchestrate fascist mass ornaments. This view was developed, for example, in Kracauer's 1942 analysis 'Propaganda and the Nazi War Film', later included in his *From Caligari to Hitler: A Psychological History of the German Film* (2004: 273–307). Kracauer also elaborated on the connection between propaganda and film in a brief excursus in the subsequent *Theory of Film: The Redemption of Physical Reality* (1960). Recalling classical crowd-psychological vocabulary, Kracauer here remarked that '[t]he moviegoer is much in the position of a hypnotized person. Spellbound by the luminous rectangle before his eyes – which resembles the glittering object in the hand of a hypnotist – he cannot help succumbing to the suggestions that invade the blank of his mind. Film is an incomparable instrument of propaganda' (1960: 160). For a discussion of this part of Kracauer's work, see Jay (1993: 374, 377). See also Witte (1977: 339–41), who quotes an unpublished Kracauer essay entitled 'Masse und Propaganda. Eine Untersuchung über die fascistische Propaganda' in which Kracauer examined the technical propaganda means by which the fascists sought to govern the masses.

Whereas Kracauer's essay revolved around aesthetic developments and how they related to broader structural–economic features, Fromm was more concerned with the modern individual. But Fromm alluded to Kracauer's observations in order to provide an additional illustration of how the modern individual was exposed to a feeling of isolation. In the mass ornament the individual is part of a mass, a collective, but he or she feels alone because there is no room for individual personality, no way of being distinguishable from others. And this, Fromm asserted, captured a broader feeling experienced by the modern individual, alienated as he or she was by urbanization, modern technology, popular culture (jazz), etc.

In contrast to, for example, Ortega's moral examination of the rise of the mass individual, Fromm attended to the psychological implications arising with this modern subject. Specifically, he argued that three so-called 'mechanisms of escape' from powerlessness and isolation were available to the modern individual. One was *authoritarianism*, which referred to 'the tendency to give up the independence of one's own individual self and to fuse one's self with somebody or something outside of oneself in order to acquire the strength which the individual self is lacking' (1941: 141). According to Fromm, authoritarianism was prone to result in a masochistic striving for submission or in a sadistic striving for domination. In either case the individual would escape his or her feeling of powerlessness and isolation, as he or she would be part of a social bond (for example, by being part of the masses celebrating their common leader). Yet the escape would assume an essentially negative form. Equally negative was the second mechanism described by Fromm, namely *destructiveness*, which 'aims at the removal of all objects with which the individual has to compare himself' (1941: 181).

Finally, the third mechanism of escape was termed 'automaton conformity'. This category is particularly interesting, as it signalled a return to classical crowd-theoretical ideas. The escape through automaton conformity took the following form: 'the individual ceases to be himself; he adopts entirely the kind of personality offered to him by cultural patterns; and he therefore becomes exactly as all others are and as they expect him to be' (1941: 185–6). More specifically, Fromm posited, each individual usually believes that he or she acts and thinks on his or her own account; that is, that his or her 'thoughts, feelings, wishes are "his"' or hers (1941: 186). Yet when the individual adopts an automaton conformity, these thoughts, feelings and wishes are not genuinely attributable to the individual but rather 'induced from the outside' (1941: 190). There are two interesting dynamics at play here. First, for Fromm the adoption of ideas, feelings, etc. from the outside amounted to a protective strategy. 'The person who gives up his individual self and becomes an automaton, identical with millions of other automatons around him, need not feel alone and anxious any more' (1941: 186). As described in Chapter 1, the notion of the automaton also stood centrally in Le Bon's description of the crowd. In Fromm's version, the Le Bonian notion was transplanted from the isolated crowd incident onto a more general societal level ('millions of other automatons'), once again demonstrating how the traits usually associated with crowd behaviour were semantically reconfigured to analyse mass society and mass individuals. Moreover, a Tardean legacy materialized in Fromm's explanatory register. Thus, when accounting for how individuals become automatons, Fromm had recourse to hypnosis. The hypnotic experiment:

shows in the most unmistakable manner that, although one may be convinced of the spontaneity of one's mental acts, they actually result from the influence of a person other than oneself ... The phenomenon, however, is by no means to be found only in the hypnotic situation. (1941: 190)[27]

Similar to Tarde, therefore, Fromm seemed to posit that the idea of hypnotic suggestion might work as a general social model. There was one crucial difference in their conceptions, though. Whereas Tarde was in no way offended by the idea of somnambulistic imitation, Fromm expressed serious concerns. Thus, as a second important dynamics pertaining to automaton conformity, the adoption of externally induced feelings, ideas, etc. 'leads eventually to the replacement of the original self by a pseudo self' (1941: 205).[28] This distinction presupposed precisely the (liberal) notion of a real self or a kernel in the self, which Tarde's theory of suggestion undermined. Fromm further argued that the replacement of the original self by the pseudo self was prone to result in a pathological state. 'The loss of the self and its substitution by a pseudo self leave the individual in an intense state of insecurity', even 'panic' (1941: 206). So although the automaton conformity appeared at first sight as a protective strategy, it would ultimately place the individual in an ever-graver situation. Indeed, argued Fromm, an individual adopting the automaton conformity would be 'ready to submit to new authorities which offer him security and relief from doubt' (1941: 206).

---

[27] Fromm repeated this conviction in *Man for Himself* from 1947, a book which was conceived by Fromm as an accompanying volume to *Escape from Freedom*: 'The reaction of people to a leader equipped with a strong power of suggestion is an example of a semi-hypnotic situation' (1999: 202).

[28] According to Fromm, '[t]he original self is the self which is the originator of mental activities. The pseudo self is only an agent who actually represents the role a person is supposed to play but who does so under the name of the self' (1941: 205).

This all formed the backdrop to Fromm's examination of the psychology of Nazism.[29] Briefly put, this analysis pivoted around two of the three character types mentioned above, namely the authoritarian person and the automaton. It was precisely these two character types which, argued Fromm, played a key role in the emergence of Nazism – buttressed, he added, by the specific socio-economic conditions of the time (e.g. inflation). More specifically, the Nazi movement was an example of an authority that grew strong because of the security (escape) it offered the panicking, isolated individuals. On Fromm's analysis, '[t]he despair of the human automaton is fertile soil for the political purposes of Fascism' (1941: 256).

Fromm was not entirely pessimistic, though; he acknowledged that modern freedom might also give way to democratic rather than fascist impulses. The character type corresponding to a democratic order was, in Fromm's eyes, to be found in the spontaneous individual, crystallized most notably in the artist, but inherent as a potential in any individual. The spontaneous person is one, who acts, thinks, feels, etc. on his or her own account, without being induced to do so from the outside. Or as Fromm put it, '[s]pontaneous activity is free activity of the self and implies, psychologically, what the Latin root of the word, *sponte*, means literally: of one's free will' (1941: 258, italics in original). By fostering spontaneity positive freedom would emerge, Fromm posited. This would imply not only 'the full affirmation of the uniqueness of the individual', but equally importantly the realization of a true democratic order, where no one is suppressed by others (1941: 263). In line with Mannheim, Fromm argued that such a development might be supported by 'a planned economy', which he described as 'democratic socialism' (1941: 272). In other words, planning was seen by Fromm as a means through which society could avoid the dangers of Nazism.

'It is difficult', Bramson has noted, 'to do justice to the impact of a work like *Escape from Freedom*, especially on young social scientists in the United States, many of whom were introduced to an interdisciplinary approach to social problems through such books' (1961: 127). This is true, and Fromm's work certainly exhibited a great leverage on particularly the Frankfurt School associates.[30] One specific contribution that

---

[29] The analysis of the psychology of Nazism was based mainly on excerpts from Hitler's and Goebbels' writings (see also Fromm 1999: 202–3).

[30] To be sure, not all Frankfurt scholars were equally fond of Fromm's work. Herbert Marcuse, for one, referred positively to Fromm's notion on the sadomasochistic character in an unpublished article from around 1972–3 (2001: 170), but he was highly critical of Fromm's reading of Freud. This is not a debate I want to engage in. Let me only refer the reader to their 1955–6 encounter in the journal

might be seen as an offshoot of Fromm's ideas was *The Authoritarian Personality*, the result of a collaboration between Adorno, Else Frenkel-Brunswik, Daniel J. Levinson and R. Nevitt Sanford. The principal problem addressed in this book, which was first published in 1950, was similar to what especially Reich and Fromm had struggled with. Thus, it was stated in the opening of the book, its 'major concern was with the *potentially fascistic* individual, one whose structure is such as to render him particularly susceptible to anti-democratic propaganda' (Adorno *et al.* 1950: 1, italics in original). Compared to the 1920s discussions of propaganda and mass media that were touched upon in Chapter 4, Adorno *et al.* did not problematize propaganda as such. Rather the real problems were the social structures that rendered propaganda successful by paving the way for a new kind of subject, the authoritarian (i.e. potentially fascistic) personality.

Similar to the other positions presented previously in this chapter, Adorno *et al.* saw the rise of the authoritarian personality as inherent to the emergence of modern society. As Horkheimer summarized in the preface he wrote to the book in his capacity as the Director of the Institute for Social Research, the authoritarian personality represented a peculiar hybrid, mixing 'ideas and skills which are typical of a highly industrialized society with irrational or anti-rational beliefs' (1950: ix). In addition to this, *The Authoritarian Personality* drew on a social-psychological apparatus and thereby demonstrated an affinity to especially Reich and Fromm. This interdisciplinary set-up ran once again counter to Theodor Geiger's recommendations, but corresponded to a more general tendency among especially German researchers. It thus seems as if the totalitarian experience convinced many scholars at this time that a proper theoretical framework, which aimed to understand contemporary society in general and totalitarianism in particular, could not begin from a strict separation of psychology and sociology, but should rather attempt to combine approaches and ideas from each of these disciplines.[31]

The Authoritarian Personality was based on comprehensive quantitative studies as well as clinical interviews. As indicated above, the book

---

Dissent (e.g. Fromm 1959; Marcuse 1959). On Fromm and Marcuse, see also Kellner (2001: 22, 27).

[31] There were exceptions to this pattern. One is Curt Geyer's study *Macht und Masse. Von Bismarck zu Hitler*, which traced Hitler's ascent to power without giving psychological explanations a prominent status (1948). In some of his previous work, however, Geyer had drawn explicitly on crowd-psychological vocabulary. See, for instance, his discussion of the leader and crowd suggestion in *Führer und Masse in der Demokratie* (Geyer 1926: 54ff.).

employed this data to distil a specific character profile, the authoritarian personality, which was seen as particularly inclined to prejudiced and fascist attitudes (although not always explicitly realized by the individual who held this personality). Counting especially Fromm's *Escape from Freedom* but also Reich's *The Mass Psychology of Fascism* as some of their explicit inspirational sources (1950: 231, n. 1), Adorno *et al.* presented the authoritarian, anti-democratic personality as one which was susceptible to submit to authoritarian figures (the strong leader, the father, etc.). This reflected a masochistic side, which was supplemented by more sadistic tendencies, namely in aggressive, even violent, propensities, directed against outgroups (1950: 231ff.). Such outgroups might include religious minorities or people whose sexual preferences were seen as deviant. Echoing Reich, Adorno *et al.* wrote that the authoritarian personality's 'strong inclination to punish violators of sex mores (homosexuals, sex offenders)' suggested, among other things, 'that the subject's own sexual desires are suppressed and in danger of getting out of hand' (1950: 241).

The important point of the book was that the authoritarian personality was far more pronounced than one might have expected in a liberal society such as that of the USA where the study was carried out. Indeed, the book seemed to lend empirical support to the idea that the authoritarian personality, the potentially fascistic individual, could be identified on a mass scale in the USA. What to do with the problem of the authoritarian personality? Adorno *et al.* were brief on this issue in the book, but reiterated an observation from classical crowd theory, arguing that '[r]ational arguments cannot be expected to have deep or lasting effects upon a phenomenon [authoritarian prejudices] that is irrational in its essential nature' (1950: 973). The authoritarian personality was portrayed as irrational because it subscribed to ideas and actions which ran counter to the individual's material interests (see also Adorno 1991b: 129).[32] Since an anti-fascist politics could not rely on rational arguments, an alternative political approach consisted in utilizing politically the fact that 'appeals to [the authoritarian individual's] conventionality or to his submissiveness toward authority might be effective' (1950: 973) – although no suggestions were offered as to how to do this more specifically. The authors also argued that anti-fascist strategies might pivot around parent–child relationships. Even if Adorno *et al.* acknowledged that it was an extremely vulnerable strategy to hope for, and seek to instigate, more caring and loving family relations, such an approach was

---

[32] Obviously, this was not an unproblematic definition of irrationality: how to determine what should count as material interests?

said to be critical in order to prevent authoritarian personalities from emerging. Indeed, as they put it in the – almost Whitmanesque or Reichian – closing remark of *The Authoritarian Personality*: 'If fear and destructiveness are the major emotional sources of fascism, *eros* belongs mainly to democracy' (1950: 976, italics in original).

Re-problematizing mass culture

Whereas *The Authoritarian Personality* was inspired partly by Fromm and his work on the authoritarian character, other Frankfurt School investigations zeroed in on a problematization of mass culture. The most famous example of this was Horkheimer and Adorno's *Dialectic of Enlightenment*, first published in 1944 (2002). In particular the chapter entitled 'The Culture Industry: Enlightenment as Mass Deception' was quintessential of the Frankfurt School's critical attitude towards the cultural fabric of the time. As the title of the essay indicated, modern cultural advances might have appeared as progressive achievements (in terms of technology, emancipation, etc.), but in reality they made manifest a grand deception. According to Horkheimer and Adorno, this deception generalized to the mass scale what was previously seen as mainly reserved for crowd incidents, namely an annulment of subjectivity by de-individualizing standardization, leading to the 'withering of imagination and spontaneity' in the modern individual (2002: 100, 116, 124–5). More devastating, perhaps, the masses purportedly 'insist unwaveringly on the ideology by which they are enslaved' (2002: 106). This was the incredible deception created through mass culture.[33]

While semantically alike, the notion of culture in Horkheimer and Adorno differed from Mannheim's conception in that the former had a much more aesthetic and medial character.[34] Hence the Frankfurt

---

[33] Herbert Marcuse would later propose a related, but more radical analysis. He argued in *One-Dimensional Man* from 1964 that the individual in the modern, industrialized society was subjected to a transformation of his or her needs from 'true' into 'false' ones. In opposition to the true needs, the false needs 'are those which are superimposed upon the individual by particular social interests in his oppression' and to which Marcuse counted '[m]ost of the prevailing needs to relax, to have fun, to behave and consume in accordance with the advertisements, to love and hate what others love and hate' (1991: 5). In other words, the modern 'one-dimensional man' was exposed to an external regulation, or even suppression, of his or her needs, so that rather than reflecting the individual's 'true' desires, these needs were designed so as to reflect the needs of the technological and administered capitalist society. On this view, the deceit that Horkheimer and Adorno diagnosed had entered the realm of needs: people did not realize that their needs were not their own.

[34] Another difference concerned the vertical point of reference, as it were. Whereas Mannheim and Ortega took as their starting point the ascent of the masses from

scholars' observations revolved around what could be described as a transformation from high culture or modernist culture to low or mass culture, that is, from classical music, literature and theatre to popular film, radio, jazz and magazines.[35] If, for Le Bon, the crowd signified the re-emergence of an archaic (intellectual) barbarianism, the contemporary mass culture signalled the regression into an '[a]esthetic barbarianism' (2002: 104). In all their critique of mass culture, Horkheimer and Adorno arrived at a position which, in some important respects, came surprisingly close to conservative critiques of modern culture as voiced by Ortega. To be sure, in the preface to the *Dialectic of Enlightenment*, Horkheimer and Adorno (2002: xvii) explicitly distanced themselves from Ortega, but the concrete analyses easily tended to obfuscate such assumed differences. At one point, for example, Horkheimer and Adorno complained that '[c]onnoisseurship and expertise are proscribed as the arrogance of those who think themselves superior' (2002: 106), for being superior was no longer allowed (or valued) in modern culture. This, they contended, came to the fore in 'the hostility inherent in the principle of entertainment to anything which is more than itself' (2002: 108). This all fitted well with Ortega's diagnosis. Yet whereas Ortega took as his starting point the entrance of the masses in societal spheres in which they had previously been denied access, Horkheimer and Adorno argued that the masses had not gained access to a, for them, new and higher level; rather, the level of culture had been lowered so that it now matched that of the masses (2002: 130; see also Marcuse 1991: 57).

below, Horkheimer and Adorno's notion of culture industry reflected how the masses were an object of powers coming from above. This difference was the reason why they preferred the notion of culture industry over that of mass culture, as the latter seemed to mark 'something of a culture that arises spontaneously from the masses themselves', as Adorno put it in a retrospective comment on the culture industry analysis (1991a: 85). Precisely this emergence from below was undermined by the culture industry which 'intentionally integrates its consumers from above' (1991a: 85).

[35] Adorno's contempt for jazz is legendary and much more elaborated than Fromm's mere reference to the beating rhythm of jazz (which, however, is interesting because of its underlying allusion to the stamping rhythms of 'primitive' peoples). In the famous 1936 essay 'On Jazz', Adorno unfolded his social critique of jazz, noting, for instance, that '[t]he more deeply jazz penetrates society, the more reactionary elements it takes on, the more completely it is beholden to banality, and the less it will be able to tolerate freedom and the eruption of phantasy, until it finally glorifies repression itself as the incidental music to accompany the current collective. The more democratic jazz is, the worse it becomes' (1989–90: 50). Replacing 'jazz' with 'crowd', this verdict could have appeared in classical critical accounts on the burgeoning era of crowds. See also Adorno's 1938 discussion of the masses' purportedly regressive way of listening (1991c). For a critical discussion of Adorno's view on jazz, see Witkin (2000). See also Jay (1973: 182ff.) who examines Adorno's work on other music genres.

While there is no doubt that most Frankfurt scholars, especially Horkheimer and Adorno, were utterly critical of mass culture, this did not amount to a wholesale rejection of all aspects of it. As Martin Jay has demonstrated, many Weimar scholars – including Kracauer and Walter Benjamin – in fact 'welcomed the crisis of high culture that accompanied the end of the Second Reich and cheered the new democratic, technological, modernist mass art they hoped would replace it' (1993: 365). For example, in spite of his remarks on film propaganda, Kracauer was particularly interested in the transformative potentials of films. Rather than seeing them as a medium for a grand cultural delusion, he believed they provided an important access to modern reality. Even key Frankfurt scholars such as Horkheimer did in fact acknowledge some advantages of *modernist* culture as compared to the traditional kinds of culture it replaced. According to Jay, Horkheimer was attracted by modernist autonomous art because its concern with art itself separated it from the capitalist economy and broke with the traditional 'positive model of harmony into which the aesthetic consumer could escape as a refuge from unhappiness in the real world' (1993: 370; cf. Horkheimer 1941; Marcuse 1988a). The Frankfurt scholars' concern with mass culture was therefore just as much a concern with the demise of modernist impulses since in mass culture capitalist economy and cultural achievements would merge into a consumerist bastard whose primary aim was to distract attention from objective repression.

One of the aspects of mass culture that Horkheimer and Adorno were most critical of was its alleged production and reproduction of sameness. 'Culture today is infecting everything with sameness', they wrote, alluding to the contagious and pathological nature which, similar to classical observations of crowds, was believed to be inherent to mass culture (2002: 94).[36] The continuous reproduction of sameness was an effect of mechanical standardization and constituted a key difference from previous cultural achievements which were characterized by their uniqueness. This echoed some crucial points from Walter Benjamin's 1936 analysis in 'The Work of Art in the Age of Mechanical Reproduction' (2007). Although Benjamin asserted that any work of art could be reproduced, the ability to reproduce art technically had fundamentally eliminated the *aura* that surrounded traditional artworks. The loss of aura had become

---

[36] This critical view was slightly modified in a 1956 essay entitled 'Masses', jointly authored by the members of the Institute. In this article, which drew extensively on crowd theorizing from Le Bon to Freud, the Frankfurt scholars distanced themselves from a common 'hostility toward the masses' as well as from a usual 'condemnation of the masses' (Frankfurt Institute for Social Research 1973: 72, 73).

particularly visible with the new artistic inventions of photography and especially the film. In both of these domains, the traditional aura had been replaced by an emphasis on the reproduction of sameness.

In a sense Benjamin's analysis transferred observations from crowd and mass semantics to the field of objects since they too were now believed to have lost their individuality, their aura. This loss was not just negative, however. According to Benjamin, the aura of artworks had its basis in cult and ritual, and precisely this ritual embeddedness had been surpassed: 'for the first time in world history, mechanical reproduction emancipates the work of art from its parasitical dependence on ritual ... Instead of being based on ritual, it begins to be based on another practice – politics' (2007: 224). This political opening had both positive–progressive and negative–reactionary potentials:

Mechanical reproduction of art changes the reaction of the masses toward art. The reactionary attitude toward a Picasso painting changes into the progressive reaction toward a Chaplin movie. The progressive reaction is characterized by the direct, intimate fusion of visual and emotional enjoyment with the orientation of the expert. Such fusion is of great social significance. (2007: 234)

Similar to Kracauer, Benjamin was particularly interested in films and argued that they could serve 'revolutionary functions' (2007: 236), as their close-ups, their explorations of otherwise hidden details, etc. were believed to illustrate hitherto unknown aspects of (social) life. In this sense, '[t]he camera introduces us to unconscious optics as does psycho-analysis to unconscious impulses' (2007: 237). While this reflected the positive side of films, Benjamin was also careful to emphasize their possible negative sides. Once again akin to Kracauer, he argued that films were employed as a crucial medium of propaganda by fascist regimes (see also Benjamin 2007: 251, n. 21).

Due to their rather univocal scepticism towards mass culture, Horkheimer and Adorno mainly subscribed to the negative views of Benjamin and referred affirmatively, i.e. in a critical vein, to the notion of 'mechanical reproducibility' (2002: 100). Although the idea of mechanical reproduction was conceived within an art-related horizon, it was embedded as well in an underlying Marxist framework that addressed property, proletarianization, etc.[37] Horkheimer and Adorno's analysis of

---

[37] This was visible not least in Benjamin's analysis of fascism: '[t]he growing proletarianization of modern man and the increasing formation of masses are two aspects of the same process. Fascism attempts to organize the newly created proletarian masses without affecting the property structure which the masses strive to eliminate' (2007: 241). In other words, fascism used films not just to generate masses as such, but equally as a tool to endow the masses with an identity, i.e. with a means

mass culture shared this Marxist inspiration which was evidenced by their systemic critique of the culture industry as well as by the latter's purported mechanisms of reification. Culture industry referred not only to the capitalistic interests in mass culture, but also to the assertion that cultural products had become similar to industrial products, that is, standardized reified commodities characterized by sameness and promoted by advertisement. In fundamental respects culture and industry had become alike, as Kracauer had also claimed.

Importantly, for present purposes, Horkheimer and Adorno did not simply complain about the predominance of standardization. The more important observation was that mass culture provided a crucial platform for fascism (see also Horkheimer 1993). In particular the radio was said to link mass culture and totalitarianism:

In fascism radio becomes the universal mouthpiece of the *Führer*; in the loudspeakers on the street his voice merges with the howl of sirens proclaiming panic, from which modern propaganda is hard to distinguish in any case. The National Socialists knew that broadcasting gave their cause stature as the printing press did to the Reformation. The *Führer's* metaphysical charisma, invented by the sociology of religion, turned out finally to be merely the omnipresence of his radio addresses, which demonically parodies that of the divine spirit. The gigantic fact that the speech penetrates everywhere replaces its content. (2002: 129, italics in original; see also 150)[38]

This marked an interesting difference from Le Bon. While he focused on the techniques a leader could use to seduce the crowd, e.g. by repeating specific phrases in his or her speeches, Horkheimer and Adorno saw the medium of broadcasting as the seductive device. Furthermore, they implicitly argued that the distinction between crowd and public, which Tarde had pinned his faith on, was no longer operative. The radio 'democratically makes everyone equally into listeners, in order to expose them in authoritarian fashion to the same programs put out by different stations' (2002: 95–6). And as a part of this, the public had become an integral part of the culture industry, not an external platform for rational reflection and critique.

Compared to *The Authoritarian Personality*, the discussion of mass culture in the *Dialectic of Enlightenment* was surprisingly meagre in its

---

through which they could observe themselves. According to Benjamin, the fascist 'introduction of aesthetics into political life' was pre-empted by Marinetti's futuristic programme (2007: 241).

[38] The celebration and penetration of loudness was, for Adorno, one of mass culture's characteristic traits. 'Loudspeakers are installed in the smallest of night clubs to amplify the sound until it becomes literally unbearable: everything is to sound like radio, like the echo of mass culture in all its might' (1991d: 58).

utilization of psychological explanations.[39] However, Adorno would express his indebtedness to psychological thinking anew in a discussion of 'Freudian theory and the pattern of fascist propaganda' from 1951 (1991b). This article made plain that for Adorno at least, Freud remained the major inspirational source when searching for explanations of fascism. Again and again Adorno stressed that Freud's essay *Group Psychology and the Analysis of the Ego* predicted the subsequent fascist developments.[40] 'It is not an overstatement if we say that Freud, though he was hardly interested in the political phase of the problem, clearly foresaw the rise and nature of fascist mass movements in purely psychological categories' (1991b: 115; see also 121). At the same time, Adorno argued, Freud's theory had to be supplemented with an understanding of mass culture to be fully adequate.

As should be clear by now, the Frankfurt School contributed to transferring many of the negative traits previously attributed to crowds (not least, de-individualization and the propensity to destruction and totalitarian rule) to a much broader and more general level of mass society, a society which appeared horrifying because it knew no outside. That said, the Frankfurt diagnoses of the modern, mid-twentieth-century mass society did not just entail a massification of crowd characteristics. Or, to be more precise, this massification must be understood

---

[39] This is not to suggest that the *Dialectic of Enlightenment* was entirely devoid of psychological reasoning. Especially the concluding essay on 'Elements of Anti-Semitism' drew on Freud's work (e.g. 2002: 149, 158–9, 162).

[40] Adorno also referred positively to the psychoanalytical work of Ernst Simmel, 'to whom we owe valuable contributions to the psychology of fascism' (1991b: 120). In 1946 Ernst Simmel edited a volume entitled *Anti-Semitism: A Social Disease*, which contained papers by several Frankfurt School associates, including Horkheimer and Adorno (1946a). Adorno's article in this book identified and discussed anti-Semitic and fascist propaganda in and among 'some West Coast agitators, pamphlets, and weekly publications' in the USA at the time (1946: 125). Simmel's own contribution to the volume, an article entitled 'Anti-Semitism and Mass Psychopathology', sought to understand why anti-Semitism could spread contagiously on a mass scale. Answering this question Simmel turned to the crowd and mass psychology of Le Bon and Freud. The Le Bonian leverage was evident: according to Simmel, 'the *individual* anti-Semite is not a psychotic – he is normal. It is only when he joins a group, when he becomes a member of a mass, that he loses certain qualities which determine normality, and thereby becomes instrumental in helping to produce a mass delusion, belief in which is shared by all the other group members' (1946b: 44, italics in original). Yet, Simmel noted, compared to the ephemeral 'crowd mind', anti-Semitism had a much more 'chronic character' (1946b: 66). When explaining anti-Semitism in more detail Simmel had recourse to Freud and argued that superego weaknesses, produced and/or enhanced by parent conflicts, accounted for the tendency towards aggressive anti-Semitism. This aggression would compensate for the weakness of the individual. In a word, Simmel pointed to how individual ego conflicts and their panicking implications paved the way for anti-Semitic action, an idea which was similar to what Hermann Broch proposed.

against the backdrop of the kind of structural transformation of society that formed the basis of the Frankfurt scholars' analyses, but was visible to some extent in Broch's work too. Most significantly, perhaps, the entire media landscape looked radically different when the Frankfurt scholars conducted their investigations than it did when the classical crowd theories of, say, Le Bon and Tarde appeared. While Tarde acknowledged the importance of newspapers, it was still possible at Tarde's time, i.e. at the end of the nineteenth century, to maintain a separation between physically co-present individuals and crowds, on the one hand, and the mass-mediated public, on the other. This became increasingly difficult due to a series of developments that vastly enhanced the societal significance of the mass media in the first half of the twentieth century. In Chapter 4, I discussed how the mounting importance of the media had been critically scrutinized in the 1920s by Lippmann and others, but while the mass media were already playing a decisive role at that time, it was barely comparable to the magnitude it would assume in the years to come. To give but a few indications of the changing situation, daily newspaper circulation almost doubled in the USA in the time-span from 1910 to 1930 (Gorman and McLean 2003: 21). In the same period, film assumed a most prominent function as a mass entertainment medium. Radio broadcasting experienced a veritable breakthrough especially in the 1930s and 1940s, and while advertising was already firmly established as a mass medium at this point, the radio gradually came to play a key role in advertising from the late 1920s (Gorman and McLean 2003: 68). Not to forget television, which boomed in the 1950s and 1960s.

This all added up to the impression guiding much Frankfurt School work, that society had become deeply enmeshed in mass medial influence. Gorman and McLean have argued that, '[b]efore World War II the media – movies, mass-circulation newspapers and magazines, national radio – had been forces for cultural integration' (2003: 168). While the Frankfurt scholars would passionately contest the notion of cultural integration, their analyses in effect subscribed to the double message that: (1) a mass audience had evolved due to the mass media; and (2) that this audience was exposed to more or less the same media (in contrast to later developments, such as cable and satellite networks, which contributed to a disintegrated composition of the mass media audience). That is, from everywhere radios could be heard, just as film, television, advertising and newspaper headlines relentlessly affected the individual, Adorno, Fromm, Kracauer, etc. argued. One central corollary of the veritable media bombardment of the modern individual was that the public sphere was constantly immanent in all social life. Hence the distinction between the physically co-present individuals and crowds, on one side, and the mass-mediated public, on the other, was hardly possible to sustain. This structural transformation marked a significant difference from the late nineteenth century and the crowd theories it inspired, but it also set the two mass-society plateaus I have analysed in this and the preceding chapter apart. Thus, the work of, say, Mannheim and Ortega was based much less on a notion of society in which the mass media had permeated all sociality and ways of thinking. This only became an integral part of the mass-society diagnosis that was championed by the Frankfurt scholars.

Mass society and the lonely crowd

The Frankfurt School's diagnosis and its centring upon the notion of mass culture received acclaim far beyond the School's confines. One example of this appeared in the work of Dwight Macdonald, an American intellectual and editor of the journal *Politics*.[41] In an article entitled 'A Theory of Mass Culture', Macdonald drew on resources from the Frankfurt School and presented a critique of mass culture which, although it was claimed to be different from that of both 'Marxian radicals and liberals', argued rather similarly to these purported alternatives that '[t]here are theoretical reasons why Mass Culture is not and can never be any good' (1953: 13). Macdonald offered arguably the most explicit illustration of how the semantics of mass society transferred features usually associated with the crowd to the level of society as such:

a mass society, like a crowd, is so undifferentiated and loosely structured that its atoms, in so far as human values go, tend to cohere only along the line of the least common denominator; its morality sinks to that of its most brutal and primitive members, its taste to that of the least sensitive and most ignorant. And in addition to everything else, the scale is simply too big, there are just *too many people*. (1953: 14, italics in original)[42]

---

[41] For fuller descriptions of Macdonald and his journal, see Pells (1985: 23–4, 174–82).
[42] A somewhat different diagnosis of mass society, which nevertheless recalled many elements discussed by the Frankfurt scholars, was presented by C. Wright Mills in his 1956 study *The Power Elite* (1956: ch. 13). In a counter-Tardean manner, referring to Le Bon, Ortega, Lippmann and others, Mills argued that in modern society publics had been replaced by masses. This, he asserted, had produced a highly asymmetrical social structure, separating a small power elite from the broad masses. Although Mills did not claim that this had yet resulted in totalitarianism (at least not in the USA), he did maintain that at the end of the 'road [of mass society] there is totalitarianism' (1956: 304). This critical observation was followed by descriptions of mass individuals that could almost have been written by Fromm: 'life in a society of masses implants insecurity and furthers impotence; it makes men uneasy and vaguely anxious; it

Although scholars from diverse branches subscribed to various aspects of the mass culture/mass society semantics, some of the key ideas underpinning this semantics were passionately contested, as the Geiger discussion from the previous chapter exemplifies. While Geiger's critique appeared in German, a central English-language problematization of the mass society semantics was articulated by Daniel Bell in a 1956 article entitled 'The Theory of Mass Society: A Critique'. According to Bell, the theory (he talked of it in the singular) of mass society was, next to Marxism, 'probably the most influential theory in the Western world today' (1956: 75). But, Bell asserted, this semantic corpus – he referred to the work of Arendt, Jaspers, Jünger, Lederer, Mannheim, Ortega, etc. – was not sustained by empirical evidence. For example, Bell (1956: 80–1) argued, the atomization depicted by several proponents of the mass society diagnosis ignored that it had been empirically ascertained that community life was actually flourishing, among ethnic groups and others. This was just one illustration of the underlying problem displayed by the mass society diagnosis, according to Bell: on a descriptive level, this semantics was inadequate and merely served 'as an ideology of romantic protest against contemporary society' (1956: 83).

Bell's critique was echoed by Edward Shils who, shortly after Bell's assessment, wrote a critical–polemical review article of an anthology entitled *Mass Culture: The Popular Arts in America* (Rosenberg and White 1957), which included contributions by and extracts from Adorno, Horkheimer, Macdonald, Ortega, among many others (Shils 1957). Similar to Bell, Shils argued that the whole semantics of mass society and especially of the various vices attributed to it (moral and aesthetic degradation, the emergence of the atomized mass individual, etc.) rested on a poor empirical foundation and was an effect of equally meagre analytical skills. Rather than applying an emphatic approach and taking seriously the actual desires of modern individuals, scholars adhering to the mass semantics promoted a 'German sociological romanticism', Shils claimed, which saw pre-modern society as better and more harmonious than empirical analysis could actually testify and hence believed that the transition to modernity had fundamentally changed individuals for the worse (1957: 598).[43] But on an empirical level, things were simply not as grave as diagnosed by the mass-society theorists, Shils

---

isolates the individual from the solid group; it destroys firm group standards. Acting without goals, the man in the mass just feels pointless' (1956: 323).

[43] A somewhat similar point was made by D. W. Brogan (1954) whom Shils also referred to (1957: 598, n. 25).

argued; the asserted decline was an illusion. Furthermore, Shils continued, the analyses offered by the critics of mass society were 'arbitrary and melodramatic' and the conclusions they drew went 'far beyond' the actual observations and often introduced 'utterly baseless prejudices' (1957: 602). On this basis, he concluded that '[t]he root of the trouble lies not in mass culture but in the intellectuals themselves' (1957: 606; for somewhat similar views, see also Shils 1960). There were a few exceptions to this picture, Shils admitted. One was David Riesman and his work on the so-called lonely crowd.

Although Shils was not entirely convinced of Riesman's respect for mass culture,[44] the latter's work nevertheless had a different anchoring than that of the Frankfurt School, just as its empirical foundation was stronger, on Shils' view. Riesman's most famous book (and the one which, for example, Kornhauser referred to) was *The Lonely Crowd: A Study of the Changing American Character*, which was published in 1950 and based on work conducted in collaboration with Nathan Glazer and Reuel Denney (1950). Similar to the tradition dating back to Ortega and Mannheim, Riesman was occupied in this book with the relation between character and social structure.[45] *The Lonely Crowd* was built on two main assertions, the first being that every society imposes some social character on its individuals. This social character was defined by Riesman as 'the more or less permanent, socially and historically conditioned organization of an individual's drives and satisfactions' (1950: 4). The second assertion was that in spite of the tendency towards permanence, the social forms generating social character were open to change, and such a transformation was precisely what Riesman observed in the American society of his time where a new social

---

[44] According to Shils, Riesman and others subscribing to his stance 'defend mass culture, but they do so largely because it is looked down upon by European anti-American intellectuals and by American xenophile intellectuals; they defend mass culture because they resent mere empty snobbery'; however, '[n]either Prof. Riesman, [nor any of the scholars expressing similar views] approves of the content of most of popular culture as it exists at present' (1957: 594–5).

[45] Riesman's work was also clearly inspired by the Frankfurt School. In a retrospective view on *The Lonely Crowd* Riesman described his and his associates' endeavour as follows: 'Working in the vein of *Escape from Freedom* and of the research tradition that led to *The Authoritarian Personality*, we saw character as molded at the "knee of society" primarily in childhood, to operate in relative independence of institutions thereafter ... following Fromm, we saw modern industrial society as primary, and as having an impact on child-rearing through the parents as transmission belts for the social imperatives' (1961: 434). Although Riesman did refer to Freud, he placed his work in opposition to that of 'orthodox Freudians' (1961: 434). It should be noted that Riesman's relation to the Frankfurt School was not unidirectional; his work also fed into that of the Frankfurt scholars (e.g. Bettelheim 1974).

character was believed to emerge. Before going deeper into that, a few remarks on Riesman's theoretical and conceptual framework are warranted.

Somewhat similar to Ortega, who, however, was only mentioned in passing in *The Lonely Crowd* (1950: 301), Riesman's starting point was demographic. Yet whereas Ortega was merely concerned with the rapid increase in the European populations from around 1800 to 1914, Riesman related various generic demographic phases to their implications for social structure and hence social character. Specifically, he distinguished between three overall phases of an S-shaped development and their corresponding social character types. First, a society characterized by high mortality and fertility rates would have a high population potential by bringing down mortality. In such a society conformity among individuals would be ensured by a social character type that Riesman called 'tradition-directed', which referred to a *Gemeinschaft*-like emphasis on the individual's embeddedness in particular clans, castes, etc. (1950: 10, 13). Second, a society which managed to bring down mortality but had not yet adjusted its fertility in a corresponding manner would be characterized by transitional growth. This growth, claimed Riesman, would make the tradition-directed character socially inadequate, and pave the way for a new type of social character, the so-called 'inner-directed' type. The point was that in such a society, 'a splintering of tradition' would occur (1950: 16) which would require of the individual that he or she could internalize societal goals and, through this, adjust to situations where no fixed standards for conduct were available beforehand. Riesman referred to Weber's (2001) Protestant ethic as an example of this inner-directedness.

Finally, and most importantly for Riesman's study, a society that experienced an incipient decline of the population – as a result of a diminishing need for high fertility rates due, for example, to improved life conditions and a transition from scarcity to abundance – would face new characterological challenges. 'The hard enduringness and enterprise of the inner-directed types are somewhat less necessary under these new conditions. Increasingly, *other people* are the problem, not the material environment' (1950: 18–19, italics in original). For the ensuing character type, the so-called 'other-directed' person, the views, behaviours, aspirations, etc. of peer groups would be crucial. Indeed, Riesman posited, the other-directed person was characterized by 'an exceptional sensitivity to the actions and wishes of others' (1950: 22). While Riesman's emphasis on how the social character was imposed on the individual by society and its social forms resembled a basically Durkheimian framework, the other-directed type amounted to a

Tardean individual whose entire approach to life was based on imitations of what his or her peers were believed to find important and right.[46]

Riesman was careful to stress that the various character types were merely ideal types and that in reality no society would be characterized by just one type. Still, the typology was believed to possess strong diagnostic qualities. Thus, whereas the analysis of the transition from tradition-direction to inner-direction amounted to a rather conventional modernization theory, the examination of other-direction was an attempt to come to terms with late-modern developments.[47] On Riesman's analysis, 'unless present trends are reversed, the hegemony of other-direction lies not far off' (1950: 21), and it is already, and in particular, 'becoming the typical character of the "new" middle class – the bureaucrat, the salaried employee in business, etc.' (1950: 21).

According to Riesman, the development towards a hegemony of other-direction constituted a severe societal and characterological predicament which was analysed in the book along several lines (work life, family life, school life, political life, etc.). For example, the whole problematization of the other-directed character type revolved around the assertion that it undermined the notion of individual autonomy. Rather than resting on their own judgements, the other-directed persons were keen on imitating their peers. This, further, was believed to lead to anxiety, caused by the permanent need for screening others' behaviours and wishes in order to find standards to imitate and adjust to (e.g. 1950: 26). Riesman argued that such adjustment would erode intimate social relations; the other-directed person 'remains a lonely member of the crowd because he never comes really close to the others or to himself' (1950: v; see also 373). This amounted to saying that this emerging social character was alienated, and that real and true personal and social relations could only be established if the individual acquired a more autonomous character. However, and this was the final crucial point, Riesman was not very optimistic about a (re)birth of autonomous individualities. 'It is much more likely', he stated at the end of the book, 'that, out of impatience with uncertainty and with the "sluggish

---

[46] Bringing Tarde's account of the individual back in helps to highlight the critical ambitions of Riesman's analysis. Thus, similar to the classic somnambulist, the other-directed character type purportedly renounced 'autonomy' and was characterized by 'false personalization' (1950: 311). In short, the other-directed character was yet another example of how qualities usually ascribed to the crowd now became predominant features of the social character corresponding to a late-modern society. Put differently, it was another warning that the liberal subject was in the line of fire.

[47] This also highlighted the difference to Tarde's analysis. Whereas the latter described sociality as such as following a somnambulistic logic, Riesman's diagnosis suggested that this was only specific to a particular social structure.

masses," parties and authoritarian movements will force people toward goals which are neither commonsensical nor utopian but merely regressive' (1950: 370; see also 1961: 455–8). So while Riesman did not explicitly refer to totalitarianism as an inherent problem of modern society, he did point to a potential propensity to regressive politics which was derived from the transition to other-direction. Related to this, Riesman's analysis suggested that it was the new middle class that was most susceptible to regressiveness, not the people with 'the fewest opportunities to participate in the formal and informal life of the community', as Kornhauser (1960: 212) would have it.

Riesman repeated his pessimism in a companioning volume to *The Lonely Crowd*, published two years later and entitled *Faces in the Crowd* (1952). This book presented a comprehensive interview-based analysis of individuals who embodied each of the three character types. The book ended with some reflections on the ability of other-directed characters to become autonomous. Again, the outlook was not too optimistic. 'Loneliness may be the inescapable destiny of many Americans', Riesman prophesied (1952: 740). To illustrate the magnitude of his pessimism, Riesman was only able to pin his faith on literature as a means through which to achieve autonomy; through literature 'we can become reconciled with ourselves and thus ready for further ventures toward autonomy' (1952: 739). But Riesman did not seem too convinced about this empowering ability attributed to literature. At any rate, he concluded the investigation by maintaining that 'the moving about between being in the crowd and being in the wilderness, between society and solitude (in Emerson's phrase), contains much of the American experience and the American tension' (1952: 740).

The approaching hegemony of the other-directed character type had obvious political implications. For example, Riesman argued that a grand transformation of politics was becoming visible where people no longer engaged in political activity because of its intrinsic value; rather they conceived of politics as parallel to consumption and looked at it in terms of its possible glamour as well as a field where 'acceptable opinions' could be acquired (1950: 208, 211).[48] According to Riesman, the mass media, and popular culture more generally, enhanced this development, as their constant display of new ideas and fashions propelled the reproduction of other-directedness. Similar views would later be expressed with great force in postmodern conceptualizations of masses (see Chapter 8).

---

[48] This development applied as well to the political leaders who were said to be guided by an (other-directed) 'psychological need to be continuously judged by others' (1950: 265).

Another significant transformation of the political realm, which the transition to other-directed stimulated, regarded a transfer of power from a ruling class to what Riesman called veto groups. Riesman described how American politics was once dominated by one 'mercantile-aristocratic group' (1950: 242) and how this had been replaced by a great number of lobbying veto groups who each fought for their own narrow interests. This appeared to resemble the kind of pluralism Kornhauser wished for. Yet it seems more correct to conceive of Riesman's account of other-direction in terms of Kornhauser's diagnosis of mass society, namely as a society where the elites can be influenced by the non-elites (the veto groups) and where non-elites are readily available for mobilization by the elites (other-direction).

Riesman's studies inspired much debate (e.g. Lipset and Lowenthal 1961), which I will not dwell on here. Instead I will pinpoint how his investigations differed from other contributions to crowd and mass semantics. Compared to the other scholars examined in this chapter, Riesman's work stands out in its rather non-explicit way of addressing crowds and masses. Except from the (admittedly, significant) titles of his books, *The Lonely Crowd* and *Faces in the Crowd*, and a few isolated passages here and there, Riesman seemed rather unconcerned with the semantic tradition investigated in the present book. He nevertheless contributed to this tradition in three important ways. First, in very general terms he adopted the diagnostic approach used by, for example, Le Bon and mapped the emergence of a new social structure which had a number of crucial individual, cultural and political effects. More importantly, second, a new social character type was registered, which possessed an urge for imitating others' ideas, opinions and behaviours. Although not conceived of in terms of hypnotic suggestion, this image of the other-directed person reiterated classical features attributed to co-present crowds, especially the reliance on the ideas of others. Yet the characteristics also differed: the other-directed person was not dependent on physical co-presence, but made use instead of mass media. Further, in addition to being attracted by the sociality offered by the crowd (at times Riesman used 'crowd' and 'society' as synonymous terms, e.g. 1952: 740), the other-directed character was simultaneously seized by a feeling of loneliness.

There is a third aspect of Riesman's work that makes it significant in comparison with the previous semantics of crowds. This aspect relates less to theoretical or conceptual content and more to *methods*. Although Ortega had referred briefly to demographic developments and to his visual experiences with masses, and Kornhauser drew on statistical data in his analysis of the politics of mass society, Riesman's methodological set-up was unique in its comprehensive use of empirical data, especially interviews which were conducted by a large group of research associates (for discussions of Riesman's methodology, see also Brodbeck 1961; Kecskemeti 1961). This empirical foundation marked a strong difference from earlier crowd theories which were much more conceptual (or in a pejorative formulation, speculative) in character.[49] As I shall argue in the final part of the chapter, it makes sense to see Riesman's interest in quantitative methods as an outcome of developments in mass communications research.

Questioning mass manipulation: the emergence of the primary group

Critiques of the mass society diagnosis not only emanated from the Bell–Shils camp. The idea that the mass media occupied a crucial role in everyday life, and contributed not a little to the isolation of individuals, was challenged by a series of studies that endorsed a less critical and more positivist agenda. As demonstrated in Chapter 4, there had been a waxing problematization in the 1920s of the relations between mass media, propaganda and public opinion. The Frankfurt School's analyses of the culture industry might be seen as an offshoot of this kind of problematization. Critiques of such mass media and propaganda studies now evolved on the basis of a booming interest in the mass media. Much of this work was pioneered by Paul F. Lazarsfeld, an Austrian *émigré* mathematician, who was director of the Office of Radio Research at Princeton University. This Office – whose inner circle also counted Frank Stanton and Hadley Cantril, and which later transferred to Columbia University, where it was renamed the Bureau of Applied Social Research, with Merton as a close collaborator – conducted several empirical studies of the role of the radio in contemporary American society. Yet Lazarsfeld and his research group also carried out comprehensive investigations of the societal influence of other media of mass communication.

According to Lazarsfeld, a problematic consensus had evolved in previous studies of mass media, from Robert E. Park to propaganda theorists, that people, the audience of mass communication, comprise a docile mass of atomistic individuals that can be directed, or manipulated, at will through the mass media (e.g. Katz and Lazarsfeld 1955: 16).

---

[49] To be sure, the Chicago School is famous for its empirical case studies, but with respect to the crowd topic, even the Chicago scholars adhered to more theoretico-conceptual investigations.

This image was being called into question by Lazarsfeld's empirical work. Indeed, this research demonstrated, people's beliefs and behaviours are not simply manipulated through the mass media. Much more, he showed in seminal studies, such as *The People's Choice: How the Voter Makes up His Mind in a Presidential Campaign* from 1944, these beliefs and behaviours are moulded through people's contact with family members, colleagues and local 'opinion leaders' (Lazarsfeld *et al.* 1968: 49). Accordingly, to fully understand the relation between the mass media and the people it was necessary to take into account an intermediary level, namely the primary group, which operated as an 'intervening variable' between the mass media and the people, as it was put in the quantitative parlance of Elihu Katz and Paul F. Lazarsfeld (1955: 34).[50]

This empirical finding had two central implications. First, the Frankfurt scholars' mass society diagnosis of the atomization of individuals in modern society was deemed inadequate, because important ties could be identified between singular individuals and primary groups. Second, and relatedly, the intervening variable of the primary group entailed that the manipulative force attributed to the mass media was exaggerated, as it would have to pass through the primary groups, or more precisely the opinion leaders in them – a process captured by the notion of the so-called 'two-step flow of communication' (Katz and Lazarsfeld 1955: ch. 14; Lazarsfeld *et al.* 1968: 151).

There is insufficient space here to go further into this tradition of mass communications research and its multifaceted contributions. Let me just make two points. First, and most importantly for present purposes, a decisive shift in interest was effected by this branch of research, from seeing the individual in his or her relation to a crowd or mass towards understanding how a primary group, itself neither crowd nor mass, impacted on the choices and desires of the individual. That is, by placing a premium on the primary group in whatever form it might assume, the importance of crowds and masses (in their

---

[50] Much of this mass communications research revolved around the so-called 'rediscovery of the primary group' (e.g. Katz and Lazarsfeld 1955: 33ff.). While the notion of the primary group had enjoyed an early career in American sociology due to the work of Charles H. Cooley, for whom it was employed to account for the socialization of individuals as well as for their basic collective affiliations, it was now reutilized in a new theoretical setting and linked to methodologies that differed markedly from those of Cooley. The rediscovery of the primary group was inspired as well by findings beyond the field of mass communications research, such as Elton Mayo's work on industrial sociology. In the famous Hawthorne study, Mayo had detected a strong peer-group effect among workers, which bore some affinity to the idea of the primary group. The connection of Mayo's work to crowd semantics is analysed by Frezza (2007: ch. 6).

classic attire) was in effect sliding rapidly down the sociological agenda. Or, as Leach has put it in his analysis of this development, one significant consequence of the rediscovery of the primary group was that it 'eroded the progressive conceptions of crowd and mass' (1986: 111).

This erosion was buttressed, second, by a shift in methodological emphasis. Thus, the mainly qualitative and conceptual framework of most exciting crowd and mass semantics was severely challenged by the predominantly quantitative approaches adopted within the mass communications research. As mentioned in Chapter 4, a wave of positivism swept American sociology from the 1920s onwards. In his analyses of the development of American sociology George Steinmetz has argued that, after 1945, this methodological positivism evolved as the new *doxa* in the American sociological landscape (2007). Lazarsfeld played a key role in this positivist tide, not merely through his own writings, but also institutionally via the influential research centres that he founded at Princeton and Columbia. Although Lazarsfeld acknowledged the need for qualitative work, his chief contribution to sociology lay in his insistence on and innovation of quantitative methods, especially survey techniques and other means of quantitative data gathering. The increasing dominance of these quantitative methods contributed – not necessarily purposefully – to contesting most crowd and mass semantics, relying as the latter did on qualitative and conceptual approaches. This might explain why books such as Adorno *et al.*'s *The Authoritarian Personality* and Riesman's *The Lonely Crowd* endorsed a quantitative set-up.[51] Adapting to a quantitative programme became one means of legitimizing a continued interest in crowd and mass issues. That said, the immense efforts of Reich, Broch and the Frankfurt School associates demonstrate that, even if the positivist agenda became increasingly dominant in American sociology, crowd and especially mass semantics actually thrived in some theoretical sectors – not least through the blend of sociological and psychological/psychoanalytical approaches.

When considering the temporal extension of the semantic plateau analysed in this chapter, it appears that the problematization of totalitarianism gradually changed, in the course of time, as the temporal distance to Hitlerism increased. From being a concern with the actual experiences

---

[51] In the 1930s, Lazarsfeld and Adorno entertained rather close ties, but the relationship later cooled down; see Calhoun and VanAntwerpen (2007: 395) and Steinmetz (2007: 327). Riesman briefly related his work to Lazarsfeld's in a discussion of opinion leaders in *The Lonely Crowd* (1950: 78, n. 2).

with fascism, as expressed in particular in the Hitler case, scholars began little by little to look beyond the German example and examine the possible proto-totalitarian inclinations in other societal settings, such as the USA. From being an *actual* problem, totalitarianism, in other words, transformed into an ever-lurking *potentiality*. Interestingly, although these proto-totalitarian potentialities were located in a wide range of fundamental structural features, from sexual inhibition over the culture industry to demographic constellations, many of the specific suggestions for how to deal with the observed calamities resorted to some form of Enlightenment strategy. If only the masses could be educated, then the dangerous potentials could be kept at bay. At the same time, some of the structural transformations, such as the rapidly changing media landscape and the immanence that the media now assumed in social life, hardly left much hope for the efficacy of Enlightenment schemes.

Let me finally note that due to the fusion of sociological and psychological or psychoanalytical registers, this semantic plateau obviously did not police disciplinary boundaries. The whole endeavour was to utilize various disciplines simultaneously so as to arrive at a more complete understanding of modern society. As the next chapter will show, this theoretical attitude was contested in two modalities of crowd thinking that appeared in the 1950s and 1960s. One would pursue a distinctive non-disciplinary approach, while the other would seek to squeeze out psychological elements or at least to base crowd thinking on what was conceived of as solid sociological grounds.

7 The culmination and dissolution of crowd semantics

The semantic transformation from crowd to mass, which was enacted within social theory from around 1930 to 1960, obtained an extremely influential position in the theorization on collectivities, culture and society. Yet its dominance was not absolute. From the late 1950s and with increasing intensity in the 1960s and 1970s, a series of alternative positions emerged that attended to crowd and collective phenomena in new fashions. This upsurge in crowd semantics did not last long, however, for simultaneous with the revitalization of crowd thinking there were dedicated attempts to marginalize the notion of crowds and replace it with a focus on social movements. I shall discuss the battles between the sociology of crowds and collective behaviour, on the one hand, and social movement studies, on the other, at the end of this chapter.

Before getting to these struggles, the chapter examines some of the mid-twentieth-century attempts to reinvent crowd theory. I first deal with what is arguably the pinnacle of crowd theory, namely Elias Canetti's *Crowds and Power*. I realize that referring to this book as the culmination of a long semantic tradition is bound to be contested. The label is warranted, however, if only because the efforts Canetti devoted to this project were exceptional. He spent more than thirty years on the book which ran to almost 500 pages in the English translation and nearly 600 pages in the German version. To the extent that *Crowds and Power* marked the apex of the tradition of crowd theorizing, this was a paradoxical culmination. The book attempted to transcend the existing crowd theory tradition and establish an entirely new edifice for discussing crowds, but this new analytical platform was almost completely silenced within sociological circles because Canetti resisted adhering to standard scientific procedures and because his deliberate ignorance of any explicit dialogue with, say, Le Bon, Park, Freud or Geiger left hardly any points of connection.

Canetti's destiny is different from but nevertheless related to the faith of a group of American sociologists who, in the second half of the twentieth century, invested much academic capital in reviving the notion of crowds. These scholars sided with Canetti in their ambition to go beyond previous crowd theorizing. Although some parallels can be identified in their conceptions of crowds and collective behaviour, the sociologists naturally situated their work more firmly in ongoing socio-logical debates. Moreover, much more markedly than Canetti the sociolo-gists reconfigured the conception of crowds, so that almost all traditional content relating to the irrationality of crowds was erased and substituted with a rational understanding of crowds and collective behaviour. These radical changes turned out to be much more successful than Canetti's, and they altered sociological crowd semantics in ways that are visible even today – especially in those sociological corners where the study of social movements did not entirely displace the interest in crowds and collective behaviour.

An inside view: Elias Canetti's phenomenology of crowds

Early personal experiences as well as broad historical circumstances propelled Canetti's continuous interest in the crowd issue, an interest which culminated with his comprehensive study *Crowds and Power*, published in 1960 (1984). This book aimed to change profoundly the conception of crowds, and it did so not least by replacing psychological and sociological approaches to the topic with a phenomenological account that described the crowd from the inside rather than from the outside, as Canetti believed most previous crowd theory had mistakenly and inadequately done. Since Canetti's own experiences with crowd incidents would have a significant bearing on his phenomenological take on the crowd issue, I will begin by briefly describing these events as they are conveyed in his memoirs.

Canetti's first personal acquaintance with the crowd was related to the outbreak of the First World War. On 1 August 1914, he and his brothers were playing in a park in Baden near Vienna when it was announced that Germany had declared war on Russia. A band entertaining in the park began playing the Austrian imperial and then the German anthem and people joined in singing. Canetti, who had just turned 9 years old, and who had previously lived for a couple of years in Manchester, recognized the tune, but since the German anthem 'Hail to Thee in Victor's Laurels' was the same tune as 'God Save the King', he began singing the latter 'at the top of [his] lungs': 'Since we were in the thick of the crowd, no one could miss it. Suddenly, I saw faces warped with rage all about me and arms and hands hitting me' (1988: 90). As Canetti later recalled, 'I didn't quite understand what I had done, but this first experience with a hostile crowd was all the more indelible' (1988: 91).

The next significant experience unfolded in late June 1922. On 24 June the German Foreign Minister Walther Rathenau was assassinated and this elicited a workers' demonstration in Frankfurt where Canetti lived at the time. Although he was not part of the demonstration, Canetti witnessed it first-hand and this left an unforgettable impression on him. 'The memory of this first demonstration that I consciously witnessed was powerful. It was the physical attraction that I couldn't forget. I was so anxious to belong to the march' (1989: 80). Indeed, he later confessed, after this experience, the crowd 'was so deeply on my mind, having become the enigma of enigmas for me' (1989: 81). Still, up until then, Canetti had only been external to the crowd, either as the object of the crowd's anger or as a curious spectator. This would change with his third formative encounter with the crowd which took place in Vienna on 15 July 1927.

The background was the following.[1] During a demonstration some months before, two demonstrators associated with the Social Democratic Party had been shot. A trial was set for the murderers, but on 15 July they were not only declared not guilty, the *Reichspost*, a Viennese newspaper, announced that this was a 'just verdict' (Canetti 1989: 245). Especially the latter statement offended the workers. Therefore:

From all districts of the city, the workers marched in tight formations to the Palace of Justice, whose sheer name embodied the unjust verdict for them. It was a totally spontaneous reaction: I could tell how spontaneous it was just by my own conduct. I quickly biked into the center of town and joined one of these processions. (1989: 245)

Arriving at the Palace of Justice the agitated crowd set it on fire. The police intervened and killed ninety people. In his memoirs, Canetti gave detailed accounts of specific episodes during this crowd event. I will return to some of these below. Of greatest immediate importance is the general impression he acquired of crowds and their behaviour. 'Fifty-three years have passed', wrote Canetti in his memoirs:

and the agitation of that day is still in my bones. It was the closest thing to a revolution that I have physically experienced ... I became part of the crowd, I fully dissolved in it, I did not feel the slightest resistance to what the crowd was doing. (1989: 245)

Precisely this kind of personal experience was entirely missing in the work on crowds from Le Bon to Freud, Canetti complained, and '[t]o describe [the crowd] without experiencing it was virtually misleading'

---

[1] For a full account of the events of this day, see Stieg (1990) as well as Hanuschek's comprehensive biography of Canetti. As is the case with Canetti's memoirs, an entire chapter of Hanuschek's book is devoted to 15 July 1927 (2005: 138–49).

(1989: 149).[2] Their purely external descriptions of crowds prevented them from recognizing the *positive* features of crowds. Canetti, by contrast, 'knew the crowd from the inside' and 'had never forgotten how *gladly* one falls prey to the crowd' (1989: 148, italics in original). In order to account for his experiences, i.e. in order to understand the dynamics he had been exposed to and which had driven him on these crucial days of his life, Canetti devoted the next three decades to the study of crowds.

The endeavour to understand crowds was also incited by larger societal events. Here Canetti's situation was not different from that of many other scholars described previously in this book. As he put it in a retrospective comment from 1962:

> A contemporary of the events of the last 50 years since the outbreak of World War One, who has experienced first wars, then revolutions, inflations and then fascist dictatorship, cannot help feeling the necessity under the pressure of these events of trying to come to terms with the question of crowds. (1996b: 5)

So, in Canetti's view, whether or not one had been physically absorbed in actual crowds, the historical developments simply compelled an interest in the crowd topic. The result of Canetti's endeavours was put forward in *Crowds and Power*, which, in addition to responding to the self-experienced enigma of crowd attraction, was an attempt to understand the roots of fascism.[3]

Crowd dynamics

In spite of the societal events that prompted Canetti's interest in the crowd, the analysis in *Crowds and Power* did not take the form of a general societal problematization of crowds. The book did not espouse the view of, say, Le Bon and Tarde, that crowds threatened the fabric of modern society. Quite the opposite, for on the one hand, Canetti's investigations had convinced him that the crowd was no specifically

---

[2] According to Canetti:

> [n]early all these writers had closed themselves off against masses, crowds; they found them alien or seemed to fear them; and when they set about investigating them, they gestured: Keep ten feet away from me! A crowd seemed something leprous to them, it was like a disease. They were supposed to find the symptoms and describe them. It was crucial for them, when confronted with a crowd, to keep their heads, not be seduced by the crowd, not melt into it. (1989: 147)

Freud in particular was the target of Canetti's contempt. His *Group Psychology and the Analysis of the Ego* 'repelled me from the very first word, and still repels me no less fifty-five years later', Canetti declared (1989: 147; see also 1996b: 12–13).

[3] Similar to Broch, Canetti's fictional work also included crowd-theoretical reflections. This applied especially to his 1936 novel *Auto da Fé* (2005). For discussions of the relation between this novel and *Crowds and Power*, see Arnason and Roberts (2004).

modern phenomenon. Although Europe's totalitarian past could not be understood without taking seriously the crowd, the latter could be identified at all times and in every society, Canetti claimed. On the other hand, the terms Canetti employed to describe the crowd were not mainly negative, but drew primarily on a vocabulary of freedom and emancipation. I say 'primarily' because Canetti also did point to violent crowd excesses, as will be clear below. In spite of this possible dialectics between crowds and violence, it was crucial to Canetti to draw a sharp distinction between the two phenomena. This is also the reason why the book was entitled *Crowds and Power*: the conjunction 'and' was meant to stress that crowds need not be enmeshed in power.

The chief problematization underpinning the book was of a descriptive and explanatory nature. As stated, Canetti wanted to furnish an inside view of the crowd which emphasized its positive features. This was the descriptive side. On the explanatory level, he did not have high thoughts about sociological and, much less, psychological approaches to crowds. It seems warranted to say that, for Canetti, the existing sociological and psychological work on crowds was deemed inadequate because its external perspective tended to reduce the crowd to some negative and violent entity. The solution to this double problematization was found in his anthropological and phenomenological account.[4]

The book opened with such an anthropological observation, which put forward in general anthropological terms what Erving Goffman (1983: 4) would later describe as a crucial feature of the interaction order of public space:

There is nothing that man fears more than the touch of the unknown. He wants to *see* what is reaching towards him, and to be able to recognize or at least classify it . . . The fear of burglars is not only the fear of being robbed, but also the fear of a sudden and unexpected clutch out of the darkness.[5] The repugnance to being touched remains with us when we go about among

---

[4] Reflecting his idiosyncratic style, Canetti's anthropological approach did not pay systematic attention to developments within the anthropological discipline. This has been demonstrated by Ritchie Robertson (2000) who shows that to some extent *Crowds and Power* drew on outdated anthropological observations. At the same time, Robertson notes, 'its more successful passages, notably the description of crowd behaviour, anticipate the interpretive turn in social anthropology, and the literary technique of thick description recently adopted by the new breed of historical anthropologists' (2000: 168).

[5] For some reason the English translation has omitted a passage at this point where Canetti explains how the feared clutch is often symbolized by the hand shaped as a claw (see Canetti 1980: 13). This is a rather grave omission since, as I shall return to below, Canetti's theory of power is based on the notion of the seizing hand. So when the book's opening paragraphs made reference to the hand/claw this was a clear, albeit implicit, vestige of how crowds and power may be related.

people; the way we move in a busy street, in restaurants, trains or buses, is governed by it. Even when we are standing next to them and are able to watch and examine them closely, we avoid actual contact if we can. If we do not avoid it, it is because we feel attracted to someone; and then it is we who make the approach. (1984: 15, italics in original)

It was this fear of being touched, elevated by Canetti to an anthropological constant, which was relieved in and by the crowd:

It is only in a crowd that man can become free of this fear of being touched. That is the only situation in which the fear changes into its opposite. The crowd he needs is the dense crowd, in which body is pressed to body. (1984: 15)

This observation of the crowd's claustrophilia, as it were, was merely the starting point for Canetti's comprehensive investigation of the internal dynamics of crowds, of which I shall highlight only the most important aspects.[6] To begin with, Canetti portrayed the crowd as being driven by a spontaneous, self-organizing energy. 'A few people may have been standing together – five, ten or twelve, not more; nothing has been announced, nothing is expected. Suddenly everywhere is black with people' (1984: 16).[7] This pull of people satisfied 'the urge to grow', which, according to Canetti, 'is the first and supreme attribute of the crowd' (1984: 16).

A second crucial attribute was *equality*. Indeed, Canetti asserted, 'one might even define a crowd as a state of absolute equality' (1984: 29). This equality had a profoundly physical nature. The tight bodily composition of the crowd entailed that 'no distinctions count, not even that of sex ... Suddenly it is as though everything were happening in one and the same body' (1984: 15, 16). The equality would grow stronger, the denser the crowd were, and this is the reason why the crowd was believed to desire density (1984: 29). According to Canetti, the culmination of equality occurs in the discharge. The discharge also demonstrates that the yearning for density and equality is not merely stirred

---

[6] It should be clear by now that the kind of crowds Canetti was interested in was physical crowds, i.e. crowds composed of physically co-present members. Some of his analyses touched on *mass* states as well, as when, for instance, he characterized nations according to their alleged crowd symbols, defining the English by the sea, the Dutch by the dyke, the Germans by the marching forest in the form of the army, the French by the revolution, etc. (1984: 169ff.). All these national crowd symbols were believed to be effective in the individuals, irrespective of whether people were physically together.

[7] To be sure, Canetti admitted, '[i]n its innermost core it is not quite as spontaneous as it appears, but, except for these 5, 10 or 12 people with whom actually it originates, it is everywhere spontaneous' (1984: 16). Canetti had no interest in this core. It was merely a condition of the crowd's emergence, but it could not account for, let alone determine, the crowd's development or organization.

by physical factors; it is founded as well on specific social conditions. Thus, posited Canetti, in our everyday life various so-called 'burdens of distance' are imposed on people which cannot be relieved by the singular individual (1984: 18). 'Only together can men free themselves from their burdens of distance; and this, precisely, is what happens in a crowd' when 'distinctions are thrown off and all feel *equal*' (1984: 18, italics in original).

What was the content of these burdens of distance that were relieved in the crowd's eruption? One answer to this question appeared, as McClelland (1989: 299) has noted, in Canetti's discussion of commands. According to Canetti (1984: 305), every time an individual carries out a command, a sting is left in him or her where it lodges for ever. These stings continuously remind the individual of the commands that were imposed on him or her from outside and which he or she submitted to. In other words, they remind the individual of the inequalities that exist in society. It is the accumulation of these stings, piled up over many years, that, claimed Canetti, constitutes a major part of the individual's burdens of distance (see also Canetti 1996b: 15). McClelland argues that burdens of distance and stings of command 'add up to what sociologists call social structure, or the distribution of social power' (1996: 24). This is true of burdens of distance, but less so for the stings of command since these referred, for Canetti, to the lasting psychological imprints of power.

Returning to the crowd, what takes place here is a collective battle against the taxing stings of command. Whereas the outside world is full of commands and social hierarchies, the crowd provides a space liberated from these structures of inequality. 'Within a crowd all are equal; no-one has a right to give commands to anyone else', Canetti stated, and this had the crucial implication that:

Not only are no new stings formed, but all the old ones are got rid of for the time being. It is as though people had slipped out of their houses, leaving their stings piled in the cellars. This *stepping out of* everything which binds, encloses and burdens them is the real reason for the elation which people feel in a crowd. Nowhere does the individual feel more free and if he desperately tries to remain part of a crowd, it is because he knows what awaits him afterwards. When he returns to his house, to *himself*, he finds them all there again, boundaries, burdens and stings. (1984: 324, italics in original)

In brief, all social inequalities are suspended in the crowd and this constitutes its real attractiveness, as it produces a new sense of freedom for the individual. Canetti described this moment of equality and freedom as 'an immense feeling of relief' and claimed that '[i]t is for the sake of this blessed moment, when no-one is greater or better than another, that people become a crowd' (1984: 18). The image of the crowd emerging here is one of temporary liberation from and resistance to existing power structures.[8] Against this background, the key anthropological assumption guiding Canetti's entire analysis comes to the fore: people have a, not necessarily reflected, threefold urge for: (1) equality; (2) the associated suspension of power hierarchies; and (3) the resulting freedom which the crowd purportedly generates. It follows from this that the kind of inquiry that triggered Reich's work (why do people desire their own submission?) was hardly compatible with Canetti's horizon.

It is possible to derive from these parts of Canetti's analysis a novel perspective on *individuality* that redefined the general image presented in the classical European crowd semantics of Le Bon and Tarde. First of all, according to Canetti's account, it makes no sense to imagine an antagonistic relation between the crowd and the individual; quite the contrary, the crowd actually seems to constitute the condition of possibility of individuality, and in certain respects it actually appears to pre-date the individual, both anthropologically and from an explanatory point of view. Endre Kiss has argued that, in contrast to Freud who 'reaches the problem of the crowds from that of the individual, Canetti portrays crowds as *prior* to individualization' (2004: 728, italics added). Moreover, rather than being a de-individualizing force, Canetti suggested that the crowd opens up transformative potentials for the individual. 'In the crowd the individual feels that he is transcending the limits of his own person', wrote Canetti (1984: 20). The crowd simply endows the individual with the possibility of becoming a new person. Or as Moscovici has put it in a discussion of Canetti's crowd theory, '[f]ar from being squashed and ground down by the crowd, as is commonly supposed, the individual thus expands within it and is expanded by it. He goes beyond himself, and then returns within himself, transformed' (1987: 49). The interest in this transformative power was partly an effect of Canetti's own crowd experiences and partly related to the inspirational sources he employed to conceive of crowds, and which consisted to a large degree of primitive myths that placed transformation centrally. These myths asserted that human beings have at their core an ability to transform themselves, and for this reason there could be no talk of

---

[8] Canetti acknowledged that an alternative and more fundamental strategy to become free might be to simply resist or 'evade [the commands] in the first place' (1984: 306), but he offered no in-depth analysis of this option. For a discussion of resistance in Canetti, see Brighenti (2011).

de-individualizing crowd tendencies, because human individuals were always already transformed and transforming.[9]

Canetti's emphasis on the positive features associated with the crowd (freedom, individuality, equality) was a reflection of his basically vitalist interpretation of crowd behaviour. This vitalism was not just a result of the life impulses he had experienced in the crowd, but equally – and perhaps even more so – related to another early personal experience, which impacted on him for the rest of his life, namely his father's death when Canetti was only 7 years old. The importance of this event is highlighted by the fact that Canetti described 15 July 1927 as 'the most crucial day of my life after my father's death' (1989: 246). It is not my aim here to psychologize Canetti (his hostility towards Freud does not invite that kind of endeavour). But this early experience had an important bearing on his subsequent work, including his crowd theorizing, in that Canetti became obsessed with the idea to fight death. 'So long as death exists', wrote Canetti programmatically, 'any utterance is an utterance against it' (1976a: 7). Moscovici (1987) sees in Canetti's appraisal of crowds one of the latter's manifold attacks on death, something which associated him with Broch and the latter's notion of the 'urge of life' that seeks to deflect death.[10] In Canetti's analysis, the crowd is life and its urge to growth is a propensity to promote this life ever further, i.e. to incorporate new bodies and to liberate more individuals. The tendency to at once expand and intensify the bodily compression is, in other words, the crowd's fundamental contribution to life.

The vitalist conception of crowds placed Canetti on a par with especially Whitman, who also associated the massified bodily contact with joy, pleasure and liberation. At the same time, however, the vitalist impulse was also what set Canetti and Whitman apart, for it was the crowd's vitalist inclinations that led Canetti to observe the possible dark sides of the transformation created by crowds. Canetti's argument ran as follows: the individual who experiences freedom in the crowd 'wants what is happening to him to happen to others too' (1984: 20), no matter what means might be required to this end. Ultimately, the vitalist

---

[9] I will not go into detail with Canetti's view of transformation. See for this purpose Arnason and Roberts (2004) as well as Paulsen (2005: 76–9).

[10] It is beyond the scope of the present investigation to delve into the relations between the crowd theories of Broch and Canetti. Suffice it to say that the main separating point was whether, as Broch thought, an understanding of crowds and masses should be founded in psychology (whether of a Freudian flavour or not), or if, as Canetti believed, a non-psychological venture was needed. For discussions of Broch and Canetti, see Borch (2008: 73–6), Moscovici (1987: 54–8), Müller-Funk (2003), Schmid-Bortenschlager (1985) and Weigel (1993).

inclination may depend on its opposition, death, for the only way for the crowd to promote (its) life may be to end life elsewhere.

While this might seem to echo Le Bon's racist biopolitics, Canetti proposed a more anthropological and bodily–theoretical reasoning. His basic point was that, '[i]f body-to-body contact with a living individual frees us of our fear of being touched in the crowd, body contact with a lifeless individual frees us of the fear of death' (Moscovici 1987: 53). By imposing death the crowd could strengthen its own feeling of being alive (see also Arnason and Roberts 2004: 116). According to Canetti, the deathly destruction that the crowd might turn to finds its most dramatic expression in the use of fire:

[The fire] can be seen from far off and it attracts ever more people. It destroys irrevocably; nothing after a fire is as it was before. A crowd setting fire to something feels irresistible; so long as the fire spreads, everyone will join it and everything hostile will be destroyed. After the destruction, crowd and fire die away.[11] (1984: 20)

Before looking more closely at the relation between crowds and power I will emphasize one final general feature of Canetti's crowd analysis. Thus, one of the elements that distinguished his phenomenological account sharply from much previous crowd theory was his insistence that the crowd is not dependent on a leader.[12] Although, he said, a '[d]irection is essential for the continuing existence of the crowd' (1984: 29), this direction is not defined by a leader. Canetti's argument against the constitutive function of the leader was based on two grounds. First, once again, his personal crowd experience on 15 July 1927 had convinced him that 'the crowd needs no *leader* to form, notwithstanding all previous theories in this respect. For one whole day, I watched a crowd that had formed *without a leader*' (1989: 251, italics in original). Second, and

---

[11] This was one of many insights that Canetti derived directly from his personal experiences with the crowd on 15 July 1927. In his memoirs, he recalled the import of the fire for the continuation of the crowd:

> I had come to see that a crowd has to fall apart, and I had seen it fearing its disintegration; I had watched it do everything it could to prevent it; I had watched it actually see itself in the fire it lit, hindering its disintegration so long as this fire burned. It warded off any attempt at putting out the fire; its own longevity depended on that of the fire. (1989: 251)

[12] Moebius (2006: 497) notes that Canetti's view of the crowd as a positive collective entity that operated independently of a leader came close to what had been argued within the Collège de Sociologie about social collectives, such as festivals (see also Chapter 2). One might point to an additional similarity, for in Canetti, as well as in the work of both Durkheim and the Collège de Sociologie, religion (and myths of religious practices) played a crucial role. Canetti discussed the relation between packs and religion at length in *Crowds and Power* (see 1984: 125–65).

more theoretically, the emphasis on absolute equality in the crowd implied that no one person was positioned higher than another; all such hierarchical structures were annulled by the crowd. In spite of the centrality ascribed to equality, Canetti granted that in *some* cases crowds might be incited by leaders. In a 1962 radio discussion with Adorno, for example, he acknowledged that lynching crowds may at times have a leader. Still, the leader was only ascribed a secondary role, as Canetti argued for the existence of 'a lynching crowd before and beyond these directed, leader-related crowds' (1996b: 13).

Canetti's move from a basic asymmetry (leader–crowd) to a fundamental symmetry (absolute equality) had the important consequence, as McClelland attentively observes, that '[i]t is not until one reads *Crowds and Power* that one realizes how implicitly Hobbesian all other crowd theory was. It was always assumed that when the crowd comes together it creates power for its leader' (1989: 297). Crucially, therefore, when Canetti theorized the crowd independently of the leader, he not only dissociated himself from a Hobbesian horizon, but in fact distanced himself from much of crowd theory's association with images of the body politic – clearly indicated by Tarde's observation of the crowd's 'head' (see Chapter 2).[13]

Relatedly, Canetti's rejection of the leader's constitutive importance and his converse insistence on equality permitted him to go beyond the major psychological approaches to the crowd. Both the suggestion doctrine and Freud's libido theory installed the kind of difference between leader and crowd Canetti discarded in order to separate crowds and power. Although adherents to the suggestion doctrine such as Sighele and Stoll were mentioned in the comprehensive bibliography of *Crowds and Power*, the book deliberately proposed a view on crowds that did not square with previous psychological conceptions and explanations. Indeed, Canetti embodied a profound hostility to abstract theorizing and concepts. As Adam Paulsen has argued, Canetti never tired of criticizing 'abstract, scientific and systematic rationality' instead of which he enthusiastically defended 'a worldview that sustains the respect for the concrete, immediately sensuous phenomenon' (2005: 60). This also explains his radical phenomenological approach, his interest in the crowd as it was experienced, rather than observing it through categories established by previous crowd theories. There is a connection here to his

---

[13] Canetti's relation to Hobbes is far from exhausted by these few remarks. Contrary to McClelland's interpretation, which I endorse here, Honneth (1996) has argued that Hobbes' theory of the state of nature is important to Canetti. See also Canetti (1986: 115ff.), Arnason and Roberts (2004: 112ff.) and Balke (2008).

fascination with myths since they were seen as representing 'the *opposite* of system' (1996a: 68, italics in original). That is, the myths were believed by Canetti to contain a truth whose source was not derived from scientific rationality, but was founded instead on concrete experiences (see Paulsen 2005: 70).

It might be argued that this approach was not academically sustainable and that Canetti himself, in spite of all intentions, ended up establishing a grand conceptual framework of the kind he wished to escape from.[14] More importantly, his resistance to ordinary methods – one 'should beware of any method', he said (quoted in Paulsen 2005: 68) – created a huge explanatory chasm between his work and existing and subsequent crowd semantics. It was almost impossible for sociologists and social theorists to build on and engage with Canetti's work on crowds since the latter was formulated in clear opposition to common disciplinary, theoretical and methodological frameworks.[15] The lack of reception of his work in social theory bears witness to this.[16] To be sure, there have been some discussions of his work among other crowd and mass theorists. But often these have been marked by a clear dislike of Canetti's 'non-scientific' approach. Two examples of this will suffice.

One appeared in the above-mentioned discussion between Adorno and Canetti where the former could not hide his aversion to the latter's peculiar framework. '[W]hat strikes me first of all about your book', Adorno declared, 'and what is – if I may say so openly – something of a scandal, is what I would call the subjectivity of thought, the subjectivity of the author' (Adorno, in Canetti 1996b: 2). While Adorno was sympathetic to Canetti's unwillingness to submit to disciplinary boundaries, he believed that *Crowds and Power* was driven more by imaginations than by real facts, an accusation Canetti, not surprisingly, refuted. Another and later example of the uneasiness Canetti's work provoked can be found in a book review of *Crowds and Power* written by Ralph H. Turner, who was one of the key figures in redirecting American sociological thinking on crowds and collective behaviour in the 1960s,

---

[14] Paulsen (2005: 69), for one, voices this reservation, although he defends Canetti by pointing to how the latter's concepts were at least based on sensory facets.

[15] In contrast to, for example, Geiger who aimed to develop a strictly sociological theory of crowds, Canetti had no respect for disciplinary boundaries whatsoever. 'My whole life is nothing but a desperate attempt to overcome the division of labor', he noted at some point, referring especially to the policing of scientific borders (Canetti 1986: 36).

[16] Illustratively, it was still possible in 2004 to state that 'Elias Canetti remains an outsider, whose significance as a seminal cultural–diagnostic thinker of our century has not been adequately recognized. His distinctive anti-systematic form of theorizing, which cuts across the customary boundaries between genres and between imagination and theory, confronts the interpreter with particular difficulties' (Arnason and Roberts 2004: 1).

and whose work will be discussed later in this chapter. According to Turner, Canetti's book was a homage to 'pre-social-science modes of thought' characteristic of the nineteenth century; it employed a 'method of provocative half-truths'; and one could 'only regret that Canetti's creativeness was not tempered by training in the methods of disciplined scholarship' (1980: 142, 143, 144; for a similar critique, see McCarthy 1991: xviii, n. 6). The opposition to the particular approach which, in Canetti's eyes, was necessary in order to arrive at the creative insights could hardly be more pronounced.[17]

Relations to power

Having described the general characteristics of crowds, Canetti delineated a large number of specific crowd types. These included, among others, *open and closed crowds* (defined according to whether or not they have physical limits to their growth); *rhythmic crowds* (identified by rhythmic movements); *stagnating crowds* (characterized by their waiting and patience); *slow crowds* (defined by having a remote goal they move towards with keen determination); *invisible crowds* (crowds that are simply not visible, such as spirits); *baiting crowds* (which have a clearly defined and attainable goal); *flight crowds* (which are formed because of a threat); *prohibition crowds* (which impose a prohibition on themselves); *reversal crowds* (which accomplish a collective escape from outside commands); *feast crowds* (where the goal is the feast that marks an exception to the customary life, not unlike what Caillois understood by the festival); as well as *crowd crystals* (i.e. 'the small, rigid groups of men, strictly delimited and of great constancy, which serve to precipitate crowds', see 1984: 73); *crowd symbols* (which do not consist of humans, but are still collective units, such as fire, the sea and rain, which are felt by humans to be crowds); and *packs* (small groups which predate crowds and crowd crystals and which cannot grow).

It is beyond the scope of the present study to more than merely mention this variety of crowds (and related formations) which Canetti examined prior to embarking, after around 200 pages of *Crowds and Power*, on his explicit investigation of power. The fact that his reflections of power were only unfolded so late in the book served his point that crowds and power should be seen as separate phenomena. Still, a relation between crowds and power was posited, so how are they connected, according to Canetti?

---

[17] For a very different assessment of Canetti's contribution, see McClelland for whom 'Canetti's *Crowds and Power* is the only masterpiece of crowd theory' (1989: 293).

I have already addressed some connections between crowds and power above (relating to stings of command, burdens of distance, death, fire), but none of these were really key to Canetti's exposition of the so-called 'entrails of power' (1984: 201ff.). This discussion of power focused instead on seizure and incorporation. Specifically, Canetti here put forward a bodily theory of power that revolved around the fear of being touched which was also at the base of the opening scene of *Crowds and Power*. The reason why we fear this touch, it was argued, is that it reactualizes the relation between hunter and prey, for it is through the act of seizing that the powerful touches the prey. 'The fingers of the attacker feel what will soon belong to his whole body', Canetti wrote (1984: 203–4). Since the seizure anticipates the annihilation or rather incorporation of the prey, the grip is the 'central and most celebrated act of power ... the highest concentration of power' (1984: 206).

Canetti's 'animalistic' theory of power, which also included reflections on teeth, gorge and excrements, was an extreme bodily manifestation of what really constituted the core of his notion of power, namely the longing for survival. 'The moment of *survival* is the moment of power. Horror at the sight of death turns into satisfaction that it is someone else who is dead', Canetti asserted (1984: 227, italics in original), thereby touching upon the deathly vitalistic image of fire that was mentioned above. The connection to the discussion of seizure and incorporation was obvious: 'The lowest form of survival is killing' (1984: 227). In order to analyse this aspect of power Canetti took an apparent detour by scrutinizing the case of Daniel Paul Schreber, a former judge who suffered from paranoia and who described his illness and delusions in his memoirs, published in 1903. Canetti was profoundly fascinated by Schreber's case, devoting the final theoretical discussion of *Crowds and Power* to it, because it purportedly opened a window into power in its ultimate form.[18] Indeed, he asserted, thinking especially of Hitler, '[w]e shall find in Schreber a political system of a disturbingly familiar kind' (1984: 443–4).

One of the crucial features of Schreber's system of delusions was his insistence that he was the last true human being alive. All other figures he saw were mere 'appearances' and 'shadows' (1984: 442). Schreber explained this in different ways, referring to how a major earthquake,

---

[18] Schreber's case had been studied by Freud in 1911 (Freud 1958), and Canetti used this fact to direct yet another critique against Freud's work. Without mentioning Freud by name, Canetti remarked that there had been 'a well-known attempt' to explain Schreber's illness through 'repressed homosexuality'; but according to Canetti, one could hardly have made 'a greater mistake' interpretation-wise (1984: 449).

glaciation, epidemics, etc. had eradicated the rest of humankind, whereas Schreber himself was protected from such dangers by benign rays. Schreber could not help feeling some satisfaction in the destruction of all other human beings, and this, Canetti stated, was the reason why he incarnated power:

> Schreber is left as the sole survivor because this is what he himself wants. He wants to be the only man left alive, standing in an immense field of corpses; and he wants this field of corpses to contain all men but himself. It is not only as a paranoiac that he reveals himself here. To be the last man to remain alive is the deepest urge of every real seeker after power. (1984: 443)

Surviving the rest of the human race in other words endowed Schreber with a magnificent power over his fellow (now former) human beings. There was an important crowd element in this, for the ultimate power manifested herein required precisely an 'immense field of corpses', i.e. a huge crowd of people that could testify to the powerful individual's aim and ability to survive. As Canetti put it elsewhere in the book, '[t]he leader wants to survive, for with each survival he grows stronger' (1984: 241). This is important for understanding how Canetti's assessment of the crowd differed from that of the more conservatively inclined crowd scholars who saw the crowd with fear. For Canetti, the crowd as such was not judged negatively, as detailed above. In principle the crowd was a positive, vital entity, something that produced freedom from power. Yet since the core of power consists in survival, the crowd became an obvious means for leaders who wanted to acquire, sustain and increase their power.

There is one more layer of Canetti's analysis of the Schreber case that needs highlighting. It is no coincidence that he repeatedly characterized Schreber's reflections on his paranoia in systemic terms, referring for instance to his 'delusional system', his 'political system', etc. (1984: 435, 444, 447). On Canetti's analysis, Schreber became synonymous with rational thinking, for as a part of his illness, he was possessed by 'a mania for finding causal relations', and for 'unmasking' the purported reasons behind his experiences (1984: 452, 453; Paulsen 2005: 74–6). So Schreber's delusions not merely embodied power in its purest form, his case also offered insights into the workings of absolute rationality and systemic thinking. There is only a small step from here to asserting that Canetti's examination depicted power and systemic rationality as two sides of the same coin – and saw power and rationality as pathological forms, in contrast to the crowd.

This squared nicely with Canetti's general problematization of systemic thinking; yet it also suggested an underlying societal, diagnostic problematization which in some respects was not so different from what several other crowd and mass scholars had argued – whereas in other respects it directly confronted existing crowd/mass semantics. Thus the significant advances in technology and rationalization usually ascribed to modern society suggested a corresponding increase in power and therefore in the possibility of violence, destruction and death. This resembled the general history of decline that was identified in much crowd and mass semantics. However, contrary to, say, Mannheim's call for more rationality and planning as the central solution to the problems of modern society, including totalitarianism, Canetti was more on a par with the Frankfurt scholars (and much later Zygmunt Bauman 1989) when arguing that rationality was in fact a main condition of totalitarian rule, not its opposite. Similarly, but here Canetti stood more alone, the crowds were not to blame for the totalitarian perils of modern society. It was the people who longed for power and who employed the crowds for this purpose who were to blame. In fact, rather than being the cause of societal problems, the crowd might be the best liberating agent that individuals could pin their faith on. Accordingly, Canetti's political programme suggested, the main societal task was to separate the crowd even further from power. Although Canetti was not too specific about how to accomplish this, the epilogue to *Crowds and Power* demonstrated that this was the kind of problem his real concerns revolved around. In order to counteract power, which in the years preceding the publication of the book had procured new technological means of mass destruction, Canetti argued for the need 'to deal with the survivor himself' (1984: 469). In order to do so an examination of the anthropology of power and commands was needed. 'If we would master power we must face command openly and boldly, and search for means to deprive it of its sting', the final sentence of *Crowds and Power* reads (1984: 470).

Canetti deployed this explanatory horizon to understand Hitler's totalitarianism, arguing that any real understanding of Hitler would have to take seriously the relations between crowds and power. This analysis ran along several lines. For example, *Crowds and Power* contained a chapter on how inflation in the 1920s had prepared the way for Hitler's hostile reaction towards Jews (1984: 183–8; see also Borch 2008: 73–6). Canetti also studied Hitler's passion for architecture as an ambition to at once provide spaces for the emergence of the crowds Hitler needed to acquire power, and as a means to maintain this power by eternalizing his life – immortalized, as it was supposed to be, in stone (1976b, 1976c). I cannot go into detail with these analyses. Instead I would like to sum up the discussion of Canetti and give a sense of the complex status of his work in the history of sociological crowd semantics.

To begin with, *Crowds and Power* clearly reinvigorated the crowd tradition going back to Le Bon and Tarde, although Canetti's perspective and approach was entirely different. What he shared with Le Bon and Tarde was a wholehearted interest in the crowd itself as a particular social phenomenon. But contrary to his sociological and psychological forerunners, Canetti did not establish any necessary connection between modernity and the prevalence of crowds. Crowds, he believed, were a common social occurrence in all types of society, although the rise of modern totalitarianism had triggered the need for an understanding of modern crowds.

Moreover, the entire explanatory framework put forward by Canetti differed profoundly from previous more psychological references to hypnotic suggestion, libido, etc., just as his inside view was far more pronounced than what had been presented in the past. This inside perspective lent support to Canetti's crucial assertion that the crowd as such is not evil, destructive or pathological, although it might be utilized for destructive purposes. This in effect added up to a *normalization* of crowds. The gaze had shifted from conceiving of crowds as problematic, pathological eruptions of violence and disorder to portraying them as essentially positive, normal incarnations of sociality and freedom.

Interestingly, this notion of the crowd as a normal, non-pathological entity aligned Canetti in a rather surprising manner with key developments that took place in American sociological crowd semantics from the 1950s onwards. As I shall demonstrate below, parallel to but independently of Canetti's efforts, a number of American sociologists challenged the idea of the crowd as a pathological entity, which had been at the base of both popular and scholarly semantics since the nineteenth century. This was a surprising alignment because the theoretico-methodological preferences of the American scholars were perpendicular to Canetti's seemingly loose methodological approach, as is evident from the Turner remark quoted above.

Finally, while I have argued that Canetti took the crowd as such very seriously, Peter Sloterdijk has contended that, in a sense, and despite all intentions, Canetti contributed to 'dissolving the concept of crowd into such differentiated variants [open, closed, rhythmic, stagnating, etc.] that there could be no talk of a uniform meaning to the expression' (2008: 57, n. 1). That is, Canetti's elaborate differentiation of various crowd forms potentially undermined the idea of understanding the crowd *as such* and thereby, possibly and paradoxically, undermined crowd semantics from within. It can be argued against this interpretation that Canetti was far from the first to differentiate between different forms of crowds. A parallel interest in the crowd's general characteristics as well as in different crowd types and manifestations can be traced back to Le Bon's *The Crowd* – and many other scholars (from Tarde to Blumer) followed similar paths. Still, Sloterdijk has a point since Canetti went much further in this respect than his predecessors. Thus, McClelland has calculated, altogether Canetti's classification 'produces 280 different types of crowd if they are classified according to pure forms' (1989: 303). Acknowledging such multiplicity risked shifting the interest from the crowd per se to its numerous specific expressions.

Conceptual rebirth: towards a rational agenda

In spite of his meticulous efforts, Canetti's work was almost entirely overlooked by especially American sociologists. This is not to suggest a complete ignorance of Canetti's theorizing among North American scholars. Marshall McLuhan, for one, lauded *Crowds and Power* – particularly its analysis of the relation between inflation and crowds – in his seminal 1964 book *Understanding Media* (1964: ch. 11). This recognition from a renowned communications, culture and media scholar was significant, especially in the light of how Lazarsfeld and others' mass communications research had contributed not a little to eroding the foundation for crowd and mass semantics.

Even if Canetti's book was rather indigestible to many American sociologists, its basic ambition to set a new agenda for discussing crowds resonated with similar efforts in American sociology around the same time. Despite the rediscovery of the primary group and the kinds of research it induced, a number of American sociologists began, in the 1950s and 1960s, to revitalize discussions of crowds and collective behaviour without resorting to comprehensive quantitative analysis, but in ways that nonetheless signified a watershed in the history of crowd semantics. Instead of problematizing crowds and masses in light of underlying subversive, violent and non-democratic threats, this new wave of theorizing shifted attention to collective behaviour more generally. Furthermore, this body of literature essentially turned one of the key attributes of classical conceptions of crowds on its head. Rather than conceiving of crowds as basically irrational entities, they were now portrayed as inherently rational. This echoed some of Canetti's ideas, but the rationalizing and normalizing image of crowds and collective behaviour was touted much more radically by the sociologists, and on the basis of entirely different theoretical frameworks.

Although the work of Mead and Parsons had varying explicit bearings on the scholars who advocated a fresh take on crowds and collective behaviour, this new generation of crowd studies reflected the change in theoretical climate which Mead and Parsons had contributed to bringing about (see Chapter 4). As a result, the study of crowds and collective behaviour became increasingly associated, not with hypnotic suggestion but rather with normative restraints on individual actors or, in more radical accounts, with explaining collective phenomena by reference to rational subjects. As will be demonstrated in the discussion of the most significant contributions below, this profoundly altered the connotations and implications of the concept of crowds.

One of the initial contributions to this literature was the first American textbook on collective behaviour, Ralph H. Turner and Lewis M. Killian's *Collective Behavior* (1957), which partly drew upon and partly revised the Le Bon–Tarde and Park–Blumer traditions.[19] Turner and Killian shared with Tarde the idea that collective behaviour is an emergent phenomenon. But contrary to the Frenchman, Turner and Killian asserted that collective behaviour gives rise to a normative order. 'Thus the collectivity is a group governed by emergent or spontaneous norms rather than formalized norms' (Turner and Killian 1957: 12).

The notion of emergent norms marked the distinguishing feature of Turner and Killian's theoretical reorientation: they normalized what was seen as intrinsically irrational and abnormal in the early European semantics. What the early European scholars conceived of as a subversive social outburst was now reinterpreted within a normative framework. This had two central dimensions. On the one hand, collective (and hence crowd) behaviour was defined by 'the operation of some kind of group norms' (1957: 12). On the other hand, the emergent norms of the crowd were as a rule believed to be in opposition to society's existing norms (1957: 143). It is likely, the authors posited, 'that the basic condition out of which crowd behavior arises is one of cultural conflict, of a breakdown of normative integration' (1957: 84). Which was to say that if the normative fabric of society were destabilized, crowds might emerge which, not dissimilar to what Park had suggested, could pave the way for alternative normative foundations.

Turner and Killian's substitution of an analytical platform of irrationality and impulsiveness with a normative horizon was deliberate. Although, they acknowledged, irrationality might be useful for understanding individual behaviour, the concept was of no help when

---

[19] Although the works of Durkheim, Freud, Le Bon, Martin, Ortega, Park, Ross, Sidis, Sorel, Tarde, Wallas, etc. were briefly reviewed at the outset, the legacy of Blumer was particularly pronounced in the book. For example, Turner and Killian adopted (in revised form) Blumer's distinction between active and expressive crowds (1957: 85–6; see also vi).

accounting for the collective domain. The assumption of an irrational 'homogeneity among members of collectivities is not supported by our knowledge', they stated (1957: 17). In addition to this, they argued, it is impossible to maintain a meaningful difference between rational and irrational action, as the same act might be assessed as being both rational and irrational according to the applied criteria. What appears as rational from one perspective may appear irrational when judged by a different yardstick. In spite of such reservations I claim that Turner and Killian's account was characterized by a fundamentally rational tenet. For example, they acknowledged that individual crowd members display a:

heightened suggestibility, but this suggestibility is not of an unfocused, indiscriminate nature. It amounts to a tendency to respond uncritically to suggestions that are *consistent with the mood, imagery, and conception of appropriate action that have developed and assumed a normative character.* (1957: 84, italics added)

This amounted to saying that the 'selective individual suggestibility' (1957: 84), which in Turner and Killian's view could be identified in the crowd, was essentially a function of the latter's normative order. This emphasis on norm-conforming behaviour tacitly introduced an aspect of rationality: crowd members follow the norms of the group not because of contagious suggestion, but because of an extensive pressure towards conformity.[20]

Turner and Killian represented one perspective on the normative–rational approach to crowds. A somewhat different effort to study the influence of norms upon individual crowd members was provided by Neil J. Smelser in his *Theory of Collective Behavior* (1962). Drawing upon the 'logic and substance' of Parsons' work, Smelser set out to examine, among other things, 'the conditions under which new norms arise and become established through a norm-oriented movement' (1962: 23, 27). Smelser's theory was an explicit attempt to move beyond the heritage of Le Bon, Tarde, etc. whose work and explanatory concepts he dismissed as plainly psychological and superficial. This move entailed, he contended, that concepts such as imitation, contagion and suggestion be excluded or at least subsumed under 'the sociological approach' which asks: 'Under what social conditions do these psychological variables come into play as parts of collective

---

[20] The notion of emergent norms was further elaborated in a 1972 revised edition of Turner and Killian's book (1972). The overall message and approach remained the same, however.

behavior?' (1962: 21; see also 152–3, 257ff.).[21] As is evident from this, Smelser did not grant the late-nineteenth-century European crowd semantics any sociological value.

In order to account for the above-mentioned social conditions, Smelser developed a comprehensive explanatory framework which focused on so-called 'determinants of collective behavior' (1962: 12ff.). These included what Smelser called structural conduciveness, structural strain, generalized belief, precipitating factors, mobilization of participants for action as well as social control. I will not discuss the content of these dimensions here. Suffice it to say that by employing this explanatory model, Smelser promoted an external view of collective behaviour. Similar to Geiger, but from a different vantage point, Smelser sought to account for the structural reasons behind crowd and collective behaviour. As a result, crowd and collective behaviour were reduced to the *effects* of specific social conditions. Consequently, moreover, Smelser's account moved away from the spontaneity previously attributed to crowds.

In spite of his efforts to transcend the Le Bon tradition, one feature from classical crowd semantics resurfaced in Smelser's account. Although his theory suggested that collective behaviour could be explained as an attempt, for instance, to change societal norms, the existing norms constituted the yardstick against which collective behaviour was measured. As a result, collective behaviour was seen from the outset as a challenge to society's normative fabric, meaning that Smelser somehow retained an underlying notion of the abnormality of much collective behaviour.

Whereas Smelser showed little respect for more classical approaches to crowds and collective behaviour, a more sympathetic attitude towards the existing traditions was presented by Kurt and Gladys Engel Lang in their book *Collective Dynamics* (1961). This was manifest, for instance, in the great indebtedness that was paid to especially Blumer. Nonetheless a certain ambivalence was at stake, for in spite of recognizing this more classical heritage, the Langs shared with Turner and Killian and Smelser the impression that a new platform for understanding collective phenomena was urgently needed. The state of affairs was lucidly described in the preface to their book:

---

[21] The conceptual exclusion also covered the notion of irrationality: 'The definition we have presented does not, by itself, involve any assumptions that the persons involved in an episode are irrational, that they lose their critical faculties, that they experience psychological regression, that they revert to some animal state, or whatever' (Smelser 1962: 11).

In recent years, the study of collective behavior has somewhat fallen into disrepute among professional sociologists. It is evident that recent research in this field has not kept pace with developments in other fields of sociological inquiry, and for most sociologists impressionistic observations of the bizarre – the crowd, the fad, the hysterical epidemic, witchcraft, etc. – do not represent a legitimate accretion to scientific knowledge. Broadly speaking, the field has suffered a decline; more than being rechristened, it needs to be reborn. (1961: vi)

A sound academic conception of collective phenomena would have to move beyond the 'inadequacy of the conventionally recognized categories of collective behavior – that is, crowd, mass, public, social movements, etc.' (1961: vi). The new alternative framework offered by the Langs revolved, as the title of the book indicated, around a purportedly *dynamic* approach. The key point was to emphasize that collective behaviour is characterized by 'a lack of structure' (1961: 3). Accordingly, collective dynamics, the new term and research field inaugurated by the authors, was defined as '*those patterns of social action that are spontaneous and unstructured inasmuch as they are not organized and are not reducible to social structure*' (1961: 4, italics in original).

The proposed research programme entailed an explicit redefinition of the status of the crowd. 'We have especially resisted the tendency to treat crowd behavior as if it were the central element in collective dynamics', it was remarked (1961: vii). Although this was another attempt to leave the allegedly outdated tradition behind, the Langs nevertheless drew heavily on classical resources from Le Bon onwards (once again displaying their ambivalent stance to this tradition). Also, even if the crowd should not figure at the centre of interest, crowd behaviour was in fact analysed extensively in the book. But here too new winds were blowing. The Langs thus stood on the shoulders of recent research – they referred to Westley (1957) – which had demonstrated that people who are part of a crowd 'are not so carried away and so unresponsible for their actions as some theorists have held' (1961: 112). In short, crowd behaviour was not as unconscious and irrational as previously claimed. This idea was further substantiated by the way in which the Langs introduced an element of rationality into their examination of the formation of crowds. It might be, they argued, that crowd dynamics generate a heightening of feelings and produce a common mood, but people still retain their critical abilities and their capacity to judge the situation. Indeed, the authors stated:

The crowd situation offers (1) positive *rewards* which temporarily outweigh any realistic assessment of consequences, (2) as well as a strategy for *guilt evasion*. Even though it may lead to his arrest, the fan who throws the bottle at the umpire enjoys his notoriety more or less consciously. (1961: 121, italics in original)

This notion of strategic considerations, as well as the prospect of achieving specific gains through the participation of crowd behaviour, clearly ran counter to what was entailed by the suggestion doctrine and references to an intrinsic irrationality in crowds.

While the approaches discussed above all subscribed to a turn towards a rational conceptualization of crowds and collective behaviour, none were as radical in this transition as that of Richard A. Berk. Berk did not hesitate dismissing as 'outdated' the entire body of literature (represented in particular by Le Bon, Freud and Blumer) that placed contagion, suggestion, irrationality, etc. centrally for the understanding of crowds (1974a: 20ff.). Inspired by Turner (1964), Berk voiced several critiques of this tradition, including its purported lack of 'empirical verification' and its inability to account for a possible division of labour within crowds (1974a: 34). In the light of these drawbacks, Berk proposed game theory as a more sophisticated analytical avenue. According to this perspective, 'crowd participants (1) exercise a substantial degree of rational decision-making and (2) are not defined a priori as less rational than in other contexts' (Berk 1974b: 356). Further, rather than signifying a spontaneous occurrence, 'the gathering of a crowd is viewed as an *opportunity* in which individuals can experience certain rewards and certain costs' (1974a: 67, italics in original). As should be clear from this, the idea underpinning the gaming approach was to place the individual actor and his/her rational decisions at the centre of the theoretical–analytical apparatus. Consequently this approach assumed the existence of precisely those qualities that were questioned by the suggestion doctrine. Moreover, Berk's model effectively erased the difference between crowd behaviour and other forms of behaviour, as they could all be boiled down to the pursuit of individual optimizing strategies.

From a historical vantage point, the significance of Berk's work lies not least in how it embodied the momentary culmination of a long American tradition of rationalizing and individualizing what was, in its initial European formulations, an idea of irrationality and a destabilization of the notion of individuality. In Berk's work, all the distinguishing and radical features of the early crowd semantics had vanished and been profoundly reconfigured. But this was a semantic transition which had been prepared by the specific adoption and/or critique of crowd theory that a long series of American scholars from Park to Parsons had propagated. Put differently, it is hardly possible to conceive of the emergence of Berk's rational choice interpretation of crowd and collective behaviour without taking into consideration all the minor steps previous American scholars had made in this direction. So although this achievement should not be underrated, Berk simply completed a conceptual–analytical architecture which had been anticipated, and was visible in nascent form, through the numerous building blocks that had already been laid down.

It should also be mentioned that, even if Canetti too espoused a normalizing and rationalizing view of the crowd, there was a gulf separating him from Berk. Most importantly, in Canetti's case the rationalizing dimension was far more ambiguous than what Berk advocated. Canetti's acknowledgement of how individual crowd members could gain from being part of crowds (e.g. the benefits made manifest by the suspension of power hierarchies) was always analysed with a view to the underlying spontaneity which was believed to characterize the crowd. Such spontaneity was absent in Berk's 'superrationalistic' model (I take this notion from Killian 1980: 282–3).

From collective behaviour to social movements: crowd semantics fading in the background

It is clear that lumping together Killian and Turner, Smelser, the Langs and Berk as belonging to one and the same semantic layer undoubtedly glosses over important differences between them. For example, the normative framework of Turner and Killian found no resonance in Berk's account which emphasized instead the individual gains and costs of specific actions (see also Berk 1974a: 69). In addition, the individualistic account was much more pronounced in Berk's model than in, for example, Smelser's. Still, such differences should not overshadow the unity of this new mode of theorizing, which lay partly in the attempt to conceive of crowds and collective behaviour in rational terms (whether or not this rationalization was linked to a normative undercurrent), and partly in the consensus that a distinctively sociological perspective was needed to revitalize the field (although there was a wide stretch from flagging norms and structural strain to endorsing an essentially economic viewpoint as Berk did).

It is also plain that focusing merely on the contributions of Killian and Turner, Smelser, the Langs and Berk means attending to a tiny, though significant, part of the rationalizing/normalizing view of crowds and collective behaviour that evolved in the 1950s and 1960s and was further elaborated in the following decades. Several other sociologists were part of this movement (e.g. Couch 1968, 1970; McPhail 1969), and I shall come back to some of them below. However, rather than marshalling all facets of this semantic change, it is worthwhile situating the new sociological ideas in a broader social and academic context, for the particular sociological mode of theorizing crowds and collective behaviour that

I have sketched above did not transpire in a vacuum. It evolved more or less concurrently with other somewhat interrelated developments.[22]

For example, a growing number of historical investigations began to question the image of irrational crowds propagated by classical crowd scholars, particularly Le Bon. I mentioned the historical work by Lefebvre, Rudé, Thompson and Hobsbawm in the Introduction to this book and will not rehearse their arguments for a more rationalistic understanding here. Suffice it to say that while the first contributions to this body of research appeared in the 1930s, a new wave swept in during the late 1960s and early 1970s. For instance, seminal work by Thompson and Hobsbawm was published in the early 1970s, i.e. more or less at the same time as Berk argued for a rational approach. This suggests that despite significant conceptual and methodological differences somewhat similar rationalizing endeavours were being unfolded across the disciplines of history and sociology, and that these endeavours lent support and credibility to one another.[23]

It was not just European historians like Lefebvre, Rudé, Thompson and Hobsbawm who challenged the crowd image associated with Le Bon. American contributions to this literature can also be identified, most notably in the work of Charles Tilly. Being a historical sociologist, Tilly had (and still has) a foot planted in both the historical and the sociological camps; and it makes sense to see his work as bridging the historians' attempt to challenge the irrational image of crowds and the sociologists' parallel wish to found a new approach to crowds and collective behaviour on the basis of more rational notions – although, as I shall come back to shortly, the kinds of sociology he championed exhibited rather uneasy ties with the collective behaviour tradition discussed above.

One example of this bridging accomplishment was delivered in Tilly's influential article 'Collective Violence in Europe' (1969). The article demonstrated that, from a historical vantage point, collective violence was intrinsic to the Western civilization and therefore a normal rather than abnormal phenomenon. At the same time, the specific forms of collective violence had changed during the past 300 years, reflecting a transformation from what Tilly termed primitive collective violence over

---

[22] In order to keep this discussion within reasonable limits, I shall ignore semantic developments that took place within social psychology (the work of Neil E. Miller, John Dollard, Muzafer Sherif and others). An overview of this work is available in McPhail (1991).

[23] Canetti's flirtation with a rational conceptualization of crowds also appears to have been influenced by some of these historical studies. For example, Lefebvre's work was cited in the bibliography of *Crowds and Power*.

reactionary to modern collective violence. It followed from this that collective violence, including that committed by crowds, had not disappeared. While this entailed an argument for a continued appreciation of crowd theory, Tilly sided with the European historians in articulating an alternative to a classical image of irrational action. Specifically, and this is where he aligned as well with the sociological endeavours at the time, he advocated a rationalist approach, arguing for the need to understand 'the logic of collective violence' by studying the organizational base of political action as well as its relation to the existing power structure (1969: 29). This call was further elaborated in books such as *From Mobilization to Revolution*, in which Tilly outlined a theory of collective action that was situated not only vis-à-vis historical studies, but also in the context of sociological theorizing from Marx, Durkheim and Weber to (rational) collective choice theorists such as James Coleman and Mancur Olson. The book retained a strong rationalist perspective, defining collective action as 'people acting together in pursuit of common interests. Collective action results from changing combinations of interests, organization, mobilization, and opportunity' (Tilly 1978: 7). By taking these parameters seriously, it would be clear that one had to raise 'fundamental doubts about any effort to single out a class of spontaneous, expressive, impulsive, evanescent crowd actions', it was argued (Tilly 1978: 171).

In addition to pioneering discussions of collective action and collective violence Tilly has left a lasting imprint on the study of social movements. The sociological interest in social movements dates back a long way. As Tilly observes, the notion of social movements was coined in 1850 by Lorenz von Stein (Tilly 2004: 5; see also Wennerhag 2010). Interestingly, until well into the twentieth century, a clear semantic line was rarely drawn between crowds and masses, on the one side, and social movements, on the other. For example, in Park and Burgess' *Introduction to the Science of Sociology*, the index entry on 'social movements' referred the reader to another entry, that of 'mass movements' (1921: 1038; see also 895ff.). A similar semantic conflation appeared in Hadley Cantril's seminal 1941 study *The Psychology of Social Movements*, which set out from a social psychology angle to explain a series of social movements, which included everything from lynching mobs to the Nazi Party (2002).

Things began to change in the late 1960s and early 1970s when a distinctive sociology of social movements crystallized. This was not least a response to the previous semantic conflation, which lent an air of abnormality and irrationality to the notion of social movements. To avoid the association with the register of abnormality, irrationality, crowds and masses, scholars now argued for a more rational conception of social movements where these were seen as entities aiming to achieve specific, commonly shared purposes. In a way, this research agenda joined hands with the tradition of Turner and Killian, the Langs, Smelser and Berk, which strived to endow collective behaviour with a more rational edifice. This was no firm coalition, however. Doug McAdam thus notes that many social movement scholars felt that Turner and Killian, etc. had merely poured old wine in new bottles (2007: 420–1). In particular, McAdam states, Smelser's work provoked reaction because it was invested with a normative framework in which social movements protest would almost inevitably come out as abnormal. In order to enact a clear separation from any old leftovers that might, unintentionally, have slipped into the new collective behaviour agenda, the study of social movements was therefore launched as a distinctive sociological inquiry, and defined in stark opposition to the entire crowds and collective behaviour paradigm. The net result was 'the rise of social movement studies at the expense of the older field of "collective behavior"', including its 1960s and 1970s incarnations (McAdam 2007: 420).

It is critical to dwell for a moment on this intra-disciplinary sociological struggle between the reinvigorated collective behaviour framework, on the one hand, and social movement studies, on the other. It thus appears that, paradoxically, the attempt to revitalize discussions on collective behaviour ended up having the opposite effect. The dismissal of the irrational modes of theorizing crowds and collective behaviour backfired in the sense that, irrespective of the new conceptual efforts, the critiques of previous explanatory horizons rendered collective behaviour inopportune as a field of study. In Clark McPhail's retrospective comment, 'the rejection of the Le Bon–Park–Blumer psychological explanation for collective behavior was tantamount to the repudiation of collective behavior as a legitimate sociological phenomenon to be explained' (1991: 152). Hammering down previous work in this tradition had shaken the scaffold itself.

This was only one side of the coin, though. The other was, as indicated above, that social movement scholars found the new collective behaviour agenda too closely linked to the old one(s). One problem was Smelser's flirtation with an abnormal image of protest. Just as important, however, it was difficult to see that a profound change had been effected on a semantic level. By retaining a notion of collective behaviour the ties to previous work in this tradition had not been properly cut. In an American sociological context, the notion of collective behaviour could not help evoking how Park and Burgess had launched the term and how, in their work, it was intimately linked to discussions of crowds and mobs, themselves recalling the work of Le Bon. Therefore a new conceptual apparatus was needed, social movement scholars felt, which carried no allusions to the irrational horizon of the French classics. This semantic problematization was made explicit by Tilly:

> Mob, disorder, and mass movement are top-down words. They are the words of authorities and elites for actions of other people – and, often, for actions which threaten their own interests. The bottom-up approach we have taken identifies the connections between the collective actions of ordinary people and the ways they organize around their workaday interests. (1978: 227)

Just as Tilly's notion of collective action was coined in part to avoid any elitist–pejorative connotations, so the notion of social movements served to break away radically from any irrational baggage silently carried along by the reference to collective behaviour.

The need for a new semantic register which revalorized the behaviour of collectivities was also prompted by external events in the form of the new types of protests that evolved in many Western countries with the 1968 student protests. It was felt that these protests opened a cleavage between the empirical reality and the old, inherited conceptual frameworks. Tilly has summarized this transformation in social movement protests as follows:

> From reactions to 1968's conflicts in the United States and elsewhere developed the idea that 'old' social movements on behalf of power for workers and other exploited categories had passed their time. 'New' social movements oriented to autonomy, self-expression, and the critique of post-industrial society, many observers thought, were supplanting the old. (2004: 70)

While such events were also a central reason for the collective behaviour scholars' reinvigoration of their conceptual horizon, the changing modes of protest nonetheless rendered a corresponding shift in explanatory framework necessary, meaning that notions of social movements and collective action were deemed fitter to account for the new reality (to be sure, the purported novelty of the 'new social movements' was later contested).

The semantic struggle between crowds and collective behaviour, on one side, and social movements, on the other, ended to the latter's advantage. It therefore seems warranted to say that, despite the upsurge of new approaches to collective behaviour in the 1950s–1970s, the social movement studies gradually became the more dominant mode of theorizing and eventually practically ousted the crowds and collective behaviour traditions (McAdam 2007: 420–2). So whereas references to and studies of crowds and collective behaviour became less common within American sociology from the 1970s onwards, a wide array of work was conducted which carried on the baton from the late 1960s and early

1970s rationalizing accounts on collective action and social movements (examples are legion, including Tarrow 1998; Waddington 1992, 2008).

Although social movement studies and its various outgrowths ended up replacing the sociological semantics of crowds, this does not amount to saying that sociological work on crowds and collective behaviour completely dried out, and that nothing new has happened to American crowd semantics since the 1970s. One effort to once again bring new energy into this tradition appeared in the early 1980s, when John Lofland set out to remedy what he saw as a significant lack in much existing work on collective behaviour, namely its ignorance of crowd joys (1981, 1982). According to Lofland, the reinvigoration of collective behaviour theorizing since the late 1960s (i.e. Turner and Killian, Berk, etc.) had rightly taken leave of references to contagion and similar notions associated with early crowd semantics and its preference for the suggestion doctrine. While this was commendable, the new wave of theorizing was characterized, he believed, by a resistance to discuss and analyse emotional aspects of crowds. The reason was, he contended, that it was feared that addressing such dimensions would lead right back to the world of Le Bon, Freud and Blumer. 'We encounter, that is, among contemporary collective behaviorists the anomaly that what seems to be a quite conspicuous feature of the topic – aroused emotions – is at the same time one that is most suppressed from explicit consideration' (1982: 377). Arguing that taking crowd emotions seriously need not entail a return to Le Bon, Lofland made a plea for a renewed investigation of what he called the dominant emotion of crowds. Such emotions could include the kinds of fear Le Bon associated with crowds, but it could just as well refer to all sorts of joy, such as those described by Whitman (who was not referenced by Lofland). Joyful components should be carefully analysed, according to Lofland, who took a first step by presenting a taxonomy of collective joy, thereby submitting to the central programmatic statement of the article: 'I propose that we bring joy back into the study of collective behavior and elevate it once again to a prominent place' (1982: 355–6).

Lofland's corrective did not change the rationalist track which the semantics of crowds and collective behaviour had embarked upon, but nor did it go unnoticed. For example, his emphasis on emotions was credited as 'an extremely important contribution' to the study of collective phenomena by Clark McPhail in the latter's book *The Myth of the Madding Crowd* (1991: 141). This book itself constituted an important attempt to revive the discussions that grew out of the interest in collective behaviour in the 1950s and 1960s. McPhail had been an active voice in these debates since the late 1960s, and *The Myth of the Madding*

Crowd essentially summarized and marked the culmination of his work in this field. The title of the book gave an indication of the task the author set himself, namely to puncture the alleged myth of the madding, i.e. inherently irrational, crowd. According to McPhail, scholars such as Le Bon, Park and Blumer were to blame for the image of the madding crowd. They had all championed the idea that some sort of transformation takes place in crowds which alters the state of the crowd members. This transformation hypothesis, as McPhail called it, held 'that crowds transform individuals, diminishing or eliminating their ability to control their behavior rationally' (1991: 1). McPhail found the transformation hypothesis fundamentally flawed in several respects. Among other things, the explanatory apparatus (contagion, suggestibility, hypnosis) was deemed inadequate and circular, if not outright tautological; empirical observations were said to contradict the irrationality attributed to crowds; just as a separation between crowded and non-crowded occurrences could not be as sharply drawn as was assumed in this literature (1991: 13–20).

Dismantling the transformation hypothesis and, thereby, the notion of the madding crowd was merely the first step, however. In the search for a positive alternative to the tradition of Le Bon, Park and Blumer, McPhail critically reviewed the work of subsequent scholars in the field, including Berk, Lofland, Tilly as well as Turner and Killian. While the theories presented by these sociologists had all challenged the myth of the madding crowd, and therefore, in McPhail's eyes, signified valuable improvements to the literature, these theories also contained their own particular limitations (not to be discussed here). Against this backdrop, McPhail then outlined his own alternative to the purported myth. This alternative consisted in a complex model, which spiced up the best of Lofland, Tilly, etc. with a *mélange* of insights from Mead and a specific mode of socio-cybernetic theorizing that revolved around purposive action.

I noted above that *The Myth of the Madding Crowd* was the apex of McPhail's decades-long work on crowds and collective behaviour. But, more than that, the book captured the essence of the transformations in crowd semantics that had taken place in American sociology since the 1950s, although some developments had a slightly different accent in McPhail's theorizing than in the work of other sociologists during this period. I would like to end the discussion of this wave of American crowd semantics by summing up how it manifested itself in McPhail's book. This has four closely related dimensions, some of which I shall attend to more briefly than others. First of all, as already mentioned, McPhail subscribed to the *rationalizing* agenda that had dominated American sociological crowd semantics from the 1950s onwards. In McPhail's book this translated into a showdown with the myth of the inherent irrationality of crowds and an argument for basing the study of collective phenomena on a notion of purposive action.

Second, the antagonism between crowds and individuality, which was guiding much classical crowd theory (especially of the sort that revolved around the suggestion doctrine), and which had been severely challenged by collective behaviour scholars since the mid-twentieth century, was being undermined by McPhail as well. Rather than seeing crowds and collective behaviour as de-individualizing phenomena, McPhail and others took as their analytical starting point the singular individual. In McPhail's book this showed in how Mead – not without a certain irony – had transformed from being a stern critic of imitation-suggestion, the key principle underpinning Tarde's as well as much early crowd theorizing, to forging the theoretical platform on which an updated, late-twentieth-century contribution to crowd semantics was formulated. This transition testified to the radical *individualization* that American sociological crowd semantics had effected.

Third, McPhail continued along the *normalizing* track, which ana-lysed crowd behaviour not as an abnormal phenomenon, but rather as a normal occurrence. This profound difference to earlier crowd seman-tics materialized in one of the fundamental conceptual choices guiding McPhail's theoretical model. Although the title of McPhail's book made explicit reference to the semantics of *crowds*, one of his chief objectives was to enact a conceptual shift from crowds to *gatherings*, defined as 'a collection of two or more persons in a common place in space and time' (1991: 153). This minimal definition was neutral with respect to the valorization of the gatherings and as such evaded the pejorative connotations associated with the transformation hypothesis. The terminological move from crowds to gatherings also served McPhail's ambition to blur the boundary between crowded and non-crowded events, as the notion of gatherings could account for both. Certainly, the conceptual preference of gatherings over crowds opened up a more comprehensive reservoir of collective behaviour, which gave no a priori primacy to crowded events. But while this expanded the analytical potentials of the theoretical apparatus, it was also indicative of how thoroughly normalized the understanding of collective behav-iour had become.

This normalizing gesture becomes very lucid when considering the inspirational background for emphasizing gatherings rather than crowds. As McPhail remarked, the notion of gatherings was inherited from Goffman's *Behavior in Public Places: Notes on the Social*

Organization of Gatherings (1963). What McPhail failed to note in the book was that Goffman drew a clear line between crowds and (non-crowded) gatherings. Goffman acknowledged the uniqueness of crowds and simply wanted to give credit to and examine a different domain, that of gatherings. In Goffman's own words from *Behavior in Public Places*:

> To be sure, one part of 'collective behavior' – riots, crowds, panics – has been established as something to study. But the remaining part of the area, the study of ordinary human traffic and the patterning of ordinary social contacts, has been little considered. It is well recognized, for instance, that mobs can suddenly emerge from the peaceful flow of human traffic, if conditions are right. But little concern seems to have been given to the question of what structure this peaceful intercourse possesses when mob formation is not an issue. It is the object of this report to try to develop such a framework. (1963: 4)

So, for Goffman, crowds signified an *extraordinary* social phenomenon, whereas the central study object of his book, gatherings, referred to the flow of *ordinary* events. In McPhail's theory, by contrast, this distinction dissolved and the extraordinary was subsumed under the ordinary, under the normal.

Fourth, and finally, McPhail's book offered an interesting, though probably unintended, testimony to the *marginalization* of the semantics of crowds and collective behaviour that had taken place due to the predominance of social movement studies. Although not addressed by McPhail, the opposition between social movement studies and the now much less influential crowd semantics was touched upon in a foreword to the book, written by John D. McCarthy. According to McCarthy, McPhail provided much-needed tools to remedy a central weakness in social movement studies, namely that:

> contemporary researchers of social movements have been inattentive to temporary gatherings, primarily because their theoretical perspectives blind them to the whole range of less routine behavior and social organizational forms that make up ongoing movements, and because the contributions of past scholars [in the crowd theory domain] have been unfairly stigmatized. (1991: xvii)

The inattentiveness to these aspects could only be overcome by bringing crowd theory of a McPhailian fashion back in, McCarthy intimated. And this would not only correct a drawback in social movement studies; much more importantly, it would reconcile any tensions between social movement studies, on the one hand, and theories of crowds and collective behaviour, on the other – and thereby help rehabilitate the latter. 'If enough scholars choose to follow McPhail's lead, the prevailing barrenness of the marriage between collective behavior and social movement studies may be finally overcome', McCarthy's pious hope read (1991: xiii).[24]

The dissolution of sociological crowd theory

Despite the efforts of the collective behaviour scholars it is safe to say that, from the 1960s and 1970s onwards, notions of crowds and collective behaviour were slowly displaced from the centre of sociology and eventually came to occupy an outsider position. McPhail's 1991 book might be seen as the final desperate cry for taking seriously the crowd in sociology, at least in the kind of sociology that adheres to the dominant US American research agendas.[25] Why did this marginalization take place? I have pointed to some events that contributed to it, such as the rise of the 'history from below' work as well as the success of the social movement studies. It might be argued that a full explanation of this development would have to dig further into a range of institutional and biographical aspects, a kind of excavation I shall not embark on in the present context. Instead I would like to end this chapter by proposing – and I offer this more as a speculation or hypothesis than a fully-fledged analysis – that the gradual marginalization of sociological crowd semantics was also propelled by a more deep-seated development. Specifically, I suggest, in addition to the intra-disciplinary battles between the crowd and collective behaviour tradition, on one side, and social movement studies, on the other, the sociological marginalization of the crowd topic occurred as an effect of a broader reinterpretation or, better, collapse of the social within sociological theorizing.

This relates to what Peter Wagner, in his penetrating studies of modernity and the social sciences, has called the crisis of classical sociology (1994, 2001). Wagner argues that the legitimacy of turn-of-the-nineteenth-century sociology hinged in great part on its ability to develop a science of society, which was associated, if only ambivalently,

---

[24] One adoption of McPhail's perspective in the more curious end has been put forward by David Schweingruber and Ronald T. Wohlstein (2005). They examined fifty sociology textbooks and found that these often depicted crowds in ways that McPhail had dismissed as myths of the madding crowd. According to Schweingruber and Wohlstein, this recurrence of crowd myths was so distressing that they prescribed how textbook chapters on crowds should be written ('What Should a Crowd Chapter Look Like?'), just as they recommended that the textbook review process be changed (2005: 146–8).

[25] To be sure, McPhail has published more recent work than *The Myth of the Madding Crowd*. But this work is derivative of the main perspective set out in that book (e.g. 2006).

with Enlightenment ideals and which aimed to understand the relation between individual and society (2001: ch. 1). Within such a conceptual landscape the problem of crowds could well occupy a lead position, pointing as it did in early sociological accounts to a de-individualizing force that threatened to undermine society and the social from within. Moreover, as long as the constitution of society and the social achieved primary sociological consideration, the relational dynamics between individuals, be they family, group, crowd or other relations, would naturally attract analytical interest. Once again, within such a horizon, the study of crowds and their interpersonal relations, including the relations between leader and crowd members, could well achieve socio-logical prominence. However, when the crowd was approached as a basically individualistic mode of action, i.e. when the sociality of crowds was reduced to and replaced by primarily individualistic categories as was the case with the majority of the American crowd and collective behaviour theorists I have analysed in this chapter, then this might be taken as a sign that the social had ceased to be the paradigmatic model for human interaction.

In Wagner's parlance, and I am aware I am pushing his analysis somewhat beyond its original context, this might be seen as a corollary of the end of classical sociology, which refers to the situation where '[t]he discourse of classical sociology lost its cognitive affinity to the structure of the society which it dealt with' (2001: 22). Put differently, what I am suggesting is that the individualistic turn in the 1960s and 1970s American crowd theorizing was a reflection, even culmination, of a longer process that had gradually questioned classical conceptions of the social and, as a side effect, rendered its corresponding categories and modes of problematization – including that of crowds – obsolete or at best marginal (see also Wagner 2001: 79). In the crowd semantics domain, this move away from the social was prefigured by early-twentieth-century liberal problematizations, as Chapter 4 delineated. Writing about a structurally analogous development, Wagner has aptly character-ized the ensuing post-1960s and 1970s situation as follows: 'Social theoris-ing that insists on addressing the problématiques of the classical tradition finds itself, though not threatened in its existence, in an uncomfortably marginal position' (2001: 24). This is what happened to sociological crowd semantics.

Yet caution is called for here, for as I shall demonstrate in the next chapter, a sociological perception of the end of the social took shape among a number of European scholars in the 1970s that gave new impetus to a series of engagements with the problem of crowds and masses. So while the marginalization of the crowd might be impelled by the end of classical sociology and its concern with the social, the end of the social itself inspired a fresh perspective on contemporary crowds. But, crucially, since this renewed interest in crowds and masses, in addition to taking leave of the social as a guiding category, put into question the foundations of sociology and its disciplinary constitution, it would not be successful in restoring crowd semantics as a key sociological concern.

This chapter has explored different attempts to insist on the topic of crowds, in spite of the mass society semantics and its critics. Although there is more that divides than unites Canetti and the American sociologists who strived to enliven the collective behaviour tradition, the few ideas they share are nonetheless important. Thus, the picture I have tried to paint in this chapter has demonstrated how the notions of crowds and collective behaviour gradually became semantically reconfigured. Whether in Canetti's deliberate anti-systemic account or in the sociologists' work, earlier references to the irrationality, abnormality and de-individualizing implications of collectivities were replaced with a new conception which gave much more room to the purported rationality, normality and co-individualizing aspects of crowds and collective behaviour. This shift is highly significant in the history of crowd semantics, as is, of course, the marginalization of the problematization of crowds that followed suit in especially American sociology. The latter addition is not unimportant, for as intimated above, a number of European scholars enthusiastically revived notions of crowds and masses from the late 1970s onwards, but in ways that called into question the boundaries between sociology and adjacent disciplines, which many of the American sociologists examined above were keen on policing.

Concurrent with the struggles in American sociology between social
movement studies and the reinvigorated collective behaviour paradigm
a number of especially European philosophers and social theorists began
to shake the scaffold of existing sociological theorizing. On their analysis, society was undergoing a profound transition which rendered familiar sociological categories obsolete. In itself there was nothing new
about problematizing the foundations of sociological inquiry on the
basis of a diagnosis of purported reconfigurations of society and the
social. In some ways, sociological crowd and mass semantics had been
doing so from the very outset. Also, registering significant changes in
modern society's constitution was obviously not an exclusively
European affair. In the USA, Daniel Bell was on a similar track when
asserting *The Coming of Post-Industrial Society* (1974). In Europe a
somewhat different semantics gained footing, namely that of postmodernity. Here Jean-François Lyotard's *The Postmodern Condition* from
1979, which contained a critical discussion of the notions of society
in both Parsonian and Marxist sociology, presented the arguably most
famous articulation of the idea that society had entered a postmodern
state (1984). But the diagnosis of an epochal shift from a modern to a
postmodern society was promoted by countless other scholars and
received a veritable breakthrough in European social theorizing in the
late 1970s and early and mid-1980s (and soon also among North
American scholars, although perhaps more in the humanities than in
the social sciences).

I am not so interested in the semantics of postmodern society per se.
Yet discussions of postmodernity can hardly be ignored in a historical
investigation of crowd semantics, for the idea of a transition into postmodernity had a bearing on the conception of crowds and masses.
In fact, several discussions of postmodern society were wedded to a
novel understanding of masses. The present chapter examines how the
diagnosis of postmodernity entailed a renewed attention to (and reconfiguration of) crowd and mass semantics, which, however, would not

succeed in bringing back this semantics to the centre of sociology. The discussion concentrates on the work of Jean Baudrillard, Peter Sloterdijk and Michel Maffesoli, respectively. As I shall argue, one of the common features running through these scholars' conceptions of postmodernity is the idea that the masses of today have entered a *post-political* era, i.e. a situation in which traditional understandings of politics are annulled, suspended or transcended.

This post-political condition is one that puts into question what Chantal Mouffe has distilled as the two main models of contemporary liberal political thought. One is the so-called 'aggregative' model, which 'envisages politics as the establishment of a compromise between differing competing forces in society', and in which '[i]ndividuals are portrayed as rational beings, driven by the maximization of their own interests and as acting in the political world in a basically instrumental way' (2005: 12–13). Berk's gaming approach incarnates this liberal view on politics. The other model is the so-called 'deliberate' one which problematizes the instrumental understanding of politics and replaces it with an emphasis on how politics is intertwined with ethics and morality. This model, embodied by Jürgen Habermas' work (1997), suggests 'that it is possible to create in the realm of politics a rational moral consensus by means of free discussion', as Mouffe puts it (2005: 13).

The contemporary masses, postmodernists such as Baudrillard and Maffesoli have argued, will have none of this, and refuse to take part in politics on either of these liberal premises. Indeed, the postmodern masses seem to renounce politics altogether. This is not to suggest that the postmodern masses have lost all contact with the political domain. As I shall demonstrate in the final part of the chapter, scholars such as Michael Hardt and Antonio Negri have argued for a reconceptualization of masses (multitudes) that take a most active part in redefining contemporary politics. Here too the understanding of politics as advanced in the two above-mentioned liberal paradigms is critiqued, but in ways that contain more positive notes on what a redefined political order might look like.

The chapter seeks to capture central semantic developments from the late 1970s until today, which in one fashion or another charted new directions for placing crowds and masses centrally in sociological analysis, thereby in effect challenging the marginalization of this semantic field that the previous chapter described. Two remarks are warranted before venturing into the discussion of the postmodern plateau. First, the postmodern problematization of crowds and masses is a less homogeneous body of literature than, for instance, the new wave of collective behaviour theorizing in the USA. In that sense, the fragmentation that postmodern analyses often stress as a significant feature of postmodern society is mirrored in the semantic corpus itself.

Second, although I limit myself below to work that falls into the postmodern register, the renewed interest in masses it at once embodied and stimulated can hardly be understood independently of a more or less simultaneous revival of crowd semantics that occurred in other domains of European social theory. I am thinking here especially of the work of the French social psychologist Serge Moscovici whose seminal book *The Age of the Crowd: A Historical Treatise on Mass Psychology* was published in French in 1981 (1985). Through a thorough reinterpretation of the work of Le Bon, Tarde and Freud, this book aimed to revive classical crowd psychology in a contemporary setting. Specifically, Moscovici, who did not hide his reservations to parts of this tradition, argued that crowd psychology provided an indispensable reservoir for conceiving the power exercised by leaders. If one were to understand the power of leaders, it would simply be inexcusable not to take seriously this rich body of literature. In Moscovici's own words, 'I find it astonishing that even today we believe that we can ignore [crowd psychology's] concepts and dispense with them' (1985: 4).

Moscovici's was an honest attempt to legitimize classical crowd semantics in social theory. Although it would only have a marginal bearing on subsequent American sociology – McPhail's denunciation of this tradition was published only a few years after the English translation of Moscovici's book came out – it did inspire a new consideration of crowds in social psychology. When in spite of this I have decided not to embark on a detailed discussion of Moscovici's work in this chapter it is because *The Age of the Crowd* exhibited a closer affinity to a modern than a postmodern constellation, as it were. Moscovici's objective was not to furnish a distinct reinterpretation of society as such. His book remained within the semantic horizon of Le Bon, Tarde and Freud (although its concluding remarks did point to the need for a more globalized understanding of crowd phenomena; see 1985: 384–5). To be sure, some of Moscovici's other work on crowds and related topics went significantly beyond classical crowd psychology. This applied in particular to the book series on changing conceptions in social psychology he co-edited with Carl F. Graumann, where one volume was devoted to *Changing Conceptions of Crowd Mind and Behavior* (Graumann and Moscovici 1986). But neither in this book was modernity as such being questioned.

Something similar might be said of, for instance, Klaus Theweleit's work. In 1977–8 Theweleit published a comprehensive, two-volume study entitled *Male Fantasies*. This project presented a new theory of fascism, based on an empirical core of German *Freikorps* publications from the 1920s. In particular the second volume analysed fascism with respect to mass categories (Theweleit 1989). Theweleit's investigation did not change the course of sociological crowd semantics, but his original work did give impetus to a reconsideration of crowd and mass theorizing. So, similar to the case of Moscovici, he contributed to legitimizing the relevance of this semantic corpus, and thereby stimulated the postmodern engagements with crowd theory that I now turn to.[1]

The masses and the implosion of the social

One of the most significant attempts to grapple with the question of crowds and masses under postmodern conditions was put forward by the French philosopher and social theorist Jean Baudrillard in his influential 1978 essay *In the Shadow of the Silent Majorities* (1983). This essay went beyond existing critical conceptions of crowds and masses, especially those presented by the Frankfurt scholars. There was an echo here of Baudrillard's previous work which had attacked Marxism's privileging of production at the expense, Baudrillard thought, of consumption. But *In the Shadow of the Silent Majorities* was also a critical comment on Le Bon's prophecy of the era of crowds as well as on sociology and the social sciences more generally.

Baudrillard opened the essay by acknowledging the intimate relation between the social and the crowd/mass upon which classical crowd theory was built: 'The whole chaotic constellation of the social revolves around that spongy referent, that opaque but equally translucent reality, that nothingness: the masses [*les masses*]', read the first sentence of the essay (1983: 1). Indeed, he contended, 'the mass is characteristic of our modernity' (1983: 2). He further alluded to classical crowd psychology by referring to ideas about the mesmerization and magnetization of masses. The resemblance to this older mode of crowd theorizing was only superficial, however, as Baudrillard's image of the masses was almost perpendicular to Le Bon's and Tarde's accounts of violent, barbarous entities. Whereas the latter evoked an idea of noisy crowds in the street, Baudrillard's diagnosis pointed towards the exact opposite phenomenon: postmodern masses that are completely silent. Furthermore, he argued, contrary to the old conception of the social, which was tied to the referent of the (noisy) masses, '[*t*]*he only referent which still*

---

[1] While *Male Fantasies* tried to come to terms with early-twentieth-century fascism, Theweleit later published an application of Canetti's crowd theory to turn-of-the-century events, such as the death of Lady Diana (1998).

functions is that of the silent majority', and this was an imaginary referent since it had no 'real' social foundation (1983: 19, italics in original):

> The masses are no longer a referent because they no longer belong to the order of representation. They don't express themselves, they are surveyed. They don't reflect upon themselves, they are tested. The referendum (and the media are a constant referendum of directed questions and answers) has been substituted for the political referent. (1983: 20)

So rather than referring to some collective subject or real actor possessed by a group mind – the mass 'has no sociological "reality." It has nothing to do with any *real* population, body or specific social aggregate' (1983: 5, italics in original) – the mass was said only to surface in surveys, statistics, opinion polls, etc. Accordingly, Baudrillard contended, the masses are *simulated*, meaning that they are generated 'by models of a real without origin or reality: a hyperreal' (1994b: 1). This simulation was a characteristic trait of the postmodern society. Baudrillard argued that, whereas modernity was characterized by industrial production and reproduction – he recalled Benjamin's analysis of technical reproduction (Baudrillard 1993: 55–6) – a radical mutation had occurred after the Second World War, signifying a postmodern phase, which amounted to an era of simulation. This entailed '[t]he end of labour. The end of production. The end of political economy' (1993: 8). In more positive terms a circulation of signs, codes, models and representation had taken over, a process that was buttressed not least by the mass media, and which bid farewell to any external referents or any 'real' foundation. In this new era of postmodern simulation, 'signs and modes of representation come to constitute "reality", and signs gain autonomy and, in interaction with other signs, come to constitute a new type of social order in which it is signs and codes that constitute "the real"' (Kellner 1989: 63). That is, representations and models came to assume a more real character than the 'reality' they represented. As mentioned, one corollary of this was that the masses no longer signified a bodily entity. This took final leave of the physical crowd of Le Bon and Tarde. But the assertion that the masses have no real foundation also entailed that the mass as a concept dissolved; it referred to nothing real (1983: 4).

The media were attributed a key role in this simulation, as they circulate the simulated reality. When discussing media Baudrillard was careful not to ascribe to them an educating, enlightening or manipulating power. The information streaming from the media did not inform the masses, nor did it guide their behaviour. The information simply 'produces even more mass' (1983: 25). To undermine the idea of any manipulating power of the media, Baudrillard highlighted Lazarsfeld's 'two-step flow model of communication', which suggested that the mass is no passive receiver of media messages, but (and this was Baudrillard's addition) is capable of absorbing and decoding the media, without this implying a transfer of meaning (1983: 42). Just as important, he argued that the masses show no interest in the messages conveyed by the media. Quite the contrary, he contended, McLuhan (1964: 7) was right in asserting that 'the medium is the message'; the spectacle of the media is what fascinates the masses (1983: 35). But Baudrillard could not resist the temptation to reformulate McLuhan's famous dictum in a way that acknowledged this interrelatedness of media and masses: 'The mass and the media are one single process. Mass(age) is the message' (1983: 44).[2]

Intimately linked to Baudrillard's analysis of the silent simulated masses was his diagnosis of the end of the social. The one was the flipside of the other. The idea of the social as a field proper was tied to the rise of modernity in the eighteenth century and quickly became a site of political intervention and subsequently of sociological analysis, giving rise to notions of social class, social relations, etc. In the postmodern society of simulation, however, the social 'with all its idealized resonances of human interaction, communication, civility and the rest' had imploded into the masses (Kellner 1989: 85):[3]

these masses that one wants us to believe *are* the social, are on the contrary the site of the implosion of the social. *The masses are the increasingly dense sphere in which the whole social comes to be imploded, and to be devoured in an uninterrupted process of simulation.* (1994a: 68, italics in original; see also 1983: 4)

As Jonathan S. Fish has noted, this diagnosis not only entailed a critique of Marxism; it was just as much a 'tacit attack on Durkheim and

---

[2] The dissolution of message and its substitution with spectacle was visible in the political field, Baudrillard argued. Here, he claimed, the masses no longer follow political debates because of their content, but because the political has developed into a spectacular TV game (1983: 37). He added that as a consequence of this development 'people have become a public' (1983: 37, italics in original). This public carried no links to Tarde's notion, where the public was the antithesis of the masses. Nor did it allude to Lippmann's conceptualization and its critique of the separation between reality and our conception of it, an analytical scheme Baudrillard would entirely reject. Instead Baudrillard's notion of the public referred to the masses' position as audience in a theatre. They had become spectators to a political performance.

[3] According to Baudrillard, part of the reason for this implosion could be found in the hyperconformity of the masses. Instead of resisting the social from an external position, they pushed it to and beyond its limits. As an example, Baudrillard mentioned how medical consumption had rapidly escalated because the masses demand more treatment, more medication, etc. This had not led to medical alienation, Baudrillard stressed. Quite the contrary, the masses 'are in a process of ruining its institution, of making Social Security explode, of putting the social itself in danger by craving always more of it, as with commodities' (1983: 47).

Parsons' understanding of the social as an objective realm, which requires rational, scientific investigation' (2003: 260). Even more ramifying, Baudrillard's thesis articulated a devastating critique of sociology as such since sociology had failed to acknowledge this purported implosion of the social. Sociology kept taking the social domain for granted as if it could be studied as an objective reality, or it presumed that the social were grossly similar to how it was conceived in the eighteenth century. On Baudrillard's view, failing to acknowledge the implosion of the social, the dissolution of any real social foundation, rendered the endeavours of sociologists obsolete (e.g. 1983: 67–8).

But the implosion of the social also marked the end of classical politics. This had several dimensions in Baudrillard's analysis. First of all, the entire essay on the silent masses was guided by a problematization of the idea that masses are manipulated by power, whether this power acquires a personal (the leader) or structural incarnation (e.g. the culture industry). He was particularly critical of the position adopted by many Frankfurt School scholars that modern capitalism had produced mass individuals whose purported isolation and alienation led to ignorance and indifference towards the 'real' societal problems. Baudrillard believed that an entirely different image of masses was needed and illustrated this by referring to that night in 1977 when the German terrorist Klaus Croissant was extradited. While a few hundred people were on the streets in Paris, protesting against the extradition, 'twenty million people spent their evening glued to the screen', because France played an important football match (1983: 12). According to Baudrillard, a Frankfurt School-inspired interpretation of this preference of football over social justice would emphasize the apparent indifference of the masses, which would likely be explained by the manipulation of the masses that this would be taken as a sign of – Fromm would probably speak of automaton conformity as a mechanism of escape from isolation. In Baudrillard's eyes, such an interpretation rested on a misconception of both masses and power. In Baudrillard's own words, 'power manipulates nothing, the masses are neither misled nor mystified' (1983: 14).

At first sight this claim might bear some resemblance to what was argued by Canetti, the American collective behaviour sociologists as well as by the historians pursuing 'history from below'. However, Baudrillard was far from subscribing to, say, the rational-choice agenda of Berk. In fact, he effectively undermined the rational edifice of Berk's work, but also the call for a rational taming of power underpinning the perspective of both Frankfurt scholars and conservative crowd theorists such as Tarde. Baudrillard asserted that, rather than being subjected to power, the masses help to stabilize an outdated image of power. The indifferent position the masses assumed in the case of Croissant covered over the impotence, not of the masses, but of power: power might attribute to itself all sorts of capabilities and associate itself with enlightenment strategies of all kinds, but this could not change the fact that, according to Baudrillard, 'this indifference of the masses is their true, their only practice' and all they long for (1983: 14). The alliance between the masses and power surfacing here was therefore one where power continuously strived to educate and liberate the masses, while the latter tolerated this ambition, but were unaffected by it and entirely consumed by something else.

Precisely this point was fundamental to Baudrillard's critique of especially socialist/Marxist thinking, whether in Frankfurt guises or not. Crowd thinking of a socialist leaning had always been governed by one chief desire, he asserted: 'Whatever its political, pedagogical, cultural content, the plan is always to get some meaning across, to keep the masses *within reason*' (1983: 9, italics in original). This, he contended, was illustrative of the essential 'contempt for the masses' inherent to any attempt to endow the masses with meaning and rationality, features they purportedly lacked (1985: 586). Indeed, with few exceptions, the masses were typically seen as representing an irrational problem that prompted education or other measures through which to endow them with rationality. While the American collective behaviour scholars would refute this image of irrationality, dismissing it as an example of the myth of the madding crowd, Baudrillard's critique lay elsewhere. According to his interpretation, the desire of the masses simply did not correspond to that of their alleged educators: 'the masses scandalously resist this imperative of rational communication. They are given meaning: they want spectacle' (1983: 10).

The notion of the spectacle alluded to the 1967 book *The Society of the Spectacle*, written by the intellectual, situationist and filmmaker, Guy Debord. In this book Debord developed a comprehensive critique of contemporary society, arguing that the mass media and the capitalist mode of production had created a veritable society of spectacle, where representation reigned at all levels. This spectacle, defined as 'a social relationship between people that is mediated by images', was deeply de-individualizing, alienating and isolating, according to Debord (1995: 12). Baudrillard's use of the term did not contain the same critical twist as in Debord. For Baudrillard, it was no real scandal that the masses preferred the spectacle of football. The true scandal was that social theorists kept scorning the masses for this; that these theorists adhered to a conception of basically irrational masses in need of guidance, and that they thereby ignored that this image of the masses had been surpassed in practice. In fact, Baudrillard speculated, rather than being an expression of suppression and alienation, the silence of the masses (their preference of the TV screen over physical demonstrations) could be an *active* act. Rather than being a sign of incompetence and powerlessness, the silence might amount to a kind of resistance. The masses' 'withdrawing into the private [sphere] could well be *a direct defiance of the political*, a form of actively resisting political manipulation' (1983: 39, italics in original). In a subsequent paper this was expressed in bolder terms as 'an original strategy, an original response in the form of a challenge' to the enlightenment attempts (1985: 578).

This was related to other political dimensions of Baudrillard's analysis. Ever since the French Revolution, he contended, it had been widely accepted that the political was tied to representation, encapsulated in the notion that politicians represent and speak on behalf of others, the people. Yet the silent postmodern masses evaded this representation, and therefore altered the parameters of politics. Their silence 'isn't a silence that does not speak, it is a silence which *refuses to be spoken for in its name* . . . No one can be said to represent the silent majority, and that is its revenge' (1983: 22, italics in original).

Furthermore, the implosion of the social meant the end to the political, whether in the form of an exchange of arguments (the deliberate model) or as an instrumental pursuit of interests (the aggregative model). Since there was nothing 'real' to fight over, and since the masses absorbed all mass-mediated attempts to guide, improve and communicate with them, Baudrillard's analysis suggested that the postmodern society gave birth to a *post-political* situation. In contrast to the tradition from Le Bon to Tilly where crowds, masses and social movements were almost always conceived of as essentially political entities which tried either to recast society or to correct injustices, Baudrillard intimated that the connection between the masses and the political had evaporated. As a mere spectator to the political spectacle, the masses assumed no active position in the political game. Indeed, he posited, as a final political act the masses had delegated their power in order to enjoy themselves instead:

the mass is very snobbish; it . . . delegates in a sovereign manner the faculty of choice to someone else by a sort of game of irresponsibility, of ironic challenge, of sovereign lack of will, of secret ruse. All the mediators (men of the media, politicians, intellectuals, all the heirs of the *philosophes* of the Enlightenment in contempt for the masses) are really only adapted to this purpose: to manage by delegation, by procuration, this tedious matter of power and will, to unburden the masses of this transcendence for their greater pleasure and to turn it into a show for their benefit. (1985: 586, italics in original)

Certain tensions might be observed in Baudrillard's conception of the masses. On the one hand, for instance, Baudrillard clearly dismissed the idea of the masses being a subject. This permitted him to avoid references to alienation and revolutionary aspirations: 'no longer being (a) subject, *they can no longer be alienated*', meaning also '[t]he end of revolution' (1983: 22, italics in original). The non-subjective character of the masses was further highlighted by the notion of simulation and the assertion that the masses are fictional entities in the sense that they have no 'real' foundation. On the other hand, Baudrillard's analysis was fraught with allusions to the existence of subjective *agency* on the side of the masses. For example, the masses were said to actively defy the political, their silence was seen as an active form of revenge, etc. There seemed in other words to be an additional layer to the masses than their simulation suggested. This impression was enhanced by Baudrillard's reflections on the masses in 'The Beaubourg Effect: Implosion and Deterrence' (1994a) which was originally published in 1977, i.e. shortly before *In the Shadow of the Silent Majorities*.

'The Beaubourg Effect' presented a discussion of the Pompidou Centre in Paris which had been officially inaugurated in late January 1977 and soon became a popular success. Baudrillard's analysis of the museum placed the masses centrally. He argued that the Pompidou Centre was nothing but 'a museal scenario that only serves to keep up the humanist fiction of culture', but that it actually effected 'the death of culture' which was the reason why 'the masses are joyously gathered' (1994a: 65):

The masses rush toward Beaubourg as they rush toward disaster sites, with the same irresistible élan. Better: they *are* the disaster of Beaubourg. Their number, their stampede, their fascination, their itch to see everything is objectively a deadly and catastrophic behavior for the whole undertaking. Not only does their weight put the building in danger, but their adhesion, their curiosity annihilates the very contents of this culture of animation. This rush can no longer be measured against what was proposed as the cultural objective, it is its radical negation, in both its excess and success. It is thus the masses who assume the role of catastrophic agent in this structure of catastrophe, it is *the masses themselves who put an end to mass culture*. (1994a: 66, italics in original)

In this quote Baudrillard depicted the masses as an agent that threatened, by its sheer weight, to make the building implode. All simulation aside, this connoted a rather traditional image of the masses as *physical-bodily* subjects that go on the streets, or here in a museum, to evoke effects (see also his discussion of implosive violence of the masses, 1994a: 69). To be sure, Baudrillard asserted that the masses act 'without knowing it' (1994a: 69), but that too aligned his analysis with classical crowd psychology, rather than setting it apart from this tradition. The physical image resurfaced later in 'The Beaubourg Effect' when Baudrillard contended that mass production is not simply a production of goods for the masses, but also a production of the masses themselves, visible in the 'stockpiles of people – the line, waiting, traffic jams, concentration, the camp' (1994a: 68). He even used the notion of the 'crowd' [*foule*] to describe this stockpiling (1994a: 68). Once again, this connotation of the physical composition of the masses ran counter to Baudrillard's insistence on the simulated character of the masses. Such tensions did not really undercut the diagnosis of a shift towards a post-political situation, though. What the masses did at Beaubourg was not a traditional political act and could not be adequately understood within a classical sociological and political register. Therefore, Baudrillard intimated, however one looked upon it, the postmodern constellation could not help but produce an embarrassment in existing sociological theory.

The politics of contempt

There are striking parallels but also important differences between Baudrillard's views on masses from the late 1970s and early 1980s and the ideas subsequently put forward by the German philosopher Peter Sloterdijk in his essay *Die Verachtung der Massen* from 2000. As the title laid bare, Sloterdijk here proposed a problematization of masses through a discussion of the contempt that surrounds them. This contempt had two dimensions. One materialized in one of the main tenets of the essay which was to avoid a particular conception of crowds and masses that, in Sloterdijk's view, had been hegemonic in most of the twentieth century. Akin to Hegel's axiom of the development of substance as subject, the aim underpinning the bulk of previous theorizations had been to cultivate the crowd/mass as subject, Sloterdijk (2000: 9) argued – echoing Baudrillard's critique of problematizations of crowds and masses which drew, in one way or other, on enlightened attempts to rationalize the purportedly irrational collectivities and transform them into proper political subjects. On Sloterdijk's analysis, and here too he sided with Baudrillard, this cultivating enterprise signified a profound contempt for the masses because these were reduced to an object of a patronizing gaze (2000: 30–1).

According to Sloterdijk, who paid no explicit attention to Baudrillard, only one scholar had resisted this wish to mould the crowd/mass into something politically digestible. This exception to the general contempt for the masses was Canetti, whom Sloterdijk lauded in high tones for having 'fixated theoretically the stage in modernization' in which the physical crowd was a principal force (2000: 16).[4] As the years had passed, however, Canetti's parlance had acquired a certain 'patina', rendering it less fitting for turn-of-the-century diagnostic purposes (2000: 15). Yet the declining relevance of Canetti's analytical reservoir was not equivalent to a waning importance of the crowd/mass topic as such, although a view of the sociological landscape would easily lend that impression. In Sloterdijk's words, the end to the predominance of physical crowds (which now merely manifested themselves in occasional eruptions) had seduced the 'majority of today's sociologists ... into believing that the era has vanished in which the management of the masses is the central problem for modern politics and culture. Nothing could be more wrong than this belief' (2000: 19). Indeed, Sloterdijk stressed, the masses continue to play a prominent role in contemporary society, although their mode of organization and ways of expression have changed radically when compared to the crowds of the street that Canetti and many other crowd scholars used to analyse. What had emerged in postmodern society was above all a new state of non-physical massification. 'The crowd has transformed into a programme-related mass, which per definition has emancipated itself from assembling physically in some public space. In it one is mass as individual. One is now mass without seeing the others' (2000: 17).

One of the central differences between modern and postmodern masses was traced to a shift from the 'leader principle' of crowds, focused on discharge, to the (mass media) 'programme principle' of the current masses, aiming at non-political entertainment (2000: 20). It might be critically argued that speaking about a leader principle just after the celebration of Canetti obscured the latter's intentions, but it resonated with the theories of Le Bon, Tarde and Freud that were also cited in the essay. More importantly, Sloterdijk contended that the leader principle and the programme principle were emblematic of two different political modes of organizing affects, namely a fascist one and one deployed by mass democracies, respectively. The fascist mode was illustrated by reference to the kinds of mobilization Hitler envisaged at the NSDAP rallies, where '[d]uring the "missa hypnotica" the fusion of mass and leader pretended to be a successful sealing of the project of bringing around the mass as subject' (2000: 21–2).[5] While Hitler sought

---

[4] Strictly speaking Canetti was not the only scholar who did not dream of an enlightenment of the masses. Le Bon, for one, also did not buy into that ideal, although for different reasons. Le Bon simply did not grant the masses the ability to think rationally so, on his view, any enlightenment strategy was doomed to fail.

[5] Some years after *Die Verachtung der Massen* was published Sloterdijk ventured into a new discussion of crowds. In an article entitled 'Foam City' (2008; extracted from 2004), he

to achieve this in part through architectural means, the programme principle of the contemporary mass media operates on a far more viral and much less material basis, Sloterdijk argued. Here collectivities ensue, not as body-to-body encounters, but rather as crystallizations of 'discourses, fashion, programmes and famous people', where masses emerge as similar patterns of imitation (2000: 17). In other words, when the programme principle is at play, masses are not oriented towards some leader, but rather towards whatever ideas, fads, celebrities, etc. are popular at a given moment.

According to Sloterdijk, this emergence of a postmodern mass – which does not 'feel its own pulsating physis' and which, akin to Baudrillard's diagnosis of silence, 'does not produce any common cry' (2000: 17) – had changed the conditions of politics:

> Masses that no longer assemble on a co-present basis risk losing the consciousness of their political potency. They no longer sense their weight of punch, the frenzy of their congregation and their authority to demand and storm as in the golden age of crowds and parades. The postmodern mass is mass without potential, a sum of micro-anarchism and loneliness. (2000: 18)

As a result of the change from 'political discharge to non-political entertainment' the political had practically imploded (2000: 28). What used to be manifest expressions of political battle had dissolved into mere amusement in the postmodern mass-mediated society. Clearly, there was not a long way from this to Baudrillard's analysis. Yet the central motif of Sloterdijk's text was not so much to theorize the rupture between modernity and postmodernity, such as Baudrillard had done in his discussion of the demise of representation, but instead to pinpoint the common thread running through both epochs, and this common thread was located in what Sloterdijk saw as the inherent resentment of crowds and masses.

A key conceptual frame to study this resentment was Sloterdijk's distinction between so-called vertical and horizontal difference. Vertical difference referred to the acknowledgement of fundamental differences between people. Some are cleverer, faster, better, more talented than others. Some have qualities others simply do not possess. All the attempts throughout history to enlighten the masses and develop them as subject essentially subscribed to a notion of vertical difference: the educators were better than the masses but benevolently offered their

---

demonstrated how Hitler's mobilization of the masses was predicated on early modern forms of crowd orchestration that materialized in the aftermath to the French Revolution. That analysis did not tap into the discussion of contempt.

assistance so as to take the latter to new and higher levels. But, Sloterdijk contended, what these educators failed to realize was that the masses have always resisted vertical difference. This was the second (and undisguised Nietzschean) aspect of the politics of contempt analysed by Sloterdijk: the masses have a profound contempt for difference. They disapprove of everything that sticks out and which claims to be better than something else. Accordingly, the identity of the masses consists in their radical egalitarianism, which in Sloterdijk's view was another way of saying their profound 'indifference' to any vertical difference (2000: 85). Instead of vertical difference, the masses endorse and embody horizontal difference, i.e. the idea that no one is better than anyone else, that all should have equal rights and possibilities, irrespective of what they have accomplished.

There were two things at stake here. One was Sloterdijk's assertion that previous crowd and mass theorizing adopted a vertical view. Another and more important thing was his claim that this vertical perspective found no resonance in the masses because, ever since the inception of modern society (and continuing through postmodernity), the real problem was that the masses had flatly refused vertical difference and substituted it with horizontal difference. This observation constituted Sloterdijk's central problematization of modern and postmodern society. Due to the horizontal difference of the masses, the difference between the talented/the elite and the mass had dissolved and had no currency in political life. The modern individual had been accustomed not to look up to a gifted person; he or she would only accept others if they resembled him or herself, Sloterdijk's critique went.

There is, as Steen Nepper Larsen (2002: 14) has observed, a clear echo here of Ortega's diagnosis of how the mass individual had ousted the select individual, although there was no mention of Ortega in Sloterdijk's essay. Indeed, as should be clear, Sloterdijk rehearsed many fundamental problematizations from within the earlier mass society semantics, aligning his analysis both with this literature and with the kinds of postmodern thinking otherwise discussed in this chapter. For example, in continuation of the reference to Ortega, it might be argued that Sloterdijk subscribed to Ortega's uneasiness about the decline of the select individual and how it was replaced with an other-directed social character (Riesman), i.e. one that adjusts his or her behaviour according to what his or her peers do. Yet what distinguished Sloterdijk from the mass society forerunners was above all his insistence on the need for escaping the contempt for the masses. More on this shortly.

As indicated above, the predominance of horizontal difference at the expense of vertical difference was not particularly a postmodern occurrence. On Sloterdijk's analysis, it was emblematic of modernity as such, and both the leader and the programme principle were guided by it. This might appear contradictory, as crowd semantics had often emphasized the vertical difference between the leader and the mass. But on Sloterdijk's interpretation, even the most radical incarnation of the leader principle in modern society, Hitler, testified to the prevalence of horizontal difference. Thus, Sloterdijk posited, Hitler was not extraordinary in any sense, nor was he particularly gifted or talented. His popularity had entirely different grounds: he mirrored his followers and this guaranteed his success. When Hitler became *Führer*, he did 'not at all stand out as an adversary from the masses he ruled; rather, he was their deputy and their' concentrate. He always held the imperative mandate of the *Gemeinheit*' (2000: 25). In brief, people could recognize themselves in Hitler; they did not have to submit to standards beyond their own sphere. Drawing the line to the present, Sloterdijk asserted that what applied to the masses gathering around Hitler applies no less to the contemporary masses that are integrated through the mass media. 'The secret of the leader of that time and the celebrities of today consists in the fact that they resemble their dullest admirers more strongly than any person involved dares imagine' (2000: 25).

While, for Sloterdijk, the masses' dismissal of vertical difference signalled a devastating cultural decline, he did not opt for the vertical perspective of previous crowd and mass theorists. Patronizing critical sociology of a Frankfurt bent showed no way out, he argued. Rather than pinning his faith on sociological educators, he envisaged a new politics of difference whose impetus was derived from fields not usually associated with crowd/mass education. Specifically, he argued that the arts, sports and financial speculation all deserved attention as domains where permanent competition and struggle are legitimate, and where contempt for difference has not sedimented:

This is why in modern society sports, financial speculation and not least the arts must become ever more significant psycho-social regulators, for in the stadiums, at the exchanges and in the galleries those who compete for success and recognition rank themselves more or less on basis of results. Since such rankings are self-co-produced distinctions, they reduce hatred although they do not offer reconciliation. They do not make elemental envy evaporate, but they lend it a form in which it can move. (2000: 91)

Fields such as these could demonstrate to the masses that the latter's indifference had not (yet) achieved absolute hegemony and that something in fact deserved to be valorized over something else. Sloterdijk seemed to suggest that a new postmodern (psycho) politics might transpire on this basis that neither insulted the masses (through vertical

communication) nor simply flattered them (through horizontal communication) (2000: 31). This, in brief, would be the way out of the post-
political predicament.

Sloterdijk's analysis was both more and less radical than Baudrillard's.
It was less radical because its treatment of the non-political entertainment of the programme-related masses was not founded in an
elaborated discussion of the operative modus of the mass media.
Here Baudrillard's examination of postmodern simulation had more
to offer. Yet Sloterdijk's diagnosis was more radical in the sense that
it demonstrated how the intertwinement of masses and the politics of
contempt had run through modernity as well as postmodernity. That
is, Sloterdijk's interest in the relation between masses and contempt
was triggered by the postmodern situation, but it ended up unravel-
ling a more profound problematique.

Postmodern tribes: an affirmative view

While Baudrillard's diagnosis of the silent, absorbing masses espoused
an 'ironic' (1985: 578; better, perhaps, cynical) view of postmodern
politics and sociality, and Sloterdijk's analysis was outright dismissive
of the masses' purported endorsement of horizontal difference, the
French sociologist Michel Maffesoli presented an image of postmodern
collectivities that was painted in much warmer colours. Continuing
in the footsteps of Whitman and Canetti he outlined a decisively
affirmative theory of postmodern crowds. This theorization was driven
by a twofold problematization of: (1) the tradition that looked upon
crowds and their associated formations with terror; and (2) the idea that
a consideration of crowds had become more or less obsolete in
late-twentieth-century society, and that focus should be shifted towards
individuals and their behaviour. The latter problematization targeted
anything from harsh methodological individualism to assertions about
an increasing individualization of society.

Maffesoli has articulated his alternative diagnosis in various works.
Seminal for present purposes is not least his book *The Time of the Tribes:
The Decline of Individualism in Mass Society*, originally published in 1988
(1996b). The title was telling. The present age is not an era of crowds in a
classical sense, but also not of its opposite, individualism. Maffesoli was
straightforward in his rejection of individualism. It is plainly incorrect, he
asserted, to work on the assumption of a constituent, more or less free-
floating individual and to take as the starting point for sociological analysis the individual's actions. Maffesoli's entire work might be seen as one
big attempt to prove 'individualism and its various theories ... invalid.

Each social actor is less acting than acted upon' (1996b: 145). Not surprisingly, therefore, the centre of his attention lay elsewhere. He argued that a new kind of collectivity had imposed itself on postmodern society, marking an era of tribes or neo-tribes, understood as affectively loaded micro-groups. In line with his reservations towards individualism, and contrary to the 'refurbished' collective behaviour tradition of American sociology that emerged in the 1950s and 1960s and which, as in Berk's case, put the purposeful individual first in the study of collective life, Maffesoli's focus on tribes championed the idea that collectivities operate on an independent plane and should be studied with this in mind. Reducing collective behaviour to a projection of individual strategies failed to recognize this, he believed. In other words, Maffesoli's book was informed by the underlying agenda that a fresh perspective on postmodern sociality was needed and that existing work on mass society and crowds and collective behaviour had not been able to furnish a persuasive account of the new conditions.

To get an impression of the nature of late-twentieth-century postmodern society, Maffesoli juxtaposed it with its modern forerunner. According to Maffesoli, the central difference between the two rested on modernity's emphasis on rationality, individuation and differentiation, which had been replaced by the allegedly more 'emphatic period' of postmodernity, where differentiation is no longer outspoken and where, rather than individuation, 'a "loss" in a collective subject' takes place, namely in the neo-tribes (1996b: 11). Relatedly, during modernity crowds signified exceptions to the rational order, hence Le Bon and others' concern with how otherwise rational individuals might dissolve in momentary crowd frenzies. The postmodern situation was different, Maffesoli posited. Here the separation between individual and collectivity had become the exception; the normal postmodern state of affairs was that individuals were 'absorbed into' all sorts of successive ephemeral tribal groupings, one after the other (1991: 15). In their postmodern everyday life, Maffesoli argued, people are part of numerous fragmented and shifting neo-tribes, self-organized around their distinct values and carrying no connections to one another. For example, people might form a neo-tribe with their closest colleagues, after work they might join a shopping neo-tribe, be active in a fan club, be part of a techno neo-tribe at night, etc. Maffesoli's point was that rather than undermining the individual, these affective neo-tribal communities have become the central locus of the postmodern individual's desires and enjoyments, and this applies both to 'the effervescent masses (sexual, festive, sporting, promiscuous) and the everyday masses (crowded, ordinary, consuming, following blindly)'

(1996b: 89; see also 1991: 12). As the quote demonstrated, Maffesoli did not submit to a rigorous distinction between the notions of crowds, masses and tribes. Rather than detailing the differences between them, he was interested in their common affective register, and this, he argued, is expressed most vividly today in the neo-tribal formations. This did not exclude 'classical' crowd eruptions; the collective de-individuation just manifests itself most clearly in the more ordinary spheres of everyday life.

Maffesoli's conception of neo-tribes drew on a wide register of previous theorizing. For example, he subscribed to the kind of (Bergsonian) vitalist horizon also penetrating Broch's work, arguing that the 'multiple explosions of vitalism' in today's tribes display an '"affirmative" quality of life, the societal "will to live"' (1996b: 32, 33). Maffesoli further argued along with Canetti that the neo-tribe has as its 'central responsibility to triumph over ordinary death' (1996b: 63). In contrast to what was held by Ortega and Sloterdijk, this purportedly endowed the masses with a certain 'nobility' (1996b: 63). To further enhance the affirmative interpretation Maffesoli argued that the vitalist impulse was consonant with an ethical component. New forms of solidarity would ensue from the collective affective experience, he posited ('the shared sentiment is the true social bond', 1996b: 43). Indeed, the customs, friendships, rituals, etc. of the neo-tribes would produce a distinctively ethical experience: '*the collective sensibility . . . results in an ethical connection*' (1996b: 18, italics in original).[6]

In addition to the vitalist aspect, Maffesoli's notion of neo-tribes testified to a strong legacy from Durkheim and the Collège de Sociologie (see also Moebius 2006: 451–4). Given Durkheim's ambivalence towards the crowd issue, basing a reconceptualization of crowd and mass phenomena under postmodern conditions on Durkheim's writings might appear as a surprising choice. Yet Maffesoli was not so interested in the parts of Durkheim's work that debunked crowd thinking. He turned his attention instead to Durkheim's sociology of religion and how it had uncovered a connection between religion and social collectivities. In Maffesoli's theorization this translated into two central points. First of all, the effervescence examined by Durkheim formed the backcloth to Maffesoli's description of the tribes as emotional, non-rational, Dionysian communities, tied together by shared passions (e.g. 1996b:

---

[6] The affirmative interpretation should not hide the negative sides of postmodern tribes. Maffesoli did acknowledge that tribes could be 'the cause of village racism and ostracism' (1996b: 97; see also 38), just as their 'affective contagion' might produce 'fanaticism' that is expressed violently (1996a: 134).

38–45). Second, due to their collective passions tribes were endowed with an essentially religious aura. Since the postmodern era was characterized by a purported 'multiplication of affective–religious groupings', religion had resurfaced as 'the matrix of all social life', and Maffesoli therefore found it warranted to speak of a 're-enchantment' of society through tribal associations (1996b: 42, 82, 83).

Maffesoli's Dionysian conception of neo-tribes as hedonistic collectivities of shared passions displayed some affinity to Lofland's call for a closer consideration of crowd joys. But whereas Lofland's suggestion was meant to supplement the rational agenda, so that both rational and irrational features were taken into account, Maffesoli aimed to transcend the very rational–irrational divide. On his view, postmodern tribes did not give way to an upsurge of irrationality; they were seen instead as *non-rational*. 'This term must be emphasized: the non-rational is not the irrational; it is not even defined in terms of the rational; it establishes a logic other than the one that has prevailed since the Enlightenment' (1996b: 144).

Although Maffesoli presented a more affirmative view of masses than Baudrillard and Sloterdijk, the political implications he drew were not radically different. He certainly agreed with Baudrillard that the Big Social had imploded, rendering most existing sociology obsolete (Fish 2003: 267–9). But the social had not imploded into hyperconforming masses who absorbed mass-mediated information and delegated, by way of an ironic gesture, their political powers so as to enjoy a piece of entertainment. On Maffesoli's analysis, the social had imploded into a plethora of fragmented neo-tribes that, rather than being hyperconforming and absorbing, nurtured their own particular ties, passions and values in active ways. Yet the issuing hyperfragmentation of values following from this, the 'polytheism of values' as Maffesoli called it, signified a zero degree or better an annulment of classical politics: 'It seems to me that polytheism goes beyond the political order; structurally, we might say, since the relativity of values results in *undecidability*. What can be more antithetical to the logic of politics?' (1996b: 110, italics in original). In a different context, Maffesoli laid a further plank to this argument by asserting that the hedonistic, postmodern condition entailed a veritable 'transfiguration of the political': 'one intends less to "act" on the social, to affect society, than to take from it all the well-being one can and to best enjoy this well-being', though this was not thought of as a subversive strategy of hyperconformity (1996a: 48). In other words, the neo-tribes had no interest whatsoever in engaging in deliberate versions of liberal democracy, nor were they politically instrumental in the sense of promoting essentially economic interests. Their hedonistic fragmented value communities were enough for them.

From a Sloterdijkean view, the fragmentation of values resulting from the postmodern neo-tribes was tantamount to hammering the final nail in the coffin of vertical difference. There was no longer a common understanding of what was better or more worthy of esteem (and indeed esteem had been replaced by hedonism). Instead a multiplicity of horizontal differences had emerged, Maffesoli's analysis suggested. In fact, the tribal differentiation of values drafted gloomier prospects for a reinsertion of vertical difference than Sloterdijk's hopes for sports, financial speculation and the arts projected. Due to the fragmentation, there was little likelihood that possible vertical differences in one neo-tribe could transfer and be accepted by other tribes. In Maffesoli's parlance this was a question of '[h]ow are these tribes and masses going to accommodate each other? How will their respective idols tolerate each other, or will they reach a compromise?' (1996a: 138). As Maffesoli's diagnosis of postmodern society left little room for successful political intervention in the social realm, he located the possible solution at the level of the masses themselves and simply hoped for the development of a future 'equilibrium' between the tribes (1996a: 139). But, as he admitted, this was a rather 'utopian' dream (1996a: 140).

The emergence of a new revolutionary subject: the multitude

The same year as Sloterdijk's cultural–critical treatise on the contemporary masses came out, the American political philosopher Michael Hardt and his Italian colleague Antonio Negri published their investigation *Empire* (2000). This book would soon become a crucial resource for left-wing debate and activism because of its emphasis on a new revolutionary agent, the multitude, which was meant to replace and transcend the old concept of the crowd. *Empire* had a double agenda. On the one hand, it outlined a diagnosis of the global order after the collapse of Soviet communism. On the other hand, it set the frame for not only analysing, but actually inspiring and effecting resistance against the predominant order.[7] In this sense the book transformed Le Bon's

---

[7] To be sure, in a later context, Hardt and Negri noted that, in their work on the multitude and its resistance, they did 'not propose the concept as a political directive – "Form the multitude!" – but rather as a way of giving a name to what is already going on and grasping the existing social and political tendency' (2004: 220). However, given the difficulties the authors had in pointing to existing forms of resistance that merited the name of multitude (see especially 2000: 399–400), it is hard not to ascribe a mobilizing agenda to their work.

objectives: rather than being a manual for how to control the modern crowds, *Empire* in effect pitched instructions for the self-organization of the multitude in a global, postmodern order.[8]

The basic hypothesis of the book was that the current world is governed by a new power, a new form of postmodern sovereignty, which Hardt and Negri named Empire. One of the crucial features of Empire was that it was said to operate as 'a *decentered* and *deterritorializing* apparatus of rule that progressively incorporates the entire global realm within its open, expanding frontiers' (2000: xii, italics in original). The decentred nature entailed that no nation state is standing behind the scene, pulling the strings. Empire referred to a distinctively global capitalist logic that goes beyond nation-state boundaries. In their dissection of Empire Hardt and Negri further argued that, in addition to its global scale, Empire is characterized by new logics of control (Deleuze 1995) and biopower (Foucault 1990) as well as by the fusion of this biopower with increasingly immaterial labour (2000: 22ff.). In short, Empire embodies an entirely new assemblage of capitalism and power which, the authors posited, produces new forms of exploitation.

In the present context the diagnosis of Empire as a new order of power and sovereignty is less important than Hardt and Negri's reflections on the new revolutionary subject they pinned their faith on. Thus, the starting point of their strategy of postmodern resistance was the assertion that, although Empire 'wields enormous powers of oppression and destruction', the new global order also opens up 'new possibilities to the forces of resistance. Our political task, we will argue, is not simply to resist these processes but to reorganize them and redirect them toward new ends' (2000: xv). Crucially, therefore, contemporary resistance should no longer be forged around the idea that society could and should be changed from the outside, or through mere sabotage (2000: 212). On the contrary, postmodern resistance must use the logics of Empire (e.g. its decentralized network organization) and turn them against Empire from within. This amounted to a call for resistance that operates through an *immanent* strategy: counter-power has to work at once '*within* Empire and *against* Empire' (2000: 61, italics in original). The similarity to Baudrillard's idea of the masses imploding the social through their hyperconforming behaviour is evident. Yet Hardt and Negri, who drew

---

[8] It might be argued that *Empire* was the first truly global contribution to crowd semantics, i.e. the first book to take seriously a crowd-like entity (the vagueness of this formulation will be clear below) operating on a global scale. This global outlook was of course also essential to early Marxism, but never really translated into Marxist accounts of, for example, mass strikes.

on Marx, Lenin, Kautsky and Luxemburg, saw this as a neo-Marxist activist rebellious strategy and thereby aligned themselves with the tradition which was the primary target of Baudrillard's theoretical critique.

The political subject that was supposed to enact this postmodern resistance was the so-called multitude. The multitude was characterized abstractly as 'a multiplicity, a plane of singularities, an open set of relations, which is not homogeneous or identical with itself and bears an indistinct, inclusive relation to those outside of it' (2000: 103).[9] Moreover, the multitude was described as a collective subject characterized by creative, innovative production, by its 'biopolitical self-organization' and by making 'rebellion into a project of love' (2000: 411). More on this love will follow below.

Hardt and Negri acknowledged that their definition of the multitude was abstract so at the end of *Empire* they set out to examine how, more practically, 'the multitude is organized and redefined as a positive, political power' (2000: 398). Here they argued that 'the multitude becomes political primarily when it begins to confront directly and with an adequate consciousness the central repressive operations of Empire' (2000: 399). Although it remained unclear what was meant by 'adequate consciousness', no kind of group consciousness was alluded to as identified in early crowd theory. Indeed, Hardt and Negri were keen to stress that the multitude is distinct from the crowd. In the sequel to *Empire*, the book *Multitude*, which as the title suggested was more explicitly concerned with 'the living alternative that grows within Empire' (2000: xiii), they supplied the following characteristic which is worth quoting in its entirety:

The components of the masses, the mob, and the crowd are not singularities – and this is obvious from the fact that their differences so easily collapse into the indifference of the whole. Moreover, these social subjects are fundamentally passive in the sense that they cannot act by themselves but rather must be led. The crowd or the mob or the rabble can have social effects – often horribly destructive effects – but cannot act of their own accord. That is why they are so susceptible to external manipulation. The multitude designates an active social subject, which acts on the basis of what the singularities share in common. (2004: 100; see also 345)

This description of crowds and mobs owed a lot to the image propagated by especially Le Bon – and Hardt and Negri did in fact discuss Le Bon explicitly (see 2000: 259–60). It concurred less with other crowd theories. Applying Geiger's notion of crowds, for example, an entirely

---

[9] This was defined in contradistinction to the notion of the people which 'tends toward identity and homogeneity internally while posing its difference from and excluding what remains outside of it' (2000: 103).

different image would emerge in which the differences of crowds and multitudes were much less significant and clear-cut (see Borch 2006a). On Geiger's view, the leader cannot manipulate the crowd into following the path he or she envisages, but basically leads it in the direction it projects itself. The crowd leads the leader as much as the other way round. Accordingly, the explosive crowd Geiger analysed was characterized by the same fundamental 'self-organization' Hardt and Negri attributed to the multitude (2000: 411). Even more at odds with Hardt and Negri's conception of the crowd was Canetti's account since here no leader was needed for the crowd to act. It seems warranted against this background to assert that pitting the multitude against the crowd served a strategic semantic purpose: the crowd was pictured as something to be developed as a subject (in Hardt and Negri this image surfaced in the claim that the purported passiveness could only be transformed through the intervention of the leader), whereas the multitude had already performed this transition.

As should be clear by now, Hardt and Negri's point was that when modern society changes into a postmodern order of Empire, the conditions of doing resistance change as well. While crowd behaviour and general strikes might have been effective means in the past, today a new agent must take the place of the crowd. This was the role played by the multitude. Although the terminologies as well as the political implications that were drawn from the analyses differed, Baudrillard, Sloterdijk and Maffesoli would all subscribe to this transition argument. Indeed, Sloterdijk has heralded Hardt and Negri's semantic shift to the multitude because it purportedly indicated 'that even those remnants of the left that still concern themselves seriously with theory have finally bid farewell to the ideology of the crowds' in a classical sense, where the physical manifestation of crowds was seen as the fixation of politics (2000: 57, n. 1).

This obviously did not entail a suspension of politics. Hardt and Negri simply argued that a contemporary politics would have to adapt to the postmodern constellation. This was another way of saying that traditional political institutions had become obsolete and in need of reinvention. A new 'political lexicon' was urged, as Negri has put it, which transcended both aggregative and deliberative understandings of democracy (2008). The multitude was granted a crucial role in this postpolitical project that aimed to recast the fundamental operational modus of politics: a new democratic order should arise through the work of the multitude (for a related analysis also revolving around the notion of the multitude, see Virno 2004).

This objective was articulated most prominently in *Multitude*, which was subtitled *War and Democracy in the Age of Empire*. The subtitle indicated the difference between Empire and the multitude. As Hardt and Negri put it at one point, 'when Empire calls for war for its legitim-ation, the multitude calls on democracy as its political foundation. This democracy that opposes war is an "absolute democracy"' (2000: 90–1). The notion of absolute democracy was inherited from Spinoza and referred to a 'democracy of *everyone*' (2000: 240, italics in original). Hardt and Negri's point was that, while the democracy of everyone, rather than just of the many, was formally endorsed in many modern constitutions, it had never been realized full-scale. Actually establishing such a democracy of everyone, which would change the practical parameters of politics, was purportedly what the post-political subject of the multitude desired to do. Hardt and Negri endorsed the coming of an absolute democracy and argued that this new democratic order and the novel kind of society it would give rise to would at once amount to and depend on love:

> People today seem unable to understand love as a political concept, but a concept of love is just what we need to grasp the constituent power of the multitude. The modern concept of love is almost exclusively limited to the bourgeois couple and the claustrophobic confines of the nuclear family. Love has become a strictly private affair. We need a more generous and more unrestrained conception of love . . . This does not mean that you cannot love your spouse, your mother, and your child. It only means that your love does not end there, that *love serves as the basis for our political projects in common and the construction of a new society. Without this love, we are nothing.* (2000: 351–2, italics added)

This resembled Whitman's political project, although there was no mention of him in *Empire* and *Multitude*.[10] For both parties politics and society rested on a broad conception of love that went far beyond family, class and nation.[11] There are also profound differences between Whitman and Hardt and Negri, though. First of all, Whitman's concep-tion of love had a more sexual tone than suggested by Hardt and Negri. Moreover, in spite of the semantic transition from crowd to multitude, Hardt and Negri's political programme carried stronger connotations to a classical crowd register than did Whitman's. Indeed, on closer inspec-tion it seems that the transcendence of the crowd tradition was not fully carried out in Hardt and Negri's work. It thus appears, I will argue, as if the significance of the notion of multitudes resided in part in its ability to evoke a classic crowd register of bourgeois fears and leftist

---

[10] Whitman was briefly mentioned in Hardt and Negri's *Commonwealth*, though (2009: 182–3).

[11] The emphasis on love as the key political value might be criticized from a Geiger-inspired point of view since it amounted to the ultimate promotion of an emotional collectivism in the form of pathos (see Chapter 6; and Borch 2006a: 14–15).

revolutionary aspirations, but doing so in an entirely retailored shape. This can be illustrated along two dimensions.

First, according to Hardt and Negri, the resistance of the multitude should be aimed directly at the existing purportedly neo-liberal and neo-conservative institutions of power and exploitation. Hardt and Negri often referred to a series of much-media-covered, turn-of-the-century globalization protests in Seattle, Genoa, Gothenburg and elsewhere as examples of how the multitude had formed and demonstrated its resistance. Interestingly, the descriptions of these events often recalled the accounts of violent crowds that had been propagated in early French crowd semantics. For example, Negri depicted the Genoa demonstrations in 2001 in a way that, through its reference to the Commune, clearly associated the multitude with a classic crowd register (see Chapter 1):

The most important episode in the struggle against neo-conservatives and neo-liberals, at the level of the contestation of neo-liberal globalization, was certainly the big Genoa demonstrations against the G8. Here a multitude, an ensemble of subjective forces unified by the refusal of capitalist domination and by the hopes for a new world – so here, in Genoa, a 'Commune' of resistance was introduced, which formed a new plan of struggle and the strategic consolidation of a new antagonism. (2008: 193)

This connection to the crowd horizon is buttressed, second, by an examination of the intellectual roots of the concept of the multitude. This concept was inspired by Spinoza's work (Hardt 1993: 110; Hardt and Negri 2000: 65–6; 2004: 194, 221). But as argued by Slavoj Žižek, Spinoza's idea of the multitude comprised not solely the positive, democratic image that Hardt and Negri identified. Rather, Spinoza's concept was broader or more neutral, as it were, as it recognized that the multitude might have both positive and destructive tendencies:

It is with regard to this neutrality that the gap that separates Negri and Hardt from Spinoza becomes palpable. In *The Empire*, we find a celebration of multitude as the force of resistance, whereas, in Spinoza, the concept of multitude qua crowd is fundamentally ambiguous: multitude is resistance to the imposing One, but, at the same time, it designates what we call 'mob,' a wild, 'irrational' explosion of violence that, through *imitatio afecti*, feeds on and propels itself. This profound insight of Spinoza gets lost in today's ideology of multitude. (Žižek 2004: 34–5; see also Balibar 1994)

So despite all the love the multitude incarnated, according to Hardt and Negri, its name and acts of resistance were prone to evoke an image of aggressive crowds.

To sum up, the work of Hardt and Negri represents a reconceptualization of the crowd-theoretical tradition under postmodern conditions.

Just as classical crowd psychology argued that modern society gave birth to the crowds, so Hardt and Negri suggested that, in the postmodern age of Empire, the multitude emerges as a new political subject. While this might be taken for an updated Le Bonian analysis, the Marxist inspiration did not fail itself. For, rather than seeing the multitude as the problem, as Le Bon surely would, Hardt and Negri believed the multitude to be the solution to the exploitation Empire purportedly confronts us with. So Hardt and Negri in effect turned Le Bon upside-down. Society is not threatened by the violent crowd; rather it is the social order itself which is the problem and which should be resisted immanently, through force and love.

I have tried in this chapter to sketch a line of problematization of crowds and masses that gained footing in especially European social theory in the late 1970s and continued to develop in the early twenty-first century. The central tenor of this semantic plateau was the idea that society had transformed into a postmodern order, which plotted new directions for crowds, masses and their political engagement. Consequently, the key argument of this semantic wave was not that notions of crowds and masses had become obsolete and therefore should be discarded from sociological attention. On the contrary, the semantic catalogue of crowds and masses was allocated a pivotal role in the postmodern diagnoses, although it often operated in a negative fashion, i.e. as a semantic register in need of reconceptualization and revalorization.

While the various contributions collected here under the umbrella of postmodern thinking differed in their emphases, they found common ground in the premise that existing sociological theory had failed to account for the transition into postmodernity and therefore had lost in analytical and explanatory relevance. Baudrillard drew the most radical consequences from this and in effect argued that sociology had become superfluous. This postmodern dismissal of inherited sociological cat-egories corresponds to what Wagner has termed 'the second crisis of modernity' (2001: ch. 5). While the match between classical sociological conceptions and the structural properties of modernity had been called into question in the first half of the twentieth century, the sociological vocabulary of the post-Second World War period were now deemed equally out of sync with the contemporary structure of society.

When viewed from the vantage point of the history of sociological crowd semantics the postmodern agenda is not least interesting because it proposed a fresh perspective on crowds and masses under current conditions, which represented an alternative to both classical crowd theories of the Le Bon fashion and more recent rationalistic–individualistic conceptions of the US American collective behaviour type. From a postmodern perspective the problem with the former was that it remained within the horizon of the social; and while the latter had effected a shift beyond the social, its alternative, the emphasis on a non-social, individualistic approach, suffered from the problem that, although the social had disappeared as a relevant referent, its dissolution gave way to new modes of post-political collectivity (silent masses, neo-tribes, etc.) that could not be adequately explained in individualistic terms (nor, of course, in classical social categories).

Although the postmodern wave of mass semantics entailed a critique of the kind of crowd behaviour tradition that emerged in the USA in the 1960s and 1970s, it hardly entertained any direct contact with the work of the American sociologists, nor vice versa for that matter. There was virtually no reciprocal referencing across the two semantic plateaus. The postmodern mass debates defined their own orbit, just as the new collective behaviour paradigm did. It might be speculated that this fact could inspire some optimism on behalf of the crowd and mass topic. If the kind of culmination of crowd thinking that had taken place with the revived collective behaviour tradition had in fact led to a marginalization of sociological crowd semantics, then the alternative postmodern positions might restore the crowd to its former glory within sociological thinking. That has not happened, though. The postmodern revival of crowds and mass semantics has not fundamentally changed the sociological status of the crowd topic; it retains its marginal role, just as the postmodern agenda seems to have been shoved into the periphery of current sociological thinking (where, perhaps, it would also prefer to be).

The fact that the American collective behaviour tradition and the postmodern theorizing developed independently of one another begs the question why this was so. How can it be that these two semantic plateaus could evolve more or less at the same time, at least with approximately the same temporal starting point, without establishing any contacts? I will propose three answers to that question, and thereby try also to elaborate on some of the issues already touched upon. A first answer is rather straightforward, namely that the two bodies of literature were occupied with different societal modalities: modern and postmodern society respectively. Yet this is not the whole story. Thus, second, there were also significant stylistic and methodological differences between the work of the American sociologists and that of the European social theorists. While the former were committed to a particular empirical imperative, the latter refrained from empirical studies that submitted to a strict sociological methodology – something that might also explain why the postmodern thinking has never gained sociological centrality. What Rob Shields (1991: 3) has said of Maffesoli's work, that '[i]n the style of French social theory, in-depth case studies are avoided', might be extended to encompass Baudrillard, Sloterdijk and Hardt and Negri as well. Or rather, the kind of case studies that might be identified in this work was of a different fashion from the more ethnographic and inter-view-based ones typically favoured in the collective behaviour tradition.

Yet vigilance is needed here, for the fact that none of the postmod-ern diagnoses submitted to established sociological methods does not entail that they are of no sociological value. This might be illustrated most vividly by the case of Sloterdijk and the more disciplinary aspects pertaining to his general approach. There is no doubt that his essay on masses had anti-sociological undertones in the sense that it scorned the bulk of previous sociological crowd and mass semantics, however sparse and implicit the interaction was with the existing sociological literature. Sloterdijk clearly preferred (and still does) to situate his theorization vis-à-vis philosophers rather than sociologists. Illustratively, a great deal of the discussion of mass contempt was based on readings of Hobbes and Spinoza. That said, Sloterdijk might well be seen as a scholar who, though not sociologist by trade, pushes the boundaries of what might count as legitimate sociology. This has been argued most forcefully by Nigel Thrift, who conceives of Sloterdijk's work, and its insistence on doing philosophy on the basis of comprehensive amounts of evidence, as a new type of sociological thinking that renders previous partitions between empirical sociology and rich conceptual thinking obsolete (Thrift 2009: 123, n. 11; Thrift in Bech *et al.* 2010: 99). Sloterdijk accomplishes both and thereby demonstrates that, for instance, the sociology of crowds need not be trapped in the chasm between empirical and 'speculative' sociology. More bluntly, this kind of work challenges the disciplinary divides underpinning the collective behaviour tradition of American sociology and demonstrates that a reinvigoration of crowds and mass thinking may rest on a broader notion of what sociology might be.

Third, and finally, the theories on postmodern masses all addressed a change in the conditions of politics, arguing that the current turn-of-the-century society had entered a post-political state. Not only had 'old politics' (arguments, debate, demonstrations) lost in significance, but the postmodern masses seemed to bypass the political as such. This was wholly different in the collective behaviour tradition of the more or less contemporary American sociologists. Consonant with a long liberal tradition, this body of theorizing typically exhibited a commitment to the aggregative model of liberalism, which postmodernity was believed to put under pressure. Of course, there were differences among the postmodern theorists with respect to depicting the post-political situation and its implications, with Hardt and Negri defending the most activist (and leftish) position. But even in their work, liberal politics in any classical sense was circumvented and a new transcending agenda was promoted.

Epilogue: the politics of crowds

This book has traced the destiny of crowd semantics from nascent sociological debates in the late nineteenth century to postmodern discussions in the early twenty-first century. The aim of this was threefold. A first objective was to cast light on the processes that transformed the crowd from being a key sociological problem to becoming a rather marginalized topic within sociological inquiry. A second and related objective was to sketch an alternative history of sociology, where the discipline's development over time was filtered through the lens of the crowd concept. A third and equally related aim of the book was to demonstrate that a great part of sociology's attempts to understand modern society has revolved around notions of crowds and masses. In that sense, the history of crowd semantics amounts to a history of conceptions of modern society. Rather than recapitulating the whole historical development I have mapped in the book I would like, by way of a conclusion, to pinpoint four central dimensions that pertain to what might be called the *sociological politics of crowds*, i.e. the struggles on how to approach the phenomenon of crowds within sociology.

First, while sociology in France, Germany and the USA took different shapes in the late nineteenth and early twentieth centuries, it was widely accepted that investigations of modern society required some form of engagement with the notion of crowds. This was a consensus that encompassed sociologists such as Tarde, Geiger and Park who concurred that modern sociality was so intimately linked to crowd behaviour that an ignorance of this phenomenon would lead to a truncated sociology. Yet the conception and problematization of crowds in early French, German and American sociology were coloured by different political horizons. Sociological crowd semantics in France was characterized in large part by conservative sympathies; in Germany, the central problematizations of crowds were of a leftish bent; and in the USA, sociological discussions of crowds reflected different types of liberal commitment. This politics of crowds surfaced for instance in how the Janus-faced nature of crowds was addressed. Thus, although much of the early theorization on crowds emphasized their purportedly irrational, violent and de-individualizing nature, it was recurringly noted that crowds are capable as well of establishing true social bonds. While the French conservative scholars primarily took notice of the irrational, socially destabilizing dimension of crowds, German sociologists such as Geiger acknowledged the ability of crowds to reconcile class tensions, whereas in the USA Park emphasized that crowds might liberate people from restraining ties.

Second, and relatedly, the very problematizations of crowds often rendered specific political responses more likely and relevant than others. Such embedded normativities have been discussed on several occasions in the course of the book. For example, the problematization of mass society generally located the perceived perils at a structural level (whether in the form of atomization, moral or cultural decline, etc.), which called for equivalent structural political responses (e.g. planning, regionalization, education, etc.).

Third, however dominant the attempt to grapple with modern society through the crowd was in sociological circles, the notion of crowds soon became entangled in rather different debates. Most importantly, Durkheim lifted the crowd from being a descriptive/explanatory/ diagnostic category to being a battlefield for the demarcation of sociology. For Durkheim, crowd semantics did not signify an important contribution to the understanding of modern society. On the contrary, he considered the sociology of crowds emblematic of the kinds of theorization that had to be purged if sociology were to materialize as a distinct science. Specifically, Durkheim was highly critical of the crowd scholars' flirtation with concepts such as suggestion that were anchored in or derived from more psychological resources. This elevation of the crowd to being a key arena for the struggle to separate sociology from adjacent disciplines embodies a central layer in the politics of crowds. While Durkheim was the first to harness the notion of crowds for this purpose, Geiger was no less insistent that the crowd formed a central fixture in the endeavour to demarcate sociology as a distinct science. But contrary to Durkheim, who in his dispute with Tarde dismissed the central categories of crowd thinking altogether, Geiger believed in the sociological centrality of the crowd topic and just wanted to arrive at an entirely sociological understanding of crowds, purified of any psychological relics.

In continuation of this, fourth, the problematizations studied in this book have been embedded in a politics of crowds that operates on a somewhat smaller scale than the Durkheim and Geiger ambitions exemplify. The crowd has not only been a vehicle for discussions of how to delineate sociology from other disciplines. Sociological debates on crowds have also been embedded in seemingly more mundane, but no less important, struggles on how to define proper approaches, methodologies, conceptual frameworks, etc. within sociology. In was not least in the wake of such battles that the crowd was relegated from a prominent to a marginal position in sociological thinking. Although, as I have argued, the branch of rejuvenated collective behaviour studies in mid- and late-twentieth-century American sociology tended to undermine its own position as legitimate sociology (because of its heavy critique of previous work in this tradition), the main charges that social movement scholars raised against it was not that it did not fall within the confines of sociology. That is, it was not contested *as sociology*, but rather because it did not fully take leave of the propositions on abnormality that characterized its forerunners in the field.

Since no hegemony is eternal, the sociological politics of crowds is never a closed battle. In this positive spirit I shall end the book with some brief reflections on a possible reopening of the politics of crowds.

The future(s) of sociological crowd theory

Crowd and mass semantics lead a rather miserable life in sociology today. The postmodern attempts to revive the notion of masses have not really changed this. As I have intimated in previous chapters, I think that the rationalization of crowd semantics that culminated with the American collective behaviour theorists in the 1960s and 1970s is partly to blame for this marginalization of crowd and mass semantics. Although these scholars strived to reinvigorate the study of crowds and collective behaviour by puncturing all the purported myths surrounding the earlier tradition, the net effect was the opposite. In their eagerness to renew the tradition by radically changing it, they threw the baby out with the bathwater: the new collective behaviour sociologists were so blinded by their wish to furnish a new theoretical and conceptual edifice that they failed to see the analytical potentials which, I think, must be granted to previous ways of theorizing crowds. This is not to suggest that the reflections on crowds which appear in the work of, say, Le Bon, Simmel and Tarde should be flatly accepted. But it is a call for reconsidering whether what they and other theorists had to say about crowds should be plainly dismissed as myths or whether there are in fact aspects of their theorizing that might be adopted for the benefit of current sociology. It might be argued that early-twenty-first-century works on 'smart mobs' (Rheingold 2002) and the purported 'wisdom of crowds' (Surowiecki 2005) point towards a fresh and undogmatic reinvention of crowd semantics at the boundary of established sociological thinking. Rather than going in those directions, however, I shall suggest three alternative routes for how a reconsideration of old ideas from the reservoir of crowd semantics might look.

First of all, as I have argued elsewhere, contemporary economic sociology, in particular social studies of finance, may profit from taking seriously the image of the irrational crowd (Borch 2007; see also Arnoldi and Borch 2007). There is a long tradition of conceiving of financial markets in crowd vocabulary (Stäheli 2006, 2007). Throughout the twentieth century traders have deployed crowd semantics as a means not only to describe themselves and their behaviour, but also as a pool for strategic action. For example, a school of so-called 'contrarian' speculation theory transpired in the USA in the 1920s and 1930s which utilized Le Bon's crowd psychology to account for what was going on in the market and to distil strategic investment guidelines from this analysis. Specifically, it was argued, the market displays the kind of irrationality Le Bon ascribed to crowds. Upon entering the financial market the investor had to be aware that he or she crossed the threshold to a highly hysteric field where one could easily fall prey to the seduction of the market's irrational pull. Accordingly, it was argued, if one were to make successful investments, one had to avoid the crowd's suggestive seduction and invest contrary to the market (Borch 2007; Stäheli 2006).

The central point here is not simply that traders then and now describe their work and strategies on the basis of crowd semantics (and that this semantics has penetrated current-day theorizing on financial markets, e.g. Shiller 2000). More importantly, by performing this semantics in their daily work, traders actually lend reality to it. That is, they transform the notion of crowds from being a 'mere' semantic register to becoming something that informs and guides actions and decisions in financial markets. For this reason alone it is premature to dismiss classical propositions on crowds as myths. It is at any rate myths that are very real and alive among actual actors (for a related analysis, see Hoggett and Scott 2010).

Second, it appears to me that the Achilles heel of the classical crowd semantics of the Le Bon and Tarde era, the notion of suggestion, might prove more analytically fruitful than its bad reputation suggests. Yet its adoption in a contemporary sociological context may require some reconceptualization. Thus, I propose, rather than seeing suggestion as a notion that describes an essentially interpersonal relationship (hypnotizer–hypnotized; leader–crowd, etc.) it makes sense to conceive of it in terms of a human–non-human relation. That is, suggestion need not be stimulated by an individual, but can be induced by objects instead. This might be illustrated in the realm of financial speculation, as I have argued elsewhere (Borch 2007: 563–4; see also Ratner 2009). For example, Karin Knorr Cetina and Urs Bruegger have demonstrated that in financial markets, the individual trader's 'subject becomes defined by the object', the market (2002: 178). This means that rather than being a fixed and constitutive entity, the trader's subjectivity is highly plastic and constantly defined by the seduction exercised by the screen that he or she follows.[1] This process is structurally equivalent to the hypnotizer–hypnotized image of the suggestion doctrine, and merely replaces the hypnotizing subject with a hypnotizing object.

The emphasis on financial markets should not lead to the impression that a contemporary reinvigoration of crowd thinking should be located exclusively or most naturally in the economic realm. To make this point, the third suggestion for how the reservoir of crowd semantics might be fruitfully exploited in current theorizing refers to the political domain. In her contribution to political sociology Mouffe has argued that crowd theory provides an important foundation for understanding the political (2005; see also Laclau 2005). In particular, she contends, the crowd theories of Canetti and Freud are important for a contemporary reconceptualization of politics because they do not suffer from what she sees as central blind spots of liberal thinking. Whereas liberal notions of politics are either too rational–instrumentalist (the aggregative model), and hence incapable of grasping that politics is not just about the pursuit of interests but also a matter of identification, or too focused on consensus (the deliberative model), and therefore fail to understand that politics is also about mobilization through conflict, crowd theory offers more adequate images of politics. According to Mouffe, '[t]he lesson to be drawn from Freud and Canetti is that, even in societies which have become very individualistic, the need for collective identifications will never disappear since it is constitutive of the mode of existence of human beings' (2005: 28). In other words, what Freud and Canetti offer, on Mouffe's analysis, is an understanding of how *passions* rather than 'reason, moderation and consensus' are key to the political (2005: 28).

To make things clear, let me conclude by remarking that I do not share Stephen Reicher's aim to restore crowd semantics 'to its rightful place at the *center* of social scientific inquiry' (2004: 232, italics added). That

---

[1] Somewhat relatedly, it has been argued that the semi-consciousness Tarde attributed to imitation-suggestion offers a valuable doorway to understanding how contemporary capitalism mobilizes affect so as to generate greater profits (see Thrift 2006).

said, I do think that crowd semantics, and its various adaptations, is of more than historical interest. The crowd offers a fascinating entry into the study of the history of sociology. But, it seems to me, crowd semantics also contains insights into the social that should not be forgotten or too rapidly expelled from view. Therefore, let the spectre of crowds once again haunt sociological thought!

References

Abbott, A. 1999. *Department and Discipline: Chicago Sociology at One Hundred.* Chicago, IL: University of Chicago Press.

Adler, A. 1934. 'Zur Massenpsychologie', *Internationale Zeitschrift für Individualpsychologie* 12(3): 133–41.

Adorno, T. W. 1946. 'Anti-Semitism and Fascist Propaganda', in E. Simmel (ed.), *Anti-Semitism: A Social Disease.* New York: International Universities Press, pp. 125–37.

1989–90. 'On Jazz', *Discourse* 12(1): 45–69.

1991a. 'Culture Industry Reconsidered', in *The Culture Industry: Selected Essays on Mass Culture.* London: Routledge, pp. 85–92.

1991b. 'Freudian Theory and the Pattern of Fascist Propaganda', in *The Culture Industry: Selected Essays on Mass Culture.* London: Routledge, pp. 114–35.

1991c. 'On the Fetish Character in Music and the Regression of Listening', in *The Culture Industry: Selected Essays on Mass Culture.* London: Routledge, pp. 26–52.

1991d. 'The Schema of Mass Culture', in *The Culture Industry: Selected Essays on Mass Culture.* London: Routledge, pp. 53–84.

Adorno, T. W. *et al.* 1950. *The Authoritarian Personality.* New York: Harper.

Agamben, G. 1998. *Homo Sacer: Sovereign Power and Bare Life*, trans. D. Heller-Roazen. Stanford, CA: Stanford University Press.

Allport, F. H. 1924. *Social Psychology.* Boston, MA: Houghton Mifflin.

Allport, G. W. 1954. 'The Historical Background of Modern Social Psychology', in G. Lindzey (ed.) *Handbook of Social Psychology, Vol. 1: Theory and Method.* Cambridge, MA: Addison-Wesley, pp. 3–56.

Anders, G. 1956. *Die Antiquiertheit des Menschen, Vol. 1. Über die Seele im Zeitalter der zweiten industriellen Revolution.* Munich: Verlag C. H. Beck.

1987. *Die Antiquiertheit des Menschen, Vol. 2. Über die Zerstörung des Lebens im Zeitalter der dritten industriellen Revolution.* Munich: Verlag C. H. Beck.

Arendt, H. 1951. *The Origins of Totalitarianism.* New York: Harcourt, Brace.

1970. 'Hermann Broch, 1886–1951', in *Men in Dark Times.* London: Jonathan Cape, pp. 111–51.

Arnason, J. P. and D. Roberts 2004. *Elias Canetti's Counter-Image of Society: Crowds, Power, Transformation.* Rochester, NY: Camden House.

Arnoldi, J. and C. Borch 2007. 'Market Crowds between Imitation and Control', *Theory, Culture & Society* 24(7–8): 164–80.

Arppe, T. 2005. 'Rousseau, Durkheim et la constitution affective du social', *Revue d'Histoire des Sciences Humaines* 13(2): 5–32.

2009. 'Sorcerer's Apprentices and the "Will to Figuration": The Ambiguous Heritage of the Collège de Sociologie', *Theory, Culture & Society* 26(4): 117–45.

Asch, S. 1952. *Social Psychology.* New York: Prentice-Hall.

Bagehot, W. 1872. *Physics and Politics, or Thoughts on the Application of the Principles of 'Natural Selection' and 'Inheritance' to Political Theory.* London: Henry S. King.

Baier, H. 1987. 'Geleitwort zum Nachdruck', in T. Geiger *Die Masse und ihre Aktion. Ein Beitrag zur Soziologie der Revolution.* Stuttgart: Ferdinand Enke Verlag.

Baldwin, J. M. 1894. 'Imitation: A Chapter in the Natural History of Consciousness', *Mind* 3(9): 26–55.

1897. *Social and Ethical Interpretations in Mental Development: A Study in Social Psychology.* New York: Macmillan.

1968. *Mental Development in the Child and the Race: Methods and Processes.* New York: Augustus M. Kelly.

Balibar, E. 1994. 'Spinoza, the Anti-Orwell: The Fear of the Masses', in *Masses, Classes, Ideas: Studies on Politics and Philosophy Before and After Marx*, trans. J. Swenson. New York and London: Routledge, pp. 3–37.

Balke, F. 2008. 'Canettis Theorie der Souveränität', in S. Lüdemann (ed.) *Der Überlebende und sein Doppel. Kulturwissenschaftliche Analysen zum Werk Elias Canettis.* Freiburg i.Br.: Rombach Verlag, pp. 247–67.

Bannister, R. C. 2003. 'Sociology', in T. M. Porter and D. Ross (eds.) *The Cambridge History of Science, Vol. 7: The Modern Social Sciences.* Cambridge: Cambridge University Press, pp. 329–53.

Barnes, H. E. 1920. 'A Psychological Interpretation of Modern Problems and of Contemporary History: A Survey of the Contributions of Gustave Le Bon to Social Psychology', *American Journal of Psychology* 31(4): 333–69.

Barrows, S. 1981. *Distorting Mirrors: Visions of the Crowd in Late Nineteenth-Century France.* New Haven, CT and London: Yale University Press.

Barrucand, D. 1967. *Histoire de l'hypnose en France.* Paris: Presses Universitaires de France.

Baschwitz, K. 1923. *Der Massenwahn. Seine Wirkung und seine Beherrschung.* Munich: C. H. Becksche Verlagsbuchhandlung.

Baudrillard, J. 1983. *In the Shadow of the Silent Majorities or The End of the Social.* New York: Semiotext(e).

1985. 'The Masses: The Implosion of the Social in the Media', *New Literary History* 16(3): 577–89.

1993. *Symbolic Exchange and Death*, trans. I. Hamilton Grant. London: Sage.

1994a. 'The Beaubourg Effect: Implosion and Deterrence', in *Simulacra and Simulation*, trans. S. F. Glaser. Ann Arbor, MI: University of Michigan Press, pp. 61–73.

1994b. 'The Precession of Simulacra', in *Simulacra and Simulation*, trans. S. F. Glaser. Ann Arbor, MI: University of Michigan Press, pp. 1–42.

Bauman, Z. 1989. *Modernity and the Holocaust.* Cambridge: Polity Press.

Bech, H., S. N. Larsen and C. Borch 2010. 'Resistance, Politics, Space, Architecture: Interview with Nigel Thrift', *Distinktion: Scandinavian Journal of Social Theory* 21: 93–105.

Bechterew, W. 1899. *Suggestion und ihre soziale Bedeutung.* Leipzig: Verlag von Arthur Georgi.

  1905. *Die Bedeutung der Suggestion im sozialen Leben.* Wiesbaden: Verlag von J. F. Bergmann.

  1928. *Die kollektive Reflexologie. Halle,* Saale: Carl Marhold Verlagsbuchhandlung.

Beetham, D. 1977a. 'From Socialism to Fascism: The Relation between Theory and Practice in the Work of Robert Michels: Part I. From Marxist Revolutionary to Political Sociologist', *Political Studies* 25(1): 3–24.

  1977b. 'From Socialism to Fascism: The Relation between Theory and Practice in the Work of Robert Michels: Part II. The Fascist Ideologue', *Political Studies* 25(2): 161–81.

Beirne, P. 1987. 'Between Classicism and Positivism: Crime and Penality in the Writings of Gabriel Tarde', *Criminology* 25(4): 785–819.

Bekhterev, V. M. 1998. *Suggestion and Its Role in Social Life,* ed. L. H. Strickland, trans. T. Dobreva-Martinova. New Brunswick, NJ and London: Transaction.

  2001. *Collective Reflexology: The Complete Edition,* ed. L. H. Strickland, trans. E. Lockwood and A. Lockwood. New Brunswick, NJ: Transaction.

Bell, D. 1956. 'The Theory of Mass Society: A Critique', *Commentary* 22(1): 75–83.

  1974. *The Coming of Post-Industrial Society: A Venture in Social Forecasting.* London: Heinemann.

Bendersky, J. W. 2007. '"Panic": The Impact of Le Bon's Crowd Psychology on US Military Thought', *Journal of the History of the Behavioral Sciences* 43(3): 257–83.

Benjamin, W. 2007. 'The Work of Art in the Age of Mechanical Reproduction', in *Illuminations,* trans. H. Zohn. New York: Schocken, pp. 217–51.

Bentley, A. F. 1897. 'Book Review: Gustave Le Bon: The Crowd', *American Journal of Sociology* 2(4): 612–14.

Berk, R. A. 1974a. *Collective Behavior.* Dubuque, IA: Wm. C. Brown.

  1974b. 'A Gaming Approach to Crowd Behavior', *American Sociological Review* 39(June): 355–73.

Berking, H. 1984. *Masse und Geist. Studien zur Soziologie in der Weimarer Republik.* Berlin: Wissenschaftlicher Autoren-Verlag.

Bernays, E. L. 1923. *Crystallizing Public Opinion.* New York: Boni and Liveright.

  1935. 'Moulding Public Opinion', *Annals of the American Academy of Political and Social Science* 179: 82–7.

  1938. 'Public Education for Democracy', *Annals of the American Academy of Political and Social Science* 198: 124–7.

  2005. *Propaganda.* Brooklyn, NY: Ig Publishing.

Bernheim, H. 1891. *Hypnotisme, suggestion, psychothérapie. Études nouvelles.* Paris: Octave Doin.

Bettelheim, B. 1974. 'Individual Autonomy and Mass Controls', in T. W. Adorno and W. Dirks (eds.) *Sociologica: Aufsätze. Max Horkheimer*

zum sechzigsten Geburtstag gewidmet. Frankfurt am Main: Europäische Verlagsanstalt, pp. 245–62.
Blackman, L. 2007. 'Reinventing Psychological Matters: The Importance of the Suggestive Realm of Tarde's Ontology', *Economy and Society* 36(4): 574–96.
    2008. 'Affect, Relationality and the Problem of Personality', *Theory, Culture & Society* 25(1): 23–47.
Blackman, L. and V. Walkerdine 2001. *Mass Hysteria: Critical Psychology and Media Studies.* Basingstoke and New York: Palgrave.
Blumer, H. 1933. *Movies and Conduct.* New York: Macmillan.
    1935. 'Moulding of Mass Behavior through the Motion Picture', *American Sociological Society* 29: 115–27.
    1939. 'Collective Behavior', in R. E. Park (ed.) *An Outline of the Principles of Sociology.* New York: Barnes & Noble, pp. 219–80.
    1951. 'Collective Behavior', in A. M. Lee (ed.) *New Outline of the Principles of Sociology.* New York: Barnes & Noble, pp. 165–222.
Blumer, H. and P. M. Hauser 1933. *Movies, Delinquency, and Crime.* New York: Macmillan.
Boadella, D. 1985. *Wilhelm Reich: The Evolution of his Work.* London: Arkana.
Borch, C. 2005. 'Urban Imitations: Tarde's Sociology Revisited', *Theory, Culture & Society* 22(3): 81–100.
    2006a. 'Crowds and Pathos: Theodor Geiger on Revolutionary Action', *Acta Sociologica* 49(1): 5–18.
    2006b. 'Crowds and Total Democracy: Hermann Broch's Political Theory', *Distinktion: Scandinavian Journal of Social Theory* 13: 99–120.
    2007. 'Crowds and Economic Life: Bringing an Old Figure Back in', *Economy and Society* 36(4): 549–73.
    2008. 'Modern Mass Aberration: Hermann Broch and the Problem of Irrationality', *History of the Human Sciences* 21(2): 63–83.
    2009. 'Body to Body: On the Political Anatomy of Crowds', *Sociological Theory* 27(3): 271–90.
    2010. 'Between Destructiveness and Vitalism: Simmel's Sociology of Crowds', *Conserveries mémorielles* 8.
    2011. *Niklas Luhmann (Key Sociologists).* London and New York: Routledge.
Borch-Jacobsen, M. 1988. *The Freudian Subject.* Stanford, CA: Stanford University Press.
Bottomore, T. 2002. *The Frankfurt School and Its Critics.* London and New York: Routledge.
Boyer, P. 1978. *Urban Masses and Moral Order in America, 1820–1920.* Cambridge, MA: Harvard University Press.
Bramson, L. 1961. *The Political Context of Sociology.* Princeton, NJ: Princeton University Press.
Brand, D. 1991. *The Spectator and the City in Nineteenth-Century American Literature.* Cambridge: Cambridge University Press.
Briggs, A. 1985. 'The Language of "Mass" and "Masses" in Nineteenth-Century England', in *The Collected Essays of Asa Briggs, Vol. I: Words, Numbers, Places, People.* Sussex: Harvester, pp. 34–54.

Brighenti, A. M. 2011. 'Elias Canetti and the Counter-Image of Resistance', *Thesis Eleven* 106(1): 73–87.

Brill, L. 2006. *Crowds, Power, and Transformation in Cinema*. Detroit, MI: Wayne State University Press.

Broch, H. 1947. 'Review of Paul Reiwald, *Vom Geist der Massen*', *American Journal of International Law* 41(1): 358–9.

1970. *Massepsykologi*. Copenhagen: Gyldendals Uglebøger.

1978a. 'Bemerkungen zur Utopie einer "International Bill of Rights and of Responsibilities"', in P. M. Lützeler (ed.) *Politische Schriften. Kommentierte Werkausgabe*, vol. 11. Frankfurt am Main: Suhrkamp, pp. 243–77.

1978b. 'Trotzdem: Humane Politik. Verwirklichung einer Utopie', in P. M. Lützeler (ed.) *Politische Schriften. Kommentierte Werkausgabe*, vol. 11. Frankfurt am Main: Suhrkamp, pp. 364–96.

1979. *Massenwahntheorie. Beiträge zu einer Psychologie der Politik*. Frankfurt am Main: Suhrkamp.

1981. 'Die Straße', in *Briefe I (1913–1938). Dokumente und Kommentare zu Leben und Werk*. Frankfurt am Main: Suhrkamp, pp. 30–5.

1983. *The Death of Vergil*, trans. J. S. Untermeyer. Oxford: Oxford University Press.

1996. *The Sleepwalkers: A Trilogy*, trans. W. and E. Muir. New York: Vintage.

Brodbeck, A. J. 1961. 'Values in *The Lonely Crowd*: Ascent or Descent of Man?', in S. M. Lipset and L. Lowenthal (eds.) *Culture and Social Character: The Work of David Riesman Reviewed*. New York: Free Press, pp. 42–71.

Brogan, D. W. 1954. 'The Problem of High Culture and Mass Culture', *Diogenes* 2(1): 1–13.

Bryder, T. 1989. 'Graham Wallas: an introduction to his political psychology', manuscript, University of Copenhagen.

Buk-Swienty, T. 2008. *The Other Half: The Life of Jacob Riis and the World of Immigrant America*, trans. A. Buk-Swienty. New York: W. W. Norton.

Burgess, E. W. 1939. 'The Influence of Sigmund Freud upon Sociology in the United States', *American Journal of Sociology* 45(3): 356–74.

Bush, G. W. 1991. *Lord of Attention: Gerald Stanley Lee and the Crowd Metaphor in Industrializing America*. Amherst, MA: University of Massachusetts Press.

Caillois, R. 1988. 'Festival', in D. Hollier (ed.) *The College of Sociology (1937–39)*, trans. B. Wing. Minneapolis, MN: University of Minnesota Press, pp. 279–303.

Calhoun, C. (ed.) 2007a. *Sociology in America: A History*. Chicago, IL and London: University of Chicago Press.

2007b. 'Sociology in America: An Introduction', in C. Calhoun (ed.) *Sociology in America: A History*. Chicago, IL and London: University of Chicago Press, pp. 1–38.

Calhoun, C. and J. VanAntwerpen 2007. 'Orthodoxy, Heterodoxy, and Hierarchy: "Mainstream" Sociology and Its Challenges', in C. Calhoun (ed.) *Sociology in America: A History*. Chicago, IL and London: University of Chicago Press, pp. 367–410.

Cameron, S. 1981. *The Corporeal Self: Allegories of the Body in Melville and Hawthorne*. Baltimore, MD and London: Johns Hopkins University Press.

Canetti, E. 1976a. 'Herman Broch', in *The Conscience of Words*, trans.
J. Neugroschel. London: Andre Deutsch, pp. 1–13.

1976b. 'Hitler, According to Speer', in *The Conscience of Words*, trans.
J. Neugroschel. London: Andre Deutsch, pp. 65–72.

1976c. 'The Arch of Triumph', in *The Conscience of Words*, trans.
J. Neugroschel. London: Andre Deutsch, pp. 73–96.

1980. *Masse und Macht*. Frankfurt am Main: Fischer Taschenbuch Verlag.

1981. 'Hermann Broch. Rede zum 50. Geburtstag, Wien, November 1936', in
Das Gewissen der Worte. Essays. Frankfurt am Main: Fischer, pp. 11–24.

1984. *Crowds and Power*, trans. C. Stewart. New York: Farrar, Straus and
Giroux.

1986. *The Human Province*, trans. J. Neugroschel. London: Picador.

1988. *The Tongue Set Free: Remembrance of a European Childhood*, trans.
J. Neugroschel. London: Andre Deutsch.

1989. *The Torch in My Ear*, trans. J. Neugroschel. London: Andre Deutsch.

1996a. *Aufzeichnungen 1992–3*. Munich: Carl Hanser Verlag.

1996b. 'Elias Canetti: Discussion with Theodor W. Adorno', *Thesis Eleven*
45: 1–15.

2005. *Auto da Fé*, trans. C. V. Wedgwood. London: Harvill.

Cantril, H. 2002. *The Psychology of Social Movements*. New Brunswick,
NJ: Transaction.

Cappetti, C. 1993. *Writing Chicago: Modernism, Ethnography, and the Novel*.
New York: Columbia University Press.

Castronovo, R. 2007. *Beautiful Democracy: Aesthetics and Anarchy in a Global Era*.
Chicago, IL and London: University of Chicago Press.

Cetina, K. K. and U. Bruegger 2002. 'Traders' Engagement with Markets:
A Postsocial Relationship', *Theory, Culture & Society* 19(5–6): 161–85.

Chakotin, S. 1971. *The Rape of the Masses: The Psychology of Totalitarian Political
Propaganda*. New York: Haskell House.

Clark, T. N. 1968a. 'Émile Durkheim and the Institutionalization of Sociology
in the French University System', *Archives européennes de sociologie* 9(1):
37–71.

1968b. 'The Structure and Functions of a Research Institute: The *Année
sociologique*', *Archives européennes de sociologie* 9(1): 72–91.

1969. 'Introduction', in G. Tarde *On Communication and Social Influence.
Selected Papers*. Chicago, IL and London: University of Chicago Press,
pp. 1–69.

Colm, G. 1924. 'Die Masse. Ein Beitrag zur Systematik der Gruppen', *Archiv für
Sozialwissenschaft und Sozialpolitik* 52(3): 680–94.

1931. 'Masse', in A. Vierkandt (ed.) *Handwörterbuch der Soziologie*. Stuttgart:
Ferdinand Enke Verlag, pp. 353–60.

Conway, M. 1915. *The Crowd in Peace and War*. London: Longmans, Green
and Co.

Cooley, C. H. 1907. *Human Nature and the Social Order*. New York: Charles
Scribner's.

1909. *Social Organization: A Study of the Larger Mind*. New York: Charles
Scribner's.

Couch, C. J. 1968. 'Collective Behavior: An Examination of Some Stereotypes', *Social Problems* 15(3): 310–22.

    1970. 'Dimensions of Association in Collective Behavior Episodes', *Sociometry* 33(4): 457–71.

Davis, M. M. 1909. *Psychological Interpretations of Society*. New York: Columbia University Studies in History, Economics and Public Law.

Debord, G. 1995. *The Society of the Spectacle*, trans. D. Nicholson-Smith. New York: Zone Books.

Deleuze, G. 1995. 'Postscript on Control Societies', in *Negotiations, 1972–1990*, trans. M. Joughin. New York: Columbia University Press, pp. 176–82.

Deleuze, G. and F. Guattari 1983. *Anti-Oedipus: Capitalism and Schizophrenia*, trans. R. Hurley *et al.* Minneapolis, MN: University of Minnesota Press.

Dewey, J. 1917. 'The Need for Social Psychology', *Psychological Review* 14(6): 266–77.

    1922. *Human Nature and Conduct: An Introduction to Social Psychology*. London: George Allen & Unwin.

    1954. *The Public and Its Problems*. Denver, CO: Alan Swallow.

    1966. *Democracy and Education: An Introduction to the Philosophy of Education*. New York: Free Press.

Doob, L. W. 1935. *Propaganda: Its Psychology and Technique*. New York: Henry Holt.

Doob, L. W. and E. S. Robinson 1935. 'Psychology and Propaganda', *Annals of the American Academy of Political and Social Science* 179: 88–95.

Dubiel, H. 1985. *Theory and Politics: Studies in the Development of Critical Theory*, trans. B. Gregg. Cambridge, MA: MIT Press.

Durkheim, E. 1895. 'Crime et santé sociale', *Revue Philosophique* 39: 518–23.

    1947. *The Elementary Forms of the Religious Life: A Study in Religious Sociology*, trans. J. W. Swain. Glencoe, IL: Free Press.

    1951. *Suicide: A Study in Sociology*, trans. J. A. Spaulding and G. Simpson. New York: Free Press.

    1961. *Moral Education: A Study in the Theory and Application of the Sociology of Education*, trans. E. K. Wilson and H. Schnurer. New York: Free Press.

    1964. *The Rules of Sociological Method*, trans. S. A. Solovay and J. H. Mueller. New York: Free Press.

Durst, D. C. 2004. *Weimar Modernism: Philosophy, Politics, and Culture in Germany 1918–1933*. Lanham, MD: Lexington Books.

Ebine, T. 2004. 'Ekstasis. Zum Massendiskurs in der Weimarer Republik', *Neue Beiträge zur Germanistik* 3(1): 164–82.

Ellenberger, H. F. 1970. *The Discovery of the Unconscious. The History and Evolution of Dynamic Psychiatry*. London: Allen Lane/Penguin Press.

Ellwood, C. A. 1901. 'The Theory of Imitation in Social Psychology', *American Journal of Sociology* 6(6): 721–41.

Elsenhans, T. 1912. *Lehrbuch der Psychologie*. Tübingen: Verlag von J. C. B. Mohr.

Elsner, H. 1972. 'Introduction', in R. E. Park *The Crowd and the Public and Other Essays*. Chicago, IL and London: University of Chicago Press, pp. vii–xxv.

Erkkila, B. 1989. *Whitman the Political Poet*. Oxford and New York: Oxford University Press.

Essertier, D. 1927. *Psychologie et sociologie. Essai de bibliographie critique*. Paris: Félix Alcan.

Esteve, M. 2003. *The Aesthetics and Politics of the Crowd in American Literature*. Cambridge: Cambridge University Press.

Faber, D. P. 1996. 'Suggestion: Metaphor and Meaning', *Journal of the History of the Behavioral Sciences* 32(January): 16–29.

Farrenkopf, J. 2001. *Prophet of Decline: Spengler on World History and Politics*. Baton Rouge, LA: Louisiana State University Press.

Fish, J. S. 2003. 'Stjphan Meštrović and Michel Maffesoli's "Implosive" Defence of the Durkheimian Tradition: Theoretical Convergences around Baudrillard's Thesis on the "End" of the Social', *Sociological Review* 51(2): 257–75.

Forgacs, D. and S. Gundle 2007. *Mass Culture and Italian Society from Fascism to the Cold War*. Bloomington, IN and Indianapolis: Indiana University Press.

Foucault, M. 1977. *Discipline and Punish: The Birth of the Prison*. London: Penguin.

1989. 'What Our Present Is', in *Foucault Live: Interviews, 1961–1984*. New York: Semiotext(e), pp. 407–15.

1990. *The History of Sexuality, Vol. 1: An Introduction*, trans. R. Hurley. New York: Vintage.

1992. *The Use of Pleasure: The History of Sexuality*, vol. 2, trans. R. Hurley. London: Penguin.

1997. 'Polemics, Politics, and Problematizations: An Interview with Michel Foucault', in *Ethics: Subjectivity and Truth. The Essential Works of Michel Foucault 1954–1984*, vol. 1, trans. R. Hurley *et al*. New York: Free Press, pp. 111–19.

2001. *Fearless Speech*. New York: Semiotext(e).

2003. '*Society Must Be Defended': Lectures at the Collège de France, 1975–1976*, trans. D. Macey. New York: Picador.

2007. *Security, Territory, Population: Lectures at the Collège de France, 1977–78*, trans. G. Burchell. Houndmills, Basingstoke: Palgrave Macmillan.

2010. *The Government of Self and Others: Lectures at the Collège de France, 1982–83*, trans. G. Burchell. Houndmills, Basingstoke: Palgrave Macmillan.

Fournial, H. 1892. *Essai sur le psychologie des foules*. Lyon: A. Storck.

Franke, M. 1985. 'Der Begriff der Masse in der Sozialwissenschaft. Darstellung eines Phänomens und seine Bedeutung in der Kulturkritik des 20. Jahrhunderts', dissertation, Mainz.

Frankfurt Institute for Social Research 1973. 'Masses', in *Aspects of Sociology*, trans. J. Viertel. London: Heinemann, pp. 72–88.

French, F. C. 1904. 'The Mechanism of Imitation', *Psychological Review* 11(3): 138–42.

Fresenius, F. C. 1866. 'Die Natur der Masse', *Deutsche Vierteljahrsschrift* 29(3–4): 112–78.

Freud, S. 1896. 'Vorwort zur zweiten deutschen Auflage', in H. Bernheim *Die Suggestion und ihre Heilwirkung*. Leipzig and Vienna: Franz Deuticke, pp. iii–iv.

1958. 'Psycho-Analytical Notes on an Autobiographical Account of a Case of Paranoia (Dementia Paranoides)', in *Standard Edition of the Complete Psychological Works of Sigmund Freud*, vol. 12, trans. J. Strachey. London: Hogarth Press, pp. 1–82.

1989. *Group Psychology and the Analysis of the Ego*, trans. J. Strachey. New York and London: W. W. Norton & Company.

Freyer, H. 1955. *Theorie des gegenwärtigen Zeitalters*. Stuttgart: Deutsche Verlags-Anstalt.

Frezza, D. 2000. 'Masses, Crowds, Mobs: Collective Identities and Democratic Citizenship in American Social Sciences, 1890–1915', in C. A. van Minnen and S. L. Hilton (eds.) *Federalism, Citizenship, and Collective Identities in US History*. Amsterdam: VU University Press, pp. 141–64.

2007. *The Leader and the Crowd: Democracy in American Public Discourse, 1880–1941*, trans. M. King. Athens, GA and London: University of Georgia Press.

Frisby, D. and M. Featherstone (eds.) (1997). *Simmel on Culture: Selected Writings*. London: Sage.

Fromm, E. 1941. *Escape from Freedom*. New York: Rinehart.

1959. 'The Human Implications of Instinctivistic "Radicalism"', in N. Thomas (ed.) *Voices of Dissent: A Collection of Articles from Dissent Magazine*. New York: Grove, pp. 313–20.

1999. *Man for Himself: An Inquiry into the Psychology of Ethics*. London: Routledge.

2001. *The Fear of Freedom*. London and New York: Routledge.

Furet, F. 1992. *Revolutionary France 1770–1880*, trans. A. Nevill. Oxford: Blackwell.

Garofalo, R. 1968. *Criminology*, trans. R. W. Millar. Montclair, NJ: Patterson Smith.

Gay, P. 1968. *Weimar Culture: The Outsider as Insider*. New York and Evanston: Harper & Row.

Gehlen, A. 1980. *Man in the Age of Technology*, trans. P. Lipscomb. New York: Columbia University Press.

Geiger, T. 1928. *Führen und Folgen*. Berlin: Weltgeist-Bücher.

1931. 'Revolution', in A. Vierkandt (ed.) *Handwörterbuch der Soziologie*. Stuttgart: Ferdinand Enke Verlag, pp. 511–18.

1931/32. 'Eine neue Masse-Theorie. Bemerkungen zu Wilhelm Vleugels: Die "Masse"', *Kölner Vierteljahreshefte für Soziologie* 10: 87–105.

1939. *Sociologi. Grundrids og hovedproblemer*. Copenhagen: Nyt Nordisk Forlag.

1950/51. 'Die Legende von der Massengesellschaft', *Archiv für Rechts- und Sozialphilosophie* 39: 305–23.

1960. *Die Gesellschaft zwischen Pathos and Nüchternheit*. Copenhagen: Ejnar Munksgaard.

1987. *Die Masse und ihre Aktion. Ein Beitrag zur Soziologie der Revolutionen*, reprint of 1926 edn. Stuttgart: Ferdinand Enke Verlag.

Geißler, R. 1995. 'Die Bedeutung Theodor Geigers für die Sozialstrukturanalyse der modernen Gesellschaft', in S. Bachmann (ed.) *Theodor Geiger. Soziologe*

in einer Zeit "zwischen Pathos und Nüchternheit". *Beiträge zu Leben und Werk.*
Berlin: Duncker & Humblot, pp. 273–97.

Geyer, C. 1926. *Führer und Masse in der Demokratie.* Berlin: Verlag J. H. W. Dietz
Nachf.

1948. *Macht und Masse. Von Bismarck zu Hitler.* Hanover: Verlag 'Das andere
Deutschland'.

Giddings, F. H. 1896. 'Book Review: Worms, Tarde, Durkheim, Le Bon, etc.',
Political Science Quarterly 11(2): 346–52.

1909. *The Principles of Sociology: An Analysis of the Phenomena of Association and
of Social Organization.* New York: Macmillan.

1962. 'Introduction', in G. Tarde *The Laws of Imitation*, trans. E. C. Parsons.
Gloucester, MA: Peter Smith, pp. iii–vii.

Goffman, E. 1963. *Behavior in Public Places: Notes on the Social Organization of
Gatherings.* New York: Free Press.

1983. 'The Interaction Order', *American Sociological Review* 48(1): 1–17.

Good, J. M. M. 2000. 'Disciplining Social Psychology: A Case Study of
Boundary Relations in the History of the Human Sciences', *Journal of the
History of the Behavioral Sciences* 36(4): 383–403.

Gorman, L. and D. McLean 2003. *Media and Society in the Twentieth Century:
A Historical Introduction.* Oxford: Blackwell.

Graham, J. T. 2001. *The Social Thought of Ortega y Gasset: A Systematic Synthesis
in Postmodernism and Interdisciplinarity.* Columbia, SC and London:
University of Missouri Press.

Graumann, C. F. and S. Moscovici (eds.) 1986. *Changing Conceptions of Crowd
Mind and Behavior.* New York: Springer-Verlag.

Greenwood, J. D. 2000. 'Individualism and the Social in Early American
Social Psychology', *Journal of the History of the Behavioral Sciences* 36(4):
443–55.

2004. *The Disappearance of the Social in American Social Psychology.* Cambridge:
Cambridge University Press.

Gudmand-Høyer, M. 2009. *On Some Imitations and Evénementalisations in the
History of Managing Depressive Illness in 20th-Century Denmark.*
Copenhagen: Copenhagen Business School, Working Paper.

Günther, M. 2005. *Masse und Charisma. Soziale Ursachen des politischen und
religiösen Fanatismus.* Frankfurt am Main: Peter Lang.

Günzel, S. 2004. 'Der Begriff der "Masse" in Philosophie und Kulturtheorie
(I)', *Dialektik* (2): 117–35.

2005. 'Der Begriff der "Masse" in Philosophie und Kulturtheorie (III)',
Dialektik (2): 113–30.

Häberlin, P. 1927. *Die Suggestion.* Basle and Leipzig: Kobersche
Verlagsbuchhandlung.

Habermas, J. 1989. *The Structural Transformation of the Public Sphere: An
Inquiry into a Category of Bourgeois Society*, trans. T. Burger. Cambridge:
Polity.

1997. *Between Facts and Norms: Contributions to a Discourse Theory of Law and
Democracy*, trans. W. Rehg. Cambridge: Polity.

Hanuschek, S. 2005. *Elias Canetti. Biographie.* Munich and Vienna: Carl Hanser.

Hardiman, F. B. 2001. *Die Herrschaft der Gleichen. Masse und totalitäre Herrschaft. Eine kritische Überprüfung der Texte von Georg Simmel, Hermann Broch, Elias Canetti und Hannah Arendt.* Frankfurt am Main: Peter Lang.

Hardt, M. 1993. *Gilles Deleuze: An Apprenticeship in Philosophy.* Minneapolis, MN: University of Minnesota Press.

Hardt, M. and A. Negri 2000. *Empire.* Cambridge, MA: Harvard University Press.

    2004. *Multitude: War and Democracy in the Age of Empire.* New York: Penguin.

    2009. *Commonwealth.* Cambridge, MA: Harvard University Press.

Harrington, A. 2006. 'Hermann Broch as a Reader of Max Weber: Protestantism, Rationalization and the "Disintegration of Values"', *History of the Human Sciences* 19(4): 1–18.

Harrison, M. 1988. *Crowds and History: Mass Phenomena in English Towns, 1790–1835.* Cambridge: Cambridge University Press.

Heidegren, C.-G. 1997. *Preussiska anarkister. Ernst Jünger och hans krets under Weimar-republikens krisår.* Stockholm: Brutus Östlings Bokförlag Symposion.

    2002. *Antropologi, samhällsteori och politik. Radikalkonservatism och kritisk teori. Gehlen – Schelsky – Habermas – Honneth – Joas.* Gothenburg: Daidalos.

Hellpach, W. 1906. *Die geistigen Epidemien.* Frankfurt am Main: Rütten & Loening.

Hill, C. 1974. 'The Many-Headed Monster', in *Change and Continuity in Seventeenth-Century England.* London: Weidenfeld & Nicolson, pp. 181–204.

Hobbes, T. 1991. *Leviathan,* ed. R. Tuck. Cambridge: Cambridge University Press.

Hobsbawm, E. J. 1971. *Primitive Rebels: Studies in Archaic Forms of Social Movement in the 19th and 20th Centuries,* 3rd edn. Manchester: Manchester University Press.

Hoggett, J. and C. Scott 2010. 'The Role of Crowd Theory in Determining the Use of Force in Public Order Policing', *Policing & Society* 20(2): 223–36.

Holton, R. J. 1978. 'The Crowd in History: Some Problems of Theory and Method', *Social History* 3(2): 219–33.

Honneth, A. 1996. 'The Perpetuation of the State of Nature: On the Cognitive Content of Elias Canetti's *Crowds and Power*', *Thesis Eleven* 45: 69–85.

Horkheimer, M. 1941. 'Art and Mass Culture', *Studies in Philosophy and Social Science* 9(2): 290–304.

    1950. 'Preface', in T. W. Adorno *et al. The Authoritarian Personality.* New York: Harper, pp. ix–xii.

    1993. 'Egoism and Freedom Movements: On the Anthropology of the Bourgeois Era', in *Between Philosophy and Social Science: Selected Early Writings.* Cambridge, MA: MIT Press, pp. 49–110.

Horkheimer, M. and T. W. Adorno 2002. *Dialectic of Enlightenment: Philosophical Fragments,* trans. G. S. Noerr. Stanford, CA: Stanford University Press.

Horowitz, I. L. 1961. *Radicalism and the Revolt against Reason: The Social Theories of Georges Sorel.* London: Routledge & Kegan Paul.

Hughes, H. S. 1975. *The Sea Change: The Migration of Social Thought, 1930–1965*. New York: Harper & Row.

Huyssen, A. 1986. 'Mass Culture as Woman: Modernism's Other', in T. Modleski (ed.) *Studies in Entertainment. Critical Approaches to Mass Culture*. Bloomington, IN and Indianapolis: Indiana University Press, pp. 188–207.

Hynes, S. 1990. *A War Imagined: The First World War and English Culture*. London: Bodley Head.

James, W. 1897. 'Book Review: Gustave Le Bon, The Crowd', *Psychological Review* 7: 313–16.

1898. 'Introduction', in B. Sidis *The Psychology of Suggestion*. New York and London: D. Appleton, pp. v–vii.

1970. 'On a Certain Blindness in Human Beings', in *Pragmatism and Other Essays*. New York: Washington Square Press, pp. 251–69.

1981. *The Principles of Psychology*, vol. 2. Cambridge, MA: Harvard University Press.

Janowitz, M. 1970. 'Foreword', in R. E. L. Faris *Chicago Sociology 1920–1932*. Chicago, IL: University of Chicago Press, pp. vii–xii.

Jaspers, K. 1953. *The Origin and Goal of History*, trans. M. Bullock. New Haven, CT: Yale University Press.

1999. *Die geistige Situation der Zeit*. Berlin and New York: Walter de Gruyter.

Jay, M. 1973. *The Dialectical Imagination: A History of the Frankfurt School and the Institute of Social Research 1923–1950*. London: Heinemann.

1993. 'Mass Culture and Aesthetic Redemption: The Debate between Max Horkheimer and Siegfried Kracauer', in S. Benhabib, W. Bonß and J. McCole (eds.) *On Max Horkheimer: New Perspectives*. Cambridge, MA: MIT Press, pp. 365–86.

Jensen, H. 1998. *Ofrets århundrede*. Copenhagen: Samlerens.

Jonsson, S. 2000. *Subject without Nation: Robert Musil and the History of Modern Identity*. Durham, NC and London: Duke University Press.

Joravsky, D. 1989. *Russian Psychology: A Critical History*. Oxford: Basil Blackwell.

Jung, C. G. 1935/36. 'Wotan', *Neue Schweizer Rundschau* 3: 657–69.

1947. 'Individual and Mass Psychology', *Chimera* 5(3): 3–11.

1958. *Psychology and Religion: West and East*, trans. R. F. C. Hull. London: Routledge & Kegan Paul.

Jünger, E. 1964. *Essays II: Der Arbeiter, Werke*, vol. 6. Stuttgart: Ernst Klett Verlag.

Käsler, D. 1984. *Die frühe deutsche Soziologie 1909 bis 1934 und ihre Entstehungs-Milieus. Eine wissenschaftssoziologische Untersuchung*. Opladen: Westdeutscher Verlag.

Katz, E. and P. F. Lazarsfeld 1955. *Personal Influence: The Part Played by People in the Flow of Mass Communications*. New York: Free Press.

Kautsky, K. 1911. 'Die Aktion der Masse', *Die Neue Zeit* 30(1): 43–9, 77–84, 106–17.

1914. *Der politische Massenstreik. Ein Beitrag zur Geschichte der Massenstreikdiskussionen innerhalb der deutschen Sozialdemokratie*. Berlin: Buchhandlung Vorwärts Paul Singer.

Kecskemeti, P. 1961. 'David Riesman and Interpretative Sociology', in
S. M. Lipset and L. Lowenthal (eds.) *Culture and Social Character: The Work of David Riesman Reviewed*. New York: Free Press, pp. 3–14.

Kellner, D. 1984. *Herbert Marcuse and the Crisis of Marxism*. Houndmills, Basingstoke: Macmillan.

1989. *Jean Baudrillard: From Marxism to Postmodernism and Beyond*. Cambridge: Polity.

2001. 'Introduction: Herbert Marcuse and the Vicissitudes of Critical Theory', in D. Kellner (ed.) *Towards a Critical Theory of Society: Collected Papers of Herbert Marcuse*, vol. 2. London and New York: Routledge, pp. 1–33.

Kierkegaard, S. 1978. *Two Ages: The Age of Revolution and the Present Age, A Literary Review*, trans. H. V. and E. Hong. Princeton, NJ: Princeton University Press.

Killian, L. M. 1980. 'Theory of Collective Behavior: The Mainstream Revisited', in H. M. Blalock (ed.) *Sociological Theory and Research: A Critical Appraisal*. New York: Free Press, pp. 275–89.

Kiss, E. 2004. 'Does Mass Psychology Renaturalize Political Theory? On the Methodological Originality of "Crowds and Power"', *European Legacy* 9(6): 725–38.

Kitschelt, H. and H. Wiesenthal 1979. 'Organization and Mass Action in the Political Works of Rosa Luxemburg', *Politics & Society* 9(2): 153–202.

Koch, G. 1996. *Kracauer zur Einführung*. Hamburg: Junius.

Koebner, T. 1965. *Hermann Broch. Leben und Werk*. Berne and Munich: Francke Verlag.

Kolb, E. 1994. '1918/19: Die steckengebliebene Revolution', in C. Stern and H. A. Winkler (eds.) *Wendepunkte deutscher Geschichte 1848–1990*. Frankfurt am Main: Fischer, pp. 99–125.

König, H. 1992. *Zivilisation und Leidenschaften. Die Masse im bürgerlichen Zeitalter*. Reinbek bei Hamburg: Rowohlt.

Kornhauser, W. 1960. *The Politics of Mass Society*. London: Routledge & Kegan Paul.

Koselleck, R. 1992. '"Volk", "Nation", "Nationalismus" und "Masse" 1914–1945', in O. Brunner, W. Conze and R. Koselleck (eds.) *Geschichtliche Grundbegriffe. Historisches Lexikon zur politisch-sozialen Sprache in Deutschland*, vol. 7. Stuttgart: Klett-Cotta, pp. 389–420.

Kracauer, S. 1960. *Theory of Film: The Redemption of Physical Reality*. Oxford and New York: Oxford University Press.

1963. *Das Ornament der Masse*. Frankfurt am Main: Suhrkamp.

1975. 'The Mass Ornament', *New German Critique* 5(spring): 67–76.

1998. *The Salaried Masses: Duty and Distraction in Weimar Germany*, trans. Q. Hoare. London and New York: Verso.

2004. *From Caligary to Hitler: A Psychological History of the German Film*. Princeton, NJ and Oxford: Princeton University Press.

Krohn, C.-D. 1995. 'Zur intellektuellen Biographie Emil Lederers', in E. Lederer *Der Massenstaat. Gefahren der klassenlosen Gesellschaft*, trans. A. Kornberger. Graz and Vienna: Nauser & Nauser, pp. 9–40.

Laclau, E. 2005. *On Populist Reason*. London and New York: Verso.

Lang, K. and G. E. Lang 1961. *Collective Dynamics*. New York: Thomas Y. Crowell.

Larsen, S. N. 2002. 'Forord', in P. Sloterdijk *Masse og foragt. Essay om kulturkampe i det moderne samfund*. Copenhagen: Det lille Forlag, pp. 7–18.

Lasswell, H. D. 1927. *Propaganda Technique in the World War*. New York: Alfred A. Knopf.

1933. 'The Psychology of Hitlerism', *Political Quarterly* 4(3): 373–84.

Latour, B. 2002. 'Gabriel Tarde and the End of the Social', in P. Joyce (ed.) *The Social in Question. New Bearings in History and the Social Sciences*. London and New York: Routledge, pp. 117–32.

Lazarsfeld, P. F., B. Berelson and H. Gaudet 1968. *The People's Choice: How the Voter Makes up His Mind in a Presidential Campaign*, 3rd edn. New York and London: Columbia University Press.

Le Bon, G. 1960. *The Crowd: A Study of the Popular Mind*. New York: Viking.

1974. *The Psychology of Peoples*. New York: Arno Press.

2001. *The Psychology of Socialism*. Kitchener, ON: Batoche Books.

Leach, E. 1986. 'Mastering the Crowd: Collective Behavior and Mass Society in American Social Thought, 1917–1939', *American Studies* 27(1): 99–114.

Lederer, E. 1967. *State of the Masses: The Threat of the Classless Society*. New York: Howard Fertig.

Lee, G. S. 1900. 'The Dominance of the Crowd', *Atlantic Monthly* 86: 754–61.

1901. 'Making the Crowd Beautiful', *Atlantic Monthly* 87: 240–53.

1913. *Crowds: A Moving-Picture of Democracy*. New York: Doubleday, Page.

Lefebvre, G. 1965. 'Revolutionary Crowds', in J. Kaplow (ed.) *New Perspectives on the French Revolution: Readings in Historical Sociology*. New York: Wiley, pp. 173–90.

1973. *The Great Fear of 1789: Rural Panic in Revolutionary France*, trans. J. White. New York: Pantheon.

Lehmann, G. 1928. *Das Kollektivbewusstsein. Systematische und historisch/kritische Vorstudien zur Soziologie*. Berlin: Junker und Dünnhaupt Verlag.

1932. 'Prolegomena zur Massensoziologie', *Archiv für angewandte Soziologie* 5: 40–56.

Lepenies, W. 1977. 'Das Altern der Kulturkritik: Wieder gelesen: Ortega y Gassets "Aufstand der Massen"', *Frankfurter Allgemeine Zeitung*, 14 January.

1988. *Between Literature and Science: The Rise of Sociology*, trans. R. J. Hollingdale. Cambridge: Cambridge University Press.

Lethbridge, R. 1993. 'Introduction', in É. Zola *Germinal*. Oxford: Oxford University Press, pp. vii–xxviii.

Leys, R. 1993. 'Mead's Voices: Imitation as Foundation, or, The Struggle against Mimesis', *Critical Inquiry* 19(2): 277–307.

Liebersohn, H. 1988. *Fate and Utopia in German Sociology, 1870–1923*. Cambridge, MA: MIT Press.

Liebknecht, K. 1969. 'Die Krisis in der USP', in H. Weber (ed.) *Der Gründungsparteitag der KPD. Protokoll und Materialien*. Frankfurt am Main: Europäische Verlagsanstalt, pp. 52–66.

Lindner, R. 1996. *The Reportage of Urban Culture: Robert Park and the Chicago School*, trans. Adrian Morris. Cambridge: Cambridge University Press.

Lippmann, W. 1961. *Drift and Mastery: An Attempt to Diagnose the Current Unrest*. Englewood Cliffs, NJ: Prentice-Hall.

1991. *Public Opinion*. New Brunswick, NJ: Transaction.

1993. *The Phantom Public*. New Brunswick, NJ: Transaction.

Lipset, S. M. and L. Lowenthal (eds.) 1961. *Culture and Social Character: The Work of David Riesman Reviewed*. New York: Free Press.

Llobera, J. R. 2003. *The Making of Totalitarian Thought*. Oxford and New York: Berg.

Lofland, J. 1981. 'Collective Behavior: The Elementary Forms', in M. Rosenberg and R. H. Turner (eds.) *Social Psychology: Sociological Perspectives*. New York: Basic Books, pp. 411–46.

1982. 'Crowd Joys', *Urban Life* 10(4): 355–81.

Lüdemann, S. 2005. 'Die Masse im Feld der Anschauung. Über Elias Canettis "Masse und Macht"', *Text+Kritik* 28: 54–66.

Luhmann, N. 1989. 'Individuum, Individualität, Individualismus', in *Gesellschaftsstruktur und Semantik*, vol. 3. Frankfurt am Main: Suhrkamp, pp. 149–258.

1995. *Social Systems*, trans. J. Bednarz, Jr. Stanford, CA: Stanford University Press.

1998. 'Contingency as Modern Society's Defining Attribute', in *Observations on Modernity*, trans. W. Whobrey. Stanford, CA: Stanford University Press, pp. 44–62.

Lukes, S. 1985. *Emile Durkheim: His Life and Work. A Historical and Critical Study*. Stanford, CA: Stanford University Press.

Lützeler, P. M. 1973. *Hermann Broch. Ethik und Politik. Studien zum Frühwerk and zur Romantrilogie "Die Schlafwandler"*. Munich: Winkler Verlag.

1979. 'Editorische Notiz', in H. Broch *Massenwahntheorie. Beiträge zu einer Psychologie der Politik*. Frankfurt am Main: Suhrkamp, pp. 579–83.

1985. *Hermann Broch. Eine Biographie*. Frankfurt am Main: Suhrkamp.

1990. 'Vom "Zerfall der Werte" zur "Theorie der Demokratie": Hermann Broch als Philosoph und Politologe', in H. Koopmann and C. Muenzer (eds.) *Wegbereiter der Moderne*. Tübingen: Max Niemeyer Verlag, pp. 163–70.

2003. 'Introduction: Broch, Our Contemporary', in P. M. Lützeler *et al. Herman Broch, Visionary in Exile: The 2001 Yale Symposium*. Rochester, NY: Camden House, pp. 1–10.

Luxemburg, R. 1969. 'Unser Programm und die politische Situation', in H. Weber (ed.) *Die Gründungsparteitag der KPD. Protokoll und Materialien*. Frankfurt am Main: Europäische Verlagsanstalt, pp. 172–201.

1972. 'Massenstreik, Partei und Gewerkschaften', in *Gesammelte Werke, Band 2: 1906 bis Juni 1911*. Berlin: Dietz Verlag, pp. 91–170.

Lyotard, J. F. 1984. *The Postmodern Condition: A Report on Knowledge*, trans. G. Bennington and B. Massumi. Minneapolis, MN: University of Minnesota Press.

Macdonald, D. 1953. 'A Theory of Mass Culture', *Diogenes* 15(1): 1–17.

Maffesoli, M. 1991. 'The Ethic of Aesthetics', *Theory, Culture & Society* 8(1): 7–20.

1996a. *The Contemplation of the World: Figures of Community Style*, trans. S. Emanuel. Minneapolis, MN: University of Minnesota Press.

1996b. *The Time of the Tribes: The Decline of Individualism in Mass Society*, trans. D. Smith. London: Sage.

Mandler, G. 2007. *A History of Modern Experimental Psychology: From James and Wundt to Cognitive Science*. Cambridge, MA: MIT Press.

Mann, T. 1956. *Betrachtungen eines Unpolitischen*. Frankfurt am Main: S. Fischer Verlag.

Mannheim, K. 1934. 'The Crisis of Culture in the Era of Mass-Democracies and Autarchies', *Sociological Review* 26(2): 105–29.

1935. *Mensch und Gesellschaft im Zeitalter des Umbaus*. Leiden: A. W. Sijthoff's Uitgeversmaatschappij.

1939. 'Mass Education and Group Analysis', in J. I. Cohen and R. M. W. Travers (eds.) *Educating for Democracy*. London: Macmillan, pp. 329–64.

1940. *Man and Society in an Age of Reconstruction*. London: Routledge & Kegan Paul.

1991. *Ideology and Utopia: An Introduction to the Sociology of Knowledge*. London and New York: Routledge.

1992. 'The Democratization of Culture', in *Essays on the Sociology of Culture*. London and New York: Routledge, pp. 171–246.

1997. *Diagnosis of our Time: Wartime Essays of a Sociologist*. London and New York: Routledge.

Marcuse, H. 1959. 'The Social Implications of Freudian "Revisionism"', in N. Thomas (ed.) *Voices of Dissent: A Collection of Articles from Dissent Magazine*. New York: Grove, pp. 293–312.

1988a. 'The Affirmative Character of Culture', in *Negations: Essays in Critical Theory*, trans. J. J. Shapiro. London: Free Association Books, pp. 88–133.

1988b. 'The Struggle against Liberalism in the Totalitarian View of the State', in *Negations: Essays in Critical Theory*, trans. J. J. Shapiro. London: Free Association Books, pp. 3–42.

1991. *One-Dimensional Man: Studies in the Ideology of Advanced Industrial Society*. London: Routledge.

2001. 'The Historical Fate of Bourgeois Democracy', in D. Kellner (ed.) *Towards a Critical Theory of Society: Collected Papers of Herbert Marcuse*, vol. 2. London and New York: Routledge, pp. 165–86.

Marinetti, F. T. 1971. 'The Founding and Manifesto of Futurism', in *Selected Writings*, trans. R. W. Flint and A. A. Coppotelli. New York: Farrar, Straus and Giroux, pp. 39–44.

Martin, E. D. 1920. *The Behavior of Crowds: A Psychological Study*. New York and London: Harper.

Martin, E. D. and E. L. Bernays 1929. 'Are We Victims of Propaganda? A Debate', *Forum* 81: 142–9.

Marx, K. and F. Engels 1974. *Werke, Band 2*. Berlin: Dietz Verlag.

Matthews, F. 1977. *Quest for an American Sociology: Robert E. Park and the Chicago School*. Montreal and London: McGill-Queen's University Press.

Mazzarella, W. 2010. 'The Myth of the Multitude, or, Who's Afraid of the Crowd?' *Critical Inquiry* 36(4): 697–727.

McAdam, D. 2007. 'From Relevance to Irrelevance: The Curious Impact of the Sixties on Public Sociology', in C. Calhoun (ed.) *Sociology in America: A History*. Chicago, IL and London, pp. 411–26.

McCarthy, J. D. 1991. 'Foreword', in C. McPhail *The Myth of the Madding Crowd*. New York: Aldine de Gruyter, pp. xi–xviii.

McClay, W. M. 1993. 'Introduction to the Transaction Edition', in W. Lippmann *The Phantom Public*. New Brunswick, NJ: Transaction, pp. xi–xlviii.

McClelland, J. S. 1989. *The Crowd and the Mob: From Plato to Canetti*. London: Unwin Hyman.

1996. 'The Place of Elias Canetti's Crowds and Power in the History of Western Social and Political Thought', *Thesis Eleven* 45: 16–27.

McDougall, W. 1920. *The Group Mind: A Sketch of the Principles of Collective Psychology with Some Attempt to Apply Them to the Interpretration of National Life and Character*. New York and London: G. P. Putnams's.

McLuhan, M. 1964. *Understanding Media: The Extensions of Man*. London and New York: Routledge.

McPhail, C. 1969. 'Student Walkout: A Fortuitous Examination of Elementary Collective Behavior', *Social Problems* 16: 441–55.

1991. *The Myth of the Madding Crowd*. New York: Aldine de Gruyter.

2006. 'The Crowd and Collective Behavior: Bringing Symbolic Interaction Back In', *Symbolic Interaction* 29(4): 433–64.

Mead, G. H. 1899. 'Review: Gustave Le Bon, The Psychology of Socialism', *American Journal of Sociology* 5(3): 404–12.

1930. 'Cooley's Contribution to American Social Thought', *American Journal of Sociology* 35(5): 693–706.

1934. *Mind, Self, and Society: From the Standpoint of a Social Behaviorist*. Chicago, IL and London: University of Chicago Press.

1987. 'Rezension von John Dewey: Human Nature and Conduct', in Hans Joas (ed.) *Gesammelte Aufsätze*, vol. 1. Frankfurt am Main: Suhrkamp, pp. 347–54.

Melville, H. 2001. *Moby-Dick, or The Whale*. London: Penguin.

Merton, R. K. 1960. 'The Ambivalences of Le Bon's *The Crowd*', in G. Le Bon *The Crowd: A Study of the Popular Mind*. New York: Viking, pp. v–xxxix.

1970. *Science, Technology and Society in Seventeenth Century England*. New York: Howard Fertig.

Meyer, T. 2001. *Die Soziologie Theodor Geigers. Emanzipation von der Ideologie*. Wiesbaden: Westdeutscher Verlag.

Michels, R. 1926. 'Psychologie der antikapitalistischen Massenbewegungen', in G. Albrecht (ed.) *Grundriss der Sozialökonomik, 9. Abteilung: Das soziale System des Kapitalismus, 1. Teil*. Tübingen: Verlag von J. C. B. Mohr (Paul Siebeck), pp. 241–359.

1959. *Political Parties: A Sociological Study of the Oligarchical Tendencies of Modern Democracy*, trans. E. and C. Paul. New York: Dover Publications.

1970. *Zur Soziologie des Parteiwesens in der modernen Demokratie. Untersuchungn über die oligarchischen Tendenzen des Gruppenlebens. Neudruck der zweiten Auflage*. Stuttgart: Alfred Kröner Verlag.

1987a. 'Der Aufstieg des Faschismus in Italien', in *Masse, Führer, Intellektuelle. Politisch-soziologische Aufsätze 1906–1933*. Frankfurt and New York: Campus Verlag, pp. 265–97.

1987b. 'Über die Kriterien der Bildung und Entwicklung politischer Parteien', in *Masse, Führer, Intellektuelle. Politisch-soziologische Aufsätze 1906–1933*. Frankfurt and New York: Campus Verlag, pp. 298–304.

Milet, J. 1970. *Gabriel Tarde et la Philosophie de l'Histoire*. Paris: Vrin.

Mill, J. S. 1859. 'Civilization', pp. 160–205 in *Dissertations and Discussions: Political, Philosophical, and Historical*, vol. 1. London: John W. Parker.

1948. *On Liberty and Considerations on Representative Government*. Oxford: Basil Blackwell.

Miller, J. 1973. 'Walt Whitman's Omnisexual Vision', in M. J. Bruccoli (ed.) *The Chief Glory of Every People: Essays on Classical American Writers*. Carbondale and Edwardsville, IL: Southern Illinois University Press, pp. 231–59.

Miller, M. C. 2005. 'Introduction', in E. L. Bernays *Propaganda*. Brooklyn, NY: Ig Publishing, pp. 9–33.

Milles, J. 1987. 'Brüche und Kontinuitäten eines radikalen Intellektuellen. Zur Einführung in die Politische Soziologie Robert Michels', in R. Michels *Masse, Führer, Intellektuelle. Politisch-soziologische Aufsätze 1906–1933*. Frankfurt and New York: Campus Verlag, pp. 7–30.

Mills, C. W. 1956. *The Power Elite*. New York: Oxford University Press.

Mitscherlich, A. 1972. *Massenpsychologie ohne Ressentiment*. Frankfurt am Main: Suhrkamp Verlag.

Moebius, S. 2006. *Die Zauberlehrlinge. Soziologiegeschichte des Collège de Sociologie (1937–1939)*. Constance: UVK Verlagsgesellschaft.

Moede, W. 1915. 'Die Massen- und Sozialpsychologie im kritischen Überblick', *Zeitschrift für pädagogische Psychologie* 16: 385–404.

1973. *Experimentelle Massenpsychologie. Beiträge zur Experimentalpsychologie der Gruppe*. Darmstadt: Wissenschaftliche Buchgesellschaft.

Mosca, G. 1939. *The Ruling Class*, trans. H. D. Kahn. New York and London: McGraw-Hill.

Moscovici, S. 1985. *The Age of the Crowd: A Historical Treatise on Mass Psychology*. Cambridge: Cambridge University Press.

1987. 'Social Collectivities', in *Essays in Honor of Elias Canetti*. New York: Farrar, Straus and Giroux, pp. 42–59.

Mouffe, C. 2005. *On the Political*. London and New York: Routledge.

Mucchielli, L. 2000. 'Tardomania? Réflexions sur les usages contemporains de Tarde', *Revue d'Histoire des Sciences Humaines* 3: 161–84.

Müller-Funk, W. 2003. 'Fear in Culture: Broch's Massenwahntheorie', in P. M. Lützeler *et al. Herman Broch, Visionary in Exile: The 2001 Yale Symposium*. Rochester, NY: Camden House, pp. 89–104.

Murphy, F. 2004. 'Introduction', in W. Whitman *The Complete Poems*. London: Penguin, pp. xxvi–xlii.

Musil, R. 1997. *The Man Without Qualities*, trans. S. Wilkins and B. Pike. Basingstoke and London: Picador.

Negri, A. 2008. 'Let us Reform the Political Lexicon!', in *Empire and Beyond*, trans. E. Emery. Cambridge: Polity, pp. 191–5.

Nicolas, S. and A. Charvillat 2001. 'Introducing Psychology as an Academic Discipline in France: Théodule Ribot and the Collège de France (1888–1901)', *Journal of the History of the Behavioral Sciences* 37(2): 143–64.

Nisbet, R. A. 1943. 'The French Revolution and the Rise of Sociology in France', *American Journal of Sociology* 49(2): 156–64.

1952. 'Conservatism and Sociology', *American Journal of Sociology* 58(2): 167–75.

Nye, R. A. 1973. 'Two Paths to a Psychology of Social Action: Gustave Le Bon and Georges Sorel', *Journal of Modern History* 45(3): 411–38.

1975. *The Origins of Crowd Psychology: Gustave Le Bon and the Crisis of Mass Democracy in the Third Republic*. London: Sage.

Ortega y Gasset, J. 1960. *The Revolt of the Masses*. New York and London: W. W. Norton & Company.

Ozouf, M. 2002. 'Introduction', in H. Taine *The French Revolution*, vol. 1. Indianapolis, IN: Liberty Fund, pp. xi–xxix.

Parell, E. 1934. 'Einwände gegen Massenpsychologie und Sexualpolitik', *Zeitschrift für politische Psychologie und Sexualökonomie* 3(4): 146–52.

Pareto, V. 1965. *Les systèmes socialistes. Œuvres complètes*, vol. 5. Geneva: Librairie Droz.

1984. *The Transformations of Democracy*, trans. R. Girola. New Brunswick, NJ: Transaction.

1991. *The Rise and Fall of Elites: An Application of Theoretical Sociology*. New Brunswick, NJ: Transaction.

Park, R. E. 1904. *Masse und Publikum. Eine methodologische und soziologische Untersuchung*. Berne: Buchdruckerei Lack & Grunau.

1915. 'The City: Suggestions for the Investigation of Human Behavior in the City Environment', *American Journal of Sociology* 20(5): 577–612.

1928. 'Book Reviews: *Das Gesetz der Macht* by Friedrich Wieser; *Die Masse und ihre Aktion* by Theodor Geiger', *American Journal of Sociology* 33(4): 642–5.

1972. *The Crowd and the Public and Other Essays*. Chicago, IL and London: University of Chicago Press.

Park, R. E. and E. W. Burgess 1921. *Introduction to the Science of Sociology*. Chicago, IL: University of Chicago Press.

Parsons, T. 1937. *The Structure of Social Action: A Study in Social Theory with Special Reference to a Group of Recent European Writers*. New York: McGraw-Hill.

Paulsen, A. 2005. 'System og forvandling: Aspekter af Elias Canettis rationalitetskritik', in A. Paulsen (ed.) *Dødsfjenden: Om Elias Canettis forfatterskab*. Copenhagen: Rævens Sorte Bibliotek, pp. 60–85.

Pells, R. H. 1985. *The Liberal Mind in a Conservative Age: American Intellectuals in the 1940s and 1950s*. New York: Harper & Row.

Peukert, D. J. K. 1991. *The Weimar Republic: The Crisis of Classical Modernity*, trans. R. Deveson. London: Allen Lane/Penguin Press.

Pickering, W. S. F. 1984. *Durkheim's Sociology of Religion: Themes and Theories*. London: Routledge & Kegan Paul.

Plato 1994. *Republic*, trans. R. Waterfield. Oxford and New York: Oxford University Press.

Plotz, J. 2000. *The Crowd: British Literature and Public Politics*. Berkeley, CA: University of California Press.

Poe, E. A. 2003. 'The Man of the Crowd', in *The Fall of the House of Usher and Other Writings*. London: Penguin Books, pp. 131–40.

Poggi, C. 2002. '*Folla/Follia*: Futurism and the Crowd', *Critical Inquiry* 28(3): 709–48.

2009. *Inventing Futurism: The Art and Politics of Artificial Optimism*. Princeton, NJ and Oxford: Princeton University Press.

Price, R. 1993. *A Concise History of France*. Cambridge: Cambridge University Press.

Procacci, G. 1991. 'Social Economy and the Government of Poverty', in G. Burchell, C. Gordon and P. Miller (eds.) *The Foucault Effect: Studies in Governmentality*. Chicago, IL: University of Chicago Press, pp. 151–68.

Pross, H. 1978. 'Hermann Broch: "Massenpsychologie" und "Politik"', pp. 89–100 in J. Strelka (ed.) *Broch heute*. Berne and Munich: Francke Verlag.

Rackelmann, M. 1994. 'Was war die Sexpol? Wilhelm Reich und der *Einheitsverband für proletarische Sexualreform und Mutterschutz*', *Emotion* 11: 56–93.

Rammstedt, O. 1986. 'Masses – From an Idealistic to a Materialistic Point of View? Aspects of Marxian Theory of the Class', in C. F. Graumann and S. Moscovici (eds.) *Changing Conceptions of Crowd Mind and Behavior*. New York: Springer-Verlag, pp. 163–76.

Ratner, H. 2009. 'Suggestive Objects at Work: A New Form of Organizational Spirituality?', *Distinktion: Scandinavian Journal of Social Theory* 19: 105–21.

Reeh, H. 2002. *Den urbane dimension. Tretten variationer over den moderne bykultur*. Odense: Syddansk Universitetsforlag.

Reich, W. 1933. *Massenpsychologie der Faschismus. Zur Sexualökonomie der politischen Reaktion und zur proletarischen Sexualpolitik*. Copenhagen, Prague, Zurich: Verlag für Sexualpolitik.

1934. *Dialektischer Materialismus und Psychoanalyse*. Copenhagen: Verlag für Sexualpolitik.

1971. *The Function of the Orgasm*, trans. T. P. Wolfe. New York: World Publishing.

1975. *The Mass Psychology of Fascism*, trans. V. R. Carfagno. Harmondsworth: Penguin.

Reicher, S. 2004. 'The Psychology of Crowd Dynamics', in M. B. Brewer and M. Hewstone (eds.) *Self and Social Identity*. Oxford: Blackwell, pp. 232–58.

Reiwald, P. 1946. *Vom Geist der Massen. Handbuch der Massenpsychologie*. Zurich: Pan-Verlag.

Reschke, R. 1992. '"Pöbel-Mischmasch" oder vom notwendigen Niedergang aller Kultur: Friedrich Nietzsches Ansätze zu einer Kulturkritik der Masse', in N. Krenzlin (ed.) *Zwischen Angstmetapher und Terminus: Theorien der Massenkultur seit Nietzsche*. Berlin: Akademie Verlag, pp. 14–42.

Rheingold, H. 2002. *Smart Mobs: The Next Social Revolution*. Cambridge, MA: Basic Books.

Riesman, D. 1950. *The Lonely Crowd: A Study of the Changing American Character*, in collaboration with R. Denney and N. Glazer. New Haven, CT: Yale University Press.

1952. *Faces in the Crowd: Individual Studies in Character and Politics*, in collaboration with N. Glazer. New Haven, CT: Yale University Press.

1961. '*The Lonely Crowd*: A Reconsideration in 1960, with the Collaboration of Nathan Glazer', in S. M. Lipset and L. Lowenthal (eds.) *Culture and Social Character: The Work of David Riesman Reviewed*. New York: Free Press, pp. 419–58.

Robertson, R. 2000. 'Canetti as Anthropologist', in D. Darby (ed.) *Critical Essays on Elias Canetti*. New York: G. K. Hall, pp. 158–70.

Rosenberg, B. and D. M. White (eds.) 1957. *Mass Culture: The Popular Arts in America*. New York: Free Press.

Ross, D. 1991. *The Origins of American Social Science*. Cambridge: Cambridge University Press.

Ross, E. A. 1897. 'The Mob Mind', *Popular Science Monthly* July: 390–8.

1901. *Social Control: A Survey of the Foundations of Order*. New York: Macmillan.

1908. *Social Psychology: An Outline and Source Book*. New York: Macmillan.

Roth, G. 1978. 'Introduction', in M. Weber *Economy and Society: An Outline of Interpretive Sociology*. Berkeley, CA and London: University of California Press, pp. xxxiii–cx.

Rudé, G. 1959. *The Crowd in the French Revolution*. Oxford: Oxford University Press.

1981. *The Crowd in History: A Study of Popular Disturbances in France and England, 1730–1848*, rev. edn. London: Lawrence & Wishart.

Satow, L. 1921. *Hypnotismus und Suggestion. Kulturpsychologische Betrachtungen*. Berlin: Oldenburg.

Schettler, K. 2006. *Berlin, Wien … Wovon man spricht: das Thema Masse in deutschsprachigen Texten der zwanziger und Anfang der dreißiger Jahre. Versuch einer historisch-diskursanalytischen Lesart von Texten*. Tönning: Der andere Verlag.

Schmid-Bortenschlager, S. 1985. 'Der Einzelne und seine Masse. Massentheorie und Literaturkonzeption bei Elias Canetti und Hermann Broch', in K. Bartsch and G. Melzer (eds.) *Experte der Macht: Elias Canetti*. Graz: Verlag Droschl, pp. 116–32.

Schmidt-Dengler, W. 2003. '"Kurzum die Hölle": Broch's Early Political Text "Die Straße"', in P. M. Lützeler (ed.) *Hermann Broch, Visionary in Exile: The 2001 Yale Symposium*. Rochester, NY: Camden House, pp. 55–66.

Schmitt, C. 2007. *The Concept of the Political*, expanded edn. Chicago, IL and London: University of Chicago Press.

Schmitz, H. W. 1987. 'Der Begriff der "conversation" bei Gabriel Tarde', *Kodikas/Code* 10(3/4): 287–99.

Schnapp, J. T. 2005. *Revolutionary Tides: The Art of the Political Poster 1914–1989*. Milan: Skira.

Schnapp, J. T. and M. Tiews (eds.) 2006. *Crowds*. Stanford, CA: Stanford University Press.

Schnapp, J. T. and M. Tiews 2006. 'Introduction: A Book of Crowds', in J. T. Schnapp and M. Tiews (eds.) *Crowds*. Stanford, CA: Stanford University Press, pp. ix–xvi.

Schor, N. 1978. *Zola's Crowds*. Baltimore, MD and London: Johns Hopkins University Press.

Schorske, C. E. 1981. *Fin-de-Siècle Vienna: Politics and Culture*. New York: Vintage.

Schultz, E. and E. Jünger 1933. *Die veränderte Welt: Eine Bilderfibel unserer Zeit*. Breslau: Wilh. Gottl. Korn Verlag.

Schuyler, S. 2006. '"Multitude": English', in J. T. Schnapp and M. Tiews (eds.) *Crowds*. Stanford, CA: Stanford University Press, pp. 124–7.

Schweingruber, D. and R. T. Wohlstein 2005. 'The Madding Crowd Goes to School: Myths about Crowds in Introductory Sociology Textbooks', *Teaching Sociology* 33: 136–53.

Seager, F. H. 1969. *The Boulanger Affair: Political Crossroad of France 1886–1889*. Ithaca, NY: Cornell University Press.

Seeling, O. 1925. *Hypnose und Suggestion. Eine Handreichung für jeden Gebildeten, insbesondere für Eltern und Erzieher, Juristen und Polizeibeamte*, 2nd, rev. edn. Berlin: Pyramidenverlag Dr. Schwarz.

Seidler, V. J. 1989. *Rediscovering Masculinity: Reason, Language and Sexuality*. London and New York: Routledge.

　1994. *Unreasonable Men: Masculinity and Social Theory*. London and New York: Routledge.

Sharaf, M. 1983. *Fury on Earth: A Biography of Wilhelm Reich*. London: Andre Deutsch.

Shepard, W. J. 1909. 'Public Opinion', *American Journal of Sociology* 15(1): 32–60.

Shibutani, T. (ed.) 1970. *Human Nature and Collective Behavior: Papers in Honor of Herbert Blumer*. Englewood Cliffs, NJ: Prentice-Hall.

Shields, R. 1991. 'Introduction to "The Ethic of Aesthetics"', *Theory, Culture & Society* 8: 1–5.

Shiller, R. J. 2000. *Irrational Exuberance*. Princeton, NJ: Princeton University Press.

Shils, E. 1957. 'Daydreams and Nightmares: Reflections on the Criticism of Mass Culture', *Swanee Review* 65: 587–608.

　1960. 'Mass Society and Its Culture', *Daedalus* 89(2): 288–314.

Shorter, E. and C. Tilly 1974. *Strikes in France 1830–1968*. Cambridge: Cambridge University Press.

Sidis, B. 1898. *The Psychology of Suggestion: A Research into the Subconscious Nature of Man and Society*. New York and London: D. Appleton.

Sieber, S. 1918. *Die Massenseele. Ein Beitrag zur Psychologie des Krieges, der Kunst und der Kultur*. Dresden and Leipzig: "Globus", Wissenschaftliche Verlagsanstalt.

Sighele, S. 1897. *Psychologie des Auflaufs und der Massenverbrechen*, trans. H. Kurella. Dresden and Leipzig: Verlag von Carl Reissner.

　1901. *La Foule criminelle. Essai de psychologie collective*, 2nd edn. Paris: Félix Alcan.

　1975. *Psychologie des Sectes*. New York: Arno.

Simmel, E. (ed.) 1946a. *Anti-Semitism: A Social Disease*. New York: International Universities Press.

Simmel, E. 1946b. 'Anti-Semitism and Mass Psychopathology', in E. Simmel (ed.) *Anti-Semitism: A Social Disease*. New York: International Universities Press, pp. 33–78.

Simmel, G. 1950a. 'Fundamental Problems of Sociology (Individual and Society)', in *The Sociology of Georg Simmel*, ed. K. H. Wolff. New York: Free Press, pp. 1–84.

1950b. 'On the Significance of Numbers for Social Life', in *The Sociology of Georg Simmel*, ed. K. H. Wolff. New York: Free Press, pp. 87–104.

1950c. 'The Social and the Individual Level: An Example of General Sociology', in *The Sociology of Georg Simmel*, ed. K. H. Wolff. New York: Free Press, pp. 26–39.

1950d. 'Superordination and Subordination', in *The Sociology of Georg Simmel*, ed. K. H. Wolff. New York: Free Press, pp. 179–303.

1950e. 'The Metropolis and Mental Life', in *The Sociology of Georg Simmel*, ed. K. H. Wolff. New York: Free Press, pp. 409–24.

1971. 'Sociability', in D. N. Levine (ed.) *Georg Simmel on Individuality and Social Forms: Selected Writings*. Chicago, IL and London: University of Chicago Press, pp. 127–40.

1989. 'Über sociale Differenzierung: Sociologische und psychologische Untersuchungen', in H.-J. Dahme (ed.) *Georg Simmel Gesamtausgabe*, vol. 2. Frankfurt am Main: Suhrkamp, pp. 109–295.

1992. *Soziologie. Untersuchungen über die Formen der Vergesellschaftlichung*, ed. O. Rammstedt. Frankfurt am Main: Suhrkamp.

1999a. 'Book Review: Gabriel Tarde, *Les lois de l'imitation*', in K. C. Köhnke (ed.) *Georg Simmel Gesamtausgabe*, vol. 1. Frankfurt am Main: Suhrkamp, pp. 248–50.

1999b. 'Book Review: Gustave Le Bon, *Psychologie des Foules*', in K. C. Köhnke (ed.) *Georg Simmel Gesamtausgabe*, vol. 1. Frankfurt am Main: Suhrkamp, pp. 353–61.

1999c. 'Book Review: Scipio Sighele, Psychologie des Auflaufs und der Massenverbrechen', in K. C. Köhnke (ed.) *Georg Simmel Gesamtausgabe*, vol. 1. Frankfurt am Main: Suhrkamp, pp. 388–400.

1999d. 'Der Krieg und die geistigen Entscheidungen', in G. Fitzi and O. Rammstedt (eds.) *Gesamtausgabe*, vol. 16. Frankfurt am Main: Suhrkamp, pp. 7–58.

1999e. 'Grundfragen der Soziologie', in G. Fitzi and O. Rammstedt (eds.) *Gesamtausgabe*, vol. 16. Frankfurt am Main: Suhrkamp, 59–149.

2003. 'Deutschlands innere Wandlung', in U. Kösser, H.-M. Kruckis and O. Rammstedt (eds.) *Gesamtausgabe*, vol. 15. Frankfurt am Main: Suhrkamp, pp. 271–85.

Sloterdijk, P. 1983. *Kritik der zynischen Vernunft*. Frankfurt am Main: Suhrkamp.

2000. *Die Verachtung der Massen. Versuch über Kulturkämpfe in der modernen Gesellschaft*. Frankfurt am Main: Suhrkamp.

2004. *Sphären III. Schäume*. Frankfurt am Main: Suhrkamp.

2008. 'Foam City', *Distinktion: Scandinavian Journal of Social Theory* 16: 47–59.

Small, A. W. 1898. 'Review: Gabriel Tarde, *Les Lois Sociales*', *American Journal of Sociology* 4(3): 395–400.

Smelser, N. J. 1962. *Theory of Collective Behavior*. New York: Free Press.

Smith-Rosenberg, C. 1972. 'The Hysterical Woman: Sex Roles and Role Conflict in 19th-Century America', *Social Research* 39(4): 652–78.

Sofroniew, A. K. T. 2006a. '"Turba": Latin', in J. T. Schnapp and M. Tiews (eds.) *Crowds*. Stanford, CA: Stanford University Press, pp. 30–4.

2006b. '"Vulga": Latin', in J. T. Schnapp and M. Tiews (eds.) *Crowds*. Stanford, CA: Stanford University Press, pp. 354–6.

Sombart, W. 1924. *Der proletarische Sozialismus. Zweiter Band: Die Bewegung*. Jena: Verlag von Gustav Fischer.

1938. *Vom Menschen. Versuch einer geistwissenschaftlichen Anthropologie*. Berlin: Buchholz & Weisswange.

Sorel, G. 1895. 'Revue critique: G. Le Bon, *Psychologie des Foules*', *Le Devenir social* April: 765–70.

1999. *Reflections on Violence*, ed. J. Jennings. Cambridge: Cambridge University Press.

Sørensen, V. 1961. *Hverken – eller. Kritiske betragtninger*. Copenhagen: Gyldendal.

Spencer, H. 2002. *The Principles of Sociology. In Three Volumes*, vol. 1. New Brunswick, NJ and London: Transaction.

Spengler, O. 1980a. *The Decline of the West, Vol. 1: Form and Actuality*, trans. C. F. Atkinson. London: George Allen & Unwin.

1980b. *The Decline of the West, Vol. 2: Perspectives of World-History*, trans. C. F. Atkinson. London: George Allen & Unwin.

Spinoza, B. 2002. 'Political Treatise', in *Complete Works*, trans. S. Shirley. Indianapolis, IN and Cambridge: Hackett, pp. 676–754.

Stäheli, U. 2003. 'Populationernes opstand', in C. Borch and L. T. Larsen (eds.) *Perspektiv, magt og styring. Luhmann og Foucault til diskussion*. Copenhagen: Hans Reitzels Forlag, pp. 60–82.

2006. 'Market Crowds', in J. T. Schnapp and M. Tiews (eds.) *Crowds*. Stanford, CA: Stanford University Press, pp. 271–87.

2007. *Spektakuläre Spekulation. Das Populäre der Ökonomie*. Frankfurt am Main: Suhrkamp.

Stein, A. 1955. 'Adolf Hitler und Gustave Le Bon. Der Meister der Massenbewegung und sein Lehrer', *Geschichte in Wissenschaft und Unterricht* 6: 362–8.

Steinmetz, G. 2007. 'American Sociology before and after World War II: The (Temporary) Settling of a Disciplinary Field', in C. Calhoun (ed.) *Sociology in America: A History*. Chicago, IL and London: University of Chicago Press, pp. 314–66.

Stewart-Steinberg, S. R. 2003. 'The Secret Power of Suggestion: Scipio Sighele and the Postliberal Subject', *Diacritics* 33(1): 60–79.

Stieg, G. 1990. *Frucht des Feuers. Canetti, Doderer, Kraus und der Justizpalastbrand*. Vienna: Edition Falter im ÖBV.

Stieler, G. 1929. *Person und Masse. Untersuchungen zur Grundlegung einer Massenpsychologie*. Leipzig: Felix Meiner Verlag.

Stoll, O. 1894. *Suggestion und Hypnotismus in der Völkerpsychologie*. Leipzig: K. F. Koehler's Antiquarium.

1904. *Suggestion und Hypnotismus in der Völkerpsychologie*, 2nd, enlarged edn. Leipzig: Verlag von Veit & Comp.

Strelka, J. 1988. 'Politics and the Human Condition: Broch's Model of a Mass Psychology', in S. D. Dowden (ed.) *Hermann Broch: Literature, Philosophy, Politics. The Yale Broch Symposium 1986*. Columbia, SC: Camden House, pp. 76–86.

Surowiecki, J. 2005. *The Wisdom of Crowds*. New York: Anchor Books.

Taine, H. 2002. *The French Revolution*, vol. 1. Indianapolis, IN: Liberty Fund.

Tarde, G. 1892. 'Les crimes des foules', *Archives de l'Anthropologie Criminelle* 7: 353–86.

1893. 'Foules et sectes au point de vue criminel', *Revue des Deux Mondes* 332: 349–87.

1902. *Psychologie économique*, vol. 1. Paris: Félix Alcan.

1903. 'Inter-Psychology, the Inter-Play of Human Minds', *International Quarterly* 7: 59–84.

1905. *Underground Man*, trans. C. Brereton. London: Duckworth.

1962. *The Laws of Imitation*, trans. E. C. Parsons. Gloucester, MA: Peter Smith.

1968. *Penal Philosophy*, trans. R. Howell. Montclair, NJ: Patterson Smith.

1969. *On Communication and Social Influence. Selected papers*, ed. T. N. Clark. Chicago, IL and London: University of Chicago Press.

1989. *L'opinion et la foule*. Paris: Presses Universitaires de France.

Tarrow, S. 1998. *Power in Movement: Social Movements and Contentious Politics, Second Edition*. Cambridge: Cambridge University Press.

Theweleit, K. 1989. *Male Fantasies, Vol. 2: Male Bodies: Psychoanalyzing the White Terror*, trans. C. Turner, E. Carter and S. Conway. Cambridge: Polity.

1998. 'Canetti's Masse-Begriff: Verschwinden der Masse? Masse & Serie', in *Ghosts: Drei leicht inkorrekte Vorträge*. Frankfurt am Main and Basle: Stroemfeld, pp. 161–249.

Thompson, E. P. 1971. 'The Moral Economy of the English Crowd in the Eighteenth Century', *Past and Present* 50(February): 76–136.

Thrift, N. 2006. 'Re-Inventing Invention: New Tendencies in Capitalist Commodification', *Economy and Society* 35(2): 279–306.

2009. 'Different Atmospheres: of Sloterdijk, China, and Site', *Environment and Planning D: Society and Space* 27(1): 119–38.

Thyssen, O. 1973. *Wilhelm Reich 1927–1939: mellem Freud og Marx*. Copenhagen: Gyldendal.

Tillich, P. 1922. *Masse und Geist. Studien zur Philosophie der Masse*. Berlin and Frankfurt am Main: Verlag der Arbeitsgemeinschaft.

Tilly, C. 1969. 'Collective Violence in European Perspective', in H. D. Graham and T. R. Gurr (eds.) *Violence in America: Historical and Comparative Perspectives*, vol. 1. New York: National Commission on the Causes and Prevention of Violence, pp. 5–34.

1978. *From Mobilization to Revolution*. Reading, MA: Addison-Wesley.

2004. *Social Movements, 1768–2004*. Boulder, CO and London: Paradigm.

Tönnies, F. 1926. 'Die große Menge und das Volk', *Soziologische Studien und Kritiken* 2: 277–303.

Tosti, G. 1897. 'The Sociological Theories of Gabriel Tarde', *Political Science Quarterly* 12(3): 490–511.

1900. 'Book Review: G. Tarde, Social Laws', *Psychological Review* 7: 211–13.

Trappe, P. 1978. 'Theodor Geiger', in D. Käsler (ed.) *Klassiker des soziologisches Denkens. Zweiter Band. Von Weber bis Mannheim*. Munich: C. H. Beck, pp. 254–85.

Tratner, M. 2008. *Crowd Scenes: Movies and Mass Politics*. New York: Fordham University Press.

Trömner, E. 1913. *Hypnotismus und Suggestion*. Leipzig and Berlin: B. G. Teubner.

Trotter, W. 1975. *Instincts of the Herd in Peace and War*. London: T. Fisher Unwin.

Turner, B. S. 1992. 'Preface to the New Edition', in K. Mannheim *Essays on the Sociology of Culture*. London and New York: Routledge, pp. ix–xxxiv.

Turner, R. H. 1964. 'Collective Behavior', in R. E. L. Faris (ed.) *Handbook of Modern Sociology*. Chicago, IL: Rand McNally, pp. 382–425.

1980. 'Book Review: Elias Canetti, *Crowds and Power*', *Contemporary Sociology* 9(1): 142–4.

Turner, R. H. and L. M. Killian 1957. *Collective Behavior*. Englewood Cliffs, NJ: Prentice-Hall.

1972. *Collective Behavior*, 2nd edn. Englewood Cliffs, NJ: Prentice-Hall.

Uexküll, J. v. 1920. *Staatsbiologie*. Berlin: Verlag von Gebrüder Paetel.

Vaerting, M. 1928. *Die Macht der Massen*. Berlin: Dr. M. Pfeiffer.

van Ginneken, J. 1985. 'The 1895 Debate on the Origins of Crowd Psychology', *Journal of the History of the Behavioral Sciences* 21(October): 375–82.

1992. *Crowds, Psychology, and Politics, 1871–1899*. Cambridge: Cambridge University Press.

Vierkandt, A. 1923. *Gesellschaftslehre. Hauptprobleme der philosophischen Soziologie*. Stuttgart: Verlag von Ferdinand Enke.

Virno, P. 2004. *A Grammar of the Multitude: For an Analysis of Contemporary Forms of Life*, trans. I. Bertoletti *et al.* New York: Semiotext(e).

Vleugels, W. 1922/23. 'Neuere massenpsychologische Literatur', *Kölner Vierteljahreshefte für Sozialwissenschaften* 4(2): 79–82.

1923. 'Zu Freuds Theorien von der Psychoanalyse', *Kölner Vierteljahreshefte für Soziologie* 3(1): 42–59, 170–5.

1926. 'Der Begriff der Masse. Ein Beitrag zur Entwicklungsgeschichte der Massentheorie', *Jahrbuch für Soziologie* 2: 176–201.

1927. 'Zur Diskussion über die Massentheorie Le Bons', *Kölner Vierteljahreshefte für Soziologie* 6(2): 168–85.

1930. *Die Masse. Ein Beitrag zur Lehre von den sozialen Gebilden*. Munich: Verlag Duncker & Humblot.

von Wiese, L. 1924. *Allgemeine Soziologie als Lehre von den Beziehungen und Beziehungsgebilden der Menschen. Teil 1. Beziehungslehre*. Munich and Leipzig: Verlag Duncker & Humblot.

1929. *Allgemeine Soziologie als Lehre von den Beziehungen und Beziehungsgebilden der Menschen. Teil 2. Gebildelehre*. Munich and Leipzig: Verlag Duncker & Humblot.

Waddington, D. 1992. *Contemporary Issues in Public Disorder: A Comparative and Historical Approach*. London and New York: Routledge.

2008. 'The Madness of the Mob? Explaining the "Irrationality" and Destructiveness of Crowd Violence', *Sociological Compass* 2(2): 675–87.

Wagner, P. 1990. *Sozialwissenschaften und Staat: Frankreich, Italien, Deutschland 1870–1980*. Frankfurt am Main: Campus.

1994. *A Sociology of Modernity: Liberty and Discipline*. London and New York: Routledge.

2001. *A History and Theory of the Social Sciences: Not All that Is Solid Melts into Air*. London: Sage.

Wallas, G. 1914. *The Great Society: A Psychological Analysis*. London: Macmillan.

1929. *Human Nature in Politics*. London: Constable's Miscellany.

Wang, M. S. 2006. '"Mob": English', in J. T. Schnapp and M. Tiews (eds.) *Crowds*. Stanford, CA: Stanford University Press, pp. 186–90.

Weber, M. 1975. *Max Weber: A Biography*, trans. H. Zohn. New York: John Wiley.

1978. *Economy and Society: An Outline of Interpretive Sociology*, ed. G. Roth and C. Wittic. Berkeley, CA and London: University of California Press.

2001. *The Protestant Ethic and the Spirit of Capitalism*, trans. T. Parsons. London and New York: Routledge.

Weigel, R. 1993. 'Elias Canettis *Masse und Macht* und Hermann Brochs *Massenwahntheorie*: Berührungspunkte und Unterschiede', in J. P. Strelka and Z. Széll (eds.) *Ist Wahrheit ein Meer von Grashalmen? Zum Werk Elias Canettis*. Berne: Peter Lang, pp. 121–45.

Weigel, R. G. 1994. *Zur geistigen Einheit von Hermann Brochs Werk. Massenpsychologie. Politologie. Romane*. Tübingen and Basle: Francke Verlag.

Welge, J. 2006. 'Far from the Crowd: Individuation, Solitude, and "Society" in the Western Imagination', in J. T. Schnapp and M. Tiews (eds.) *Crowds*. Stanford, CA: Stanford University Press, pp. 335–58.

Wennerhag, M. 2010. 'Another Modernity is Possible? The Global Justice Movement and the Transformations of Politics', *Distinktion: Scandinavian Journal of Social Theory* 21: 25–49.

Westley, W. A. 1957. 'The Nature and Control of Hostile Crowds', *Canadian Journal of Economics and Political Science* 23(1): 33–41.

Whitehead, A. N. 1978. *Process and Reality: An Essay in Cosmology*. New York: Free Press.

Whitman, W. 2004. *The Complete Poems*, ed. and with Introduction and Notes by F. Murphy. London: Penguin.

Wieser, F. 1926. *Das Gesetz der Macht*. Vienna: Verlag von Julius Springer.

Williams, R. 1963. *Culture and Society 1780–1950*. Harmondsworth: Penguin.

Williams, R. H. 1982. *Dream Worlds: Mass Consumption in Late Nineteenth-Century France*. Berkeley, CA: University of California Press.

Wistrich, R. S. 1983. 'Karl Lueger and the Ambiguities of Viennese Antisemitism', *Jewish Social Studies* 45(3/4): 251–62.

Witkin, R. E. 2000. 'Why Did Adorno "Hate" Jazz?', *Sociological Theory* 18(1): 145–70.

Witte, K. 1977. 'Nachwort', in S. Kracauer *Das Ornament der Masse: Essays*. Frankfurt am Main: Suhrkamp, pp. 333–47.

Wordsworth, W. 1994. *The Collected Poems of William Wordsworth*. London: Wordsworth Poetry Library.

Wundt, W. 1892. *Hypnotismus und Suggestion*. Leipzig: Verlag von Wilhelm Engelmann.

1911. *Probleme der Völkerpsychologie*. Leipzig: Ernst Wiegandt.

1917. *Völkerpsychologie. Eine Untersuchung der Entwicklungsgesetze von Sprache, Mythus und Sitte. Siebenter Band: Die Gesellschaft. Erster Teil*. Leipzig: Alfred Kröner Verlag.

Žižek, S. 2004. *Organs without Bodies: Deleuze and Consequences*. New York and London: Routledge.

Zola, É. 1993. *Germinal*, trans. P. Collier. Oxford: Oxford University Press.

Index

Lightning Source UK Ltd.
Milton Keynes UK
UKOW04f1030220115

244902UK00001B/113/P